THE SMALL GULF STATES

Small states are often believed to have been resigned to the margins of international politics. However, the recent increase in the number of small states has increased their influence and forced the international community to incorporate some of them into the global governance system. This is particularly evident in the Middle East where small Gulf states have played an important role in the changing dynamics of the region in the last decade.

The Small Gulf States analyses the evolution of these states' foreign and security policies since the Arab Spring. With particular focus on Oman, Qatar and the United Arab Emirates, it explores how these states have been successful in not only guaranteeing their survival, but also in increasing their influence in the region. It then discusses the security dilemmas small states face, and suggests a multitude of foreign and security policy options, ranging from autonomy to influence, in order to deal with this. The book also looks at the influence of regional and international actors on the policies of these countries. It concludes with a discussion of the peculiarities and contributions of the Gulf states for the study of small states' foreign and security policies in general.

Providing a comprehensive and up-to-date analysis of the unique foreign and security policies of the states of the Gulf Cooperation Council (GCC) before and after the Arab Spring, this book will be a valuable resource for students and scholars of Middle East studies, foreign policy and international relations.

Khalid S. Almezaini is Lecturer at Qatar University and a Visiting Research Fellow at LSE. Prior to joining Qatar University, Almezaini taught Middle East Politics at the universities of Exeter, Edinburgh and Cambridge. His research interests range from international relations, Middle East politics and security to foreign aid and political economy.

Jean-Marc Rickli is Lecturer at the Department of Defence Studies of King's College London and at the Qatar Joint Command and Staff College in Doha. He is also an Associate Fellow of the Geneva Center for Security Policy. His previous appointment includes Assistant Professor at the Institute for International and Civil Security at Khalifa University in Abu Dhabi.

THE SMALL GULF STATES

Foreign and security policies before and after the Arab Spring

Edited by Khalid S. Almezaini and Jean-Marc Rickli

First published 2017
by Routledge
2 Park Square, Milton Park, Abingdon, Oxon OX14 4RN

and by Routledge
711 Third Avenue, New York, NY 10017

Routledge is an imprint of the Taylor & Francis Group, an informa business

© 2017 Gulf Research Centre Cambridge

The right of the editors to be identified as the authors of the editorial material, and of the authors for their individual chapters, has been asserted in accordance with sections 77 and 78 of the Copyright, Designs and Patents Act 1988.

All rights reserved. No part of this book may be reprinted or reproduced or utilised in any form or by any electronic, mechanical, or other means, now known or hereafter invented, including photocopying and recording, or in any information storage or retrieval system, without permission in writing from the publishers.

Trademark notice: Product or corporate names may be trademarks or registered trademarks, and are used only for identification and explanation without intent to infringe.

British Library Cataloguing in Publication Data
A catalogue record for this book is available from the British Library

Library of Congress Cataloging in Publication Data
Names: Almezaini, Khalid S., editor. | Rickli, Jean-Marc, editor.
Title: The small Gulf States : foreign and security policies before and after the Arab Spring / edited by Khalid S. Almezaini and Jean-Marc Rickli.
Description: New York, NY : Routledge, [2017]
Identifiers: LCCN 2016027664 | ISBN 9781138665972 (hardback) | ISBN 9781315619576 (ebook) | ISBN 9781138665989 (pbk.)
Subjects: LCSH: Persian Gulf States–Foreign relations. | National security–Persian Gulf States. | Gulf Cooperation Council.
Classification: LCC DS247.A138 S63 2017 | DDC 327.536–dc23
LC record available at https://lccn.loc.gov/2016027664

ISBN: 978-1-138-66597-2 (hbk)
ISBN: 978-1-138-66598-9 (pbk)
ISBN: 978-1-315-61957-6 (ebk)

Typeset in Bembo
by Sunrise Setting Ltd, Paignton, UK

CONTENTS

	Contributors	vii
1	Small states in the Gulf *Khalid Almezaini and Jean-Marc Rickli*	1
2	Theories of small states' foreign and security policies and the Gulf states *Jean-Marc Rickli and Khalid Almezaini*	8
3	The changing security dynamic in the Middle East and its impact on smaller Gulf Cooperation Council states' alliance choices and policies *Victor Gervais*	31
4	Gulf security policy after the Arab Spring: considering changing security dynamics *Andreas Krieg*	47
5	The United States and its key Gulf allies: a new foundation for a troubled partnership? *David Goldfischer*	64
6	Iran and the Gulf Cooperation Council sheikhdoms *Shahram Akbarzadeh*	89
7	Oman's independent foreign policy *Abdullah Baabood*	107

8	Evolving foreign and security policies: a comparative study of Qatar and the United Arab Emirates *Emma Soubrier*	123
9	Risk diversification and the United Arab Emirates' foreign policy *Leah Sherwood*	144
10	Gulf states' engagement in North Africa: the role of foreign aid *Lisa Watanabe*	168
11	The foreign policies of the small Gulf states: an exception in small states' behaviours? *Khalid Almezaini and Jean-Marc Rickli*	182
	Bibliography	*191*
	Index	*219*

CONTRIBUTORS

Shahram Akbarzadeh is research professor of Middle East & Central Asian Politics and holds the prestigious ARC Future Fellowship on foreign policy making in Iran. He is deputy director (international) at the Alfred Deakin Institute for Citizenship and Globalization at Deakin University (Australia) with an active research interest in the politics of Islam and the Middle East. He has led many research projects on Middle East politics and maintains an active publication record, including 4 authored books, 13 edited books, and over 70 research chapters and journal articles. These publications include *Uzbekistan and the United States: Authoritarianism, Islamism, and Washington's Security Agenda* (Zed Books, 2005), *US Foreign Policy in the Middle East: The Roots of Anti-Americanism* (Routledge, 2008), *Muslim Active Citizenship in the West* (Routledge, 2014) and *The Routledge Handbook of Political Islam* (Routledge, 2011).

Khalid Almezaini is visiting research fellow at the London School of Economics and Political Science (LSE), and a lecturer at Qatar University (in Qatar), teaching foreign aid and foreign policies of the Gulf states. Prior to joining Qatar University, Dr Almezaini was a research fellow at LSE and the University of Cambridge, and taught Middle East politics at the universities of Exeter and Edinburgh. He received his PhD from the University of Exeter. In 2013 he published a book on UAE foreign policy and foreign aid.

Abdullah Baabood is director of the Gulf Studies Center at Qatar University. He holds a Master in business administration (MBA), a Master in international relations (MA) and a Doctorate in international political economy (PhD) from the University of Cambridge. His academic interest focuses on the Gulf states' economic, political, security and social development and their external relations.

Abdullah has held several positions in business and academia and his last post was director of the Gulf Research Centre, Cambridge, at the University of Cambridge.

Victor Gervais is assistant professor at the Emirates Diplomatic Academy (EDA), Abu Dhabi. Prior to joining the EDA, he was assistant professor at the Institute for International and Civil Security at Khalifa University and visiting researcher at the Emirates Center for Strategic Studies and Research (ECSSR), Abu Dhabi. Dr Gervais has also worked as a researcher for the Kuwait Program at Sciences Po, Paris.

David Goldfischer is associate professor at the Josef Korbel School of International Studies, where he was founding director of the Programs in International Security and Homeland Security. From 2010 until 2013, he served as director of the Institute for International and Civil Security at Khalifa University in Abu Dhabi. His research has focused on the fields of nuclear policy, human rights and security, globalization and security, and US foreign policy toward the Middle East. Publications in the latter field include: 'Belligerent Fundamentalism and the Legacy of European Fascism', with Micheline Ishay, (*The Fletcher Forum*, Winter 2009), and 'The Strange Case of Dr Saud and Mr Jihad' (Open Democracy, March 2016). He is currently working on a book on United States Middle East policy since 1945.

Andreas Krieg is lecturer for defence studies at King's College London. He is currently seconded to the Joaan Bin Jassim Joint Command and Staff College in Doha, Qatar. Dr Krieg's research in the field of security and conflict studies particularly focuses on the Middle East as a region in transition. Dr Krieg has just published a book with Palgrave named *Commercializing Cosmopolitan Security* and is due to publish another book with Palgrave on Middle East security named *Socio-Political Order and Security in the Arab World*.

Jean-Marc Rickli is lecturer at the Department of Defence Studies of King's College London, as well as at the Joaan Bin Jassim Joint Command and Staff College in Doha, Qatar. He is also a senior researcher at the Near East Centre for Security and Strategy of King's College London, an associate fellow at the Geneva Centre for Security Policy (GCSP) and a senior advisor to the Artificial Intelligence Initiative of the Future Society at Harvard Kennedy School. Prior to his current position, he was assistant professor at the Institute for International and Civil Security at Khalifa University in Abu Dhabi. He holds a PhD and an MPhil in international relations from the University of Oxford, where he was also a Berrow scholar at Lincoln College.

Leah Sherwood is deputy director of research at TRENDS Research and Advisory in Abu Dhabi. Previously, she was senior officer at the Institute for International and Civil Security at Khalifa University. Her areas of expertise are international security, foreign policy analysis, small states and non-traditional security threats.

Emma Soubrier is a PhD candidate in political science/international relations at Auvergne University (Clermont-Ferrand), working in association with the Strategic Research Institute (IRSEM) of the French Ministry of Defence in Paris. Her research focuses on GCC countries' evolving security issues, defence policies and procurement strategies.

Lisa Watanabe is senior researcher at the Center for Security Studies, Swiss Federal Institute of Technology. She is co-author of *Critical Turning Points in the Middle East: 1915–2015* (2011), author of book chapters on terrorism and state formation in Algeria, and regularly writes on the transitions in North Africa.

1
SMALL STATES IN THE GULF

Khalid Almezaini and Jean-Marc Rickli

Most small states in the Middle East are located in the Gulf, with the exceptions of Lebanon, Israel, Jordan and Tunisia. Those states include Oman, Bahrain, Qatar, Kuwait and the United Arab Emirates (UAE). The small Gulf states, however, emerged in the regional system late, unlike other states in the Middle East. The continuous political instability and the hostile environment that characterize international relations in the Middle East present small states with major security challenges. Conflicts with Israel (occupied Palestine) and Iran have, for many years, been among the main security threats these states faced. New geopolitical tensions have, however, emerged. In addition, the rise of non-state actors in the region has created new security problems for both large and small states.

Scholars of international relations have very often argued that small states are confined to the margins of international politics. In contrast, the behaviour of larger states contributes to shaping regional politics and regional security dynamics. This, in turn, forces small states to modify their behaviour so as to adapt to the characteristics of their environments. Although most small states endure their new environment, some try to contribute to the construction and maintenance of regional dynamics or security, such as Qatar and the UAE, for the stability of the Gulf environment. The end of the Cold War magnified this phenomenon. Indeed, due to the increasing number of small states following the collapse of the Soviet Union, the international environment dramatically changed for small states, offering them traditional security options ranging from alliances to neutrality, but also opening up the opportunity to conduct risk-management strategies based on hedging.

The increase in the number of small states, however, forced the international community to incorporate them in the global governance system and allowed some small states to play limited, but influential roles. This is evident in different regions, particularly in the Middle East, where small Gulf states have emerged and played an increasing role in regional politics. This includes the UAE, Qatar, Kuwait and

Oman. Those small states usually were weak and threatened by other states at the regional level. As a consequence, they have relied heavily on the security support of Western powers, particularly under the umbrella of the United States. Thanks to this security umbrella and their vast financial capabilities, however, the small Gulf states have managed to become important players in the changing dynamics of the Middle East in the last few years.

The so-called Arab Spring has indeed created new security challenges for the Gulf states. As a reaction, they have increased their domestic and regional activities to contain the rise of non-state actors and are playing various supporting roles in states such as Libya and Egypt. The weakening or collapse of major actors in the region such as Hosni Mubarak in Egypt, Bashar al-Assad in Syria, and Saddam Hussein in Iraq led to the creation of a power vacuum and to major instabilities in the Middle East. Surprisingly, the small Gulf states have found opportunities in these uncertainties and instabilities and have shored up not only their financial power but also their social and political influence. They have managed, for the first time, to intervene in other Arab countries that experienced the centrifugal forces of the Arab Spring by using both their military and soft power in order to control the fragmented and weak governments of their fellow Arab countries. This has been evident in the cases of Egypt, Tunisia, Libya, Syria and Yemen. For that matter, the UAE and Qatar have played a more visible and influential role in North African countries than the other small Gulf states.

During the Arab Spring, two countries indeed played a major role in the international relations of the Middle East: Qatar and the UAE. Although there are great similarities between small states in the Gulf, Qatar's and the UAE's perceptions and reactions towards the rise of non-state actors, such as the Muslim Brotherhood, differed in nature and in policy. Consequently, the differences in the support, or lack thereof, of particular groups has become one of the main determinants of their foreign policies since 2011. Very often, these two small states have ended up competing for influence using various tools and mechanisms of regional security.

One of the interesting aspects of the small states in the Gulf is that they are members of the Gulf Cooperation Council (GCC), a political organization created at the initiative of Saudi Arabia after the Islamic revolution in Iran in 1981. It is therefore expected that the small Gulf states cooperate under the umbrella of one regional organization. However, numerous concrete examples have demonstrated that their behaviours and foreign policy approaches within the organization have been different and sometimes even in opposition.

The small Gulf states' foreign and security policies exhibit unique characteristics in the behaviour of small states that are worth exploring. This book gathers the reflection started at a workshop on small Gulf states' foreign and security policies after the Arab Spring at the 2014 Gulf Research Meeting at the University of Cambridge. It presents a detailed analysis of the foreign and security policies of the small Gulf states before and after the Arab Spring. The book addresses two main questions: How do we explain the external behaviour of the small Gulf states? Why are the small states' foreign and security policies in the GCC different than other states in the Middle East? This book answers these questions by looking at specific issues in the foreign and security policies of selected small states in the Gulf (Oman, Qatar and the UAE). In addition, the book looks at the changing security dynamics in the Gulf and their impact on small states, as well as at the ways Iran and the United States perceive and influence small states in the Gulf.

The changing security dynamics in the Gulf and small states' foreign and security policies

States that are characterized as being small are very often perceived as being weak (Handel 1990). This is not only due to their small size, but also due to the hegemony of larger states. Although the decolonization period produced a great number of small states, most of them considered as vulnerable (Commonwealth Secretariat 1997), the end of Cold War and the collapse of the Soviet Union led to the creation of new small states with various degrees of power, as well as to the empowerment of some existing small states. The European Union, for instance, has provided small states with institutional mechanisms that leverage their influence if used wisely (Panke 2010, 2011; Thorhallsson 2015). Thus, globalization, though presenting major challenges for small states, also provides them with new opportunities. Indeed, the pursuit of soft power by small states allows them to play new roles in the international system (Nye 2004). Small states moved from being passive to active actors with the ability to play significant roles in different regions.

The Middle East and the Gulf region is no exception to these developments. In particular, some small states of the GCC; Oman, Qatar and the UAE have developed active foreign policy approaches which aim at influencing the regional economic, social–political and security dynamics in the Middle East. Two main factors contributed to the emergence of small states as actors in Middle East politics. First, the diversification of international and regional alliances through the pursuit of bandwagoning, balancing and hedging strategies (Rickli 2016). Second, the decline of regional powers such as Egypt under Hosni Mubarak or Iraq under Saddam Hussein. The Arab Spring, in a similar way to globalization, has weakened some small states such as Tunisia and empowered others. Qatar and the UAE in particular have found opportunities to control, support and modify some of the regional dynamics. The role that both states played in Egypt, Libya and Tunisia reflects how such small states from the GCC managed to rise at the regional level and cooperate with great powers to influence regional security dynamics.

These small states have used four main tools: foreign aid, the media, mediation and interventions. Although the GCC small states used foreign aid in the 1970s and 1980s, the new inflow of money due to the rise of the oil and gas prices in the 2000s provided them with enormous financial resources to conduct influential foreign policies in the weak Arab republics. Similarly, the establishment of the Qatar-based television channel Al Jazeera in the 1990s and its success in providing a new voice and perspectives in international affairs paved the way for similar initiatives in the 2000s, such as the Dubai-based Saudi Al Arabiya TV channel. The control of the media influence has indeed become an important area of competition among the Gulf states. Thirdly, with increased financial resources, the small Gulf states have been able to diversify and reach out further through international mediation. The fact that the centre of gravity of international security moved away from Europe to the Middle East after the Cold War also contributed to giving more importance to the mediation opportunities provided by the small Gulf states.

Finally, the weakening of regional powers and smaller states provided opportunities for the small Gulf states to conduct direct military interventions in the framework of a multinational coalition. Indeed, the shift of global security dynamics towards the Middle East has, however, not only offered new opportunities for the small Gulf states but also faced them with new threats. In particular, the political instabilities in many Arab countries as well as the rise of non-state actors such as the Muslim Brotherhood, Al Qaeda or the Islamic State, has directly posed domestic threats to the Gulf regimes and influenced the internal stability of these states. This has forced the small GCC states to adopt new external behaviours, which completely break with their foreign and security policy traditions. For instance, the military intervention of the Qatari and the Emirati air forces among a NATO-led multinational coalition in Libya in 2011, as well as their direct intervention on the ground, left many observers of international relations baffled.

Even so, more traditional security challenges related to great power politics and the regional balance of power have not faded away. The disappearance of Iraq, since the US intervention in 2003, and Egypt, since the ousting of Hosni Mubarak in 2011, as influential actors in the Middle East has directly modified the basic balance of the power equation of the small Gulf states. Similarly, the perceived disengagement of the United States from the Middle East and the Gulf under the Obama administration has changed the fundamentals of their alliance policy. This has forced the small Gulf states to review their policy towards regional powers, especially Iran. The signing of a landmark nuclear deal, the Joint Comprehensive Plan of Action, between Iran and the P5+1 group of world powers, comprising the United States, the United Kingdom, France, China, Russia and Germany in July 2015 only heightened the urgency of the redefinition of their relationship with Tehran.

These changes and the resulting new configuration of power in the Middle East and the Gulf call for new insights about the foreign and security policies of the Gulf states. Therefore, this book seeks to understand the new external behaviour of these states and the way they have managed to survive within these new security dynamics over the past five years. Moreover, contributors of this book also seek to explain the extent to which oil prices can affect the foreign policies of the small states in the Gulf. From a theoretical point of view, this book contributes to enhancing our knowledge of how small states develop different strategies to compensate for their power deficit.

The structure of the book

The ultimate purpose of the book is to provide a new and critical analysis as well as coherent and informative data of small states' foreign and security policies in the Gulf. In particular, we seek to examine the new behaviours of the GCC small states after the so-called Arab Spring. We are particularly interested in enhancing our understanding of the way these small states have adapted their foreign and security policies not only to guarantee their survival and their security but also to prosper and, for some, even to influence the regional security dynamics. Most contributions focus on the past and present of the politics of external relations.

In chapter two, Jean-Marc Rickli and Khalid Almezaini review the theories of foreign and security policy analysis and the way they could be applied to small states. They suggest that neoclassical realism provides a good starting point to think about the development of small states' foreign and security policies. Moreover, they also look at foreign policy outcomes by providing a theoretical framework that identifies foreign and security strategies available to small states. They argue that, due to their deficit of power, small states have to choose between favouring autonomy or influence in their foreign and security policies. It follows that small states can opt for one of three main strategic orientations: alignment, defence or hedging strategies. This chapter then looks at the factors that make the GCC states peculiar in the realm of international relations.

In chapter three, Victor Gervais provides a general analysis of how the changes in the security dynamics of the Middle East are impacting on the GCC states' external and internal alliance choices and policies. In particular, this chapter looks at the most active small states in the Middle East, Qatar and the UAE, and the way these states contributed to undermine the traditional alliance model established in the Gulf more than three decades ago. To do this, the chapter provides a strong theoretical analysis of the GCC small states' alliance and cooperative strategies, relying notably on Barry Buzan's concept of regional security complex theory. The changing regional dynamics that occurred since the so-called Arab Spring provided the small Gulf states with new opportunities to seek multiple cooperative strategies and alliances that can provide not only protection but also opportunities to intervene in other states in the Middle East and North Africa (MENA), yet at the expense of undermining the current alliance system of the small GCC countries.

In the fourth chapter, Andreas Krieg develops a theoretical framework revolving around a liberal normative approach to security. The latter argues that foreign and security polices of the Gulf states ought to be more individual-centric in order to achieve long-term sustainable security and stability. The author demonstrates that security in the Gulf is not a product of state-centric national security agendas, but rather depends on the ability of the monarchical regimes to cater for individual security needs. His argument is then tested in two small Gulf states: Qatar and Bahrain. These two states have adopted two different approaches to individual security, which has in turn shaped their long-term stability.

The relationship between the Arab Gulf states and the United States has been strong for many years. This has encouraged the small Gulf states to take advantage of this security umbrella for adopting sometimes passive and sometimes active roles in the Middle East. David Goldfischer examines in chapter five how the new foundations of this relationship between the United States and the GCC countries have also created some set-backs. Further, due to the active roles that the small Gulf states have played in the last five years in the MENA region, the United States has been put in an awkward position, having to constantly assess whether it should actively support these new policies or rather take some distance and stay silent. This new situation has created some risks for this relationship. In particular, the chapter aims, in the words of the author, "to partially penetrate the fog through which the United States views current Middle East dangers, and through which Saudi Arabia and the UAE struggle to understand the United States".

Sharham Akbarzadeh, in chapter six, examines Iran's foreign policy towards the smaller Gulf states since the Iranian revolution in 1979. In particular, the author highlights how the small states, despite being members of a regional organization (GCC), have not had unified policies and experiences towards Iran. Due to the regional changes in the 1980s, the 1990s and particularly since 2003, Iran's relations with the GCC until the so-called Arab Spring shifted to increase its influence in various areas of the region, specifically in Iraq, following the collapse of Saddam Hussein, Palestine (during Ahmadinejad's presidency) and Lebanon. This increased influence has also been in effect more recently in Syria since 2011, as well as in Yemen. This Iranian interventionism has increased the tension with the Gulf states, especially the destabilization of Bahrain in 2011. Due to the changes at the regional level and increased sectarianism, tensions between Saudi Arabia and Iran have been more visible, especially after the Houthis coup in Yemen and then the ensuing Saudi intervention. The author concludes that Rouhani's government has brought some cautious optimism to the GCC states, however.

In chapter seven, Abdullah Baabood provides an insightful analysis of Oman's foreign policy. There have been very few studies that have attempted to explain what makes Oman's external behaviour unique and different from all other small states in the Gulf. While the other chapters demonstrate that Qatar and the UAE have pursued very active and visible foreign and security policies, Oman in contrast has been the active invisible player in the Middle East. Its unique and pragmatic foreign policy made Oman less vulnerable than the other GCC states towards its relations to Iran. In order to demonstrate this, Baabood examines Oman's relations using foreign policy analysis approaches at three different levels of analysis: societal, state and systemic. This chapter also shows that Oman's foreign policy is not an easy case to analyse due to its unpredictable external behaviour.

The next chapter, written by Emma Soubrier, critically examines the evolving foreign and security policies of Qatar and the UAE. This chapter provides a comparative analysis of these two small states' policies that have competed for influence and control since the beginning of the so-called Arab Spring. The chapter not only looks at foreign policy outcomes but emphasizes foreign policy processes by looking at the origin of the different foreign and security policy options adopted by

Abu Dhabi and Doha. The chapter particularly looks at the role of leaders' perceptions and strategic culture.

Leah Sherwood provides an in-depth analysis of the UAE foreign and security policy strategy in chapter nine. The author seeks to understand how small states formulate security strategies that fluctuate between proactive and defensive security postures, using the UAE as a case study. Due to the regional changes, notably the threats from Iran and non-state actors such as the Muslim Brotherhood, this chapter demonstrates that the UAE has adopted risk-diversification strategies. This chapter first identifies these strategies and then examines how they are chosen. Adopting a relational perspective of power, this chapter argues that the variations of the UAE's power dictate its risk-diversification strategies and foreign policy.

In chapter ten, Lisa Watanabe provides a unique analysis of small states engaged in North Africa through the use of foreign aid. As mentioned above, foreign aid has been among the most active tools that small states in the Gulf have used over the past forty years. The author analyses the role of foreign aid in the conduct of the foreign policies of the Gulf states, with a particular focus on Qatar, Saudi Arabia and the UAE. These countries have been active and generous aid donors who, in the words of the author, "took a more interventionist stance in reaction to the uprising and transitions in North Africa". To demonstrate this, the chapter examines the impact of foreign aid on states in North Africa, with a particular focus on Egypt.

The final chapter concludes with a general discussion on the way the small Gulf states will be able to sustain their current foreign and security policies that were implemented since the outbreak of the so-called Arab Spring in 2011. The conclusions also provide an in-depth examination of the impact of the continuously low oil prices on the foreign and security policies of the small states in the Gulf. The concluding chapter posits that there is a strong relationship between the activism of small states in the Gulf and the level of the oil prices. The variation in foreign aid, the use of foreign direct investment, the development of media empires and capabilities for military interventions depend to a great extent on the cash flow stemming from oil revenues. The editors would like to thank the Gulf Research Centre Cambridge for the support provided to publish this book as well as the different authors for their contributions.

References

Commonwealth Secretariat (1997). *A Future for Small States: Overcoming Vulnerabilities*. London: Commonwealth Secretariat.
Handel, M. (1990). *Weak States in the International System*. London: Frank Cass.
Nye, J. (2004). *Soft Power: The Means to Success in World Politics*. New York: Public Affairs.
Panke, D. (2010). *Small States in the European Union: Coping with Structural Disadvantages*. London: Routledge.
Panke, D. (2011). Small States in EU Negotiations, Political Dwarfs or Power-Brokers?, *Cooperation and Conflict*, 46(2): 123–43.
Rickli, J.-M. (2016). New Alliances Dynamics and Their Impact on Small GCC States, *Third World Thematic (Thematic issue of Third World Quarterly)*, 1(1): 1–19.
Thorhallsson, B. (2015). How Do Little Frogs Fly? *NUPI Policy Papers*, Oslo: Norwegian Institute of International Affairs, no. 12.

2
THEORIES OF SMALL STATES' FOREIGN AND SECURITY POLICIES AND THE GULF STATES

Jean-Marc Rickli and Khalid Almezaini

Introduction

Small states represent the majority of countries in the international community, yet their study has been neglected. This omission is in large part due to the fact that the theoretical focus of international relations, notably through the lenses of the paradigm of realism, has been mainly on explaining the variations of the balance of power prodded by the interactions between great powers. Similarly, in terms of foreign and security policy analysis (FSPA), the focus had been on explaining the behaviour of great powers. It follows that small states were deemed irrelevant to the understanding of the dynamics of the international system and the understanding of international relations. Although other theoretical approaches, notably liberalism and constructivism, provide more room for the study of small states, the latter has remained marginal.

The interest in small states' foreign and security policies has been cyclical and is a reflection of the evolution of the international system (Neumann and Gstöhl 2004). During the decolonization period between the 1950s and 1970s, the main interest at the time concerned the survival of small states in a world characterized by the domination of the two superpowers. Some argued that it was best achieved with cooperation through alignment (Keohane 1969; Rothstein 1968; Vital, 1971) while others argued for an independent policy through neutrality (Däniker 1966; Ralston 1969). From the mid-1970s to the end of the 1980s, small states' study was neglected as the end of the period of *Détente* led to a revival of the superpowers' confrontation and therefore international relations theories were busy explaining and second-guessing the outcome of this rivalry. When this confrontation came to an end, the ensuing proliferation of small states due to the collapse of the Soviet empire led to renewed interests in small-state studies especially in Europe (Steinmetz *et al.* 2010). Some studies have looked at the impact of the EU on small states' security (Baillie 1998; Goetschel 2000; Inbar and Sheffer 1997; Molis 2006; Thorhallsson 2000; Wiberg 1996; Wivel 2005), while others have focused on the security options of small states within a military alliance (Gärtner 2001; Mouritzen 1991; Wivel 2003) and in NATO (Männik 2004; Simon 2005; Setälä 2004) or independently (Matthews and Yan 2007). There has also been an interest in small states' foreign and security policies (Fendius Elman 1995; Gvalia *et al.* 2013; Hey 2003; Jazbec 2001; Payne 1993; Swiss Political Science Review 2013), diplomacy (Cooper and Shaw 2009) and the way small states can exert influence (Bailes and Thorhallsson 2014; Björkdahl 2008, Wright 2012). A few studies have looked at small states' military policies (Bjerga and Haaland 2010; Galbreath 2014; Loo 2009; Rickli 2008). The study of small states' security strategies has mainly focused on Europe, as the landmark publication in the field demonstrates (Archer *et al.* 2014). Very few studies have specifically dealt with small Gulf states' foreign and security policies (Al-Ebraheem 1984, Al-Mashat 2008; Belfer 2014; Kamrava 2013; Khatib 2013; LSE Middle East Centre 2015; Rickli 2016b; Ulrichsen 2012, 2014).

The purpose of this chapter is to provide a theoretical framework describing how we can think about small states' foreign and security policies and what are the specificities of the environment in which small states evolve in the Gulf. This chapter, therefore, looks at both the foreign and security policy outcomes and processes of the small Gulf states. The chapter consists of six main sections. First, it reviews the traditional debate about the definition of small states, followed by the examination of small states' foreign and security policy options or foreign and security policy outcomes. Third, it reviews and examines foreign policy theoretical approaches. Building on this, section four provides a theoretical approach that combines both external and internal factors to make sense of small states' foreign and security policies. Fifth, the chapter puts these theoretical considerations into context by considering the specificities of Arab states' foreign policies and the peculiarities of the small states in the Gulf. The chapter concludes by summarizing the main points developed in this theoretical chapter.

What is a small state?

There are fierce disagreements over the definition of small states, which can be delineated by four generations of scholars (Knudsen 2002; Maass 2009). The first generation, which stems from the realist tradition, focuses on the importance of power as capability and adopts a definition based on states' physical attributes such as the geographic or demographic size of the country or its GDP (East 1973; Vital 1966, 1971). For the realists, states, considered as unitary and rational actors, all evolve in an anarchic international environment where there is no authority above states. It follows that states must compete for power in order to guarantee their survival. From this competition a balance of power emerges which defines the characteristics of the international system and the policy options available to states. Small states are therefore those considered lacking capabilities, especially military power. For the realists and the neo-realists, small states' foreign and security policy options are by definition limited and imposed by the structural dynamics of the international system. They are the product of the distribution of power or balance of threats (Fendius Elman 1995: 173). It follows that, for both the realists and the neo-realists, small states' role in the international system is marginal and therefore not worth paying much attention to. Critics of these approaches argue that realism and neo-realism fail to account for small states as international actors partly because of 'their neglect of international norms and rules in determining states' behaviour' (Thorhallsson 2012: 141).

As a reaction to this quantitative perspective, other theorists have chosen a qualitative approach. The second generation, associated with the neo-liberals, focuses on the role and the influence of small states within international institutions (de Carvalho and Neumann 2015; Keohane 1969; Rothstein 1968). The neo-liberals or liberal institutionalists also consider that states are unitary and rational actors and that they evolve in an anarchic international system. However, unlike the realists or the neo-realists, the neo-liberals consider that cooperation in the international system is possible but is hampered by the lack of trust among states. The consequences of anarchy are less severe for the neo-liberals than for the realists/neo-realists. Whereas for the latter anarchy has a direct impact on states' survival and security, the former assumes that rather it creates a risk of being cheated upon by the other states. International institutions, however, through different mechanisms can overcome this problem and encourage states to cooperate (Keohane and Nye 1977). First, international institutions reduce transaction costs by offering open channels of communications. This incentivizes states to join these organizations. Once states have joined institutions, they are locked in mechanisms that foster cooperation. By dealing with different problems across different issue-areas and by repeating states' interactions over time through continuous negotiations, international institutions dramatically decrease states' incentives for cheating on the others and thus reduce, by the same token, the lack of trust among them, allowing cooperative patterns to emerge (Müller 2002: 374–6). Instead of focusing on smallness based on whether states can maintain their security primarily with their own resources, small states' definitions drawn from this paradigm look at the role and influence that states can exert within a group and in the international system. Small states are those who 'can never, acting alone or in a small group make a significant impact' and influence the system (Keohane 1969: 296).

The third generation, influenced by the constructivists, adopts a psychological definition that maintains that smallness is a matter of self-perception (Hey 2003; Knudsen 2007). Unlike the two previous paradigms, the constructivists do not consider the material world as given. The latter does not exist independently of human perception and cognition. Social reality is constituted by rules and intersubjective meanings. These values and ideas interact in the construction of states' identities and the states set the boundaries for proper behaviours. It follows that, unlike realism and neo-liberalism, states do not have a priori interests in the constructivist paradigm. On the contrary, interests are the products of social practices that mutually constitute actors and structures (Ratti 2006: 90). For the constructivists, small states' definition is all about perceptions. Thus, 'if a state's people and institutions generally perceive themselves to be small, or if other states' people and institutions perceive that state as small, it shall be so considered (Hey: 2003: 3). This definition, anchored in psychology, does not provide any objective standards but relies on 'the perceived role of the small state in the international hierarchy' (Hey 2003: 3).

These different definitions of small states are not really helpful because they are very subjective and static. Thus, the realist definition very much focuses on the size of the state, but small and large are relative concepts. Moreover, which criteria should be considered to define a small state? Should definitions look at the size of the population, of the territory or at the national income? And then, where should the line be drawn? For instance, the World Bank defines a small state as one with a population of 1.5 million and below (World Bank 2011). Then, what about states with 1.6 or 2 million? Does this marginal quantitative difference prod different behaviours and policies? Others have adopted a cut-off point for small states' populations at 17 million and below (Molis 2006: 82). Focusing on a specific threshold has the advantage of making the operationalization of the small-state concept easy; however, fixing this threshold is purely arbitrary. Similarly, the definitions based on the role and influence in international affairs or on perceptions are also very subjective. They identify a small state at a specific moment in time and assume that it will always remain so and act according to this behavioural attribute. Consequently, categorizing states according to quantitative criteria or coming up with a definite category of small states is not very helpful as a small state's power potential varies according to the subject area and over time (Thorhallsson 2012: 139). More importantly, all these definitions do not help in the understanding of the behavioural consequences of smallness. This has consequently led some scholars to reject small states as a conceptual tool of analysis altogether (Baehr 1975; Baker Fox 1969; Handel 1990; Maass 2014).

To avoid this deadlock, a fourth generation of scholars has adopted a different perspective, which provides a more dynamic definition. Thus, instead of defining small states through a definition of smallness, it relates this concept to the one of power. Power has two dimensions: it encompasses the capacity to modify the conduct of other states, while preventing others from affecting its own behaviour (Goetschel 1998: 15). One can therefore define a small state as one that has limited power in its relation to others due to its limited ability to mobilize resources, which can be material, relational or normative (Rickli, 2008). Rather than considering small states on the basis of the power they possess, the focus is here on the power they exercise (Mouritzen and Wivel 2005: 3). This approach looks at power not as a state's attribute but rather in relational terms through its concrete exercise (Goetschel 1998; Wivel 2005; Archer *et al.* 2014). Thus, smallness does not stem from physical attributes such as the size or the population of a state, but from the lack of power that it can exert. It follows that being a small state is related to a 'specific spatio-temporal context' (Thorhallsson and Wivel 2006: 654).

Small states' foreign and security options

The approach adopted in this book concurs with the assumptions of the fourth generation. The smallness attribute of small states comes from its relation to power. Power represents the ability to remain autonomous while influencing others. The ability of states to achieve their foreign and security objectives ultimately depends on the exercise of these two dimensions (Mouritzen and Wivel 2005: 33). Foreign and security policy outcomes of small states must therefore be understood and analysed along this continuum between autonomy and influence (see Figure 1.1).

Due to their lack of resources, small states lack the power to set agendas and thus have a limited capacity to influence or modify the conduct of others. They also have limited powers to prevent others from affecting their own behaviour (Fendius Elman 1995: 171). Because of this, the objective of the security policies of small states is to minimize or compensate for this power deficit (Goetschel 1998: 19). This translates into two broad security orientations. Small states can favour either influence or autonomy (Mouritzen 1997: 101–6; Wivel 2005: 396).

A small state can choose to maximize its influence. It will thus opt for the adoption of a foreign and security strategy based on alignment by either joining an alliance or a coalition. An alliance is a 'formal association of states bound by mutual commitment to use military force against non-member states to defend the member states' integrity' (Gärtner 2001: 2). A coalition is a looser form of association that does not entail a formal security pact. Between formal alliances and coalitions, small states might also rely on less-formalized arrangements which nonetheless bind small states to great powers, because the small states endorse the general policy objectives of the great powers in return for a security guarantee and the protection against outside threats. Considering that small states' ability to project power over far distances is by definition more limited than great powers, the security concerns of small states is primarily defined by their neighbouring states rather than the more distant ones (Miller 2005: 241). It follows that a small state can either ally with (band-wagoning) or against threats (balancing) (Walt 1987).

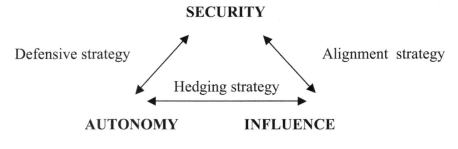

FIGURE 1.1 Small states' strategic dilemma and small states' strategic options

Source: Rickli 2016b.

Whereas band-wagoning is driven by the opportunity for gain, balancing is pursued by the desire to avoid losses (Schweller 1994: 74). In this case, an alliance is a tool for states for balancing when 'their resources are insufficient to create an appropriate counterweight to the hegemonial endeavours of one state or a group of states' (Müller 2002: 371). An alignment and more particularly an alliance policy allows the small state to benefit from the protection and the dissuasion exerted by a great power, but at the expense of its autonomy. A small state risks being entrapped by the policy of its bigger partner and forced to fight wars that are not in its direct interests. Moreover, uncertainty is always present, since protection by the bigger partner can never be taken for granted (Wiberg 1996). It follows that entrapment and the loss of strategic autonomy are therefore two risks that a small state has to accept when their foreign and security strategy relies on alignment.

In situations of mature anarchy, that is, when the system reaches a certain degree of institutionalization, small states can use a different type of alignment strategy which mainly relies on exerting influence within an international or regional organization (Keohane and Martin 1995). The United Nations, through Article 2(4) of its Charter, calls on all its member states 'to refrain in their international relations from the threat or use of force against the territorial integrity or political independence of any state' (United Nations 1945). This principle represents a strong motivation for small states to join the UN. However, the lack of enforcement power of the organization makes the UN more a symbolic tool for small states' foreign policies than an effective means to guarantee their security. Exceptions do exist, however, as the invasion of Kuwait by Iraq and the subsequent US-led coalition under a UN mandate to free the small kingdom demonstrated during the 1991 Gulf War. Nevertheless, this has rather been the exception than the norm. The true power of international organizations is not so much their protection of small states but rather the fact that they provide small states with ways to exert influence over their larger partners. Liberal institutionalists assert that small states seek membership of international institutions because laws, norms and decision-making procedures constrain larger states and therefore increase small states' room to manoeuvre. Others argue that small states' diplomatic, negotiation and leadership skills can be used for maximal influence within international organizations if small states use them within the right coalition (Thorhallsson 2012). The constructivists also argue that small states' influence within international organizations can be magnified if they use their reputation and perceived neutrality to develop new norms. Small states can act as norm entrepreneurs with the objective that the internationalization of their norms will compel other states to adopt them without external pressures (Finnemore and Sikkink 1998). Through this process of norms creation and adoption, small states are able to influence the policy of the great powers in directions that support their national interests. Norm entrepreneurship and promotion has, for instance, been a key feature of the foreign and security policies of the Nordic states to promote peace (Björkdahl 2013, 2008; Crandall and Collin 2015; Ingebritsen 2002). When it comes to alignment strategies, the end of the Cold War has opened up strategic options that small states can choose. As Duke rightly notes, 'unlike the Cold War, smaller states may now choose to involve themselves on an a la carte basis in a wide range of security commitments with an emphasis upon their own security requirements and those in the immediate vicinity' (2001: 50).

The alternative to the conduct of a foreign and security policy based on alignment is one whose central objective is the protection of autonomy. In this case, the small state adopts a defensive security strategy that favours sovereignty. In this configuration, this policy does not rely on the protection of major powers and consequently small states can expect to stay out of others' wars. The corollary to this is that the small state risks being abandoned by the great powers in times of threats to its security (Bailes et al. 2014). Traditionally this option is characterized by the adoption of a policy of neutrality (Beyer and Hofmann 2011; Reiter 1996; Rickli 2004, 2010a).

Neutrality can be defined as a 'foreign policy principle whose purpose is the preservation of the independence and sovereignty of small states through non-participation and impartiality in international conflict' (Rickli 2010b: 182). The law of neutrality was codified in three conventions: Paris (1856), the Hague (1907) and London (1909). The law of neutrality recognizes three basic obligations for the neutral states – abstention, impartiality and prevention – but solely during war time and only in the case of interstate conflicts (Schindler 1992: 379). Thus, neutral states must not provide military support either directly or indirectly to the belligerents. They must treat the belligerents impartially, which means that they must apply equally to all belligerents the rules set up by themselves with regard to their relations with belligerents. Finally, the neutrals are obliged to maintain their territorial integrity and defend their sovereignty by any means at their disposal so as to prevent belligerents from using their territory for war purposes. In the case of intra-state war, the law of neutrality does not apply and therefore the neutral state's scope of action is unhindered and left to that state's discretion. As the law of neutrality only applies in war time, if a state chooses to opt for neutrality also in peacetime it acquires the status of permanent neutral (Bindschedler 1976). In this case, the permanent neutral state has an additional duty which pertains to the impossibility of joining a military alliance (Rickli 2010b: 183). This concept of not being a member of a military alliance is also the modern understanding of non-alignment or military non-alignment (Agius and Devine 2011: 268). Historically however, non-alignment, unlike neutrality, is not a legal concept but a political one that meant adopting a policy aimed at avoiding entanglement in the superpowers' conflicts of the Cold War (Raymond 1997; Vukadinovic 1989). This understanding was formalized by the creation of the Non-Aligned Movement at the 1961 Belgrade Conference and notably comprised India, Indonesia, Egypt, Ghana and Yugoslavia.

A third alternative is when a small state opts to forego the 'security benefits of strong alignment in return for increased policy autonomy' by adopting a hedging strategy (Lim and Cooper 2015: 709). Hedging is 'a class of behaviors which signal ambiguity regarding great power alignment, therefore requiring the [small] state to make a trade-off between the fundamental (but conflicting) interests of autonomy and alignment' (Lim and Cooper 2015: 703). Whereas neutrality and alignment imply an unequivocal identification of the threats, hedging best addresses situations when small states face risk that are multifaceted and uncertain. These situations arise when the identification of friends and foes is difficult and adopting an alliance strategy could thus mean losing independence or, worse, inviting unwanted interferences from the great powers. The alternative of adopting a non-aligned position in this situation would run the risk of putting the small state at a disadvantage if the great power gains pre-eminence in the future. It follows that, in these situations, small states are likely to pursue simultaneous strategies of 'return-maximising and risk contingency' (Kamrava 2013: 52). This is best achieved by band-wagoning with a regional power while simultaneously balancing the latter through a bilateral alliance with the hegemon or the superpowers in the international system or with the regional power's adversaries. The function of bilateral alliances is to hedge against regional hegemons so as to prevent them from dominating, as well as to limit the domestic influence of regional allies. Hedging is therefore a strategy that seeks 'to offset risks by pursuing multiple policy options that are intended to produce mutually counteracting effects, under the situation of high-uncertainties and high stakes' (Cheng-Chwee 2008: 163). The ultimate objective of hedging is to reconcile 'conciliation and confrontation in order to remain reasonably well positioned regardless of future developments' (Tunsjø 2013: 2–3).

Due to its deficit of power, a small state cannot adopt an offensive strategy. This requires that it would be capable of exerting influence while guaranteeing autonomy. This configuration of power is what makes states great powers, as only they have the power to influence the structure of the international system while guaranteeing their own security (Reiter 1996: 65). Or as Morgenthau stated, 'a great power is a state which is able to have its will against a small state [...] which in turn is not able to have its will against a great power.' (1948: 129–30). Because of our focus on a relational approach, it is worth noting that small states can sometimes use offensive strategies if they are confronted with smaller states. Even so the core of their security strategies is nonetheless modelled on alignment, defence or hedging. These strategies are the only way to compensate for their power deficit vis-à-vis more powerful states.

No matter which foreign and security policy strategy small states pursue, because of their inherent deficit of power small states have to invest their resources very wisely in order to maximize their impact and get the best return on investment. The key to this is to 'prioritize and invest available resources in issues of particular importance' (Panke 2012: 317). As small states do not have the luxury to waste resources, the strategies that offer the best prospect of return on investment are those that concentrate on niche capabilities and strategies (Rickli 2008; Taulbee 2014). Niche strategies can be defined as 'strategies that channel resources in order to gain expertise and/or capabilities in one or several issue areas' (Rickli 2014: 272). It follows that small states' foreign and security policies based on niche strategies will be characterized by the conduct of niche diplomacy. The latter is characterized by the concentration of 'resources in specific areas best able to generate returns worth having rather than trying to cover the field' (Former Australian Foreign Minister

Gareth Evan, quoted in Cooper 1997: 5). This kind of diplomacy very much relies on the exercise of soft power, which relies on 'the ability to get what you want through attraction rather than coercion or payments. It arises from the attractiveness of a country's culture, political ideals, and policies' (Nye 2004: 10). Practically, this kind of diplomacy beyond a 'solid reputation for collegiality, responsibility and tact', involves 'a specific pattern of statecraft based upon entrepreneurial skill – technical leadership directed at coalition building to generate political energy around a particular issue set' (Taulbee 2014: 9). Small states' traditional niche diplomacy areas comprise peacekeeping, institution building, conflict prevention, mediation, human rights promotion or sustainable development; whereas niche capabilities in military policies involve special operations forces, medical and transportation units, logistics, water-purification capabilities, NBC (nuclear, biological, chemical) protection or counter-terrorism.

FPSA approaches

The previous section looked at small states' foreign and security policy options in terms of outcomes. This section looks at small states' foreign and security policy processes. This study is part of FPSA, which can be defined as 'the study of the conduct and practice of relations between different actors, primarily states, in the international system' (Alden and Aran 2012: 1). Whereas international relations looks at understanding the characteristics and evolutions of the international system, FPSA is interested in looking at why a specific state acts as it does when it does.

FPSA grew up out of frustrations from the dominance of realism and from a general dissatisfaction of its ability to provide credible explanations of foreign policy outcomes (Alden and Aran 2012: 1). Part of realism's inability to explain let alone predict foreign policy outcomes is due to its concept of the state, which it considers a black box. For realists, the state is considered as a unitary and rational actor where the nature of the political system, the political and strategic culture or the internal balance of power within the state among the different policymakers do not play any role (Donnelly 2000). Foreign policy only obeys one rule, which is the pursuit of national interest defined in terms of power. And because states evolve in an anarchic international system, the conduct of power should be the guiding principle of foreign policy (Morgenthau 1948: chs. 2–4, 9–12).

Some scholars frustrated by this very parsimonious concept of the state and foreign policy took the challenge to open the black box to explore how foreign policy decisions are taken (Snyder et al. 1962; Rosenau 1966). Foreign policy analysis emerged as a new branch of international relations. FPSA looks at states' sources of foreign and security policy decisions by investigating the structures and processes of decision-making, the individual decision maker's beliefs and motivations and the broader context within which these decisions are formulated.

The most straightforward way for challenging realist explanations based on rationalism is to challenge the assumption of rationality by analysing the influence of psychological and cognitive factors on foreign policy-making. Scholars looking at these factors consider individuals and no longer states as units of analysis. Here, the role of beliefs and perceptions of political leaders play an important part in explaining foreign and security policies. Beliefs serve as filters through which external factors are interpreted and are focal points that define the choice of options. Perceptions play the same role of subconscious filter which information has to go through. Whereas rational approaches consider that human beings will always choose the option that maximizes their well-being, psychological approaches question these assumptions. Misperceptions, as well as affective and cognitive biases can modify the rationality of cost–benefit calculations (Axelrod 1976; Jervis 1976). For instance, emotions or perceptual distortions, which arise from dealing with huge amounts of information, alter people's decision-making abilities. Thus, new types of rationality such as bounded rationality, which no longer aims at optimizing choices but rather at being satisfied with a good-enough option are used to explain foreign policy (Simon 1957). Proponents of these psychological approaches characterize 'foreign policy making as a far less organised, consistent and rational process than depicted by the realists' (Alden and Aran 2012: 5). These approaches are also very much in line with the constructivist assumptions and open up FPSA to new concepts such as political or strategic culture (Barnett 1999; Booth 1990; Glenn 2009; Poore 2004).

Some approaches broadened the narrow scope focusing individuals to look at the influence of the context where decision makers evolve and where they get their information from. Bureaucracies as well as institutional and decision-making processes are therefore considered as key factors influencing foreign and security policy decisions. Obvious sources of policy-making are the foreign affairs and defence ministries. Yet, other ministries and agencies, but also interest groups, play a role in the final policy outcome. These approaches rely on organizational and sociological concepts by looking at the manner in which institutional motivations and procedures impact the foreign policy process. They analyse the inner working of the government, the nature and the role of standard operating procedures, the responsibilities of agencies and the bargaining processes between institutions as well as between individuals and institutions (Allison 1971; Caldwell 1977; Drezner 2000; Kier 1995; Welch 1992). The latter approaches maintain that foreign policy outcomes are the result of 'intensive competition among decision makers and bargaining along regularised channels among players positioned hierarchically within the government bureaucracy, each with his or her own perspective on the issues at hand' (Gerner 1995: 23).

Some approaches have moved away from individuals and bureaucracies to consider the national context in which foreign and security policy decisions are taken. Here, political domestic structures and the political system are considered as having a key influence on foreign policy outcomes (Gourevitch 2002; Kaarbo 2012; Risse-Kappen 1991). The most well-known theory that considers the impact of the nature of the polity on foreign policy is the democratic peace theory (Kisangani and Pickering 2011; Rummel 1995; Russet 1993). It posits that democracies are more peaceful than other political regimes. They do not fight each other, though they might go to war with non-democratic regimes.

The end of the Cold War and the emergence of globalization have produced new approaches that look at transnational sources and influence on foreign policy. The emphasis here is on the role of non-state actors: non-governmental organizations, international institutions, multinational companies, organised-crime organizations, terrorist groups and transnational advocacy groups (Hill 1993; Risse-Kappen 1995; Strange 1996). These different actors that coexist and compete with states create a 'pluralist environment of complex interdependency' (Alden and Aran 2012: 8). Depending on the state capacity to co-opt these forces, this interdependency can increase or limit the scope of its action in foreign policy. Strong states will be able to use these actors as force multipliers in their foreign policy, while weak states will be penetrated and influenced by transnational forces. The next sections discuss foreign policy and security analysis applied to small states.

FPSA and small states

When it comes to small states' FPSA, there is no consensus about which level of analysis is the most important and which factors are the most determinant. Most argue that small states' foreign and security policies are overdetermined by structural factors. The systemic level of analysis provides the best sources of factors that influence small states' policies (Sutton 1987; Zahariadis 1994). Yet, critics argue that if that was the case, then small states' foreign policy theory would be so parsimonious that it would be an exception in international relations theories. But more importantly this theory does not pass the criterion of testing as many small states exhibit different behaviours than predicted (Hey 2003: 6). Some, however, argue that, at the unit level, domestic determinants are the most important factors explaining small states' foreign and security policies (Baillie 1998; Fendius Elman 1995). This lack of consensus calls for finding a middle ground between these two poles.

Small states' traditional security dilemma is based on a strategic choice between protecting their autonomy and maximizing their influence. Or as Goetschel rightly asserts, 'depending on the general normative nature of the international system and the specific international arrangement concerned small states have to make different kinds of reflections in order to maximize their sovereignty or to minimize their power deficit' (Goetschel 1998: 27). The means chosen to deal with this dilemma depends in turn both on the meaning of power within the international system and on the domestic acceptability of different security strategies within the given state. Although all small states evolve in the same international system, they do not necessarily respond to its challenges in similar ways. Small states' responses are conditioned by their internal foreign and security policy processes and the perceptions and interests of their decision makers.

FPSA should therefore address the structure–agency debate that divides scholars over the extent of the influence of structural factors stemming from the international system and human agency through the role of individuals in shaping the international system (Alden and Aran 2012: 2; Carlsnaes 1992). It follows that the most appropriate theoretical approach to analyse small states' foreign and security policies must account for both external (systemic and regional) and domestic factors.

Neoclassical realism, by integrating foreign policy theorizing with international relations concepts, provides an appropriate research framework to analyse small states' foreign and security policies. Neo-realism explains states' behaviour through the changing balance of power at the systemic and regional levels, and the resulting consequences on states' alignment strategies. Neo-realism seeks to explain recurring patterns of international outcomes, but does not provide a theory of security strategy explaining why a specific state acts as it does or variations of this strategy. Unlike neo-realism, which considers states as black boxes, neoclassical realism takes into account what happens within the black box. International imperatives are filtered through the medium of the state's structure, which affects how decision makers assess threats, identify and develop strategies in response to those threats and ultimately extract and mobilize societal resources to implement and sustain those strategies (Taliaferro *et al.* 2009: 3–4). In the words of the inventor of the term 'neoclassical realism', this approach argues 'that the scope and ambitions of a country's foreign [and security] policy is driven first and foremost by the country's relative material power'. Yet, he contends, 'the impact of power capabilities on foreign [and security] policy is indirect and complex, because systemic pressures must be translated through intervening unit-level variables such as decision-makers' perceptions and state's structure' (Rose 1998: 147). Neoclassical realism builds upon Putnam's two-level game of analysis concept (1988). Thus, decision makers' calculations and their threat perceptions mediated by domestic political institutions act as intervening variables between international security dynamics and states' responses in the form of foreign and security policies. It follows that neoclassical realism accounts for the subjective understanding of events and differing foreign and security policy choices of small states (Alden and Aran 2012: 117).

Neoclassical realism also offers a methodology to analyse small states' foreign and security policies. First, one has to identify the changes in the balance of power at the systemic level. Second, the perception of these changes at the domestic level has to be analysed. Elite perceptions combined with internal constraints are then factored in to develop measures deemed necessary and domestically acceptable and feasible to adjust to this new power configuration. This approach requires therefore 'demonstrating who is in power domestically and how the perceptions of the decisionmakers influence foreign policy' (Rickli 2016a: 137). The domestic perception of systemic changes is key to neoclassical realism. One can therefore legitimately ask the question whether there is a specific Arab or Gulf foreign policy tradition. The next section looks at the foreign policies of the Gulf and the Arab states.

The foreign policies of the Arab states

Studies on the foreign policies of the Gulf states have always been examined under the general analysis of the Arab states. In fact there is no study solely examining the foreign policies of the Gulf states. Over the past years, there have been only a few main studies on the foreign policies of the Arab states. The first study to have examined Arab states' external behaviour was the (1984) book by Bahgat Korany and Ali Hillal Dessouki, which then was updated in a new edition in 2008 to reflect how globalization has affected the Arab states, by notably looking at the role of international and non-governmental organizations. This study uses diverse theoretical approaches of foreign policy analysis ranging from state-centric power to psychological–idiosyncratic approaches. The book covers Egypt, Iraq, Jordan, Morocco, Sudan, Lebanon, Syria and only two cases from the Gulf: the UAE and Saudi Arabia. As the changes in the region over the last six years are considered a turning point in the political history of the Middle East, there is a need for a re-evaluation of these policies. The second major study on the foreign policies of the Arab states is by Raymond Hinnebusch and Anoushiravan Ehteshami (2002), on Middle East states' external behaviour. It has provided a specific theoretical framework and a strong understanding of Arab states' policies in general. Unlike the previous study, Hinnebusch and Ehteshami's study provides a new dimension in understanding the Arab states' foreign policies, in particular by looking at the influence of identity. For these authors, identity includes both state-level as well as supranational identity, such as Arab and Islamic identity as well as other cross-national ideologies. Moreover, the authors argue that the scope of the Arab states' foreign policies is determined by the core states of the international system. Under these circumstances, these states resort to omnibalancing strategies to ensure regime survival. Michael N. Barnett and Shibley Telhami's work '*Identity and foreign policy in the Middle East*' (2002) is also a major study that looks at several cases through in-depth theoretical frameworks. Similarly, Barnett and Telhami argue that identities and ideologies constitute important factors influencing states' behaviours in the Middle East. They prove their point by making a comparison between rationalist and constructivist analysis. These three studies provide important insights about the foreign policies of the Arab states by looking at identity and regional factors, but none of them examine any of the small Gulf states.

Gerd Nonneman's (2005) study '*Analyzing Middle East foreign policies and the Relationship with Europe*' constitutes another important scholarly work on the Middle Eastern states' external behaviour. Nonneman does not provide a particular case study from the Gulf, but analyses the dynamics and determinants of the GCC as well as the Arab states' foreign policies. Although there are major differences between the GCC states and other Arab states, the book explains that the domestic, regional and international environments determine the external behaviour of states in the Middle East.

Finally, the most recent theoretical study of Arab states' foreign policies is the one of Hassan Hamdan Al-Akim (2011). Al-Akim analyses Arab states' foreign policy-making by looking at domestic constraints in terms of political, economic and social factors, as well as at external constraints defined by the contemporary world order, the Arab regional system, the Arab–Israeli conflict and the interactions between the Arab states and their main neighbouring countries. The study relies on one very limiting assumption, however, which is that while 'heterogeneity among the Arab countries' is recognized, the author considers 'the Arab states as one political unit' (Al-Akim 2011: 12). In other words, the study considers that 'Arab states' foreign policy-making are [sic] determined by similar external and domestic variables' (Al-Akim 2011: 12). Considering the variations in domestic politics of the Gulf states, this assumption appears very constraining.

Similar to Al-Akim, Steven Wright (2011) looks at the different factors that influence the foreign policy of the GCC countries. Wright identifies history, elite-level alliances, the socio-political context, the regional geopolitical context, the relations with the United States and the rentier capacity of the state as important variables to consider. He argues for a 'multilevel and multicontextual' approach when it comes to the analysis of the foreign policy of the GCC states (Wright 2011: 93).

Other existing studies are normally single case studies. Almezaini (2012) examines the UAE's foreign policy and adapts a constructivist approach. The study looks at how ideas and identities influenced the UAE's foreign policy and foreign aid policy before the so-called Arab Spring. Further, Joseph Kechichian (1995) provides an analysis of Oman's foreign policy from a historical perspective. He examines in detail why Oman has had a different approach towards its neighbouring countries, as well as internationally. Mehran Kamrava (2013) looks at how Qatar as a small state has played big politics in the region. This study is supported by a theoretical framework that explains Qatar's foreign policy in terms of the pursuit of hedging strategies. All these studies underline that the Arab states have specific conditions for survival and for the conduct of their foreign policies. The next section looks more specifically at the peculiarities of the Gulf environment for small states.

The peculiarities of the small Gulf states

States in the Middle East in general and the Gulf in particular have always been labelled as being peculiar in the international system. Simon Bromley (1994: 99) points out that it is not that the Middle East is unique as the Orientalists have claimed, but rather that all contexts of state formation are peculiar. This does not include only the political nature of these states, but also their economies, particularly for the Gulf states. Ayubi argues that the political economy of Saudi Arabia and the Gulf states represents an obvious – if somewhat distinctive – case of what is sometimes called 'the export enclave syndrome', displaying most of the economic distortions that result from such heavy reliance on exportation (1996: 224). Even so, these states have managed to emerge regionally and internationally. Yet, they display many differences when compared with other small states outside the region. One could therefore legitimately ask what makes the Gulf states peculiar or an anomaly in the international system?

Several studies on the international relations of the Middle East reach the conclusion that Middle Eastern states are unique creatures (Bromley 1994; Ehteshami 2007; Korany and Hillal Dessouki 2008; Ayubi 1996; Nonneman 2005; Hinnebusch 2002; Wright 2011). However, very few of these studies provide a comprehensive explanation as to why these states are peculiar, with the exceptions of Hinnebusch and Ehteshami's work on foreign policy and globalization (2002 and 2007, respectively), as well as Wright (2011). In particular, Saouli's (2012) study on state formation provides a fresh analysis and looks at what makes the Arab state peculiar and different. From his work, five main factors can be identified: unusual state-formation, rentier economy, foreign policy, political system and tribal system.

Unlike the European experience, the small Gulf states were formed, to a great extent, due to external actors, mainly the role of the British in the Gulf before the 1970s. The establishment of these states does not necessarily reflect domestic struggles for independence from the British, but rather a collaboration between local elites and the British. The combination of internal (tribal politics) and external (British domination) factors significantly contributed to the formation of these states. Nonetheless, the regional system in which these states were established led to the emergence of peculiar states, particularly in their foreign policies. Adham Saouli (2012) points out that the Middle Eastern state was born in an international structure not of its own choosing; while competition between European rulers produced the European system, the Middle Eastern system was constituted externally. The international system structured the development of the Middle Eastern state and defines the possible responses to that structure. Saouli refers to this externality as an 'exogenous shock'. The responses to the development of the regional system, therefore, led to the activism of small states in order to strengthen their survival at the regional level.

Second, the rich endowment in hydrocarbons of the Gulf states has produced a specific economic system based on rent. The Gulf states heavily rely on the export of oil and for some gas as the main source of their income. Although programmes of economic diversification have been launched in the last fifteen years, oil remains nonetheless the major source of income. The impact of the decline of oil prices since 2014 reflects the extent to which these states depend on oil. Nonetheless, the rentier economy of the small Gulf states has played an important role in consolidating state–society relations. Al-Rumaihi (1975: 53) and Ayubi argue that

> oil money plays a peculiar role in most of these countries since, while it has led to social mobility and among various segments of the society, it also consolidates the role of the traditional elites who have the right to allocate most of the society's financial resources.
>
> (Ayubi 1996: 225)

The financial power of the Gulf states has contributed to their emergence as active players in the region. It is very likely that without these hydrocarbon resources, they would have been marginalized.

Third, because of their rentier state system, a traditional perspective on the GCC states' security policy holds that threats are primarily seen through the domestic lens of regime security rather than through international balance of power considerations (Gause 1994, 1997; Cooper 2003). Regime survival is considered as the primary objective of foreign and security policy, and domestic stability is seen as the key enabler. Thus, anything that upsets domestic stability is considered as a threat to the regime and becomes a matter of national security. This influences alignment policies towards omnibalancing (David 1991). The latter refers to the view that Arab states' alignment strategies are a consequence of their leaders seeking to counter internal and external threats to their rule. This is evident in most Arab republics that witnessed instabilities, such as in Egypt, Algeria, Syria, Tunisia and Yemen. Yet, small states in the Gulf have been more active than many other small states in the Middle East and North Africa (MENA) region over the past fifteen years. Qatar and the UAE used their military capabilities to contribute in the operation to oust Gaddafi in Libya in 2011 (Rickli 2016a; Ulrichsen 2016). They have been part of the international coalition to fight the Islamic State in Iraq and Syria (ISIS) in Syria and Iraq since 2014. Since 2015 they have joined the Saudi coalition to fight the Houthis in Yemen. With the exception of Oman, the small Gulf states have also joined NATO's Istanbul Cooperation Initiative since 2004. The UAE has even appointed a permanent ambassador to NATO. The emergence of these states as active players is partly due to the fact that they managed to maintain strong relations with Western powers, unlike some of the other Arab states. This gave the small Gulf states more confidence for playing influential roles at the regional level. Therefore, the foreign and security polices of the small states in the Gulf are, to a large extent, different from the other Arab small states.

Fourth, the MENA region is divided between monarchies and republics. The stability of the Gulf monarchies compared with the instabilities of the Arab republics has been remarkable and makes these states peculiar. Despite the fact that these monarchies are located in a hostile and unstable region, they have been able to survive and have experienced little or no political unrest. The support of the West and the economic capabilities of the monarchies significantly contributed to this achievement. The unique nature of the small Gulf states' political system (modern tribal system) allowed them to integrate at the regional level. Their economic powers allow them to have significant influence over other states. Their economic and financial capability channelled through foreign aid has been an important factor to consolidate their relations with the other Arab states. During the so-called Arab Spring, leaders of Egypt, Tunisia, Libya and Yemen were forced to step down by their people. Many other Arab states experienced this uprising, with the exception of the monarchies in the region, even though Oman witnessed demonstrations and Bahrain disruptions. In particular, the Gulf monarchies survived, and the experiences in other Arab countries strengthen the position and roles these states play at the regional level. Therefore, the stability and survival of monarchies of the Gulf in the twenty-first century demonstrate the resilience of these political regimes and these states.

Finally, the tribal nature of the Gulf states and societies adds more to our understanding as to why they are peculiar. In the Gulf Arab states of today, 'tribes are still central to national leadership and are presented by that leadership as part of the national construction' (Partrick 2012: 51). Further, Neil Partrick demonstrates that the leadership within the Gulf is composed of the dominant families or ruling tribes that emerged in the struggle for power during the pre-independence phase (2012). This tribal dimension in the small Gulf states is very much embedded within the current political structure, particularly in the state–society relations. The strong relationship between the tribal leadership and Gulf societies is a product of the pre-independence and the emergence of these states. Yet, even though these states have developed since then, the tribal factor remains an integral part of the politics and socio-economic relations of these states. The combination of modernity, tribalism and economic development have, to a large extent, made these small Gulf states peculiar, particularly in how they integrate within the regional and international systems.

Conclusions

This chapter has set the context for the study of small states' foreign and security policies. It has dealt with foreign and security policies both as an outcome and as a process. While the former exhibits a range of options to address the security dilemma based on autonomy and cooperation, the latter make sense of these choices based on factors located at the systemic, regional and state levels. When it comes to small states' FPSA, neoclassical realism offers a theoretical approach that combines both the influence of structural factors with the perceptions of these factors domestically. This chapter also demonstrated that Arab states' FPSA has been under-studied and that Gulf states' theoretical analysis is almost non-existent. This is partly due to the peculiarities of the small Gulf states' monarchies. The next chapters provide case studies exploring different aspects of the small Gulf states by focusing particularly on Qatar and the UAE.

Bibliography

Agius, C. and Devine, K. (2011). 'Neutrality: A really dead concept? A reprise', *Cooperation and Conflict*, vol. 46, issue 3, pp. 263–84.
Al-Akim, H.H. (2011). *Dynamics of Arab foreign policy-making in the twenty-first century: Domestic constraints and external challenges*. London: SAQI.
Alden, C. and Aran, A. (2012). *Foreign policy analysis: New approaches*. Abingdon, UK: Routledge.
Al-Ebraheem, H.A. (1984). *Kuwait and the Gulf: Small states and the international system*. Washington, DC: Center for Contemporary Arab Studies.
Allison, G.T. (1971). *Essence of decision: Explaining the Cuban Missile Crisis*, 2nd edn. Boston, MA: Little, Brown.
Al-Mashat, A.-M. (2008). 'Politics of constructive engagement: The foreign policy of the United Arab Emirates', in Korany, Bahgat and Hillal Dessouki, Ali E. (eds), *The foreign policies of Arab States: The challenge of globalization*. Cairo: The American University in Cairo Press, pp. 457–80.
Almezaini, K.S. (2012). *The UAE and foreign policy: Foreign aid, identities and interests*. Abingdon, UK: Routledge.
Al-Rumaihi, M.G. (1975). *Bahrain: A study on social and political changes since the First World War*. Kuwait: University of Kuwait.

Archer, C., Bailes, A. and Wivel, A. (2014). *Small states and international security: Europe and beyond*. London: Routledge.
Axelrod, R. (1976). *Structure of decision: The cognitive maps of political elites*. Princeton, NJ: Princeton University Press.
Ayubi, N.N.M. (1996). *Over-stating the Arab state: Politics and society in the Middle East*. London: I.B. Tauris.
Baehr, P.R. (1975). 'Small states: A tool for analysis?', *World Politics*, vol. 27, issue 3, pp. 456–66.
Bailes, A. and Thorhallsson, B. (2014). 'Instrumentalising the European Union in small states' strategies', *Journal of European Integration*, vol. 35, issue 2, pp. 99–115.
Bailes, A., Rickli, J.-M. and Thorhallsson, B. (2014). 'Small states, survival and strategy', in Archer, Clive, Bailes, Alyson and Wivel, Anders (eds) *Small states and international security: Europe and beyond*. London: Routledge, pp. 26–45.
Baillie, S. (1998). 'A theory of small state influence in the European Union', *Journal of International Relations and Development*, vol. 1, issue 3–4, pp. 195–219.
Baker Fox, A. (1969). 'Small states in the international system: 1919–1969', *International Journal*, vol. 24, issue 4, pp. 751–64.
Barnett, M. (1999). 'Culture, strategy and foreign policy change: Israel's road to Oslo', *European Journal of International Relations*, vol. 5, issue 1, pp: 5–36.
Barnett, M.N. and Telhami, S. (2002). *Identity and foreign policy in the Middle East*. Ithaca, NY: Cornell University Press.
Belfer, M. (2014). *Small state, dangerous regions. A strategic assessment of Bahrain*. Frankfurt: Peter Land.
Beyer, J.L. and Hofmann, S.C. (2011). 'Varieties of neutrality: Norm revision and decline', *Cooperation and Conflict*, vol. 46, issue 3, pp. 285–311.
Bindschedler, R.L. (1976). 'Neutralitätspolitik und Sicherheitspolitik', *Österreichische Zeitschrift für Aussenpolitik*, vol. 6, pp. 339–54.
Bjerga, K.I. and Haaland, T.L. (2010). 'Development of military doctrine: The particular case of small states', *Journal of Strategic Studies*, vol. 33, issue 4, pp. 505–33.
Björkdahl, A. (2008). 'Norm advocacy a small state strategy to influence the EU', *Journal of European Public Policy*, vol. 15, issue 1, pp. 135–54.
Björkdahl, A. (2013). 'Ideas and norms in Swedish peace policy', *Swiss Political Science Review*, vol. 19, issue 3, pp. 322–37.
Booth, K. (1990). 'The concept of strategic culture affirmed', in Jacobsen, Carl G. (ed), *Strategic power: USA/USSR*. London: Macmillan, pp. 121–8.
Bromley, S. (1994). *Rethinking Middle East politics*. Austin, TX: University of Texas Press.
Caldwell, D. (1977). 'Bureaucratic foreign policy-making', *American Behavioral Scientist*, vol. 21, issue 1, pp. 87–110.
Carlsnaes, W. (1992). 'The agency-structure problem in foreign policy analysis', *International Studies Quarterly*, vol. 36, issue 3, pp. 245–70.
Cheng-Chwee, K. (2008). 'The essence of hedging: Malaysia and Singapore's response to rising China', *Contemporary Southeast Asia*, vol. 30, issue 2, pp. 159–85.
Cooper, A. (ed) (1997). *Niche diplomacy: Middle powers after the Cold War*. New York: Macmillan.
Cooper, A.F. and Shaw, T. (eds) (2009). *The diplomacies of small states*. Basingstoke, UK: Macmillan.
Cooper, S. (2003). 'State-centric balance-of-threat theory: Explaining the misunderstood GCC', *Security Studies*, vol. 13, issue 2, pp. 306–49.
Crandall, M. and Collin, A. (2015). 'Small states and big ideas: Estonia's battle for cybersecurity norms', *Contemporary Security Policy*, vol. 36, issue 2, pp. 346–68.

Däniker, G. (1966). *Strategie des Kleinstaates*. Huber: Frauenfeld.
David, S.R. (1991). 'Explaining Third World alignment', *World Politics*, vol. 42, issue 2, pp. 233–56.
de Carvalho, B. and Neumann, I.B. (eds) (2015). *Small state status seeking: Norway's quest for international standing*. London: Routledge.
Donnelly, J. (2000). *Realism and international relations*. Cambridge: Cambridge University Press.
Drezner, D.W. (2000). 'Ideas, bureaucratic politics, and the crafting of foreign policy', *American Journal of Political Science*, vol. 44, issue 4, pp. 733–49.
Duke, S. (2001). 'Small states and European security', in Reiter, Erich and Gärtner, Heinz (eds), *Small states and alliances*. Heidelberg: Physica-Verlag, pp. 39–50.
East, M.A. (1973). 'Size and foreign policy behaviour: A test of two models', *World Politics*, vol. 25, issue 4, pp. 556–76.
Ehteshami, A. (2007). *Globalization and geopolitics in the Middle East: Old games, new rules*. New York: Routledge.
Fendius Elman, M. (1995). 'The foreign policies of small states: Challenging neorealism in its own backyard', *British Journal of Political Science*, vol. 25, issue 2, pp. 171–217.
Finnemore, M. and Sikkink, K. (1998). 'International norm dynamics and political change', *International Organization*, vol. 52, issue 4, pp. 887–917.
Galbreath, D. (2014). 'Western European armed forces and the modernisation agenda: Following or falling behind', *Defence Studies*, vol. 14, issue 4, pp. 394–413.
Gärtner, H. (2001). 'Small states and alliances', in Reiter, Erich and Gärtner, Heinz (eds), *Small states and alliances*. Heidelberg: Physica-Verlag, pp. 1–10.
Gause, F.G. III (1994). *Oil monarchies: Domestic and security challenges in the Arab States*. New York: Council On Foreign Relations.
Gause, F.G. III (1997). 'Arms supplies and military spending in the Gulf', *Middle East Report*, No. 204 (July to September), pp. 12–14.
Gerner, D.J. (1995). 'The evolution of the study of foreign policy', in Neack, Laura, Hey, Jeanne A. K. and Haney, Patrick J. (eds), *Foreign policy analysis: Continuity and change in its second generation*. Englewood Cliffs: Prentice-Hall, pp. 17–32.
Glenn, J. (2009). 'Realism versus strategic culture: Competition and collaboration?', *International Studies Review*, vol. 11, issue 3, pp. 523–51.
Goetschel, L. (1998). 'The foreign and security policy interests of small states in today's Europe', in Goetschel, Laurent (ed), *Small states inside and outside the European Union*. Dordrecht: Kluwer Academic, pp. 13–31.
Goetschel, L. (2000). *Small states and the common foreign and security policy of the EU: A comparative analysis*. Bern, Switzerland: Institut für Politikwissenschaften.
Gourevitch, P. (2002). 'Domestic politics and international relations', in Carlsnaes, Walter, Risse, Thomas and Simmons, Beth (eds), *Handbook of international relations*. New York: SAGE, pp. 309–28.
Gvalia, G., Siroky, D., Lebanidze, B. and Iashvili, Z. (2013). 'Thinking outside the bloc: Explaining the foreign policies of small states', *Security Studies*, vol. 22, issue 1, pp. 98–131.
Handel, M. (1990). *Weak states in the international system*. London: Frank Cass.
Held, D., and Ulrichsen, K. (2012). *The transformation of the Gulf politics, economics and the global order*. Abingdon, UK: Routledge.
Hey, J.A.K. (2003). *Small states in world politics: Explaining foreign policy behavior*. Boulder, CO: Lynne Rienner.
Hill, C. (1993). *The changing politics of foreign policy*. Basingstoke, UK: Palgrave.
Hinnebusch, R.A. and Ehteshami, A. (2002). *The foreign policies of Middle East states*. Boulder, CO: Lynne Rienner.

Inbar, E. and Sheffer, G. (1997). *The National Security of small states in a changing world*. London: Frank Cass.

Ingebritsen, C. (2002). 'Norm entrepreneurs: Scandinavia's role in world politics', *Cooperation and Conflict*, vol. 37, issue 1, pp. 11–23.

Jazbec, M. (2001). *The diplomacies of new small states: The case of Slovenia with some comparison from the Baltics*. Aldershot, UK: Ashgate.

Jervis, R. (1976). *Perception and misperception in international politics*. Princeton: Princeton University Press.

Kaarbo, J. (2012). *Coalition politics and cabinet decision making: A comparative analysis of foreign policy choices*. Ann Arbor, MI: University of Michigan Press.

Kamrava, M. (2013). *Qatar: Small state, big politics*. New York: Cornell University Press.

Kechichian, J.A. (1995). *Oman and the world: The emergence of an independent foreign policy*. Santa Monica, CA: Rand.

Keohane, R.O. (1969). 'Lilliputians' dilemmas: Small states in international politics', *International Organization*, vol. 23, issue 2, pp. 291–310.

Keohane, R.O. and Martin, L. (1995). 'The promise of an institutional theory', *International Security*, vol. 20, issue 1, pp. 39–51.

Keohane, R.O. and Nye, J.S. (1977). *Power and interdependence*. New York: Longman.

Khatib, L. (2013). 'Qatar's foreign policy: The limits of pragmatism', *International Affairs*, vol. 89, issue 2, March, pp. 417–31.

Kier, E. (1995). 'Culture and Military Doctrine: France between the wars', *International Security*, vol. 19, issue 4, pp. 65–93.

Kisangani, E.F. and Pickering, J. (2011). 'Democratic accountability and diversionary force: Regime types and the use of benevolent and hostile military force', *Journal of Conflict Resolution*, vol. 55, issue 6, pp. 1021–46.

Knudsen, O. (2002). 'Small states, latent and extant: Towards a general perspective', *Journal of International Relations and Development*, vol. 5, issue 2, pp. 184–200.

Knudsen, O. (ed) (2007). *Security strategies, power disparity and identity*. Aldershot, UK: Ashgate.

Korany, B. and Hillal Dessouki, A.E. (eds) (2008). *The foreign policies of Arab states: The challenge of globalization*. Cairo: American University in Cairo Press.

Lim, D.J. and Cooper, Z. (2015). 'Reassessing hedging: The logic of alignment in East Asia', *Security Studies*, vol. 24, issue 4, pp. 696–727.

Loo, B. (ed) (2009). *Military transformation and strategy: Revolutions in military affairs and small states*. London: Routledge.

LSE Middle East Centre (2015). *The new politics of intervention of Gulf Arab States*. London: LSE Middle East Centre. Collected Papers, Volume 1, April.

Maass, M. (2009). 'The elusive definition of the small state', *International Politics*, vol. 46, issue 1, pp. 65–83.

Maass, M. (2014). 'Small states: survival and proliferation', *International Politics*, vol. 51, issue 6, pp. 709–28.

Männik, E. (2004). 'Small states: Invited to Nato – able to contribute?', *Defense & Security Analysis*, vol. 20, issue 1, pp. 21–37.

Matthews, R. and Yan, N.Z. (2007). 'Small country 'total defence': A case study of Singapore', *Defence Studies*, vol. 7, issue 3, pp. 376–95.

Miller, B. (2005). 'When and how regions become peaceful: Potential theoretical pathways to peace', *International Studies Review*, vol. 7, issue 2, pp. 229–67.

Molis, A. (2006). 'The role and interests of small states in developing European security and defence policy', *Baltic Security & Defence Review*, vol. 8, pp. 81–100.

Morgenthau, H. (1948). *Politics among nations: The struggle for power and peace*. New York: Knopf.

Mouritzen, H. (1991). 'Tensions between the strong, and the strategies of the weak', *Journal of Peace Research*, vol. 28, issue 2, pp. 217–30.

Mouritzen, H. (1997). *External danger and democracy: Old Nordic lessons and new European challenges.* Aldershot, UK: Ashgate.

Mouritzen, H. and Wivel, A. (2005). *The geopolitics of Euro-Atlantic integration.* London: Routledge.

Müller, H. (2002). 'Security cooperation', in Carlsnaes, Walter, Risse, Thomas and Simmons, Beth A. (eds), *Handbook of international relations.* London: SAGE, pp. 369–91.

Neumann, I.B. and Gstöhl, S. (2004). *Lilliputians in Gulliver's world: Small states in international relations.* Reykjavik: Centre for Small State Studies, University of Iceland.

Nonneman, G. (2005). *Analyzing Middle East foreign policies and the relationship with Europe.* London: Routledge.

Nye, J. (2004). *Soft power: The means to success in world politics.* New York: PublicAffairs.

Panke, D. (2012). 'Dwarfs in international negotiations: How small states make their voices heard', *Cambridge Review of International Affairs*, vol. 25, issue 3, pp. 313–28.

Partrick, N. (2012). 'Nationalism in the Gulf states', in Held, David and Ulrichsen, Kristian (eds), *The transformation of the Gulf politics, economics and the global order.* Abingdon: Routledge, pp. 47–65.

Payne, A. (1993). 'The politics of small state security in the Pacific', *Journal of Commonwealth and Comparative Politics*, vol. 31, issue 2, pp. 103–32.

Poore, S. (2004). 'Strategic culture', in Poore, Stuart (ed), *Neorealism versus strategic culture.* London: Ashgate, pp. 45–71.

Putnam, R.D. (1988). 'Diplomacy and domestic politics: The logic of two-level games', *International Organisation*, vol. 42, issue 3, pp. 427–460.

Ralston, J.W. (1969). *The defense of small states in the Nuclear Age.* PhD dissertation: Graduate Institute of International Studies, University of Geneva.

Ratti, L. (2006). 'Post-Cold War Nato and international relations theory: The case for neoclassical realism', *Journal of Transatlantic Studies*, vol. 4, issue 1, pp. 81–110.

Raymond, G.A. (1997). 'Neutrality norms and the balance of power', *Cooperation and Conflict*, vol. 32, issue 2, pp: 123–146.

Reiter, D. (1996). *Crucible of beliefs: Learning, alliances, and world wars.* Cornell: Cornell University Press.

Rickli, J.-M. (2004). 'The Western influence on Swedish and Swiss policies of armed neutrality during the early Cold War', in Schwok, René (ed), *Interactions globales.* Genève: Institut Européen de l'Université de Genève, pp. 117–34.

Rickli, J.-M. (2008). 'European small states' military policies after the Cold War: From territorial to niche strategies', *Cambridge Review of International Affairs*, vol. 21, issue 3, pp. 307–25.

Rickli, J.-M. (2010a). *The evolution of the European neutral and non-allied states' military policies after the Cold War 1989–2004.* PhD dissertation: University of Oxford, Oxford.

Rickli, J.-M. (2010b). 'Neutrality inside and outside the EU: A comparison of the Austrian and Swiss security policies after the Cold War', in Steinmetz, Robert, Thorhallsson, Baldur and Wivel, Anders (eds), *Small states in Europe: Challenges and opportunities.* Aldershot, UK: Ashgate, pp. 181–98.

Rickli, J.-M. (2014). 'Clean energy as a niche strategy for small states to guarantee energy security. The example of the Gulf Countries', in Luciani, Giacomo and Ferroukhi, Rabia (eds), *Political economy of energy reform: The clean energy–fossil fuel balance in the Gulf.* Berlin: Gerlach Press, pp. 265–88.

Rickli, J.-M. (2016a). 'The political rationale and implications of the United Arab Emirates' military involvement in Libya', in Henriksen, Dag and Larssen, Ann Karin (eds), *Political rationale and international consequences of the war in Libya*. Oxford: Oxford University Press, pp. 134–54.

Rickli, J.-M. (2016b). 'New alliances dynamics and their impact on small GCC states', *Third World Thematic (thematic issue of Third World Quarterly)*, vol. 1, issue 1, pp. 1–19.

Risse-Kappen, T. (1991). 'Public opinion, domestic structure, and foreign policy in liberal democracies', *World Politics*, vol. 43, issue 4, pp. 479–512.

Risse-Kappen, T. (ed) (1995). *Bringing transnational relations back in: Non-state actors, domestic structures and international institutions*. Cambridge: Cambridge University Press.

Rose, G. (1998). 'Neoclassical realism and theories of foreign policy', *World Policy*, vol. 51, issue 1, pp. 144–77.

Rosenau, J. (1966). 'Pre-theories and theories and foreign policy', in Farrell, Barry (ed), *Approaches to comparative and international politics*. Evanston, IL: Northwestern University Press, pp. 27–92.

Rothstein, R.L. (1968). *Alliances and small powers*. New York: Columbia University Press.

Rummel, R. (1995). 'Democracies are less warlike than other regimes', *European Journal of International Relations*, vol. 1, issue 4, pp. 449–64.

Russet, B.M. (1993). *Grasping the democratic peace: Principle for a post-Cold War world*. Princeton: Princeton University Press.

Saouli, A. (2012). *The Arab state: Dilemmas of late formation*. London: Routledge.

Schindler, D. (1992). 'Changing conceptions of neutrality in Switzerland', *Austrian Journal of Public and International Law*, vol. 44, pp. 105–16.

Schweller, R. (1994). 'Bandwagoning for profit', *International Security*, vol. 19, issue 1, pp. 72–107.

Setälä, M. (2004). *Small states and Nato: Influence and accommodations*. Helsinki: The Atlantic Council of Finland.

Simon, H. (1957). *Models of man, social and rational: Mathematical essays on rational human behavior in a social setting*. New York: Wiley.

Simon, J. (2005). *Nato expeditionary operations: Impacts upon new members and partners*. Washington, DC: National Defence University Press.

Snyder, R., Bruck, H.W. and Sapin, B. (1962). *Foreign policy decision-making: An approach to the study of international politics*. New York: Free Press/Macmillan.

Steinmetz, R., Thorhallsson, B. and Wivel, A. (eds) (2010). *Small states in Europe: Challenges and opportunities*. Aldershot, UK: Ashgate.

Strange, S. (1996). *The retreat of the state: The diffusion of power in the world economy*. Cambridge, UK: Cambridge University Press.

Sutton, P. (1987). 'Political aspects', in Clarke, Colin and Payne, Tony (eds), *Politics, security and development in small states*. London: Allen & Unwin, pp. 3–25.

Swiss Political Science Review (2013). 'Natural born peacemakers? Ideas and Identities in foreign policies of small states in Western Europe', *Swiss Political Science Review*, Special Issue, vol. 19, issue 3, pp. 259–423.

Taliaferro, J.W., Lobell, S.E. and Ripsman, N.M. (2009). 'Introduction: Neoclassical realism, the state and foreign policy', in Taliaferro, Jeffrey W., Lobell, Steven E. and Ripsman, Norrin M. (eds), *Neoclassical realism, the state and foreign policy*, Cambridge, UK: Cambridge University Press, pp. 1–41.

Taulbee, J.L. (2014). 'Lesser states and niche diplomacy', in Taulbee, James Larry, Kelleher, Ann and Grosvenor, Peter C. (eds), *Norway's peace policy: Soft power in a turbulent world*. New York: Palgrave Macmillan, pp. 1–22.

Thorhallsson, B. (2000). *The Role of small states in the European Union*. Aldershot, UK: Ashgate.

Thorhallsson, B. (2012). 'Small states in the UN Security Council: Means of influence?', *The Hague Journal of Diplomacy*, vol. 7, issue 2, pp. 135–60.

Thorhallsson, B. and Wivel, A. (2006). 'Small states in the European Union: What do we know and what would we like to know?', *Cambridge Review of International Affairs*, vol. 19, issue 4, pp. 651–68.

Tunsjø, Ø. (2013). *Security and profit in China's energy policy: Hedging against risk*. New York: Columbia University Press.

Ulrichsen, K.C. (2012). 'Small states with a big role: Qatar and the United Arab Emirates in the wake of the Arab Spring', Discussion Paper. Durham, UK: Durham University, HH Sheikh Nasser al-Mohammed, al-Sabah Programme.

Ulrichsen, K.C. (2014). *Qatar and the Arab Spring*. Oxford: Oxford University Press.

Ulrichsen, K.C. (2016). 'The rationale and implications of Qatar's intervention in Libya', in Henriksen, Dag and Larssen, Ann Karin (eds), *Political rationale and international consequences of the war in Libya*. Oxford: Oxford University Press, pp. 118–35.

United Nations (1945). *Charter of the United Nations and Statute of the International Court of Justice*. San Francisco, CA: United Nations.

Vital, D. (1966). *The unaligned small state in its foreign relations*. PhD dissertation, Oxford: University of Oxford.

Vital, D. (1971). *The Survival of small states: Studies in small power/great power conflict*. Oxford University Press: London.

Vukadinovic, R. (1989). 'The various conception of European neutrality' in Haltzel, Michael H. and Kruzel, Joseph (eds), *Between the blocs: Problems and prospects for Europe's neutral and nonaligned states*. Cambridge, UK: Cambridge University Press, pp. 29–46.

Walt, S.M. (1987). *The origins of alliances*. Ithaca, NY: Cornell University Press.

Welch, D. (1992). 'The organizational process and bureaucratic politics paradigms', *International Security*, vol. 17, issue 2, pp. 112–46.

Wiberg, H. (1996). 'Security problems of small nations', in Bauwens, Werner, Clesse, Armand and Knudsen, Olav (eds), *Small states and the security challenge in the new Europe*. London: Brassey's, pp. 21–41.

Wivel, A. (2003). 'Small states and Alliances', *International Affairs*, vol. 79, issue 1, pp. 176–7.

Wivel, A. (2005). 'The security challenge of small EU member states: Interests, identity and the development of the EU as a security actor', *Journal of Common Market Studies*, vol. 43, issue 2, pp. 393–412.

World Bank (2011, 24 September). 'The World Bank and small states: Accelerating partnership', in *Small states forum: Sustainability of small state's development and growth*, Washington, World Bank, http://siteresources.worldbank.org/PROJECTS/Resources/40940-1118776867573/TheWorldBankandSmallStates.pdf (accessed 6 September 2016).

Wright, S. (2011). 'Foreign policy in the GCC states', in Kamrava, Mehran (ed), *International politics of the Persian Gulf*. New York: Syracuse University Press, pp. 72–93.

Wright, S. (2012). 'Foreign policies with international reach: The case of Qatar', in Held, David and Ulrichsen, Kristian (eds), *The transformation of the Gulf: Politics, economics and the global order*. London: Routledge, pp. 296–332.

Zahariadis, N. (1994). 'Nationalism and small state foreign policy: The Greek response to the Macedonian issue', *Political Science Quarterly*, vol. 109, issue 4, pp. 647–67.

3

THE CHANGING SECURITY DYNAMIC IN THE MIDDLE EAST AND ITS IMPACT ON SMALLER GULF COOPERATION COUNCIL STATES' ALLIANCE CHOICES AND POLICIES

Victor Gervais

Introduction

This chapter analyses the impact of the changing security dynamics in the Middle East on the Gulf Cooperation Council (GCC) states' external and internal alliance choices and policies, highlighting current limitations and growing contradictions. In particular, it shows that recent regional activism by smaller GCC states – in particular, Qatar and the UAE – has undermined the traditional alliance model established in the Gulf more than three decades ago.

The chapter first outlines the parameters that guide smaller GCC states' ruling elites when they make alliance decisions. Interestingly, while the international relations (IR) literature on small states claims that cooperative strategies are usually preferred by states to maximize their influence—at the expense of their autonomy—smaller GCC states have actually opted for a hedging strategy based on a multilevel alliance model that prioritizes both protection and autonomy. This contrasting alliance model embodies important and distinctive features. At the GCC level, cooperative strategies have mainly focused on internal security threats, while fears of Saudi hegemony on the part of the smaller member states have hampered progress toward security cooperation in other key areas. Military integration, in particular, has remained largely symbolic and limited to temporary bursts of coordination activity. In order to avoid any external disruption of the status quo, GCC states have opted instead to rely on extraregional protectors, each smaller member state being integrated under the U.S. security umbrella on a bilateral basis. Efforts to maintain room to maneuver within the Saudi orbit also explains smaller GCC states' willingness to rely on their own resources and capabilities when trying to shape regional dynamics and influence political developments across the region—rather than making the GCC, as a multilateral body, the main source of their regional influence.

This model has kept smaller GCC states safe and secure for more than three decades. However, due to the changing dynamics in the region, it is currently facing significant challenges. On the one hand, confidence in the United States' ability and willingness to guarantee regional stability and secure GCC states' core interests has been severely hurt by the 2003 U.S. invasion of Iraq and its aftermath, and more recently by U.S. diplomatic choices during the "Arab uprisings." On the other hand, rivalries and tensions among GCC states have been increasing as they have become more involved politically, financially, and militarily in most areas of regional unrest and compete for influence in the power vacuum created by the dislocation of the regional order. Significantly, as a result of this increasingly activist and assertive foreign policy across the region, there has been a lack of consensus among GCC states regarding the nature of internal threats and how to prioritize among them, thereby undercutting the alliance's ability to develop a common understanding of durable patterns of amity and enmity, as well as a regional approach to the continuous challenges raised by current regional political developments. Indeed, while the fear of Iranian-led Shia uprising in the Gulf and Iran's growing regional influence continue to unite GCC states, as demonstrated by the Peninsula Shield Force (PSF) intervention in Bahrain and the Saudi-led intervention in Yemen, there is a clear lack of agreement regarding the identification, assessment, and prioritization of other perceived internal threats, such as the Muslim Brotherhood.

In this regard, this chapter aims to offer new insights into the impact of the changing security dynamics in the Middle East regional system on smaller GCC states' alliance policies. It argues that these regional developments have not only created new security challenges for these states, but—more importantly—they have also strongly called into question the validity of the multilevel alliance model established in the Gulf over the past three decades in an attempt to combine both security and a degree of regional autonomy. The chapter is divided into three sections. First, it outlines the main characteristics of the smaller GCC states' security and alliance policies. Second, it examines the transformation of regional dynamics and structures in recent years and analyzes its impact on the alliance model of smaller GCC states. By looking at the interplay between the changing dynamics in the Middle East and the security policies of the smaller GCC states, it then explains the limitations and contradictions of the smaller GCC states' alliance model.

Threat perceptions and alliance choices of the smaller GCC states

There is an apparent consensus in the literature about the main characteristics of GCC states' security policies and the parameters that guide their ruling elites when they make alliance decisions. It has been asserted (Gause, 1994, 1997; Cooper, 2003) that GCC states view threats primarily through the lens of regime security rather than through more conventional balance of power considerations. They balance threats rather than aggregate power, and threats may be internal, not solely external (David, 1991).[1] In particular, rulers see threats to regime security as particularly salient because of the importance of transnational identities and ideologies in the region (Barnett, 1998; Piscatori 1983; Ajami, 1981).[2] When making alliance decisions, GCC states thus prioritize threats directed against the legitimacy and stability of their ruling regimes: regional states act more against perceived threats to their own domestic stability emanating from abroad, than attempting to counter unfavorable changes in the distribution of power or to take advantage of favorable power imbalances between states. In other words, according to Gregory Gause (2010, p. 9), they do not choose their allies based on "classic balance considerations, balancing against the strongest regional state, but on how their domestic regime security would be affected by the outcome of regional conflicts." Accordingly, we can expect successful regional cooperation to be based primarily on the convergence of regime interests relating to internal security, especially the shared perception of internally generated threats to the security of states and the stability of regimes (Ayubi, 1996, p. 62).[3]

In many ways, the GCC's trajectory is consistent with these parameters. The smaller Arab Gulf states' decision to join the Saudi-led GCC in 1981 seems, indeed, best explained by leaders' concerns about the spread of internal unrest following the Iranian revolution, rather than by fear of military spillover from the Iran–Iraq war or the possibility of direct Iranian military invasion.[4] As Barnett and Gause (1998, p. 171) put it:

> the GCC has been established to provide a safe (for GCC leaders) political alternative for citizens' loyalties against the appeals of Baghdad and Tehran by offering Gulf citizens a rhetorical and an institutional alternative identity (beyond their state identities) that would compete with Iran's Islamic revolutionary and Iraq's secular Arab nationalist platforms.

> This preoccupation – cooperation and coordination between member states to preserve security within their territorial borders – has remained one of the principal characteristics of the organization
>
> (Legrenzi, 2011)[5]

To some extent, the focus on internal threats also explains why there has been so little external security cooperation at the GCC level (Russell, 2007). While increased sharing of intelligence about political dissent and coordination on internal security issues have directly improved state security, which was, unsurprisingly, an early achievement within the GCC framework, external military cooperation, on the other hand, has remained at the margin of the organization's core purpose. Even today, GCC external defense is largely a symbolic display of unity represented by a numerically and practically limited force (Partrick, 2011; Ramazani, 1988). Thirty-five years after its establishment, the GCC remains an institutional forum for the Gulf monarchies to coordinate policies and work out their differences, but has failed to integrate them and evolve into a real military alliance. The GCC members have opted instead to rely on powerful extraregional protectors, in particular the United States, to bolster their defenses and guarantee their external protection.[6]

This system of bilateral alliances, developed in the aftermath of Saddam Hussein's invasion of the State of Kuwait on August 2 1990, has since served as the backbone of external security relations for GCC states.

Throughout the region, states' attempts to develop conventional military capabilities were similarly shaped by the seemingly contradictory objectives of protecting themselves from internal threats as well as external adversaries. Although they have invested heavily in conventional arms, the literature in the field has typically assumed that GCC states have often preferred to have weak militaries, trading over lower military effectiveness for greater ruling family control and a reduced risk of military takeover (Cooper, 2003).[7] As James A. Russell explains (2007, p. 21), it is almost universally agreed that:

> while Middle Eastern leaders historically spent lavishly on conventional arms, those arms were never primarily intended to provide credible conventional military capability to reduce external threats to state security. The reason for this is that regional regimes were motivated by a more important consideration: the overriding domestic political imperative to keep their conventional militaries weak as a way to mitigate coup threats from their militaries. Instead of protecting regimes from external threats, arms purchases served as vehicles to co-opt potential internal regime opponents while simultaneously addressing a more important purpose of cementing political relations with outside powers.[8]

GCC countries' capacity to mobilize and organize a credible deterrence is thus seen to have been hampered by the institutional legacy of state-building processes for which "coup-proofing," ruling family politics and patronage employment were the predominant motives shaping their armed forces (Hertog, 2011).

Therefore, amid a variety of conceptual perspectives, scholars in the field have generally converged around a common conclusion that, while the GCC states are facing a broad range of security and foreign policy challenges, their security policies and alignment behaviors have been shaped by one essential parameter: the stability of the ruling regimes. This, however, only partially explains smaller GCC states' preference for extraregional protection and thus fails to provide an accurate understanding of the alignment behaviors of the smaller GCC states—the UAE and Qatar in particular. Indeed, the limited coordination and cooperation at the regional (GCC) level and the ensuing reliance on external powers to guarantee external protection and stability appears to be also the result of another factor: the unequal distribution of power, or capabilities, among the GCC member states. With Saudi Arabia as the dominant and—at times—overbearing patron, smaller GCC states—Qatar, UAE, Kuwait, Bahrain, and Oman—have constantly expressed their reluctance to voluntarily dilute their sovereignty and autonomy within a larger bloc: while accepting to bandwagon with the Saudi leadership on certain issues of common concern, they have maneuvered to maintain autonomy from Riyadh whenever possible. Although the GCC has been the most resilient subregional organization in the Arab world, its evolution has thus been dictated by this regional competition. As rightly pointed out by Matteo Legrenzi (2011, p. 1), the GCC:

> was not created to serve a regional institutional purpose, but rather, was deliberately made hollow and served primarily to project a semblance of unity. As in previous cases in the history of the Arab system, the smaller member states fear the interdependence that such an institution was ostensibly designed to promote.

As such, while third parties usually provide an incentive for group action, in this case the presence of extraregional protectors has represented a strong deterrent to regional cooperation and integration: in spite of Saudi Arabia's repeated calls for greater integration, the integration of smaller GCC states under the U.S. security umbrella has enabled them to avoid the cost of regional integration and to maintain some degree of regional autonomy and room to maneuver within the Saudi orbit (Gause, 1994, 2010; Cooper 2003).

Such considerations are an important and unavoidable feature of the smaller GCC states' alliance choices and policies. They enable us to understand how the multilevel framework of alliance has allowed these states over the past decades to secure their independence and stability through alignment behaviors aimed at guaranteeing both their protection and regional autonomy—at the expense of their influence, from a collective standpoint. Each of these elements, however, is under challenge today due to changing security dynamics at the regional level. In the past years, confidence in extraregional protection has been shaken. In addition, regional disorder and fragmentation have led to the rise of new security challenges through the gradual overlapping of the sub-RSCs (Regional Security Complexes) of the Gulf and the Levant, and increased security interdependence, creating significant variations in the main patterns of amity and enmity among regional actors. As the influence of Saudi Arabia wanes, smaller GCC states have become more assertive at the regional level, playing a key role in trying to shape regional dynamics and influence political developments in most areas of regional unrest. Together these changing dynamics have greatly undermined the traditional alliance model developed in the Gulf during the past decades. To highlight these limitations, the next section examines the transformation of the regional dynamic and power structure in recent years and analyzes its impact on the alliance model of the smaller GCC states. In order to track and analyze these regional changes and their implications, it draws largely on the concept of RSCs, first introduced by Barry Buzan.

The changing security dynamics in the Middle East regional system

In many ways, security dynamics in the Middle East and the effects of regional changes on the GCC's alliance policies are best explained by viewing the area as a RSC. RSCs are defined (Buzan and Waever, 2003, p. 44) as "a set of units whose major processes of securitization and desecuritization are so interlinked that their security problems cannot reasonably be analyzed or resolved apart from each other." They are regions seen through the lens of security: their formation derives from the mutuality of threat/fear felt among members toward each other, and the intensity and the durability of their security interactions, whether positive or negative.[9] The RSC theory's focus on regional patterns of rivalry has been widely used in recent years to explain security outcomes in the Middle East and the Gulf region—the wars that took place, the alliances that have been formed, and problems of sociopolitical cohesion.[10] In particular, it has helped understand why power relations and the insecurity of ruling elites within their domestic sphere have played a significant role in shaping the dynamics of (in)security overall.

In this regard, in an interesting development of the RSC theory, Buzan and Waever (2003, p. 40) added an operational formulation of the theory, making it therefore possible to analyze changes within any region, and anticipate and explain them up to a point. As the authors claimed (2003, p. 53), RSCs have durable substructures, and internal and external boundaries that can be used to monitor continuity and change, as well as to distinguish significant change from less important events. In particular, under the condition of anarchy, RSCs are defined by two kinds of relationships: power relations and patterns of amity and enmity. As such, the essential structure of a RSC depends on four variables. First, boundaries differentiate a RSC from its neighbors.[11]

Second, a RSC has an anarchic structure composed of two or more autonomous units. The third variable is polarity, which covers the distribution of power among the units. The fourth variable is social construction, which refers to the pattern of amity and enmity among the units. From this configuration, Buzan and Waever (2003, p. 53) logically conclude that, at any given point in time, only three possible evolutions are open to a RSC:

- Maintenance of the status quo: no significant changes are observed in the RSC's essential structure.
- Internal transformation: changes in its essential structure occur within the context of the RSC's existing boundary and could be associated with changes in the anarchic structure (regional integration), in polarity (state failure, merger, conquest, different growth rates, or so on), or in the dominant patterns of amity/enmity (ideological shifts, war-weariness, changes of leadership).
- External transformation: the outer boundary of a RSC is transformed, through expansion or contraction, thus changing the RSC's membership.

Within these parameters of essential structure and evolution, we can identify and assess changes that have taken place in the Middle East in recent years. Over the last decade, the region has undergone a profound internal transformation that can be monitored by reviewing material and discursive conditions of change.

First, the structures and balances of power established in the late 1970s and amended after the end of the Cold War have collapsed. These structures and balances included a number of key elements. In the Levant, the Arab-Israeli peace process, with all its limitations, contributed to reducing existing tensions in this part of the region. Already at peace with Egypt, Israel signed a peace agreement with Jordan in 1994 and entered several rounds of negotiations with the Syrian regime, thus ensuring both formal and informal truces with all its major contiguous state opponents (Salem, 2008).[12] In addition, a weakened Palestine Liberation Organization (PLO) was coopted into the 1993 Oslo accord, while Syria's regional role was recognized and its influence in Lebanon legitimized. Meanwhile, groups opposed to this process—Hamas, Hezbollah, and other dominant Palestinian factions—were weakened, isolated, and contained. In the Gulf, Iraq was first bolstered in the 1980s, then defeated in 1991, and was preserved during the following decade as a buffer to counterbalance revolutionary Iran, under the U.S. dual containment policy. In both the Levant and the Gulf, the United States has acted as the key security broker and patron for regional states, ensuring the stability of the regional order it had contributed to shape (Roy, 1999).

Today this system is in ruins. With Saddam Hussein ousted from power in 2003 and Iraq subsequently weakened, the polarity in the region has changed as Iran has become a dominant player in the core of the Arab system. Also, the rising relative strength and confidence of Iran in the region has further provided a reinforced pole of attraction for those actors out of step with U.S. policy (Fawcett, 2013). In particular, the U.S. war on Iraq strengthened those Middle Eastern states and non-state actors that had been contained in the 1990s and were unwilling to legitimize U.S. hegemony over the region or to accept normalization with Israel. This brought new support to the so-called *front du refus* formed by Hamas and Hezbollah, under the Iranian leadership, and later joined by Syria in an attempt to challenge the regional status quo. The regional order has been further modified by the Arab Spring and the ongoing civil war in Syria, which have exposed the fragility of the state institutions both at the margin and the core of the Middle East systems. This, in turn, has created a significant power vacuum as the traditional leading Arab states, such as Egypt, Syria, and Iraq, even Libya, are now quite incapable of acting as dominant and influential powers at the regional level. As a consequence, non-Arab states—Israel, Iran, and Turkey—have played a greater role in shaping regional dynamics. GCC states have also stepped up their regional role, taking up a new leadership position in the Middle East. Second, these profound developments have altered the dominant patterns of amity/enmity in the region. By removing the Iraqi state, the U.S. invasion of Iraq not only broke the old Middle East state system of power balances and buffers, but also led to increased sectarian tensions. Indeed, the Shia–Sunni divide, instrumentalized by regional states and non-state actors, has emerged as one of the leading strategic factors in the Middle East—and as a new source of tensions and instability. In addition, the weakening of certain states' authority has provided radical Sunni organizations, such as al-Qaeda and the so-called Islamic state, with the territorial space and resources they need to (re)materialize and flourish as regional actors, thereby making counterterrorism a core feature of regional states' foreign and security policies, and alignment behaviors. These variations in the main patterns of amity and enmity in the Middle East RSC have also generated significant divisions between regional states over the Muslim Brotherhood and the prominent role this organization played at the outset of the Arab Spring. In this regard, we must observe that enmity and amity in relationships do affect interstate relations and thus polarity as well. Significantly, while the development of radical Sunni organizations in the region has been seen as a key factor leading to greater "penetration" of the Middle East RSC in the aftermath of 9/11 (Buzan and Waever, 2003), it has also reinforced the processes of security interactions between states in the region, as the rise of the Muslim Brotherhood illustrated. In particular, this has led to the gradual overlapping of the subregional security systems of the Gulf and the Levant through increased security interdependence.[13] This gradual overlapping of the previous semiautonomous subregional complexes, in turn, has generated new dynamics that go beyond the Israeli–Arab conflict and the struggle for leadership among Arab states—a phenomenon overlooked by the majority of authors who have studied Middle East and Gulf security issues.

In summary, the internal transformation of the Middle East's RSC in the past decade was driven by a mix of power and status rivalries, wars and changes of leadership, ideological competition, and ethnic, sectarian, and cultural divisions. In particular, the U.S. war on Iraq and the Arab Spring, changed some of the Middle East RSC's basic structures and have triggered sequences of events that are likely to define security dynamics in the region in the near future. These changes, in turn, pose certain difficulties for the smaller GCC states, as they raise new security concerns and call their alliance model into question. The next section identifies, in particular, two main challenges facing the smaller GCC states' alliance model and policies.

Smaller GCC states' alliance model

Challenges and uncertainties

The first of these challenges is linked to the GCC states' reassessment of the value and reliability of their strategic alliance with the Superpower. The United States has acted as the Gulf's policeman during the past three decades, with varying degrees of success. However, as American power and predominance have continued increasing in the Gulf to the point that the region is mainly dependent on the United States for its security needs, paradoxically, the differences between Washington and regional actors in terms of political outlook, purported national and regional interests, and threat assessments have multiplied and undermined mutual trust (Kahwaji, 2004). In particular, in recent years, American allies in the region have expressed growing doubts about the U.S. capacity and willingness to guarantee a regional order that could secure their core interests.

The main reasons behind current disagreements have been well documented (Gause, 2010). Tensions have been linked first to the impact of the 9/11 attacks on the U.S. perceptions of its interests in the Middle East. In the years that followed, the Bush administration did indeed make considerable efforts to fundamentally alter political and security dynamics in the region, radically shifting from a policy of managing the Middle East through containment, power balancing, conflict suppression, and crisis management to a policy of regional transformation through regime change, confrontation, and democratization. The invasion of Iraq in 2003 and its aftermath,[14] in particular, did much to undermine the U.S. credibility as a reliable security guarantor, as did the perception in the Gulf that the Iraq war paved the way for Iran to exert a stronger regional influence.

However, more that the U.S. failure in Iraq, in many ways it is the strategic confusion that has since characterized U.S. policies toward the Middle East that worries Gulf regimes the most. Indeed, hesitation, confusion, and a desire to stay in the background have defined the U.S. responses to the momentous changes in the region. In particular, its cautious and contradictory approach to the so-called Arab Spring, which at times amounted to an endorsement of the inevitable, was strongly criticized by GCC states and paved the way for the persistent idea in the Gulf that the United States was abandoning its allies—as illustrated by the U.S. call, in early 2011, for an "orderly transition" in Egypt away from the rule of Hosni Mubarak, a longstanding ally of both the GCC states and Washington.[15] Embroiled in disputes over regional policies, many became anxious that Western powers could eventually switch sides in the Gulf as well—a fear reinforced by the prospect of a gradual rapprochement between the United States and Iran following the nuclear agreement. Similarly, when Gulf countries pushed the United States into taking a more decisive, assertive, and interventionist role, Washington showed scant appetite for direct military engagement in the Middle East. In fact, events in Libya highlighted a clear U.S. desire to "lead from behind," while the case of Syria underlined the reluctance of the Obama administration to commit ground troops—or to engage in further military interventions of any kind, in contrast to the Iraq scenario in 2003.[16] As a Gulf observer put it, we are seeing a "noncommittal, wavering, fatigued United States" (Al Shayji, 2013).

In recent years, these changing dynamics have persuaded some of the smaller GCC states to opt for a more assertive regional policy. Amid regional uncertainties, they have become increasingly influential actors, using their substantive energy resources and capital accumulation during the oil price boom between 2002 and 2008 as leverage resources to play a more active role in regional security affairs.[17] The timing of the massive creation of wealth in the 2000s also coincided with a new generation of leadership in the smaller GCC states of the UAE and Qatar, and encouraged new statecraft to emerge—representing necessary but not sufficient conditions for the growing regional assertiveness of smaller GCC states. In the UAE, in particular, the emergence of a stronger and more centralized federal state has enabled the country to articulate a more unified and active foreign policy, under the leadership of Abu Dhabi's ruling family,[18] thus moving from being a neutral player, always seeking reconciliation, to an engaged force, using its oil wealth to influence regional dynamics. Qatar, similarly, has taken the lead in mediating disputes among Arab countries, particularly those involving Yemen, Lebanon, and Darfur. In recent years, the UAE and Qatar have been at the forefront of the regional responses to the pressure triggered by the disintegration of regional order and the vacillating U.S. policy toward the Arab Spring.

However, driven by the necessity to cope with new regional challenges, this increasingly assertive foreign policy has, paradoxically, further contributed to the undermining of the smaller GCC states' alliance model. Rivalries and tensions among GCC states have increased in recent years, as they have become more involved politically, financially, and militarily in most areas of regional unrest, and compete for newfound influence in the power vacuum created by the Arab Spring. With competing regional agendas, their position on security issues has become more divergent and polarized, placing additional strain on inter-GCC relations and progressively undercutting the alliance's ability to develop a common understanding of durable patterns of amity and enmity.

As a result, there has been a clear lack of consensus regarding the nature of internal threats and how to prioritize them. Indeed, while the fear of Iran's hegemonic ambition and Iran-led Shia uprisings in the Gulf continue to unite GCC states today, as illustrated by the PSF intervention in Bahrain in 2011 and the Saudi-led military intervention in Yemen in 2015, they have disagreed on the identification, assessment, and prioritization of other perceived internal threats, such as the Muslim Brotherhood: while some members have vehemently opposed the movement and labeled it as a security issue, others have opted to align themselves with the movement for political motivations. Qatar, in particular, has broken ranks with the rest of the Gulf in its enthusiastic support for Brotherhood-linked groups. For instance, Qatar gave strong support to the Muslim Brotherhood in Egypt, pouring $8 billion of financial support into the country during Morsy's year in power, giving Egypt a favorable gas deal to alleviate power shortages, and preparing plans to invest $18 billion over five years (Ulrichsen, 2014). It also backed Muslim Brotherhood-affiliated rebel brigades in Libya who helped overturn the Qadhafi regime, and gave support to opposition factions linked to the organization in Syria. On the other hand, other GCC states have seen the rise of the Muslim Brotherhood as a regional destabilizing factor and a key threat to the stability of their own political system. The election of Mohammed Morsy as President of Egypt in 2012 especially unsettled Saudi Arabia and the UAE,[19] and led to their support for the military's intervention that ousted him a year later. Despite Doha's insistence that its support for the Muslim Brotherhood does not pose a danger to GCC internal security, security measures were also stepped up in these countries. The UAE's security services arrested and sentenced dozens of Muslim Brotherhood supporters, allegedly plotting to overthrow the regime. Those arrested included a number of Qatari nationals. In addition, a row erupted between the UAE and Qatar over Yusuf al-Qardhawi, the Doha-based Islamic scholar and TV preacher, known for his support for the Muslim Brotherhood and his outspoken criticism of Saudi Arabia and the UAE. In a sermon broadcast on Qatari state television in early February 2014, he accused the UAE government of being "anti-Islamic," provoking a fierce war of words and official warnings from Abu Dhabi officials, with Qatar eventually distancing itself from al-Qardhawi's statement. This diplomatic spat between GCC states culminated in March 2014 with the decisions by Saudi Arabia, Bahrain, and the UAE to withdraw their ambassadors from Qatar. In a joint statement, they accused Doha's foreign policy in the region of undermining its fellow GCC members' security, claiming that Qatar had "failed to commit" to GCC principles. Two days later, Saudi Arabia formally designated the Muslim Brotherhood a terrorist organization, aligning itself further with Egypt's new leadership against the group.[20]

Certainly, tensions among GCC states are not unprecedented. In recent years conflicts have been caused by a wide range of issues, from unsettled border tensions and territorial disputes to accusations of espionage—although tensions and disagreement usually take place behind closed doors. What really distinguishes recent developments, however, is the GCC states' concern over a fellow member stepping out of line and not following the prescribed protocol on an issue perceived as a threat to their own domestic stability, thus undermining a key achievement of the GCC during the previous decades: the capabilities of the six member states to achieve a high level of cooperation in the field of internal security. Even though the intensity of the diplomatic crisis between Qatar and the GCC has waned, tensions remain. In addition—and crucially from the long-term cooperation perspective—because threat assessments have become deeply intertwined with GCC states' competing regional ambitions—each country framing its own policies toward the changing Middle East—the current divisions within the GCC over how to respond to perceived internal threats are only destined to reoccur and grow.

Conclusion

Over the last decade, the Middle East security complex has undergone a profound internal transformation driven by territorial disputes, power and status rivalries, wars and changes of leadership, ideological competitions, and ethnic, sectarian, and cultural divisions. These developments, combined with instability in the region triggered by the progressive dislocation of the structures and power balances, have led to significant variations in the main patterns of amity and enmity among regional actors. Faced with important challenges, smaller GCC states, in particular Qatar and the UAE, have responded to these new conditions with an increasingly activist and assertive foreign policy across the region. They have played a key role in trying to shape regional dynamics and influence political developments in most areas of regional unrest. This more assertive approach to regional policy, however, has highlighted significant limitations and growing contradictions in the smaller GCC states' alliance model and policies.

In making their alliance choices, smaller GCC states have traditionally opted for a hedging strategy that prioritizes both protection and autonomy. By relying on extraregional protectors in order to avoid any external disruption of the status quo, they have managed to maintain some room to maneuver within the Saudi orbit. They have also defined regional policies that emphasize each member state's own preferences, choices, and interests rather than making the GCC, as a multilateral body, the main source of their regional influence. At the GCC level, cooperative strategies have mainly focused on internal security threats, a choice that involved only limited integration among member states.

As this chapter has argued, this model is now facing significant challenges. In the Gulf, both bilateral security alliances—in particular with the United States—and the multilateral GCC alliance, have been framed to meet internal needs by reinforcing regimes' security—against threats from their own societies as well as from neighboring states. However, on the one hand, confidence in the United States' ability and willingness to guarantee regional stability and secure GCC states' interests has been severely hurt by the Iraq war and its aftermath, and more recently by American diplomatic choices during the Arab Spring. On the other hand, recent GCC attempts to shape regional dynamics and restore regional order have led to increased tensions and rivalry between the alliance's member states. Today, unified against the perceived threat from Iran and its regional influence, the six GCC states are unable to agree on the nature and the extent of the threats posed by groups using religion for political objectives, which prevents them from adopting a common approach to the continuous challenges raised by current regional political developments. Thus, it is becoming necessary for the smaller GCC states to further define new security and alliance policies in order to establish a regional security architecture that can provide greater stability than the current security arrangements.

Notes

1 Barnett (1998), who uses a constructivist perspective to analyze alliance decisions in the Middle East, similarly underlines that alignment patterns in the region have much more to do with maintaining domestic stability than with classical responses to external threat (see also Adib-Moghaddam, 2006).
2 In particular, transnational identities and ideologies are believed to play a significant role in shaping security dynamics by providing powerful and emotive alternative models that challenge states' efforts to develop affective linkages with their societies and administrative control over them (Buzan and Waever, 2003). They also offer ambitious leaders access to the domestic politics of their neighbors, using shared identities or ideologies with other groups across borders as levers of influence; in turn, leaders may see this as a destabilizing factor and a threat to their own regimes' stability (Gause, 2010; Barnett and Telhami, 2002). Their importance is directly related to the degree of "stateness" or sociopolitical cohesion that a state possesses. As underlined by Buzan and Waever (2003), states with higher degrees of sociopolitical cohesion will tend to find that most threats come from outside their borders; those with lower degrees of stateness are likely to be forums in which a variety of sub-state actors compete for their own security, and/or to capture the state. Similarly, scholars who have written on developing states and security issues have emphasized that state formation and state–society relations differ substantially from that which is experienced in advanced industrialized countries, and those differences lead to different security agendas (Migdal, 2001, 1988; Holsti, 1996; Buzan, 1991).
3 Preoccupied with security regimes, reactions of most GCC states toward the so-called Arab Spring can thus be seen as an attempt to prevent the rise of groups or political organizations that are deemed threatening to the fundamental legitimacy and political stability of their ruling regimes.

4 Stephan Walt's (1987) balance-of-threat theory provides an alternative security-studies explanation of the GCC. Yet it falls shorts of proposing clear and testable hypotheses about how states prioritize threats and react to them, and thus fails to explain GCC states' threat perceptions and alliance choices (see Gause, 2003; Priess, 1996).
5 Also, significant growth and increased penetration of state institutions have not fundamentally altered Gulf countries' threat assessment and prioritization, for two main reasons. On the one hand, societies remain highly segmented and divided along ethnical, tribal, and sectarian lines. On the other hand, the Middle East state system still represents a strong deterrent for cooperative strategies, since it provides multiple alternative models and support for regional players that challenge states' efforts to develop effective linkages with their societies.
6 These agreements committed the United States to the defense of these countries, permitted U.S. use of host-nation military facilities, defined the legal status of U.S. military personnel deployed in their countries, made provisions for prepositioned military equipment, and established a framework for arms sales and military exercises (Russell, 2007, p. 13). Buzan and Waever (2003, p. 47) refer to such alignment with external powers as "penetration" of RSCs, which links regional balance with the global level. As they argue, states in RSCs often make use of external powers in their efforts to balance against regional threats.
7 Also, see Quinlivan (1999) and G. Salame, unpublished thesis (1978).
8 In this regard, the development of UAE armed forces since the first Gulf War represents an important exception to this pattern. In the UAE, military effectiveness has not been perceived as a threat to the security and stability of the ruling families. Accordingly, the country has developed a range of capabilities aimed to provide deterrence in the event of a regional crisis. Extraregional protection and security agreements are deemed necessary nonetheless, as they have allowed the authorities to concentrate on long-term military development plans, ostensibly in order to develop a military force capable of deterring any first wave of attack against the country's population or most vital infrastructures, long enough for reinforcements sent by the UAE's allies to arrive (Gervais, 2011). Also, Saudi Arabia's reluctance to develop its military capabilities—if that claim still holds some truth today—has much less to do today with a coup-proofing strategy than with the Saudi state's elites' rivalries and its fragmentation into uncoordinated sets of vertically divided fiefdoms, headed by rival senior Saudi princes (Hertog, 2011, pp. 400–2).
9 As such, RSCs are socially constructed in the sense that they are contingent on actors' security practices. In order to qualify as a RSC, a group of states or other entities must possess a sufficient degree of security interdependence, both to establish them as a linked set and to differentiate them from surrounding security regions. In this respect, the RSC theory suggests an interesting analytical scheme for structuring analysis of security concerns tied together in regional formations but mutually exclusive of each other (Waever, 2004).
10 In particular, see Gause (2010).
11 As Buzan and Waever argue (2003, p. 49), these boundaries are not "necessarily arbitrarily defined." RSCs, they suggest, define themselves as a substructures of the international system by the relative intensity of security interdependence among a group of units, and security indifference between that set and surrounding units.
12 As Michael Barnett (1996–7) explains, during the 1990s the Arab system consolidated itself sufficiently to contain both domestic violence and revisionism. In particular, the Gulf War, the insistence on sovereignty as the basis of regional order, and the emergence of statism contributed to two striking developments. The first was the division of the Arab–Israeli conflict into an interstate conflict with Israel and the Arab States as opponents and an intercommunal conflict between Israel and the Palestinians. The second was the region-wide debate over the boundaries of the region, the desired regional order, security institutions, and regional organizations.

13 Thus, contrary to what Buzan and Waever argued (Buzan and Waever, 2003, chapter 7), it is only recently that the Middle East has emerged as one unified security complex, as a result of the aforementioned changes that took place at the regional level.

14 The U.S. failure in Iraq is also the direct product of a series of momentous decisions made by the Bush administration following its announcement in Iraq on May 1 2003 that major combat operations had come to an end. Having invaded Iraq with a small force—what has been called "the worst war plan in American history" (Ricks, 2006, quoted by Zakaria, 2014)—destroyed Iraq's power structure, and dismantled its army and its ruling party, the U.S. administration chose to rely on political forces opposed to Saddam Hussein, but with strong ties with neighboring Iran, paving the way for the regional transformations described and analyzed above. In this respect, Fareed Zakaria (2014) is right to mention that these moves—to disband the army, dismantle the bureaucracy, and purge Sunnis in general—might have been more consequential than the invasion itself.

15 Further differences came when protests started in Bahrain, in February 2011, even if the rift between the United States and GCC countries proved temporary. In addition, as pointed out by Kinninmont and Spencer (2013), the alleged support and development of ties between Western governments and Muslim Brotherhood-inspired governments and organizations has been seen as naïve, at best, by most of the GCC states.

16 In this context, the Obama administration's so-called Pivot to the Asia-Pacific strategic orientation, announced in November 2011, has been received with a mixture of concern and uncertainty by Gulf officials, and widely perceived as another sign of U.S. faltering resolve and diminishing ability to maintain its presence in the region.

17 These uncertainties have similarly led to various attempts in the Gulf to reduce dependency on U.S. security guarantees. During the past decade, Gulf countries have sought to diversify their political and strategic alliances, as illustrated for instance by the opening of the French joint military base in Abu Dhabi in 2009. Military spending has also increased significantly in some GCC states, in particular Saudi Arabia and the UAE, along with newfound enthusiasm among experts and former military officers for increased military integration at the GCC level. However, none of these options seem likely to provide a real alternative to the U.S. security umbrella, at least in the medium term. Medium powers, such as France and Great Britain, lack the power projection capabilities to offer credible deterrence in the Gulf, and GCC states' greater economic and strategic ties with Asian countries have yet to materialize into security guarantees. At the regional level, military integration between GCC states remains very unlikely, for the political reasons explained above. As such, despite military buildup, and in some cases growing military effectiveness, smaller GCC states are still largely reliant on external security alliances, especially in the event of all-out and prolonged attacks against a state's vital interests.

18 With the establishment of a more unified foreign policy decision-making system in the UAE, the federal capital—Abu Dhabi—feels less compelled to constantly adjust its foreign policy objectives to the often contradictory sensibilities and positions of the other federation's emirs, concerning regional issues. On the UAE's foreign policy's constraints during the previous decades, see Gause (2000).

19 Clearly, the UAE and Saudi Arabia have been at the forefront of the actions against Qatar. Other smaller GCC states—Kuwait, Bahrain, and Oman—have adopted a more conciliatory attitude toward Doha, mainly for internal reasons.

20 This designation represented a major escalation by Riyadh against the transnational Islamist movement. The Saudi terrorism list also included the local branch of the Shiite movement Hezbollah, the militant group the Islamic State of Iraq and Syria (ISIS), and the al-Qaeda-linked al-Nusra Front. This decisive move by the Saudi kingdom received strong support from the UAE.

References

Adib-Moghaddam, A. (2006) *The International Politics of the Persian Gulf: A Cultural Genealogy*, London: Routledge.
Ajami, F. (1981) *The Arab Predicament: Arab Political Thought and Practices since 1967*, Cambridge, UK: Cambridge University Press.
Al Shayji, A. (2013) Gulf Allies Losing Faith in their Allies, *Gulf News*, October 27.
Ayubi, M. (1996) *The Third World Security Predicament: State Making, Regional Conflict, and the International System*, Boulder, CO: Lynne Rienner.
Barnett, M. (1996–7) "Regional Security after the Gulf War," *Political Science Quarterly*, 111(4), 597–618.
Barnett, M.N. (1998) *Dialogues in Arab Politics: Negotiations in Regional Order*, New York: Columbia University Press.
Barnett, M.N. and Gause, F.G. III (1998) "Caravans in Opposite Directions: Society, State, and the Development of Community in the GCC," in E. Adler and M. Barnett (eds.), *Security Communities*, Cambridge, UK: Cambridge University Press, pp. 161–97.
Barnett, M.N. and Telhami, S. (2002) *Identity and Foreign Policy in the Middle East*, Ithaca, NY: Cornell University Press.
Buzan, B. (1991) *People, States and Fear: An Agenda for International Security Studies in the Post-Cold War Era*, Boulder, CO: Lynne Rienner.
Buzan, B. and Waever, O. (2003) *Regions and Powers: The Structure of International Security*, Cambridge, UK: Cambridge University Press.
Cooper, S. (2003) "State-Centric Balance-of-Threat Theory: Explaining the Misunderstood GCC," *Security Studies*, 13(2), 306–49.
David, S.R. (1991) "Explaining Third World Alignment," *World Politics*, 42(2), 233–56.
Fawcett, L. (2013) "The Iraq War Ten Years On: Assessing the Fallout," *International Affairs*, 89(2), 325–43.
Gause, F.G. III (1994) *Oil Monarchies: Domestic and Security Challenges in the Arab States*, New York: Council on Foreign Relations.
Gause, F.G. III (1997) "The Political Economy of National Security in the GCC States," in Gary Sick and Lawrence Potter (eds.), *The Persian Gulf at the Millennium: Essays in Politics, Economy, Security, and Religion*, New York: St. Martin's Press, pp. 61–84.
Gause, F.G. III (2000) "The UAE: Between Pax Britannica and Pax Americana," in Kechichian, Joseph (ed.), *A Century in Thirty Years: Sheikh Zayed and the United Arab Emirates*, Washington, D.C.: Middle East Policy Council, 213–34.
Gause, F.G. III (2003) "Balancing What? Threat Perception and Alliance Choice in the Gulf," *Security Studies*, 13(2), 273–305.
Gause, F.G. III (2010) *The International Relations of the Persian Gulf*, Cambridge, UK: Cambridge University Press.
Gervais, V. (2011) *Du Petrole a L'armee: Les Strategies de Construction de l'Etat aux Emirats Arabes Unis*, Paris: IRSEM.
Hertog, S. (2011) "Rentier Militaries in the Gulf States: The Price of Coup-Proofing," *International Journal of Middle East Studies*, 43(3), 400–2.
Holsti, K.J. (1996) *The State, War, and the State of War*, Cambridge, UK: Cambridge University Press.
Kahwaji, R. (2004) "U.S.–Arab Cooperation in the Gulf: Are Both Sides Working From the Same Script?" *Middle East Policy*, 11(3), 52–62.

Kinninmont, J. and Spencer, C. (2013) "The Arab Spring: The Changing Dynamics of West–GCC Cooperation," IAI report, in R. Alcaro and A. Dessi (eds.), *The Uneasy Balance. Potential and Challenges of the West's Relations with the Gulf States*, IAI Research Papers no. 8. Chatham House, pp. 49–69. Retrieved from www.iai.it/sites/default/files/iairp_08.pdf (accessed July 15, 2014).

Legrenzi, M. (2011) *The GCC and the International Relations of the Gulf: Diplomacy, Security and Economy Coordination in a Changing Middle East*, London: I.B. Tauris.

Migdal, J.S. (1988) *Strong Societies and Weak States: State–Society Relations and State Capabilities in the Third World*, Princeton, NJ: Princeton University Press.

Migdal, J. (2001) *State-in-Society: Studying how States and Societies Transform and Constitute One Another*, Cambridge, UK: Cambridge University Press.

Partrick, N. (2011) "The GCC: Gulf State Integration or Leadership Cooperation," *Kuwait Programme on Globalisation, Governance and Development in the Gulf*, London: London School of Economics & Political Science (LSE).

Piscatori, J. (ed.) (1983) *Islam in the Political Process*, Cambridge, UK: Cambridge University Press.

Priess, D. (1996) "Balance of Threat Theory and the Genesis of the Gulf Cooperation Council: An Interpretive Case Study," *Security Studies*, 5(4), 143–71.

Quinlivan, J.T. (1999) "Coup-proofing: Its Practice and Consequences in the Middle East," *International Security*, 24(2), 131–65.

Ramazani, R.K. (1988) *The Gulf Cooperation Council: Record and Analysis*, Charlottesville, VA: University of Virginia Press.

Ricks, T.E. (2006) *Fiasco: The American Military Adventure in Iraq*, New York: Penguin Press.

Roy, O. (1999) "Moyen-Orient: Faiblesse des Etats, Enracinement des Nations," *Critique International*, 4, 79–104.

Russell, J.A. (2007) "Regional Threats and Security Strategy: The Troubling Case of Today's Middle East," Strategic Studies Institute, Carlisle, PA: U.S. Army War College.

Salame, G. (1978) *Le Développement du rôle Régional et International de l'Arabie Saoudite*, Unpublished thesis, Paris: Université de Paris I (Panthéon-Sorbonne).

Salem, P. (2008) "The Middle East: Evolution of a Broken Regional Order," *Carnegie Papers*, 9, June. Available at http://carnegieendowment.org/files/cmec9_salem_broken_order_final.pdf (accessed September 28, 2016).

Ulrichsen, K.C. (2014) "Qatar and The Arab Spring", Carnegie Endowment For International Peace, September 24. Retrieved from http://carnegieendowment.org/2014/09/24/qatar-and-arab-spring-policy-drivers-and-regional-implications-pub-56723 (accessed October 18, 2016).

Waever, O. (2004) "Aberystwyth, Paris, Copenhagen – New Schools in Security Theory and Their Origins between Core and Periphery," Paper presented at the annual meeting of the International Studies Association, Montreal.

Walt, S.M. (1987) *The Origins of Alliances*, Ithaca, NY: Cornell University Press.

Zakaria, F. (2014) Who Lost Iraq? The Iraqis Did, with an Assist from George W. Bush, *Washington Post*, June 12.

4
GULF SECURITY POLICY AFTER THE ARAB SPRING

Considering changing security dynamics

Andreas Krieg

Introduction

The uprisings across the Arab World since 2010 have been a statement of the newly acquired confidence of the individual within the Arab World to express its thoughts, assert its needs and state its grievances. Once the barrier of fear had been broken, small groups of liberals were joined by other parts of society, transforming the so-called Arab Spring into a mass movement, eventually either severely challenging existing power structures or overthrowing them. The Arab Spring has arguably been the most severe collective security challenge for societies and states in the modern Arab World. Yet, academic scholarship and Arab regimes alike have widely failed to draw the necessary conclusion: security narratives whether academic or political ought to move from a state-centric to an individual-centric approach. Stability and regime resilience in the Arab World cannot be appreciated in isolation from the public security of individuals within the state they live in.

This chapter will develop a theoretical framework revolving around a liberal normative approach to security to demonstrate that foreign and security policies of Arab Gulf states ought to be more individual-centric in order to achieve long-term sustainable security and stability. The argument put forward in this chapter is that security and resilience in the Gulf is not a product of state-centric national security agendas or narrow regime security, but will increasingly depend on the ability of regimes to cater for individual security needs. This conceptual argument will be supported by two empirical case studies looking at Qatar and Bahrain as two small states in the region, whose different approaches to individual security domestically and, in the case of Qatar, also externally, shape their long-term stability inversely.

Although the argument in this chapter takes an opposite approach to understanding security than the small states' literature, it is intended to be complementary rather than contradictory. This chapter contends that small states' security ought to be conceived as the sum of individual security needs as opposed to the conventional understanding of security as state-centric security. State and regime security in a small state should not be divorced from the individual security needs of those bringing the state into existence. Academics and policymakers in the Gulf should move beyond the narrow realist conceptualization of security in an effort to conceptualize a small state's overall security. In particular, in regards to the widely accepted trade-off in the small states' literature between autonomy and influence, a small state's ability to cater for individual security needs, both domestically and externally, may be a means to increase overall security by breaking this trade-off, exercising influence while maintaining its autonomy.

The chapter will commence by establishing the conceptual foundation for a new security narrative in the Arab World in general and the Gulf in particular. Thereby, it will first explain the tenets of traditional security debates centering on the Gulf, before outlining why the empirical reality of increased individual civil-societal participation in the Arab World necessitates a broader, more liberal approach to formulating a security narrative. This chapter will continue by applying the conceptual framework to the cases of Bahrain and Qatar, demonstrating that discrepancies in domestic security and stability are a product of their policy approach towards defining security.

Towards a new security narrative in the Gulf

The traditional focus on regime and state

When defining the nature of security in the Arab World or the Gulf in particular, the traditional focus on security has been limited to national and international security, with the state as its key referent object of security. Both empirical evidence and conceptual academic debates seem to have reinforced the idea that security in the Gulf is an autocratic undertaking focusing on eliminating any form of external threat to the sovereignty and territorial integrity of the state, while at the same time ensuring the survival of the regime internally. Consequently, national security policies have narrowly focused on state and regime security. Also, academic security discourses in reference to the Gulf have been widely state-centric as well. In the academic literature concepts of individual or societal security have been marginalized (Bensahel and Byman, 2004; Gause, 2010; Kamrava, 2011; Koch and Long, 2003; Legrenzi, 2013; Macris, 2010; Martin, 2011; Ulrichsen, 2011) in favour of state security. In a region where autocratic hereditary monarchies reign with little or no direct participation of society, a focus on individual or societal security seems to have been considered redundant (Gause, 2011, p. 81). In the small states' literature as well, security has been defined as state security. Instead of being considered a sum of its parts, the small state's security is defined in isolation of the community of individuals it serves, trying to balance security policy within the trade-off of gaining influence while retaining autonomy (Rickli, 2008).

Ulrichsen was one of the first, in 2009, to note that, although references to human security in the academic security debate surrounding the Gulf have become more frequent, Gulf regimes have widely failed to commit to providing human security inclusively on behalf of individuals and societies (Ulrichsen, 2009). 'Human security' became something of a buzzword during the 1990s, particularly within humanitarian circles. While taking an individual-centric approach to security, the concept of human security has widely remained vague and difficult to apply by policymakers. The Arab Human Development Report 2009 makes a strong case for human security as a prerequisite for state and regime security; however, it notes that, in general, Arab regimes continue to focus on state rather than individual human security (UN Development Program, Regional Bureau for Arab States, 2009, p. 18). Until the eruption of mass protests across the Arab World in 2011, Arab regimes appeared to have failed to appreciate the link between individual and regime security – a trend that led academia to believe that security in the Arab World, and the Gulf in particular, remains a matter of national or international state affairs (Bellin, 2012). The overall neglect of individual security has to be understood within the historic socio-political context of the Arab World.

Without jumping on the Western Orientalist bandwagon trying to explain every shortcoming in the Arab World with the lack of liberal channels of democracy, socio-political communal affairs in the Arab World have never been individual-centric in nature, at least not by Western standards. Instead, the individual's self-worth has always been defined in the context of its affiliation to greater communities of kinship or patrimony (Hourani, 2002, p. 105). Communal affairs have traditionally been regulated by widely autocratic leaders who, at the top of highly centralized and personalized governance systems, provide security as they see fit (Bill and Springborg, 1999, pp. 71–3). The tradition of centralized, autocratic governance was further exacerbated by the establishment of the colonial state. Colonial powers in an effort to facilitate colonial administration created artificial territorial entities whose governance was entrusted to particular social elites. The bureaucratic organization of new colonial administrations relied on local elites, often sectarian minorities, to govern the new territorial entities, with little regard to individual desires and needs. In particular the overall strategy of 'divide and rule' created states that to a great extent developed into personal patrimonies of certain elites (Owen, 1992, p. 17). Security sectors were arranged in a way so as to guarantee that these new elites and their regimes were protected not just from external threats but particularly domestic threats from a society that was, for the most part, excluded from participating directly or indirectly in policy-making (Brooks, 2004, pp. 129–35). As a consequence, the regimes' security agendas mostly revolved around making the system 'coup-proof' against potential societal forces from within the boundaries of the state (Quinlivan, 2000). Developments in the Arab Gulf countries were not much different, although centralized autocracies were not established by colonial powers as a means of divide and rule but were founded on existing tribal dynamics (Owen, 1992, p. 56). Particularly in Kuwait, Bahrain, Qatar and the UAE, the monarchies were able to assure their control over social and political affairs through the external protection by Britain until long into the second half of the 20th century (Wright, 2011, p. 71). The rise of rentier economies further allowed ruling elites to avoid individual participation in policy-making. Yet, it is important to note here that the degree of individual participation in the Arab Gulf states directly or indirectly varies to a degree between Kuwait on one end of the scale and Saudi Arabia on the other end of the scale. Constitutionally, individuals in Kuwait are able to directly participate in policy-making through parliamentary elections; yet, the parliament has almost no direct impact on significant policy decisions (Roberts, 2011a, p. 94). In Saudi Arabia, individual participation in policy-making, whether directly through elections and consultations or indirectly through civil-society activism, is virtually non-existent. Although an increasing number of civil-society groups exist in Saudi Arabia, it appears as if ruling elites choose to respond to civil society not with accommodation but with co-option and repression (Yom, 2005). Hence, in sum, the individual in the Arab World as a whole and in the Gulf in particular, is believed to be widely excluded from directly or indirectly exercising influence over policy-making. With the individual perceived to lack the liberal political emancipation from centralized, autocratic power, international relations and security scholarship focusing on the region has neglected the individual as a considerable referent object for security. Consequently, the scholarly focus on regime and state security has often been limited to external threats emanating from other states, without accepting the fact that regime and individual security are two sides of the same coin. For small states in particular, as will be discussed in more detail later on, state and regime security depend on the ability of the state to cater for individual security needs.

The Arab public sphere

Redirecting the focus towards the individual

For many, the uprisings of the Arab Spring came as a surprise (Bellin, 2012), suddenly witnessing individuals expressing their concerns. Despite facing repressive regimes and co-opted security sectors, individuals were willing to stand their ground collectively until the public voice was heard. The Arab public sphere, which in common view has been condescendingly declared non-existent (Norton, 1995; Hawthorne, 2005; Kassem, 2004, p. 87), proved to be a powerful current, sweeping even long-living regimes off their feet. Traditionally, those sceptical or denying of an Arab public sphere have applied a Western liberal Habermasian model to the Arab public. Habermas, a German sociologist, approached the notion of the public sphere socio-historically, identifying the socio-political upheavals of 17th-century Europe as an evolutionary pillar in the development of a liberal public sphere vis-à-vis autocratic political elites. Habermas defined the public sphere as

> a realm of our social life in which something approaching public opinion can be formed. Access is guaranteed to all citizens [...] Citizens behave like a public body when they confer in an unrestricted fashion – that is with the guarantee to assembly and association and the freedom to express and publish their opinions – about matters of general interest.
>
> *(1974, pp. 49–50)*

Using this model to conceptualize an Arab public sphere, scholars have argued that, due to the authoritarian nature of Arab regimes, a true public sphere cannot emerge, as individuals are not granted the freedom to associate or to express themselves (Nawar, 2003; Zaine, 1992; Ayish, 2009, p. 47). Further, the Arab public sphere has been referred to as irrational and emotionally charged, making the formation of a 'rational public opinion', an attribute ignorantly attributed to public opinion in the West, highly unlikely (Regier and Khalidi, 2009). While it might be far-fetched to describe the Arab public sphere as vibrant and unrestrained, as in some liberal democracies, the core tenets of Habermas' theory nonetheless hold true for the Arab public as well. The Arab public sphere is in essence a platform of public discourse, which, particularly in the era of satellite or new media, has become an inclusive sphere granting virtually unrestricted access.

Since the 1990s, the new-media environment in the Arab World has been attributed a liberalizing effect, emancipating the individual from the omnipresent repression of autocratic regimes. The Arab Spring has to be understood as the pinnacle of this development that Anderson, Lynch and Alterman have predicted: the emancipation of the individual from the private confinements of the household to join public debate challenging existing power structures. The first platform allowing individuals to engage in an interactive public dialogue beyond the reach of state repression was satellite television. Lynch argues that satellite TV in the Arab World has laid the foundation for challenging and undermining the regime's control over means of communication (Lynch, 2007). Broadcasting from Qatar with little government restriction, Al Jazeera as an international Arab broadcaster, unlike state-owned national broadcasters, provided a platform for relatively unrestrained dialogue across the Arab World, addressing issues of political, social and economic concern. The individual, while domestically silenced by repression and co-option, regarded the emerging public platform of discourse as an opportunity to address grievances in a transnational Arab dialogue (Alterman, 2004). Much more powerful than satellite TV in both forming a transnational Arab public opinion and organizing public resistance, was the internet. While Internet 1.0 was limited to distribute information one-directionally, Internet 2.0 allows for instant, unrestricted, transnational interaction expanding the reach of the public sphere in terms of both size and quality (Anderson, 2003, p. 41). The increasing flood of individual communication and interaction in cyberspace becomes even more difficult for regimes to monitor and regulate. Consequently, particularly social media, which allows a growing number of individuals to join the public cyberspace from mobile devices, has become an important tool of individual liberalization in the Arab World in the past decade (Diamond, 2010).

In the absence of direct political participation and a growing gap between the autocratic regimes and the societies they rule over, the individual in the Arab World has turned to new and social media so as to partake in socio-political discourse. To that end public discourse does not only serve as a means of individual, societal interaction but most importantly as a means of bottom-up dialogue between society and regime, placing the regime at the receiving rather than emitting end.

The public sphere allows individuals to criticize regime policy, holding the regime at least normatively accountable for its policies. During the Arab Spring, this form of public accountability via new and social media had devastating effects for those regimes still convinced that the public could be dealt with through repression and co-option. In the decade leading up to the Arab Spring, new and social media fostered the disconnect between the autocratic regime and society, widening the gap between individual security needs and regime security provision (Noueihed and Warren, 2013, p. 2). The security discourse that had traditionally been one-directional, dominated by the autocratic regime from the top-down, had been widened from the bottom-up. Yet, the irresponsiveness of regimes to address individual security concerns had created a public transnational community of frustrated youths and liberals who were waiting for the trigger to act. This trigger came in December 2010 when Tunisians took to the street in response to the self-immolation of the vender Bouazizi, who had been maltreated by regime authorities. New and social media allowed for the images of the successful Tunisian mass protests to be instantly shared across the Arab public sphere, bypassing conventional state-imposed restrictions on the freedom of speech (Doran, 2011, p. 41).[1] This in turn provided Egyptians and Libyans with a trigger to overcome their initial barrier of fear to revolt (El-Din Haseeb, 2013, p. 5). Apart from merely sharing information across the public sphere, social media such as Facebook and Twitter became also pivotal platforms of social organization in the resistance against regime authorities (Doran, 2011). Despite the absence of official and direct channels of individual participation in policy-making, the individual in the Arab World through the public sphere took the initiative to challenge existing power structures not just verbally but also physically. The achieved degree of individual emancipation from the confinements of the private sphere and regime-co-opted public sphere is unprecedented in the Arab World and most likely irreversible. It is against this backdrop that the security discourse in the Arab World in general and the Gulf in particular ought to be redirected from the regime and the state as the referent object of security, to the individual at the core of the security debate.

Defining security beyond state and regime security

In this chapter the security narrative is directed away from the narrow focus on state or regime security to a broader, more liberal understanding of security as the individual's security. Nonetheless, it is important to recognize that the individual's security cannot be understood in isolation from its social context. Social Contract theory appears to provide an adequate conceptualization for how the individual can maximize their individual security desires within the context of society and state (Black, 2001, p. 22; Lambton, 1981, pp. 35–6; Lewis, 2010, p. 123; Horovitz, 1930, p. 185; Ibn Khaldun, 1858).[2]

According to Social Contract theorists such as Hobbes, Locke and Rousseau, the individual is willing to enter society as a state of compromise in an attempt to escape the state of nature. The state of nature is a state of complete freedom and lawlessness where every individual is merely responsible for themselves (Locke, 1988, §4). The lack of a central regulatory mechanism to provide security for individuals in the state of nature triggers individual sentiments of insecurity as every individual is asked to provide for its own security according to its own means – a situation where weaker individuals are exposed to the mercy of stronger individuals (Hobbes, 2004, p. 74). Consequently, as stated by Locke, the individual enters into association with other individuals to establish society and state as a regulated entity to have the individuals' lives, liberties and estates protected (Locke, 1988, §123). Thereby, in reference to the type of threat, security is not only defined as the individual's physical security, but also its socio-economic, political and identity security. The state functions as the central regulatory authority with the purpose

> to defend them from the invasion of foreigners, and the injuries of one another, and thereby to secure them in such sort, as that by their own industry, and by the fruits of the Earth, they may nourish themselves and live contentedly.
>
> *(Hobbes, 2004, p. 99)*

The state ought to protect the aggregate individual security interests as a form of integrated public security will, similar to Rousseau's concept of the *volonté générale*, which is a consolidated sum of individual wills (Rousseau, 1762/2003, p. 12). The legitimacy of the state arises thereby from its ability to provide public security, as the inclusive aggregate of individual security interests. In this respect, public security is a concept that combines a reference to the object of security, namely the individual in a communal context, with a reference to the socio-political mechanism in place to provide for it. Public security then, relates to the aggregate security of all individuals in the public sphere of the community, which the state is supposed to protect based on the Social Contract. The term 'public' describes the communal level of the discretionary association of individuals, concerning the sphere beyond the individual's exclusive private sphere (Roy, 1999; Stevensen, 2010).[3] What does that mean for the difference between private and public security? The latter is provided via the social-contractual relationship between state and the public on behalf of all individual security interests inclusively. Private security, on the contrary, is any security not provided inclusively for the benefit of all individuals within the community but exclusively for partisan individual or group security interests. Whether true public security as the aggregate security of all individuals is actually possible has been debated by critics of the normative concept of the *volonté générale*, who argue that it is impossible to empirically define an aggregate of individual wills without marginalizing some. For Talmon it leads to 'totalitarian democracy' (Talmon, 1960), which Tocqueville describes as the 'tyranny of the majority' (Tocqueville, 1838). Thus, the finding of a true common denominator within an extensive community of individuals can be difficult. However, an argument can be made that, within small states constituted by smaller communities of individuals, the empirical inclusive definition of a true public-security will is easier than in bigger societies.

At the core of the social-contractual relationship between society and state lies the idea of communal consent. Consent is granted to the state formally through elections, as in the conceptualization of Rousseau, or informally through societal acquiescence, as in the conceptualizations of Hobbes and Locke. Thus, liberal democracy is not necessarily a prerequisite to establish legitimate society–state relations within the framework of the Social Contract. The reason is that the state's communal approval is founded on its ability to inclusively provide public security for the community as what Locke would consider to be a discretionary association (Locke, 1988, §123). The discretionary association's consent can then be withdrawn when the state fails to meet the social-contractual demand of providing security as an inclusive public good for all individuals within the association. Whether consent is withdrawn formally through elections or informally by civil-societal disobedience and apathy, the state loses its legitimacy to govern. The covenantal social-contractual arrangement between the individual and the state revolving around individual security provision consequently becomes void.

Hence, in this chapter small-state security in the Gulf ought to be understood as the individual's security within the public communal context, which the state is obliged to provide. Instead of focusing on private security interests of regimes or more generic national security interests of states, the individual's increasing indirect participation in socio-political affairs through the Arab public sphere necessitates a stronger conceptual and applied political consideration of the individual's security needs. Consequently, a small state's failure to deliver public security inclusively will translate into anarchy and eventual regime insecurity, brought about by an increasingly empowered public sphere. Further, a small state's focus on individual security in its definition of foreign policy can, as will be discussed in the next section, allow the small state to overcome its security dilemma. The small state can exercise influence by empowering individuals overseas while maintaining its autonomy.

Private and public security in the Gulf

Bahrain and Qatar

The response to the Arab Spring in the Gulf could not have been more diverse. While some GCC states have responded to the increasingly active public sphere with accommodation, others have opted for repression. In terms of their ability and willingness to provide security as a public good inclusively for all individuals within society, Bahrain and Qatar find themselves on opposite ends of the same scale. Bahrain and Qatar are the smallest states within the GCC, share a common history and are geographically proximate. Yet, their approach to the concept of individual security vis-à-vis regime security varies greatly.

Bahrain finds itself at the crossroad of the Sunni and Shi'a world in the Gulf, with a highly heterogeneous population maintaining transnational relations with Saudi Arabia and Iran (Zahlan, 1998, p. 61). The two most important constituencies in Bahrain have traditionally been the indigenous Baharna people following Shi'ite Islam and the Sunni Bani Utub (Noueihed and Warren, 2013, p. 138). As a commercial hub in the region Bahrain attracted merchants of various descent over the centuries. Nonetheless, internal sectarian divides in Bahrain run along confessional lines of Shi'a and Sunni Islam. This sectarian divide was exacerbated by the defeat of the Persians in the late 18th century and the subsequent establishment of the Sunni Al Khalifa rule over Bahrain (Kinninmont, 2011, p. 32).

With the support of the British acting as the external protector of the Gulf since the 1920s, the Al Khalifa family was able to consolidate its power internally. Over the coming decades the Al Khalifa family built a closely knit power network, monopolizing political and economic control over the island state within the hands of family members and affiliated Sunni families. The Shi'a majority of the country has been widely marginalized and excluded from key positions in government, the security sector and the economy (Economist Intelligence Unit, 2011). The Al Khalifa family created a private regime providing physical, socio-economic, political and identity security predominately to its key constituency: the Sunni population. From a social-contractual point of view, the Al Khalifa regime has failed to provide public security for all individuals inclusively, particularly disregarding the security interests of the Shi'a population. Instead, the regime has focused on regime security in an effort to preserve the private interests of those in power as well as those keeping it in power. Thereby, the Shi'a majority of the country has widely been excluded from the circles of power and influence as a perceived 'other' who is believed to threaten the privatized *raison d'état* (Bellin, 2012, p. 134). Consequently, the security sector in Bahrain, both constabulary and military, have not been designed as a public security provider but as a private security provider, protecting the private security of the Al Khalifa regime and its key constituency. All key positions in the security sector, similar to all key positions in government, are held by the royal family and relatives. The Bahraini Armed Forces widely exclude the Shi'a majority of the country by recruiting Sunnis locally and abroad in Syria, Jordan or Yemen (Lutterbeck, 2013, p. 42). As a consequence, civil–military relations in Bahrain are not social contractual in nature as they fail to serve the public *volonté générale*. The disconnect between large parts of society on the one hand and the state, as well as the security sector on the other, have created feelings of public exclusion and marginalization particularly among the Shi'a majority (Noueihed and Warren, 2013, p. 142).

Over the decades Bahraini Shi'as have repeatedly protested against their exclusion from the public, particularly decrying their socio-economic insecurity. Shi'as in Bahrain have occupied lower socio-economic classes and suffered disproportionately from unemployment and low incomes compared with other communities (Noueihed and Warren, 2013, p. 142). The eruption of protests in February 2011, in solidarity with Egyptian demands for more consideration of individual security concerns, was preceded by a decade-long vibrant public discourse. The Al Khalifa's dismissal of the National Assembly in 1975 had driven political discourse to the informal public sphere of clubs and societies (Bill and Springborg, 1999, p. 208). This public sphere expanded throughout the 2000s with the increasing use of social media by young Bahrainis, both Shi'a and Sunni, who gradually appeared to withdraw their communal consent for the Al Khalifa regime. In February 2011, the regime saw itself confronted with a well-organized front of protestors who neither followed a sectarian banner nor directly called for regime change. The protests were calling for more socio-economic security of neglected communities as well as political and physical security for those exercising their freedom of expression (Underwood, 2013, p. 91). Despite the inclusive, public nature of the protests framed in reference to individual justice, not revolution, the regime in Bahrain portrayed the expressions of individual security needs through the traditional prism of state security. The Al Khalifas and loyalist media claimed that Iran was trying to incite sectarian violence within Bahrain in an effort to destabilize the country (Gause, 2011, p. 49). Consequently, the protests became a matter of national security. Failing to recognize the legitimacy of individual security needs and underestimating the individuals' willingness to stand their ground, the Bahraini regime called on its privatized security sector to use all means necessary to protect regime security. By reacting to individual demands with repression rather than accommodation, the Al Khalifa regime demonstrated that it does not acknowledge the interconnectedness of individual public security and regime security. While the mostly Saudi GCC forces coming to the Al Khalifa's rescue in March 2011 did not provide more than a show of force, the overwhelmingly Sunni security sector did not hesitate to use violence to disperse protestors (Bassiouni et al., 2011, pp. 219–317). The maltreatment of protestors by the Bahraini security sector during and after the protests exacerbated the individuals' feelings of physical insecurity. Not only did the state fail to assume its social-contractual function of providing individual security, but also the state contributed to individual sentiments of insecurity. Whereas in the short run the regime managed to suppress protests, in the aftermath the Bahraini public sphere has expanded its activities through the use of social media. Bahrainis, mostly Shi'a and left-wing Sunni, continue to publicly challenge the regime's policies, as in their eyes the Al Khalifa regime has lost its social-contractual legitimacy. Therefore, in the long run, the Bahraini people will most likely be confronted with public disobedience or revolt again if the regime continues to fail to cater for individual security needs.

In Qatar, just 50 kilometres to the east of Bahrain, the situation is a different one. Unlike Bahrain, Qatari society is homogenous, with the overwhelming majority of Qataris subscribing to conservative Wahhabi interpretation of Sunni Islam. The only significant source for heterogeneity in Qatar is the huge expat population, which accounts for approximately 85 per cent of the population. The homogeneity of the small indigenous population, the absence of any significant sectarian divides and unprecedented financial wealth, have allowed the Al Thanis to create a regime founded on public inclusion (Noueihed and Warren, 2013, p. 255). Similar to other GCC states, Qatar is an autocracy without any institutionalized form of public accountability. Nonetheless, although Qataris repeatedly express their desire for democratization (Gengler, 2011), Qatari opinion polls suggest that individual socio-economic and physical security are more important than direct participation in policy-making (Social & Economic Survey Research Institute (SESRI), 2012, p. 6). The Al Thani regime has lived up to its social-contractual duty of providing public security inclusively for Qatari citizens, whereby socio-economic and physical security are the key dimensions of public security. Even though discrepancies in terms of access and income exist between various tribes in Qatar, the overall levels of individual socio-economic security for Qatari citizens is still exceptional. The absence of a vibrant public sphere expressing public security concerns seems to imply that a general public satisfaction with the regime has led to a degree of Qatari civil-societal apathy and tacit consent (Al Jazeera, 2013).[4] As a consequence, although regime security is a major concern for the Al Thanis, the waves of public uprisings across the Arab World, particularly those shaking Qatar's neighbour Bahrain, have not exacerbated the Qatari regime's security concerns.[5] The local security sector remains the backbone for both private regime security and public security (Fromherz, 2013, p. 131). Unlike in Bahrain where the Al Khalifa regime deliberately created a rift in civil–military relations, the new Emir Sheikh Tamim Al Thani has invested in a rapprochement between society and military by introducing a four-month compulsory military service (*The National*, 2013). Apart from increasing already high levels of public confidence in the state's security sector (SESRI, 2012, p. 7), this initiative will make the security sector more responsive to public security needs. It is hard to imagine that, if friction between the regime and the public were to occur, the Qatari security sector would use the same degree of repression as its counterpart in Bahrain.

In contrast, the expat community in Qatar, which constitutes the vast majority of the public in that Gulf state, receive less consideration by the regime than Qatari citizens. In particular, repeated allegations of inhumane living conditions for migrant workers imply that this huge demographic is sometimes deprived of basic individual socio-economic or physical security (Human Rights Watch, 2013). Their public marginalization and individual sentiments of insecurity could potentially become a source of domestic instability if the Qatari state continues to fail to guarantee basic individual security for these non-citizens. Although the migrant worker's ability to form a powerful civil-societal force within the public sphere is limited, their sheer numerical superiority and often geographical concentration could become a threat to public and regime security. Qatar's ability to cater for socio-economic and physical security interests of its citizens have created a domestic realm of stability, which allows the regime to divert its attention to a more proactive policy externally. While Qatari security policy domestically seems to revolve around a symbiosis of private regime security and public security, its foreign security policy, particularly since the beginning of the Arab Spring, has prioritized individual security over regime security overseas. Unlike other Gulf states that verbally or actively supported existing regimes against revolting individuals during the Arab Spring, Qatar has actively supported those who were eager to change existing power structures. Witnessing public revolts against non-social-contractual authoritarian regimes across the Arab World, the Qatari regime started both financially and politically to support individual strives for self-determination (Wright, 2011, p. 87). Qatar's most significant support was to the Libyan and Syrian opposition, as well as the Muslim Brotherhood in Egypt. In all these conflicts it appears as if the Qatari regime tried to be on the right side of history by supporting those fighting for their individual physical, socio-economic, political and identity security. As Roberts argues, for the Al Thani regime, 'being at the forefront of popular Arab opinion and defending fellow Arabs against an onslaught from a widely hated dictator [was] a priceless commodity, both at home and abroad' (Roberts, 2011b). As part of its expansionary foreign policy, Qatar tried to seize the opportunity during the Arab Spring to win over individual hearts and minds of those asking for a stronger consideration of their individual security needs. It has to be noted here that Qatar's support for Arab public security interests was not entirely motivated by altruistic considerations but was part of an overall attempt to further extend its influence as a small state in the wider region (Roberts, 2012). The case of Qatar serves as an example of how a small state can escape the trade-off between influence and autonomy by prioritizing individual security needs. Widespread individual support for the regime domestically provides the state with an internal stability that enables Qatar to proactively engage in building relations abroad with those players who have built social bases by catering for individual security needs locally. Unlike Bahrain, who by ignoring public security needs is more reliant on external support, thereby sacrificing autonomy, Qatar maintains autonomy domestically as well as externally by building influence in communities abroad. The support for individual security needs overseas has become a means for Qatar as a small state to gain influence without surrendering its autonomy. Particularly for a small state as well-endowed financially as Qatar, an individual-centric foreign policy allows financial power to be translated into political influence. This political influence makes the small state more attractive as a partner for medium-sized or big states who are more willing to ally with the small state on almost equal terms. This in turn allows the small state to increase its external security, ultimately serving the individual's security needs domestically.

Thus, unlike peers in the Gulf, Qatar seems to have recognized the importance of considering individual security needs when conducting foreign and security policies. It has done so without being confronted with a domestic challenging public sphere. It has preemptively built a position of public accommodation across the transnational Arab sphere – a move with a questionable outcome for Qatar's overall public security. As neighbouring regimes appear to be alienated with Qatar's individual-centric foreign and security policy in the short run, in the long run it seems as if Qatar is moving in the right direction. While Qatar still lags behind Western liberal democracies' prioritization of individual security over regime security, Qatar nonetheless seems to stand out in the Arab World as the famous one-eyed in the kingdom of the blind.

Conclusion

Taking a long-term visionary approach to security in the Arab World in general and the Gulf in particular, security agendas and narratives should no longer be dominated by a narrow, realist state-centric approach to the definition of security. Despite assertions that the Arab World is far away from inspiring the development of civil society, at least when measured by liberal standards, the individual in the Arab World has been emancipated from its private sphere over the past two decades. Fuelled by evolutions in media technology, the individual has become both more aware of public affairs and more responsive to grievances in the public sphere. While this development might still be in its infant phase of a wider evolutionary process, the trend towards a greater involvement of the individual in shaping security narratives and public security awareness is irreversible – a trend that will be increasingly difficult to contain through the distribution of rents. Consequently, both academic conceptual foci on security and the regimes' policy foci on security ought to be more aware of individual security needs. In the future particularly small-state security and resilience will most likely be a product of the ability of these states to provide for inclusive security as the aggregate of individual security needs.

Looking at Bahrain and Qatar as two small states within the Gulf, two diametrically opposed images occur: on the one hand, Bahrain, whose leadership has developed a sectarian patronage network favouring one part of the public over the other in a declining rentier state economy; on the other hand, Qatar, which has developed a widely inclusive public governance system fuelled by the immense rents generated from the hydrocarbon sector. In both countries, the involvement of the individual in the public sphere is different. In Bahrain, where parts of society are deliberately excluded from the Social Contract, civil society is more active. In Qatar, on the contrary, the public appears to be widely apathetic – a phenomenon that could be explained by the Qatari regime's ability to adequately compensate the individual in the core security dimensions of physical and socio-economic security. As it will be more and more difficult to distribute rents inclusively to a growing population in the future, both states will most likely see a relative increase in individual involvement in the public sphere. This reality will have to be addressed in both their foreign and security policies. In that way, security narratives and agendas ought not to be defined exclusively from a statist point of view vis-à-vis other states in the region, but increasingly by the security demands of their publics.

Arguably, adopting a first-generation definition of small states, for a geographically and demographically small state, it might actually be easier and more important to consider individual security needs. The reason for this is that, due to an increased propensity for societal cohesion, more intimate bonds between individuals within a geographically more confined space and closer bonds between regime and society in general, the state might be better able to provide security inclusively to society at large. At the same time, society might be more inclined and more capable to mobilize inclusively to get its voice heard. Therefore, a small-state approach to understanding security in the Gulf ought to expand its analytical focus from state-centrism so as to consider other referent objects of security, which equally determine a small state's security policy.

Considering the approach of small states to foreign policy, an individual-centric approach might again, at least in respect to Qatar, be beneficial considering a fourth-generation definition of small states. In regards to the conceptual trade-off between influence and autonomy, Qatar's individual-centric foreign policy approach might be evidence of its transition away from its small-state legacy. Particularly, Qatar's ability to project power across the Arab World, supporting individual calls for more public security in all four dimensions during the Arab Spring has, to a degree, demonstrated that Qatar acts autonomously and influentially. Qatar has defied irrational pressure from its neighbours in the GCC to abandon an individual-centric agenda, which by Qatar's peers was believed to undermine private regime security. Qatar has directly and indirectly supported the *volonté générale* of publics in Libya, Egypt and Syria, choosing individual security needs over private regime security.

Notes

1 It important to note here that the bottom-up challenge of regimes through new or social media has triggered regimes to try to develop new methods of monitoring and restricting freedom of speech, which in a self-perpetuating 'arms race' has led the public to develop new means of bypassing these restrictions.
2 It is important to note that the notion of the Social Contract, although emanating from liberal Western political philosophy, is not alien to the Islamic World. In fact, in Islamic political thought the concept of the *bay'ah* as the subject's pledge of allegiance to the ruler is bound covenantally to the ruler's ability and willingness to provide for the security interests of all its citizens. The *bay'ah*, similar to the Social Contract, assigns duties to both the ruler and the ruled.
3 Conceptually the terms public and private can be traced back to the Ancient Greek dichotomy between the *oikos*, meaning 'house' or 'household', and the *polis*, namely the polity. Etymologically, the terms public and private are derivatives of the Latin *poplicus*, meaning 'of the people', and *privatus*, meaning 'withdrawn from public life'.
4 Exceptional cases of direct criticism of the Al Thani leadership exist. However, the trial against al-Ajami for insulting the Emir of Qatar in 2011 and his 15-year prison sentence remain rare in a country where the freedom of speech is relatively liberal in comparison to other countries in the region.
5 The argument that the Qatari government's rise of public service salaries and the announcement of parliamentary elections in 2011 were a direct response to the Arab Spring, remains weak. The reason is that an adjustment of public sector salaries vis-à-vis private sector salaries was overdue and parliamentary elections were actually postponed.

References

Al-Jazeera (2013). Qatari Court Upholds Poet's Jail Sentence. Al-Jazeera (21 October). Retrieved online 19 August 2016 from www.aljazeera.com/news/middleeast/2013/10/qatar-court-upholds-sentence-against-poet-20131021123723850815.html.

Alterman, J.B. (2004). The Information Revolution and the Middle East. In *The Future Security Environment in the Middle East – Conflict, Stability, and Political Change*, Nora Bensahel and Daniel L. Byman (eds). Santa Monica, CA: RAND (pp. 227–51).

Anderson, J.W. (2003). The Internet and Islam's New Interpreters. In *New Media in the Muslim World – The Emerging Public Sphere*, Dale F. Eickelman and Jon W. Anderson (eds). Indianapolis, IN: Indiana University Press (pp. 45–61).

Ayish, M.I. (2009). *The New Arab Public Sphere*. Berlin: Frank & Timme (p. 47).

Bassiouni, M.C., Rodley, N., Al-Awadhi, B., Kirsch, P. and Arsanjani, M.H. (2011). *Report of the Bahrain Independent Commission of Inquiry*. Chapter VI, Allegations of Human Rights Violations Against the Person. Manama: BICI (pp. 219–317).

Bellin, E. (2012). Reconsidering the Robustness of Authoritarianism in the Middle East. Lessons from the Arab Spring. *Comparative Politics*, Vol. 44, No. 2, pp. 127–49.

Bensahel, N. & Byman, D. (2004). *The Future Security Environment in the Middle East: Conflict, Stability, and Political Change*. Santa Monica, CA: RAND.

Bill, J.A. and Springborg, R. (1999). *Politics in the Middle East*, 5th edition. New York: Addison Wesley Longman.

Black, A. (2001). *The History of Islamic Political Thought – From the Prophet to the Present*. Edinburgh, UK: Edinburgh University Press (p. 22).

Brooks, R. (2004). Civil–Military Relations in the Middle East. In *The Future Security Environment in the Middle East – Conflict, Stability, and Political Change*, Nora Bensahel & Daniel L. Byman (eds). Santa Monica, CA: RAND (pp. 129–62).

Diamond, L. (2010). Liberation Technology. *Journal of Democracy*, Vol. 21, No. 3, pp. 69–83.

Doran, M.S. (2011). The Impact of New Media – The Revolution will be tweeted. In *The Arab awakening: America and the transformation of the Middle East*, K. Pollack (ed). Washington, DC: Brookings (pp. 39–46).

Economist Intelligence Unit (2011). *Bahrain. Country Report, September 2011*. London: Economist Intelligence Unit.

El-Din Haseeb, K. (2013). The Arab Spring Revisited. In *The Arab Spring – Critical Analyses*, Khair El-Din Haseeb (ed). London: Routledge (pp. 4–17).

Fromherz, A.K. (2013). *Qatar – A Modern History*. London: I.B. Tauris (p. 131).

Gause, F.G. III (2010). *The International Relations of the Persian Gulf*. Cambridge, UK: Cambridge University Press.

Gause, F.G. III (2011). Why Middle East Studies Missed the Arab Spring – The Myth of Authoritarian Stability. *Foreign Affairs*, Vol. 90, No. 4, pp. 81–90.

Gengler, J. (2011). Qatar's Ambivalent Democratization. *Foreign Policy* (1 November). Retrieved online 21 March 2014 from http://foreignpolicy.com/2011/11/01/qatars-ambivalent-democratization/.

Habermas, J. (1974). The Public Sphere: An Encyclopedia Article (1964), trans. Sara Lennox and Frank Lennox, *New German Critique*, Vol. 3, pp. 49–50.

Hawthorne, A. (2005). Is Civil Society the Answer? In *Uncharted Journey: Promoting Democracy in the Middle East*, Thomas Carothers and Marina Ottaway (eds). New York: Carnegie Endowment for International Peace (pp. 81–114).

Hobbes, T. (2004). Leviathan. Sioux Falls, SD: Nuvision Publications.

Horovitz, J. (1930). Ibn Qutaiba's Uyun al-Akhbar. *Islamic Culture*, Vol. 4, pp. 171–98.

Hourani, A.H. (2002). *A History of the Arab Peoples*. Harvard, MA: Harvard University Press (p. 105).

Human Rights Watch. (2013). *World Report 2013. Qatar*. New York: Human Rights Watch.

Kamrava, M. (ed) (2011). *International Politics of the Persian Gulf*. Syracuse, NY: Syracuse University Press.

Kassem, M. (2004). *Egyptian Politics – The Dynamics of Authoritarian Rule*. London: Lynne Rienner (p. 87).

Khaldun, I. (1858). *Muqaddimah*, trans. by Franz Rosenthal, Paris: Benjamin Duprat (§22).
Kinninmont, J. (2011). Bahrain. In *Power and Politics in the Persian Gulf Monarchies*, C. Davidson (ed). London: Hurst (pp. 31–62).
Koch, C. and Long, D.E. (2003). *Gulf Security in the Twenty-First Century*. London: I.B. Tauris.
Lambton, A.K.S. (1981). *State and Government in Medieval Islam: an Introduction to the Study of Islamic Political Thought: the Jurists*. Oxford: Oxford University Press (pp. 35–6).
Legrenzi, M. (ed). (2013). *Security in the Gulf*. London: Routledge.
Lewis, B. (2010). *Faith and Power – Religion and Politics in the Middle East*. Oxford: Oxford University Press (p. 123).
Locke, J. (1988). Of the Ends of Political Society and Government, Chapter IX. In *The Two Treatises of Government*, Peter Laslett (ed). Cambridge, UK: Cambridge University Press (pp. 350–4).
Lutterbeck, D. (2013). Arab Uprisings, Armed Forces, and Civil–Military Relations. *Armed Forces & Society*, Vol. 39, No. 1, pp. 28–52.
Lynch, M. (2007). *Voices of a New Arab Public – Iraq, Al Jazeera, and Middle East Politics Today*. New York: Colombia University Press.
Macris, J.F. (2010). *The Politics and Security of the Gulf: Anglo-American Hegemony and the Shaping of a Region*. London: Routledge.
Martin, L.G. (2011). *New Frontiers in Middle East Security*. London: Palgrave Macmillan.
Nawar, I. (2003). *The State of the Arab Media: The Fight for Democracy*. Annual Report 2003. London: Arab Press Freedom Watch.
Norton, A.R. (1995). *Civil Society in the Middle East*. Leiden, NL: E.J. Brill.
Noueihed, L. and Warren, A. (2013). *The Battle for the Arab Spring – Revolution, Counter-Revolution and the Making of a New Era*. New Haven, CT: Yale University Press (p. 142).
Owen, R. (1992). *State, Power and Politics in the making of the Modern Middle East*. London: Routledge.
Quinlivan, J.T. (2000). *Coup-proofing: Its Practice and Consequences in the Middle East*. Santa Monica, CA: RAND.
Regier, T. and Khalidi, M.A. (2009). The Arab Street: Tracking a Political Metaphor. *Middle East Journal*, Vol. 63, No. 1, pp. 11–29.
Rickli, J.-M. (2008). European Small States' Military Policies after the Cold War: from Territorial to Niche Strategies. *Cambridge Review of International Affairs*, Vol. 21, No. 3, pp. 307–25.
Roberts, D. (2011a). Kuwait. In *Power and Politics in the Persian Gulf Monarchies*, Christopher Davidson (ed). London: Hurst & Company (pp. 89–112).
Roberts, D.B. (2011b). Behind Qatar's Intervention in Libya. Why was Doha such as strong supporter of the rebels? *Foreign Policy* (28 September). Retrieved online 15 March 2014 from www.foreignaffairs.com/articles/libya/2011-09-28/behind-qatars-intervention-libya.
Roberts, D.B. (2012). Understanding Qatar's Foreign Policy Objectives. *Mediterranean Politics*, Vol. 17, No. 2, pp. 233–9.
Rousseau, J.J. (1762/2003). *The Social Contract or Principles of Political Right*, trans. G.D.H. Cole. Mineola, NY: Courier Dover Publications (p. 12).
Roy, J. (1999). '*Polis*' and '*Oikos*' in Classical Athens. *Greece & Rome*, Vol. 46, No. 1, p. 1.
Social & Economic Survey Research Institute (SESRI) (2012). *Annual Omnibus Survey: A Survey of life in Qatar 2012*. Doha, QA: SESRI (p. 7).

Stevenson, A. (2010). *Oxford Dictionary of English*. Oxford: Oxford University Press.
Talmon, J.L. (1960). *The Origins of Totalitarian Democracy*. London: Secker & Warburg.
The National (2013). Qatar approves compulsory military service for men: reports. *The National* (13 November). Retrieved online 13 March 2014 from www.thenational.ae/world/middle-east/qatar-approves-compulsory-military-service-formen-reports.
Tocqueville, A. (1838). *Democracy in America*. New York: Dearborn & Co.
Ulrichsen, K.C. (2009). The Evolution of Internal and External Security in the Arab Gulf States. *Middle East Policy* Vol. 16, No. 2, pp. 39–58.
Ulrichsen, K.C. (2011). *Insecure Gulf*. Colombia, NY: Colombia University Press.
Underwood, L.J. (2013). *Cosmopolitanism and the Arab Spring – Foundations for the Decline of Terrorism*. New York: Peter Lang (p. 91).
UN Development Program, Regional Bureau for Arab States (2009). *Arab Human Development Report: Challenges to Human Security in the Arab Countries*. New York: UN Development Program (p. 18).
Wright, S. (2011). Foreign Policy in the GCC States. In *The International Relations of the Persian Gulf*, Mehran Kamrava (ed). Syracuse, NY: Syracuse University Press (pp. 72–93).
Yom, S.L. (2005). Civil Society and Democratization in the Arab World. *Middle East Review of International Affairs*, Vol. 9, No. 4, pp. 14–33.
Zahlan, R.S. (1998). *The Making of the Modern Gulf States*. Reading, UK: Ithaca Press (p. 61).
Zaine, A. (1992). *Communication and Freedom of Expression in Yemen: 1974–1990*. Beirut: Contemporary Thought Press.

5
THE UNITED STATES AND ITS KEY GULF ALLIES

A new foundation for a troubled partnership?

David Goldfischer

Introduction

To say the United States and its two most important Gulf allies: Saudi Arabia and the United Arab Emirates, are at a crossroads, does not quite do justice to the level of current confusion. While it is clear that all parties have left behind an earlier stage of the journey, on which they had long traveled together, fueled by powerful synergies in security and economics, they have veered off in different directions, despite reassuring—and at least partially genuine—continuing references to "partnership" and "coalition."

Once, during the long Cold War, the U.S. foreign policy of containment had meshed powerfully with crucial objectives of the Gulf oil monarchies: all needed to keep the Soviets away from the oil on which the capitalist world depended, and all sought to crush leftist popular movements that implied ideological affinity with the U.S.S.R. That close alignment seemed, at least initially, to navigate safely the first major turn in the road, when the 1979 Khomeini revolution presented a new common threat. In retrospect, though, it is clear that 1979 was the year that clear skies gave way to deepening clouds, as the tactical appeal of mobilizing religion against communism in Afghanistan blinded the United States to Saudi Arabia's strategic embrace—in response to its own heightened sense of danger—of transnational religious radicalism.

Three-and-a-half decades later, those clouds had spread from Afghanistan to New York and Washington, over the entire Middle East and far beyond, descending in a fog so thick that the travelers themselves seemed uncertain which road they were on and where they were headed. In the darkness, a sickening synergy sprang up between Islamic State terrorists and Western demagogues, each sniffing for sites of decay in liberalism's world project, places where fear could crystallize public anxiety into a gratifying choice between two warring identities: Are you a Muslim or are you not? That specter had been nourished by stunning failures of U.S. post-9/11 Middle East policy. Dangers unleashed by the Bush Administration's 2003 invasion had been worsened by the Obama Administration's withdrawal, discrediting the foreign policy establishments of both political parties, and enhancing the American public's receptivity to simplistic alternatives.

For the moment at least, long-standing and powerful reminders of U.S. ties to the Gulf monarchs were still intact. Those ties were embedded in flows of oil and gas, in international finance, in vast, worldwide investments—by sovereign wealth funds and rich individuals—in global industry, transport, agriculture, mass media, and real estate; in humanitarian and development projects; and in Gulf state largesse, much of it charitable, but also artfully bestowed on academic Middle East programs and foreign policy think tanks (Lipton *et al.* 2014). The ties were also entrenched in the form of U.S. military bases, multi-billion dollar weapons and training contracts, joint military operations, and intelligence sharing. All of these connections were buttressed by warm relationships within elite communities of businessmen, politicians, diplomats, defense officials, and academic experts, whose cultivation over decades of shared interests, satisfying deals and personal gain, had evoked feelings of friendship, trust, even loyalty.

Those material, institutional, and psychological attachments, however, have been severely tested, from the perspective of the Saudis and Emiratis: by the U.S. 2003 invasion that empowered Iraq's Shia majority, by the U.S. infatuation with democratic politics during the "Arab Spring," by U.S. absence from the war against Syria's Bashar Al Assad, and by the "Iran deal."[1] Those concerns were matched, from the U.S. standpoint, by suspicions of Gulf Arab ambivalence toward—even collusion with—various Al Qaeda affiliates and the Islamic State.[2] As terror revisited Europe and the United States in the fall of 2015, pressure on the Gulf Arab rulers seemed bound to intensify.

How does—or should—the United States weigh the case for continuity in policy toward the Gulf states against the risk that the status quo will compound current dangers? No one has explained that risk more directly than President Obama: "If young people live in places where the only option is between the dictates of a state, or the lure of an extremist underground, no counterterrorism strategy can succeed" (The White House, Office of the Press Secretary, 2014b). Yet, with rare exceptions, the policy implications of that insight are discussed only within the sideshows of academia and mass media.[3] On the main stages of the State Department, the Department of Defense, and the White House, one mainly hears reassuring affirmations of continuity.[4] Those declarations were backed by policies such as U.S. assistance in the Saudi/United Arab Emirates (UAE) war against Yemen's Iran-backed Houthis—a campaign that strengthened America's deadliest enemies: Al Qaeda in the Arabian Peninsula and Islamic State in Iraq and Syria (ISIS).[5] In the vast space between the prevailing U.S. embrace of the Gulf Sunni autocracies, and the President's own admission that the status quo ensures failure, there is clearly a need to better understand the relationship between the United States and its Gulf partners, toward the end of evaluating the extent to which significant change is necessary and possible.

The goal of this chapter is to at least partially penetrate the fog through which the United States views current Middle East dangers, and through which Saudi Arabia and the UAE struggle to understand the United States. I select those two Gulf states, so different in wealth, size, and historical role, for three reasons: first, because their wealth, foreign policy activism, and location, give them unique regional importance; second, because the larger of the two is deeply implicated in the ideology underlying violent Sunni extremism; third, because its far smaller neighbor, hostile since its creation to political Islam, may hold the key to crafting—and becoming a beacon for—the long-sought "counter-narrative" to that ideology.[6]

The argument that follows can be summarized: first, while the strategic goal of U.S. post-war foreign policy has been, and remains, the implantation of a liberal world order, the Cold War favored tactical adoption of a realist "balance of power approach" that entailed support for "friendly dictators" throughout the developing world. The first section considers why the legacy of Cold-War realism continued to drive U.S. Gulf policy even after it was abandoned elsewhere, and describes its distorting effects. The second section looks at the U.S. abandonment of realism in favor of "neoconservatism" after 9/11, and the role of that approach in the fiasco following the U.S. invasion of Iraq. The third section considers the Obama Administration's oscillation between realist and liberal theories of foreign policy, culminating in a reactive incrementalism that has confused U.S. Gulf partners, failed to address worsening threats to regional and global security, and contributed to an incoherent debate over future policy. In the fourth section, I consider the possible collaborative role of the United States and one—or both—of the two Gulf states under consideration, in addressing the regional roots of global Islamist terrorism. I will argue that the security of all three states requires a liberal alternative to deepening regional sectarianism. Finally, the conclusion briefly assesses prospects for renewed U.S. leadership in advancing that objective.

The realist trap

U.S. Middle East policy (1945–2001)

To make sense of any nation's foreign policy, one has to consider the purposes which animate it. That is certainly true of the United States, whose combination of wealth and military power is historically unparalleled, freeing it to lead a global campaign for a liberal world order. As Robert Kagan describes that goal, U.S. post-Second World War policy has been animated by the belief that:

> American prosperity cannot occur in the absence of global prosperity …, that American freedom depends on the survival and spread of freedom elsewhere …, and that American national security is impossible without a broad measure of international security.
>
> *(1998: 28)*

Explaining the historical origins of that view, or how it became central during the Second World War, is beyond the scope of this chapter. The "shorthand" explanation—which contains much truth—is that the interwar failure by an isolationist United States to address the rise of European fascism (Nazism in particular) had inspired an elite commitment to "liberal internationalism," that is, a global free market, coupled to promotion of democracy, universal human rights, and the rule of law, all backed by U.S. power.[7]

Put another way, the United States is not merely a "great power," in the sense conveyed by "realist" theories of international relations. States are not actors at all; their action results from the purposeful behavior of those who control the reins of state power and of the citizens who serve—or share—leaders' interests. Those myriad purposes can include, for example, dedication to the spread of some ideology; protecting national territory, the domestic suppression of contending aspirants to control over the state, opulence for oneself and one's closest friends; privileges for one's class, or ethnic group, or religious sect, etc.; the well-being of all citizens; and so on. States, then, are best understood as the most important repositories and instruments of power, making control over states the single most valuable prize for advancing the purposes of any ambitious individual or group (as Al Baghdadi, unlike bin Laden, recognized).

In the case of the United States, its enormous power has long been wielded by a coalition of liberal capitalists, who, despite endless partisan bickering over the best mixture of "property rights" (cherished by Republicans) and "equality" (emphasized by Democrats), have combined, since the Second World War, in support of a revolutionary global agenda. That agenda, largely though inconsistently backed by mass electoral support, includes the defeat of challenges, whether foreign or domestic, from any of the three main anti-liberal approaches to organizing human society: fascism, communism, or dictatorship in the name of religion.

Such assaults on liberalism can take the form of subnational or transnational movements, or, most dangerously, can be spearheaded by states under the control of anti-liberal ideologues. If Kagan's claim about post-Second World War U.S. foreign policy remains correct, those who pose significant challenges to a liberal world order must ultimately contend with the most formidable military ever assembled, joined by international allies to the liberal cause, financed by the most productive form of economic organization ever devised, and animated by the universal appeal of human freedom. While one can scarcely discount the impacts of corporate greed, or demagogic nativism, or exhausted isolationism, or sheer folly on U.S. foreign policy since its Second World War emergence as a global "superpower," one cannot comprehend the survival and extension of liberty, or the vast edifice of norms, institutions, and practices that bind the "international community," without assigning centrality to the liberal internationalist dynamism of the United States.

A strategic commitment to a liberal world order in no sense suggests naïve "idealism" when facing danger. The Second World War had reinforced a compelling lesson for U.S. leaders: the importance, when confronting a major threat, of the realist adage that "the enemy of my enemy is my friend." Until 1945, that meant tactical alliance with Stalin's anti-liberal Soviet Union against the equally anti-liberal, but then far more dangerous, Nazi Germany. When allied victory supplanted the German and Japanese threats with one posed by the Soviet superpower, "realpolitik" led to the embrace of various dictators who could help contain Soviet expansionism. That "realist" tactical stance, applied without distinction throughout the Third World, seemed particularly crucial in the Middle East, whose oil and proximity to Communist Russia made it pivotal.[8] An enduring question hanging over U.S. foreign policy, including past and current policy toward the Persian Gulf, is whether and where tactical realism remains necessary for securing or advancing its core strategic objective: a liberal international order.

For U.S. policy toward most of the developing world, the end of the Cold War provided a clear, negative answer to that question. Realpolitik was largely abandoned, as the Clinton Doctrine's call for the expansion of "market democracies" supplanted U.S. support for "friendly dictators." A global wave of democratization followed. The fateful regional exception was the Middle East, where U.S. decision-making was affected by unique reasons for continuing to fear changes in the authoritarian status quo, and for continuing to pursue a balance of power politics. The following briefly describes those reasons, and then turns to the dangers they overlooked.

One unique argument for favoring Middle East continuity and stability over democratic change was an inheritance from an event that occurred near the onset of the Cold War: the 1948 creation of a Jewish State, a state that was later brought under the umbrella of U.S. protection. In contrast to other developing regions, popular Arab rage at Israel (often fed by dictators as a means to direct public anger away from themselves) raised concerns that Arab democratic transitions could produce regimes hostile to the United States. It follows that one part of the puzzle of promoting stable democratization in the Middle East would be a Palestinian–Israeli settlement based on liberal principles of universal human rights for both peoples.[9]

A second reason for continuing to elevate tactical realpolitik above the strategic goal of "market democracy" was that continued world reliance on oil put an added premium on a stable status quo. That reasoning was greatly reinforced by the shock of the 1979 Khomeini revolution, presenting a new threat of a hostile takeover of Gulf oil that, like the Soviet Union, represented a fusion of state power and transnational anti-Western ideology. Balance of power geopolitics was now applied to Iran, as reflected in the U.S. "tilt" toward Saddam Hussein's Iraq during the 1980–8 Iran–Iraq war. When Iraq, with its 1991 invasion of Kuwait, similarly threatened to overturn the Gulf's balance of interstate power, U.S. policy shifted to "dual containment" of Iraq and Iran.

Each of those threats elevated the importance of the U.S. partnership with Saudi Arabia. During the Shah's rule over Iran, Iran and Saudi Arabia were regarded as the "twin pillars" of Gulf anti-Soviet containment. With the "fall of Iran," the remaining pillar became crucial. The kingdom looked like the perfect "balancer," thanks to its wealth and size, its exchange of "petrodollars" for U.S. weapons, and its shared fear of the Soviet Union and Iran. The 1979 Soviet invasion of Afghanistan brought

U.S. realpolitik into its sharpest Gulf formulation: the Carter Doctrine's threat of war to protect the Arab oil monarchs against threats from any source. The Saudi pillar now seemed pivotal at both the regional and global levels, as Saudi money backed Iraq's war with Iran, and as the Saudis provided funding and oversight of the Islamist uprising against the Soviet occupation of Afghanistan.[10] As then U.S. National Security Advisor Zbigniew Brzezinski later expressed it: "What was more important in the world view of history? . . . A few stirred-up Muslims or the liberation of Central Europe and the end of the Cold War?" (Gibbs, 2000).

The rising costs of U.S. realpolitik would become clear. The U.S. role in sustaining the Shah's misrule fed the danger that revolution would tap deep popular hatred of the United States. Iran also demonstrated a problem that would become glaring, three decades later, during the aftermath of the Arab Spring. As described by Peter Sluglett:

> Perhaps the most unfortunate general consequence of this pathological fear, or hatred, of local communists and leftists, which the cold war encouraged . . . , was that the secular opposition was driven underground almost everywhere in the Middle East . . . . In consequence, what opposition there was drifted into the hands of religious organizations of various kinds, since, in Islamic countries, governments cannot, ultimately, close down the mosques . . . . The obsession with persecuting . . . the left has had two results, first, the maintenance of . . . dictatorial regimes of whatever political hue, and second, the rise of the religious right. In the latter, we are now faced with uncontrollable forces.
>
> *(2005)*

We know that the lens of realpolitik, through which the United States had viewed the region since 1945, masked the gathering power of two mutually hostile, violent transnational movements backed by state power: the "Shia revival" launched by Khomeini in 1979, and the Wahhabist campaign unleashed—as protection and retaliation—by the rulers of Saudi Arabia. Detailing the enormity and scope of what now transpired "invisibly," that is, below the realist radar informing U.S. foreign policy, is beyond the scope of this chapter. But the central thread is now well known, and unchallenged in serious scholarship on Saudi Arabia. With their legitimacy challenged by Khomeinism from without, and by Wahhabist extremists from within, Saudi King Fahd decided to outmaneuver those threats by championing—with an investment of billions of dollars—a worldwide campaign to draw the Sunni Muslim world into a brutally intolerant version of Islam, an ideology adopted without substantial revision by Al Qaeda, and more recently by the Islamic State.[11]

In Afghanistan, that meant that only extreme jihadist groups would be funded in fighting the Soviet-backed regime, as the United States uncomprehendingly farmed out implementation of its anti-Soviet war to the Saudis and the Wahhabist Pakistani Inter-services Intelligence (I.S.I.). The resulting empowerment of bin Laden and his new Al Qaeda organization was followed, as U.S. attention waned after Soviet withdrawal, by Saudi support for the Taliban takeover. Having driven home, domestically and throughout the Sunni world, a doctrine that encouraged violence against liberalism and all rival religious beliefs, many within the Saudi elite all but celebrated the 2001 attack on America, organized and led by Saudi nationals.[12]

Why then, was the post-9/11 rage of the George W. Bush Administration directed, in the Middle East, against Iraq rather than against the source of Sunni extremism? In one sense, it was understandable why 9/11, which dramatized the global reach of even a non-state actor like Al Qaeda, would increase U.S. concern over regimes with long-standing records of hostility to the United States—in particular that of Saddam Hussein. The general post-9/11 mood of war fever also provided an opportunity for those who had regarded the removal of Saddam Hussein's regime as the unfinished business of Desert Storm's 1991 liberation of Kuwait. Finally, a few realists had concluded that the weakening of the sanctions regime against Iraq, combined with worry over Iraqi acquisition of mass-destruction weapons, had made regime change a necessity (see Pollack, 2002). But the majority of realists, drowned out by post-9/11 passions, strongly opposed the war, maintaining that "dual containment" of Iraq and Iran was working, and presciently arguing that an invasion would benefit Iran.[13]

However problematic, security-based arguments in favor of war would now be bolstered by the ascent, within U.S. Middle East policy, of an ideologically infused movement that had first gained influence within the Republican Party during the Reagan Administration. It was animated by a two-pronged attack on competing approaches to American foreign policy: against realists for rejecting the core U.S. mission of building an "empire of liberty," and against liberal Democrats, whose rhetorical embrace of human rights, they argued, was negated by their antagonism toward the use of force.[14] In addition to bolstering the general case for war against enemy regimes, 9/11 had galvanized the belief that only the democratic transformation of the Middle East could uproot the anti-U.S. hatred—and terrorism—emanating from the region.

The neoconservative trap

U.S. Gulf policy under G. W. Bush (2003–9)

As noted earlier, realist arguments favoring regime stability over democratic change had preserved their post–Cold War appeal only when applied to the Middle East. After 9/11, that exception was bound to be questioned. The faction within the U.S. community of foreign policy advisors who had—during the Cold War—been most insistent on the forceful use of U.S. power to back friendly anti-communist dictators, now embraced a radical shift of aims.[15] These "neoconservatives" had celebrated Ronald Reagan's deep confidence in the natural desire of all humans to resist despotism, and they now applied to the Middle East his conviction that U.S.

power held the key to mobilizing those yearnings for democratic self-governance. Through that lens, the problem of Saddam Hussein and the danger revealed by 9/11 now appeared connected, as neoconservatives in the Bush Administration began to argue, as depicted by Gregory Gause, "that an American-reconstructed Iraqi polity could be a beacon of moderation and pro-Western democracy in the region, exerting pressure for reform on neighboring states that would then reduce the chances of terrorist groups developing in those states" (2005: 278–9).

When the toppling of Saddam Hussein was followed by a growing anti-U.S. insurgency, President George W. Bush's initially enthusiastic embrace of the neoconservative argument was quickly muted. Yet it is worth remembering that, in 2003, Bush's case for democracy extended beyond Iraq to include a public appeal to the rulers of Saudi Arabia, Egypt, and Bahrain to undertake democratic transitions (see The White House, 2003).

In retrospect, it is obvious that the neoconservative school of liberal internationalism was unprepared to design and implement a democratic transition in Iraq. The neoconservatives displayed a striking lack of concern with the challenges confronting efforts to transform a country ravaged by prolonged despotic rule and lacking any tradition of liberal self-governance. That oversight, in large measure, represented the foreign policy analogy to the conservative ideology that now dominated the Republican Party's domestic agenda, characterized by deep suspicion of the role of government, and a conception of "liberty" as synonymous with property rights and unregulated free enterprise. That ideological stance, whatever its merits as a domestic policy critique of the American "welfare state," contributed to engrained hostility toward the very notion of developing a serious, comprehensive plan for occupying and transforming Iraq.

The deepest flaw in the neoconservative approach to democratic transition in Iraq was its complete lack of curiosity regarding the actual nature of Iraq's culture, society, and politics. Most glaringly, the U.S. invaders undertook their occupation completely oblivious, as the late Fouad Ajami put it, of "the terrible secret that lay at the heart of Islam in the Fertile Crescent and the Gulf—the fault line between Sunni and Shia Muslims" (2014: 96). Combined, the neoconservatives' heedlessness both of the general need to supplant authoritarian structures and rebuild society, and of the specific obstacles posed by Iraqi sectarianism set the stage for the instability that now engulfs the region.[16]

From the perspective of the Sunni-led Gulf monarchies, the neoconservative enterprise in Iraq constituted a double betrayal: first, the U.S. commitment to regional democratization axiomatically threatened the one-family rule; second, the fact that Iraqi democracy would empower a Shia majority created the prospect of a vast expansion of Iran's influence. Consequent fear that the United States was retreating from its commitment to the security of their regimes has cast a lengthening shadow over the oil monarchs' perception of U.S. regional policy ever since.

From the Saudi perspective in particular, the decapitation of Saddam's regime had set in motion a progressive deterioration in relations with the United States. If Saddam had usefully dominated Iraq's Shia majority and helped contain Iran, his invasion of Kuwait had still marked him as a dangerous enemy of the Arab Gulf states. Now, with Saddam gone, the only remaining "boots on the ground" against the newly empowered Shia belonged to Al Qaeda in Iraq. Yet the danger for the Saudis of the Sunni insurgency in Iraq quickly became apparent, as bin Laden tried in 2003 to launch an uprising against the House of Saud. From then until now, the monarchy has faced a dilemma: the most effective warriors against militant Iran-backed Shia groups throughout the region belong to organizations that challenge their own claim to rule the domain containing the holiest sites of Islam.

As the U.S.-led occupation of Iraq led to a rising Sunni insurgency and deepening sectarian civil war, exhaustion with the Iraq quagmire began to transform U.S. domestic debate over foreign policy. Unfortunately, the Obama Administration's Middle East policy would reveal flaws in his more dovish variant of liberal internationalism that were at least as dangerous as those associated with neoconservatism.

The liberal trap

U.S. Gulf policy under Barack Obama (2009–16)

One might have thought that Democratic Party liberals would have embraced the toppling of the murderous Saddam Hussein and celebrated U.S. leadership aimed at democratic transition in Iraq and throughout the Middle East. Most did not. Democratic presidential candidates—from George McGovern in 1972 to Barack Obama in 2008 and 2012—would henceforth be denounced by Republicans for their unwillingness to use force in defense of freedom; they in turn would predictably accuse their Republican rivals of militaristic fantasies that would lead to disaster. In the unfolding fiasco following the 2003 U.S. invasion, most Americans would come to side with the liberal doves; Barack Obama's nomination and election were substantially attributable to his opposition to the war in Iraq, and his corresponding commitment to withdraw all U.S. troops if elected.[17]

From the vantage point of 2008, post-invasion events in Iraq had seemingly demonstrated the accuracy of dire realist and liberal "dove" forecasts, and the newly elected President Obama drew upon both of those perspectives on world politics. He now argued that withdrawal from Iraq would not threaten the Middle East balance of power, linking that realist concern to the liberal argument that Iraq's democracy would be inclusive enough to overcome mutual suspicions among Sunni, Shia, and Kurds, hence robust enough to resist Iranian expansionism. In effect, what he had denounced as a debacle from which the United States must withdraw in defeat when he ran for office, he now celebrated as a success that allowed for U.S. withdrawal with honor: the new Iraq would meet both the realpolitik requirement to contain Iran and the liberal standard of extending freedom.

Those assumptions about Iraq were embedded within Obama's broader view of the world and particularly the Middle East and North Africa (MENA) region, a set of assumptions that conveniently supported what was clearly his main wish: that U.S. military intervention would no longer be required. First, that Iraq would now demonstrate his more general argument that diplomacy should be favored over the use of military power; second, that there was no tension between support for traditional authoritarian partners and long-term hopes for progress toward democracy and human rights; third, that violent extremism, while vexing, could be managed without "boots on the ground"; fourth, that the only potentially actionable threat to the regional balance of power would be Iran's acquisition of nuclear weapons—requiring a policy of sanctions and negotiation that kept military threats "on the table" but remote. One final dimension to Obama's overall analysis gave added weight to his case for military disengagement: the accurate recognition that past U.S. interventions in the region had generated widespread anger throughout the Muslim world.

Those themes were interwoven within Obama's foreign policy addresses as early as his June 4, 2009 speech at Cairo University (The White House, 2009), highlighted by an eloquent appeal to the Islamic world that America was not an enemy. They were repeated, in varying combinations, but essentially unrevised despite breathtaking changes in the region, until as late as his May 28, 2014 speech at West Point (The White House, 2014a). A brief excerpt from the Cairo speech captures the ongoing ambiguities that would haunt U.S. policy until today:

> Today, America has a dual responsibility: to help Iraq forge a better future—and to leave Iraq to Iraqis.... I know there has been controversy about the promotion of democracy in recent years, and much of this controversy is connected to the war in Iraq. So let me be clear: No system of government can or should be imposed by one nation on any other. That does not lessen my commitment, however, to governments that reflect the will of the people. Each nation gives life to this principle in its own way, grounded in the traditions of its own people.... But I do have an unyielding belief that all people yearn for certain things: the ability to speak your mind and have a say in how you are governed;... the freedom to live as you choose. These are not just American ideas; they are human rights. And that is why we will support them everywhere.
>
> (The White House, 2009)

What precisely was the balance between Obama's realist aversion to intervening in the internal affairs of other countries, and his liberal impulse to promote the extension of human freedom? The first test was Iran, whose Green Movement arose in protest against the allegedly rigged June 2009 election of President Mahmoud Ahmadinejad. The world was riveted, first by the courageous challenge by thousands of young Iranian liberals against corrupt theocratic rule, then by its brutal suppression. As Fouad Ajami described President Obama's response: "The embattled liberals in the Arab-Islamic world watched when Obama was caught flat-footed by the turmoil . . . . He was out to conciliate the rulers, and he couldn't even find the language to speak to Iran's rebellion." (2014: 23).

The costs of having no vision—and consequently no strategy—would soon be fully demonstrated by the Arab Spring's return of mass politics to the Arab world. In the face of the Tahir Square demonstrations, Obama's realist impulse to back long-standing U.S. ally Hosni Mubarak waned as the crowds surged. A quavering liberal voice then prevailed, as Obama prodded Mubarak to step down, validated the electoral triumph of the anti-liberal Muslim Brotherhood, and denounced the Abdel Fattah al-Sisi coup. The main consequence of this confused, lip-service liberalism seemed to call into question what remained of U.S. Cold War realpolitik: the implicit U.S. commitment to regime security for dictators friendly to the United States, and the explicit U.S. commitment (dating back to the 1979 Carter Doctrine) to defend the Gulf oil monarchies against Iran.

Making matters worse, from the monarchs' perspective, the U.S. flirtation with regional democratization coincided with steps toward nuclear negotiations with Iran, which, they could imagine, might presage eventual U.S. abandonment of its Gulf Arab allies. These combined concerns soon became local and concrete, as Obama sought to persuade Bahrain's Sunni monarchy to negotiate democratic reforms with Manama's Pearl Roundabout demonstrators. From the Gulf monarchs' perspective, Bahraini democratization would have empowered a Shia majority and brought Iran to their very borders. On March 14, 2011, their response to the lofty liberal appeals of U.S. officials was to send their militaries into Bahrain to crush the democracy movement.[18]

In fact, the Obama Administration's flirtation with turning liberal rhetoric into sustained policy was winding down. The test case was the mass uprising in Syria. Having made his liberal appeal to Syrian dictator Bashir al Assad to allow democratic elections, Obama established a "red line" whose crossing would trigger U.S. intervention: the use of mass-destruction weapons. When Assad ignored the threat, Obama was confronted with a vexing question: Would he now, in effect, resurrect the neoconservative agenda he had campaigned against, using the U.S. military to democratize Syria?

On the pro-intervention side of the balance sheet was the President's liberal impulse to protect the possibility of a democratic future for the Syrian people, as well as the "responsibility to protect" civilians against crimes against humanity. On the other side of the ledger were the President's realpolitik assumptions: that there was no compelling "national interest" in using force to protect human rights, the risk that an attack would derail nuclear negotiations with Iran, and the concern that a return to military engagement in the Middle East would disrupt his geopolitical priority of a U.S. "pivot to Asia" to address the rise of China. The realist case prevailed.

For the Saudis and Emiratis, America's realist impulse to ignore its own "red line" against their common enemy Assad, and America's liberal impulse to prod their common friend, Mubarak, to step down, pointed to the same conclusion: U.S. commitments in the region were no longer credible. The United States had, in effect, rejected the Gulf monarchs' view of the Syrian civil war as one front in the Saudi-led regional struggle, on behalf of all Sunni Arabs, to contain, and hopefully reverse, Iranian expansionism in the name of a supremacist Shiite ideology.

One year after the red-line bluff confirmed the supremacy of realist-based non-interventionism in U.S. Middle East policy, all of the premises supporting that policy were swept aside by the shocking advance of Islamic State. As one faction fighting within chaotic Syria, Islamic State could be safely mislabeled as a "junior varsity" version of Al Qaeda. But when they swept into Iraq, routed the Iraqi army, and approached within hours of Baghdad, they destroyed the foundational 2009 Cairo speech premise of Obama's foreign policy in the region: "Today, America has a dual responsibility: to help Iraq forge a better future — and to leave Iraq to Iraqis." The actual consequence of leaving Iraq to the Iraqis was now painfully clear. In its haste to withdraw, the United States had left behind a government controlled by Shiite Islamists bent on vengeance against the Sunnis. That had created fertile soil for the creation of the Islamic State, whose savage war of conquest against all "infidels" drove what remained of Iraqi governance ever more deeply into the arms of Iran and Iraq's radical Shiite militias. The glaring contradiction between America's alleged "dual responsibilities" in Iraq had now become manifest in the worst of all possible ways: the emergence of a terrorist organization far more potent than Al Qaeda, posing a growing threat to the West, and requiring, inescapably, a return to U.S. military intervention in the Middle East.

There was one remaining realist illusion left to be dispelled: the belief that the Sunni Arab states, led by Saudi Arabia and the UAE, could be resurrected as effective partners against the common danger posed by the Islamic State.[19] Instead, as the United States found itself in a new war, its old Gulf allies were all but absent, preoccupied with their own wars against Iranian influence and Shia empowerment, from Bahrain to Syria to Yemen, a war in which their interests and that of the Islamic State (and its jihadist predecessor Al Qaeda) substantially coincided. Downplaying the near absence of Iraq's neighboring Sunni-led states from a war vital to U.S. national security, unreal discussions premised on a "coalition" proceeded. The United States, it was proposed, would now bring the countries of the Gulf Cooperation Council (GCC) under a common anti-Iranian missile shield.[20] In reality, rivalries between the ruling families comprising the GCC had reached a fever pitch. The Qatari rulers had supported the Muslim Brotherhood's bid for power in Egypt and beyond, an approach regarded by Saudi King Abdullah and UAE leadership, particularly Sheik Mohammed bin Zayed, as blatant efforts to delegitimize their own rule. The Omani offense, facilitating U.S. negotiations with Iran, was milder, but still revealed a weak link in the deepening conflict with Iran.

The United States had now completed its cycle of backward-looking policies: moving from realism, rendered anachronistic by 9/11; to neoconservatism, discredited by the Iraq fiasco; to the Obama Administration's dabbling in toothless liberalism; and finally back to anachronistic realism. There were apparently no strategic arrows left in the U.S. quiver. The culmination of those successive failures was now manifested in mass public anxiety over the truly maniacal Islamic State, and over the flight of millions of refugees from sectarian war, many arriving in desperation at the doorstep of the West.

The prudential value of realism never disappears in a world in which states are the most formidable instruments of power. Sometimes there are compelling reasons to choose the enemy of one's enemy as a friend, even when there is a high later price to be paid. Few question the U.S. Second World War alliance with Stalin's Russia, even though its price was the emergence of an expansionist Soviet superpower in 1945. Similarly, and without the benefit of hindsight, U.S. support for the Shah of Iran and the House of Saud can be defended as vital to the protection of the free world's oil from the Soviet threat. In 1979, had Ayatollah Khomeini succeeded in his aspiration to unite the entire Gulf region, and to harness all of its oil, under the banner of his violent Islamist vision, that new marriage of major state power and revolutionary anti-liberal ideology would have justified a new geopolitical response, in which great powers, even those hostile to each other, might have tactically united against a major common threat.

In the event, however, the Ayatollah's project bogged down almost immediately, as his calls for a Shiite uprising in Iraq prompted invasion by Saddam Hussein, and the bloodletting of an eight-year war that ended in stalemate. The Ayatollah's call for the overthrow of the House of Saud produced a very different response. Saudi King Fahd effectively warded off Iran's power by moving closer to the West economically and militarily, while countering Iran's ideological threat by embracing, and exporting, Saudi Arabia's equally puritanical form of Islam. If the alliance with the United States against the Soviet Union in Afghanistan cultivated the appearance that the Saudis stood with the liberal world, 9/11 began to unmask the kingdom's temptation to outbid the Iranian theocracy's Islamist assault on a liberal world order.

The result, coming to fruition in today's Iraq, Syria, and Yemen, and beyond, is a vicious cycle of deepening sectarian violence fed by the rulers of Iran and Saudi Arabia. The United States is right when it reassures the Saudis that it has no interest in realigning with Iran. Yet the United States will find no advantage in siding with either side in a transnational religious conflict over which form of Islamist authoritarianism should prevail, a conflict in which the one theme uniting the fiercest warriors on both sides is their sincere call for "death to America."

Today, as growing anxiety over terrorism, combined with millions of refugees fleeing that conflict, test liberal values in Europe and the United States, the West finds itself in an exhausting global game of "whack-a-mole" against multiplying targets, as geographically diverse as the outposts of Al Qaeda and the proliferating "provinces" of the Islamic State, as large as Mosul and as tiny as the troubled minds of "lone wolves." The various strands of policy developed during the Cold War and its aftermath have run their course. If U.S. foreign policy is to regain its footing, it will begin by returning to the platform it developed during its war on fascism and affirmed globally in 1945: an insistence that its own security, and that of the wider world, begins with a revolutionary commitment to the forceful defense of liberalism.

Toward a liberal regional order

Saudi Arabia, the United States, and the UAE

In contemplating U.S. paralysis in the face of the mounting threat emanating from the Middle East and threatening the viability of a liberal world order, it was not surprising that more than one historically aware observer was drawing comparisons to interwar Europe. One memorable example is from a Roger Cohen op-ed lamenting America's failure to halt the bloodletting in Syria:

> As T.S. Eliot wrote after Munich in 1938, "We could not match conviction with conviction, we had no ideas with which we could either meet or oppose the ideas opposed to us." Syria has been the bloody graveyard of American conviction.
>
> *(2016)*

Cohen is of course referring to liberals' loss of faith as they confronted the mounting threat of fascism in Europe. In today's Middle East, liberalism has again found itself mute, this time confronted by the furious confrontation between two competing strands of clerical fascism: the supremacist ideology imposed on Shiite Islam by Ayatollah Khomeini, and the extremist Sunni counterclaim fashioned out of Saudi Wahhabism. Against the force of those faith-based convictions, stand the weak reeds of monarchical legitimacy (whose leading champions are the ruling families of Saudi Arabia and the UAE), and the secular dictatorship of Egypt's Al-Sisi.

In that context, hopes for a Saudi-led coalition that contains Iran and defeats the Islamic State should be regarded as an anachronistic geopolitical fantasy. Long dependent on Wahhabism as the basis for monarchical legitimacy, the only militarily potent "counter-narrative" the Saudi rulers have been able to offer against the medieval ideology of Iran's theocracy has been the equally medieval ferocity of Sunni jihadism. That effort to appease its extremists domestically, and to mobilize them against external threats is now pointing toward a tragic conclusion, as Al Qaeda, having morphed into the more powerful Islamic State, proves more compelling than the kingdom as warriors against militant Shiism, and as ideological bulwarks against the universal appeal of liberty.

We are now witnessing the policy consequences of the House of Saud's effort to compete with the Islamic State for credentials as the most legitimate defender of the Sunni faith. As the United States tries to insist that the Saudis fight Islamic State, the Saudi ruling family asks the United States to understand (or support) its interventions from Bahrain to Yemen, and against its own Shia population concentrated in its oil-producing region. Presented to the West as containment of Iran, they are as sectarian and anti-democratic as the campaigns of Iran and its allies.

Thus far, the Obama Administration still listens to the faint echoes of Cold War era rationales for protecting the kingdom against its enemies, and, cognizant that every hint of rapprochement with Iran terrifies the ruling family, finds itself still struggling, in word and deed, to reassure the Saudi rulers. This policy inertia masks underlying reality: there remain no deeply shared interests between the United States and the Saudis, save one that is admittedly crucial: the collapse of the House of Saud would almost certainly create far more danger than its survival.

As Saudi Arabia finds itself increasingly drained, within and beyond its borders, by the enduring hold of an ancient pact with the harsh imperatives of Muhammad ibn Abd al-Wahhab, it needs to cultivate a new basis of legitimacy in order to endure. To paraphrase Cohen's quotation of T.S. Elliot, the children and grandchildren of Saudi Arabia's founding ruler Abdulaziz ibn Saud need to embrace an idea powerful enough to oppose both of the ideologies which, since 1979, have become increasingly lethal: Khomeinism and Wahhabist extremism. As the Saudi rulers sink further into a deepening quagmire, in which declining oil revenues fall short of the mounting costs of widening war and domestic security, finding a more reliable basis for legitimacy will ultimately prove the only possible path to survival.

To secure itself against external threats, from the Soviet Union, to Iran, to Saddam Hussein's Iraq, the House of Saud was compelled to turn repeatedly to the wellspring of world liberal power since 1941: the United States. The moment is approaching when the Saudi ruling family needs to appeal once more to the United States and its liberal allies worldwide, and to the ranks of its own citizens who have grown tired of being terrorized by the clerical descendants of Muhammad ibn Abd al-Wahhab. Even if the medieval foundations of Saudi society are strong enough today to crush popular aspirations to liberty, their corrosive effects weaken every aspect of the state, yielding an army that does not fight and an economy fated to decline. Deputy Crown Prince Mohammed bin Salman has produced impressive economic liberalization plans, essential for meeting basic needs of citizens and vital for sustained competition with Iran. The strictures of Salafism, interlocked with the fiefdoms of Saudi princes, however, will hobble the flexibility and entrepreneurship required to meet the challenge of moving toward a post-oil economy, preserving in place a slow-motion path toward state failure (Ignatius, 2016).

One might imagine a U.S. president privately insisting to Saudi leaders that they supplant, on an agreed-upon timetable, the current clerical establishment, its schoolbooks, and its sermons, domestically and worldwide, with one that promotes a genuinely tolerant interpretation of Islam. That request would be analogous, in a sense, to the U.S. request to King Fahd, four days after Saddam Hussein's invasion of Kuwait, to allow US forces to use Saudi territory as a staging ground for an attack on Iraq. In that case, the King, preferring national survival over Iraqi invasion, was willing to enrage Osama bin Laden and other Wahhabi purists. A quarter of a century later, those unappeasable purists couple their war on the West with internal war against the House of Saud. If that perspective ruled, the rulers would welcome such U.S. pressure.

A more pessimistic analogy would be to the U.S. demand to the Afghan Taliban, following 9/11, that they abandon Osama bin Laden and his followers. In that case, solidarity with Al Qaeda trumped Taliban prudence. The Saudi rulers, in other words, would finally find themselves at a similar fork in the road. For the United

States and its Western allies, whose soldiers and civilians have, for two decades, died at the hands of Salafist warriors spawned in Saudi-funded madrassas, it is appropriate to make that demand, and to react according to the answer they receive. By agreeing, the Saudi rulers would have the chance to face their relentless internal threat head-on, backed by reform-minded clerics, by large numbers of educated Saudis, and by the far wider appeal of freedom. In doing so, a reforming Saudi state would be forging its first durable alliance with the United States, as well as with Europe and the wider liberal world, an assemblage that has proven itself as the most formidable coalition in world history. Uprooting the foundation of Sunni-based terrorism would set the stage for Saudi Arabia to emerge as an actual "pillar" against two common adversaries: the Islamic State and supporters of theocracy in Iran.

Like the Saudis, the rulers of the UAE find themselves entrapped in a deepening regional quagmire posing existential threats. As a far smaller state, they have bandwagoned with their Saudi neighbors in common approaches to both the Arab Spring uprisings and the Iran threat, intervening together in Bahrain, supporting the al-Sisi coup in Egypt and financing its consolidation, pressuring Qatar to halt its support for the Muslim Brotherhood, and attacking the Houthis in Yemen. Yet their situation is different in several critical respects. First, while the House of Saud risks being devoured by its foundational pact with Wahhabism, the rulers of Abu Dhabi and Dubai face the problem of having literally no ideological basis for legitimacy. The UAE constitution, whose list of laws begins with the phrase "We the rulers," offers only implicit rationales for their power: the authority of tradition, the promise of benevolence toward their citizens, and the threat of coercion. The shakiness of that foundation, however, has been more than compensated, at least until now, by several advantages.

The most crucial is that, despite the monarchy's evident weakness in the realm of political theory, the ruling families of Abu Dhabi and Dubai have long recognized that Islamism poses the single greatest threat to their power. If the United States confronted the full fury of Sunni religious extremism in the year 2001, the Bedouin ancestors of the current ruling families have been episodically battling Wahhabist assaults for more than two centuries. The result has been that one crucial precondition for a democratic transition is already firmly in place: a genuine inclination toward tolerance, both of other religions and of the lifestyles of the vast numbers of secular Westerners (part of the UAE's global guest list) who arrive as workers or tourists.

Tolerance, one by-product of freedom from theological authority has also been an enabler of by far the most dynamic process of development, modernization, and Westernization in the Arab Middle East. Of course, development is fueled by other factors: the combination of vast oil wealth and small population, and the good fortune of having visionary, entrepreneurial leaders capable of translating oil wealth into stable, diverse, national development. Those rulers made the strategic decision of going beyond military alignment with the West, building educational and cultural ties that deepen and reinforce the security relationship. In short, one can respect the basic honesty of the following recent claim by Yousef Al Otaiba, the UAE Ambassador to the United States:

> We are testing a new vision for the region—an alternative, future-oriented ideology. It is a path guided by the true tenets of Islam: respect, inclusion, and peace. It empowers women, embraces diversity, encourages innovation, and welcomes global engagement.
>
> *(2015)*

Those remarkable contrasts with Saudi Arabia make political reform more likely. By eschewing religious authority as the basis for dictatorial rule and by embracing modernization, the rulers, however unwittingly, have enabled UAE citizens to recognize that their exclusion from self-governance is explained simply by the ruling families' desire to preserve their power and wealth. Moreover, by embracing women's rights in education and employment, the rulers have unleashed a latent feminist movement that presses increasingly against the sexism enshrined in Sharia law and undermines the whole concept of dynastic male rule. Finally, the rulers have created a legislative body (now headed by a woman), and extended the vote to a growing portion of its citizenry. While the Federal National Council lacks real power, its members are learning more about the rights of citizens than the leaders may have hoped.

What is missing from this "future-oriented ideology" is the rulers' willingness to tolerate even the most limited challenges to their absolute authority. Their lesson from the Arab Spring was that no space can be allowed for political activism; bloggers appealing for even modest reforms can expect arrest. Yet in contrast to the Saudis, key conditions for transition to a constitutional monarchy are already in place: de facto secularism, tolerance for diverse cultures, real steps toward gender equality, and rapid modernization that weakens adherence to the tribal traditions on which monarchic rule is founded. The UAE rulers also know well that they cannot survive without the security relationships they have built with the United States, the British, and the French.

For all of those reasons, the United States is in a position to pressure the rulers of the UAE to take one more decisive step: a commitment to the liberal core of any genuine "ideology of openness." A transition to constitutional monarchy would almost certainly enable the ruling families to preserve their wealth, would reinforce the respect of their citizens, and would bring badly needed merit-based talent, at the level of policy-making, into their remarkable national project. Should the UAE take that step, the regional impact would likely be powerful. Despite its small size, the UAE embodies the aspirations of ordinary Arabs throughout the region. Already a magnet for the region's entrepreneurs, educators, and highly skilled workers, the UAE can literally use immigration policy to become an engine of liberalism throughout the region. At that point, the Emiratis would truly have begun "testing a new vision for the region—an alternative, future-oriented ideology." Short of real progress toward secular liberalism, the UAE is destined to fail its own test.

The UAE's current, unpalatable alternative to that promising direction is to stand with the Saudis in a regional war that feeds sectarian extremism, a path that may well overwhelm the leading outpost of modernity in the Arab world. The Iranian theocracy has little to fear from the hollow Saudi state or the fierce but tiny UAE. By contrast, a combination of great wealth, a globally competitive economy, and the proclamation of a new liberal regional order, may send a shock wave across the Gulf that Iran's backward-looking theocrats may well be unable to withstand.

Conclusion

Prospects for U.S. leadership

In describing the rationale for his outline of "a new vision for the region," Ambassador Al Otaiba described "Islamic extremist violence" as "the most destabilizing and dangerous force since fascism." He is correct in his diagnosis. Fascism, he might remember, was defeated first in war, thanks to Pearl Harbor's awakening of the "sleeping giant" of U.S. global power, and then by prolonged occupations that supplanted anti-liberal ideologies in defeated Germany and Japan, and transformed those states into bastions of liberal democracy.

Seven decades later, another potential lethal assault on liberalism has surfaced, this time as a clerical variant of fascism, whose global threat takes the form not of mass armies, but of a less tangible "*blitzkrieg*" based on the global reach of terrorism, the power of social media and the internet, the fear-inspiring potential of globalized, sensationalist real-time news coverage, the destabilizing power of massive flows of refugees, and the resulting popular appeal of Western demagogues, exploiting all of those sources of global anxiety, whose anti-Muslim rantings echo the drumbeat of anti-Semitism during Hitler's rise to power.

Against such voices, the empowering liberal voice of the United States had fallen mute. As the first three sections of this chapter explained, backward-looking policies rooted in seven decades of U.S. foreign policy history since the dawn of the Cold War: realism, neoconservatism, and dovish liberalism, had followed their path-dependent policy prescriptions into new challenges for which they were entirely ill-suited. Applying realism to the region had evolved from a practical tactic for balancing major power threats to the Gulf's oil, to irrelevance in dealing with new dangers posed by transnational, revolutionary movements. The neoconservatives, by associating the spread of liberty with the simple-minded application of U.S. military power, had discredited their essential, valid insight: that U.S. security required extending the liberal world order into the Middle East.

Finally, liberal doves, their Vietnam scars reopened by the fiasco in Iraq, now regarded the defense of liberalism only as a domestic battle, directed against Republicans, over income inequality, social safety nets, and religion-inspired restrictions on individual liberty. They had long forgotten that their original hero, Franklin Delano Roosevelt, had recognized the indivisibility of local and global struggle for those values. In his 1941 State of the Union address, eleven months before Pearl Harbor animated America's enduring emergence as the leading world power, Roosevelt had called on the American people to uproot European fascism by the worldwide promotion of "four freedoms": freedom of speech, freedom of worship, freedom from want, and freedom from fear (Roosevelt, 1941). That vision, combining individual liberty, secularism, and inclusive capitalism, coupled to the security required to protect those universal aspirations, offered a strategic unity of power and purpose that uprooted fascism and shaped the U.S.-led design of the post-war international system, a vision that would fragment, under the pressure of Cold War passions, in the quagmire of the Vietnam War.

During that war, President Johnson, in a wildly wrong prediction, is widely alleged to have said that "if we quit Vietnam tomorrow we'll be fighting in Hawaii and next week we'll have to be fighting in San Francisco." By contrast, U.S. withdrawal from Iraq in 2010 cannot be fully disassociated from the Islamic State-inspired attack, five years later, in San Bernardino, California. As the United States returned to war in Iraq in the summer of 2014, airstrikes were combined with the beginnings of diplomatic pressure that had been completely absent when the United States withdrew, insisting that, for the United States to intervene successfully to stop the advance of the Islamic State, the Iraqi government had to abandon its repression of Sunni Iraqis and move decisively toward an inclusive democracy that respected minority Sunni rights.

Eighteen months later, as troops from the Shia-led Iraqi government closed in on Falluja, held by the Islamic State, the punishment of innocent Sunni civilians by Iraqi soldiers showed that no progress had been made. A reporter's interview captured the essence of the problem: "This message is to all the honest people in the world," said a woman in Falluja reached by telephone: "We are caught between the injustice of ISIS and an unknown future with the government that will accuse us of being with ISIS" (Arango, 2016). Former U.S. Ambassador to Iraq Ryan Crocker accurately described the implications for U.S. foreign policy:

> There is no political architecture that will convince any Sunni over the age of 3 that he or she has a future with the Iraqi state. The administration is trying to use a limited military weapon to defeat an adversary that only a political offensive can overcome, and we're not willing or able to make that effort.
> *(Arango, 2016)*

No serious observer of the region would likely disagree with Ambassador Crocker: unless the Iraqi government is effectively pressured to cross the liberal threshold toward becoming a secular state that respects religious and ethnic minorities, Sunni fear and anger will fuel the Islamic State. That makes the success of Iraqi democracy a core U.S. national security interest. Standing in the way of achieving that objective are the two principle sources of regional sectarianism: the Iranian theocracy and the Wahhabism-dependent House of Saud. For reasons that were well understood by American neoconservatives, the success of liberal democracy in Iraq would likely prove a direct threat to those illiberal regimes, and others throughout the region. In effect, Iran and Saudi Arabia oppose secular democracy in Iraq for the same reasons that its achievement is vital to the United States.

Breaking that logjam can only occur when the United States moves beyond the legacy of past approaches. That is a tall order, given the sheer inertia of policies long propelled by reliance on oil and hunger for recycled petrodollars; popular exhaustion with endless post-9/11 war; and the collapse of counter-terrorism policy into theoretical incoherence and partisan bickering. Equally daunting, no U.S. initiative, however innovative and bold, would likely inspire confidence among the region's terrified liberals, whose long memories include U.S. collaboration with the Shah of Iran, its sidelining of Palestinian rights, and the perversity, starting in 2003, of alternatively raising and dashing Iraqi hopes, from the promise of toppling Saddam Hussain to the chaos of occupation and the criminality of Abu Ghraib; from the promise of the "surge" and the associated "Sunni awakening," to the betrayal of leaving Iraq in the vengeful hands of Shia Islamists.

Nevertheless, it is to be hoped that some reminder of necessity, hopefully one far short of another 9/11-scale attack, will reawaken the courage of liberal convictions, in the West and in the region. Part of any viable liberal internationalist U.S. strategy for the Middle East will be pressure on its two major partners in the region, the Saudis and the UAE, to undertake reforms toward building liberal beachheads in the Middle East. In the Saudi case, the task goes to the heart of the current danger: the need to supplant violent Sunni extremism at its ideological source. In the case of the UAE, the challenge is less central but also less intractable, as the current government and society at least recognizes the need for a truly new vision for the region.

In the context of current U.S. debate, opinions about "boots on the ground" or more effective diplomacy ring hollow. Such tactical decisions will only become meaningful if they flow from a clear strategic purpose. So long as the prevailing narrative in the current Middle East is based on religious sectarianism, the threat to the West will grow; one can expect no effective "counter-narrative," in the era of mass politics in the Arab world, to flow from authoritarian monarchies or secular dictatorships. As in the case of interwar fascism and Cold War communism, liberal triumph over clerical fascism is not a "generational project"[21] to amble forward on its own, but a compelling, near-term strategic necessity requiring political leadership.

Notes

1 For depictions of those doubts, including quotations expressing the concerns of Arab Gulf state government officials, see Kahl *et al.* (2014). For concerns over the Iran deal in particular, see Solomon (2013), Boyes and Watson (2013), Sanger (2015), Lippman (2014), Spyer (January 2014), and Wehrey (2014).
2 For depictions of these suspicions see Friedman (2015), Daoud (2015), Kristof (2015), Goldberg (2015), and Rogin (2014).

3 For a notably dire, perhaps overstated forecast, by an academic expert on the Gulf, see Davidson (2012).
4 A glaring example was an outburst by Vice-President (VP) Joe Biden, accusing Turkey, Saudi Arabia, and the UAE of supporting extremist groups in their eagerness to remove the Assad regime in Syria. The VP later apologized to high-ranking officials in each country he mentioned. For an overview of his comments and subsequent "apology tour," see Holland et al. (2014) and "Biden's Apology Tour" in *The Wall Street Journal* (2014).
5 For an example of this, see Friedersdorf (2015).
6 Qatar is left unaddressed for two main reasons: first; its strong regional backing for Islamist parties (notably the Muslim Brotherhood) encountered bitter opposition from the Saudis and Emiratis (and arouses U.S. concern as well); second, because, in reaction to that opposition, Qatar has stepped from its assertive bid for regional leadership.
7 For an extended argument that U.S. foreign policy is best understood in terms of the expanding power of an increasingly global "capitalist security community," see Goldfischer (2005) "Prospects for a New World Order." For a combined biography of six men, whose careers straddled Wall Street and Washington, and who exemplified the "Establishment" that crafted U.S. security and economic policy in the early post-war years, see Isaacson and Thomas (1986).
8 The centrality of the Middle East, which animated every presidential "doctrine" from the Truman through the Carter Administrations, was well captured by Campbell (1958) cited by Hudson in Fawcett (2005: 292): "The entrenchment of Soviet power in that strategic region would bring a decisive shift in the world balance, outflanking NATO. Soviet control of Middle Eastern oil could disrupt the economy of the free world. And the triumph of communism in the heart of the Islamic world could be the prelude to its triumph through Asia, Africa, and Europe."
9 For insights into why an end to that conflict requires extending liberal human rights principles to both sides, see Ishay and Kretzmer (2016), forthcoming in Ehrenberg and Peled (2016).
10 The Saudi's even funded the Reagan Administration's 1981–8 war against the Soviet-backed Sandinista regime in Nicaragua. For an account of this, see Bronson (2006: 183–5).
11 Two excellent sources for that alternative history are Nasr (2006) and Bronson (2006).
12 For an account of this, see Lacey (2010: 228–30).
13 Many prominent realists made these points in a petition published on the op-ed page of *The New York Times*. See "War with Iraq is not in America's Best Interest," *The New York Times* (2002).
14 For a brilliant exposition of this "three-cornered" foreign policy debate in the context of its Cold War origins, see Krauthammer (1986).
15 In its post-Vietnam origins, neoconservatives had directed their anger at what they regarded as President Jimmy Carter's liberal *naiveté* in advancing human rights arguments that had weakened the Shah of Iran and other friendly dictators. Still fearing the Soviet Union, they regarded tactical support for dictators as vital. The first influential "neoconservative" contribution to the U.S. foreign policy debate was Jeane Kirkpatrick's forceful defense of the tactical need to support friendly dictators, given the near-certainty that whoever replaced them would prove more dangerous. She specifically attacked President Carter's willingness to tolerate the fall of the Shah of Iran and the Somoza dictatorship in Nicaragua. Brought to the attention of incoming President Ronald Reagan, her foreign policy views led to her selection as U.S. Ambassador to the United Nations. See Kirkpatrick (1979).
16 For a detailed depiction, see Ricks (2006).
17 The charge that liberal supporters of democracy and human rights worldwide lacked the will to defend their principles has a longer history, dating back to the post-First World War era, when Theodore Roosevelt, as cited by Kissinger (1994: 40), condemned the dangerous futility of Woodrow Wilson's "milk and water righteousness unbacked by force."

18 Defense Secretary Gates visited Manama on March 11, forcefully insisting that the rulers undertake democratic reforms. As he reflected on that encounter: "My visit had been intended as a show of support for the kingdom's royal family, but the message I delivered was hardly welcome. Separately, I told the crown prince and the king that as their strategic partner for more than sixty years, we were deeply concerned about Bahrain's political stability. I told them that they needed to take credible steps toward genuine political reform and to empower moderate voices for change . . . . The ineffectiveness of my diplomacy became apparent two days after I left Manama, when more than a thousand Saudi troops moved into Bahrain to ensure the royal family and the Sunnis remained in control" (2014: 516–17).
19 That change in outlook included the embrace of al-Sisi's rule over Egypt. As Obama put it during his remarks at West Point in May, 2014: "In countries like Egypt, we acknowledge that our relationship is anchored in security interests—from peace treaties with Israel, to shared efforts against violent extremism. So we have not cut off cooperation with the new government, but we can and will persistently press for reforms that the Egyptian people have demanded" (Obama, 2014a).
20 For more on this U.S./Gulf commitment, see Shanker (2012) and Shalal (2015).
21 Having affirmed the necessity for U.S., regional, and international security, and of a Middle East transition to democracy and universal human rights, President Obama has substituted that vague phrase in lieu of any policy for advancing those ends. See Obama's 2014 speech to the UN General Assembly (Obama, 2014b).

References

Ajami, F. (2014) *In this Arab time: the pursuit of deliverance*. Stanford, CA: Hoover Institution Press.

Arango, T. (2016) "Sunni resentment muddles prospect of reunifying Iraq after ISIS," *The New York Times*, February 13. Online. Available from: www.nytimes.com/2016/02/13/world/middleeast/sunni-resentment-muddles-prospect-ofreunifying-iraq-after-isis.html?_r=0 (accessed February 18, 2016).

Boyes, R. and Watson, R. (2013) "Saudi Arabia turns up the heat on the West over possible Iran nuclear deal," *The Times*, November 22. Online. Available from: www.thetimes.co.uk/tto/news/world/middleeast/article3929509.ece (accessed February 20, 2016).

Bronson, R. (2006) *Thicker than oil: America's uneasy partnership with Saudi Arabia*. Oxford: Oxford University Press.

Campbell, J.C. (1958) *Defense of the Middle East: Problems of American policy*, New York: Council on Foreign Relations. Cited by Hudson, M. (2005) "The United States in the Middle East," in Fawcett, L. (ed.), *International relations of the Middle East*, Oxford: Oxford University Press, pp. 285–306.

Cohen, R. (2016) "America's Syrian shame," *The New York Times*, February 8. Online. Available from: www.nytimes.com/2016/02/09/opinion/americas-syrian-shame.html (accessed February 22, 2016).

Daoud, K. (2015) "Saudi Arabia: an ISIS that has made it," *The New York Times*, November 21. Online. Available from: www.nytimes.com/2015/11/21/opinion/saudi-arabia-an-isis-that-has-made-it.html (accessed February 19, 2016).

Davidson, C. (2012) *After the Sheikhs: The coming collapse of the Gulf monarchies*. London: Hurst.

Friedersdorf, C. (2015) "How America's drone war in Yemen strengthens al-Qaeda," *The Atlantic*, September 28. Online. Available from: www.theatlantic.com/international/archive/2015/09/drone-war-yemen-al-qaeda/407599/ (accessed February 17, 2016).

Friedman, T. (2015) "Our radical Islamic BFF Saudi Arabia," *The New York Times*, September 2. Online. Available from: www.nytimes.com/2015/09/02/opinion/thomas-friedman-our-radical-islamic-bff-saudi-arabia.html (accessed February 21, 2016).

Gates, R.M. (2014) *Duty: memoirs of a Secretary at War*. London: W.H. Allen.

Gause, G. (2005) "The international politics of the Gulf," in Fawcett, L. (ed.), *International relations of the Middle East*, Oxford: Oxford University Press, pp. 278–9.

Gibbs, D.N. (2000) "Afghanistan: the Soviet invasion in retrospect," *International Politics*, 37(June): 233–46. Online. Available from: http://dgibbs.faculty.arizona.edu/sites/dgibbs.faculty.arizona.edu/files/afghan-ip.pdf (accessed January 10, 2016).

Goldberg, J. (2015) "Ashton Carter: Gulf Arabs need to get in the fight," *The Atlantic*, November 5. Online. Available from: www.theatlantic.com/international/archive/2015/11/ashton-carter-gulf-iran-isis/414591/Goldberg Nov 2015 (accessed February 21, 2016).

Goldfischer, D. (2005) "Prospects for a new world order," in Andali, E. and Rosenau, J. (eds.), *Globalization, security, and the nation-state: paradigms in transition*, Albany, NY: State University of New York Press, pp. 199–219.

Holland, S., Storey, D., and Grenon, A. (eds.) (2014) "Biden adds Saudi Arabia to his apology list over Islamic State," *Reuters*, October 7. Online. Available from: www.reuters.com/article/us-mideast-crisis-biden-idUSKCN0HW21M20141007 (accessed February 20, 2016).

Ignatius, D. (2016) "The costly blunders of Saudi Arabia's anxiety-ridden monarchy," *Washington Post*, January 5. Online. Available from: www.washingtonpost.com/opinions/the-glass-house-of-saud/2016/01/05/47583676-b3f0-11e5-9388-466021d971de_story.html (accessed February 16, 2016).

Isaacson, W. and Thomas, E. (1986) *The wise men: six friends and the world they made: Acheson, Bohlen, Harriman, Kennan, Lovett, McCloy*. London: Faber and Faber.

Ishay, M. and Kretzmer, D. (2016) "Reclaiming human rights: alternative paths for an Israeli/Palestinian peace," forthcoming in Ehrenberg, J. and Peled, Y. (eds.), *Israel and Palestine: alternative perspectives on statehood*, Lanham, MD: Rowman & Littlefield.

Kagan, R. (1998) "The benevolent empire," *Foreign Policy*, Summer. p. 28.

Kahl, C., Gfoeller, M., Katz, M., and Kimmitt, M. (2014) "U.S. Commitments to the Gulf Arab States: are they adequate?" *Middle East Policy*, 21: 2, pp. 1–33. Online. Available from: http://mepc.org/journal/middle-east-policy-archives/us-commitments-gulf-arab-states-are-they-adequate (accessed February 20, 2016).

Kirkpatrick, J. (1979) "Dictatorships and double standards" *Commentary*, November 1. Online. Available from: www.commentarymagazine.com/articles/dictatorships-double-standards/ (accessed February 21, 2016).

Kissinger, H. (1994) *Diplomacy*, New York: Simon & Schuster, p. 40.

Krauthammer, C. (1986) "In defense of interventionism," *The New Republic*, February 17, pp. 14–22.

Kristof, N. (2015) "Sentenced to be crucified," *The New York Times*, October 29. Online. Available from: www.nytimes.com/2015/10/29/opinion/sentenced-to-be-crucified.html (accessed February 20, 2016).

Lacey, R. (2010) *Inside the Kingdom: kings, clerics, modernists, terrorists, and the struggle for Saudi Arabia*. London: Arrow Books.

Lippman, T. (2014) "The U.S. and the Gulf: a failure to communicate," *LobeLog Foreign Policy* (blog), April 26. Online. Available from: www.lobelog.com/the-u-s-and-the-gulf-a-failure-to-communicate/ (accessed February 20, 2016).

Lipton, E., Williams, B., and Confessore, N. (2014) "Foreign powers buy influence at think tanks," *The New York Times*, September 6. Online. Available from: www.nytimes.com/2014/09/07/us/politics/foreign-powers-buy-influence-at-think-tanks.html (accessed February 20, 2016).

Nasr, V. (2006) *The Shia revival: how conflicts within Islam will shape the future*. New York: W.W. Norton.

Obama, B. (2014a, 28 May) Remarks by the President at the United States Military Academy Commencement Ceremony," The White House. Available from: www.whitehouse.gov/the-press-office/2014/05/28/remarks-president-united-states-military-academy-commencement-ceremony (accessed October 19, 2016).

Obama, B. (2014b, 24 September) "Remarks by President Obama in Address to the United Nations General Assembly," The White House. Available from: www.whitehouse.gov/the-press-office/2014/09/24/remarks-president-obama-address-united-nations-general-assembly (accessed October 19, 2016).

Otaiba, Y.A. (2015) "A vision for a moderate, modern Muslim world," *Foreign Policy*, December 2. Online. Available from: http://foreignpolicy.com/2015/12/02/a-vision-for-a-moderate-modern-muslim-world-uae-abu-dhabi-isis/ (accessed February 18, 2016).

Pollack, K. (2002) "Next stop Baghdad," *Foreign Affairs*, March 1. Online. Available from: www.foreignaffairs.com/articles/iraq/2002-03-01/next-stop-baghdad (accessed February 20, 2016).

Ricks, T.E. (2006) *Fiasco: the American military adventure in Iraq*. New York: Penguin Press.

Rogin, J. (2014) "America's allies are funding ISIS," *The Daily Beast*, June 14. Online. Available from: www.thedailybeast.com/articles/2014/06/14/america-s-allies-are-funding-isis.html (accessed February 18, 2016).

Roosevelt, F.D. (1941) "Four freedoms speech during Annual Message to Congress on the State of the Union," *Franklin D. Roosevelt Presidential Library and Museum*. Online. Available from: www.fdrlibrary.marist.edu/pdfs/fftext.pdf (accessed February 20, 2016).

Sanger, D. (2015) "Saudi Arabia promises to match Iran in nuclear capability," *The New York Times*, May 13. Online. Available from: www.nytimes.com/2015/05/14/world/middleeast/saudi-arabia-promises-to-match-iran-in-nuclear-capability.html?_r=0 (accessed February 20, 2016).

Shalal, A. (2015) "Missile shield for Gulf to take years, and heavy U.S. commitment," *Reuters*, May 15. Online. Available from: www.reuters.com/article/us-usa-gulf-missiledefenseidUSKBN0O00C720150515 (accessed February 21, 2016).

Shanker, T. (2012) "U.S. and Gulf allies pursue a missile shield against Iranian attack," *The New York Times*, August 8. Online. Available from: www.nytimes.com/2012/08/09/world/middleeast/us-and-gulf-allies-pursue-a-missile-shield-against-iranian-attack.html (accessed February 20, 2016).

Sluglett, P. (2005) "The Cold War in the Middle East," in Fawcett, L. (ed.), *International relations of the Middle East*, Oxford: Oxford University Press, pp. 55–6.

Solomon, J. (2013) "Iran nuclear deal raises fears of proliferation among Arab States," *The Wall Street Journal*, November 29. Online. Available from: www.wsj.com/articles/SB10001424052702303332904579228214211545256 (accessed February 20, 2016).

Spyer, J. (2014, 1 January) "Confidence game: Losing American support, the Gulf States scramble," *The Tower*. Online. Available from: www.thetower.org/article/confidence-game-losing-american-support-the-gulf-states-scramble/ (accessed February 20, 2016).

The New York Times (2002, September) "War with Iraq is not in America's best interest," Online. Available from: http://web.mit.edu/cis/pdf/TimesAd_01.pdf (accessed February 20, 2016).

The Wall Street Journal (2014) "Biden's Apology Tour," October 7. Online. Available from: www.wsj.com/articles/bidens-apology-tour-1412636332 (accessed February 20, 2016).

The White House, Office of the Press Secretary (2003) "President Bush discusses freedom in Iraq and Middle East," November 6. Online. Available from: http://georgewbushwhitehouse.archives.gov/news/releases/2003/11/20031106-2.html (accessed February 21, 2016).

The White House, Office of the Press Secretary (2009) "Remarks by the President at Cairo University," June 4. Online. Available from: www.whitehouse.gov/the-press-office/remarks-president-cairo-university-6-04-09 (accessed February 20, 2016).

The White House, Office of the Press Secretary (2014a) "Remarks by the President at the United States Military Academy Commencement Ceremony," May 28. Online. Available from: www.whitehouse.gov/the-press-office/2014/05/28/remarks-president-united-states-military-academy-commencement-ceremony (accessed February 15, 2016).

The White House, Office of the Press Secretary (2014b) "Remarks by President Obama in Address to the United Nations General Assembly," September 24. Online. Available from: www.whitehouse.gov/the-press-office/2014/09/24/remarks-president-obama-address-united-nations-general-assembly (accessed February 21, 2016).

Wehrey, F. (2014) "A new U.S. approach to Gulf security," *Carnegie Endowment for International Peace: Policy Outlook*. March 10. Online. Available from: http://carnegieendowment.org/2014/03/10/new-u.s.-approach-to-gulf-security/h30d (accessed February 18, 2016).

6

IRAN AND THE GULF COOPERATION COUNCIL SHEIKHDOMS[1]

Shahram Akbarzadeh

Introduction

Iran has long held volatile relations with members of the Gulf Cooperation Council (GCC), upon which Iran–Saudi rivalry has inevitably cast a long shadow. Saudi Arabia is the largest and most powerful member of the GCC, hosting its headquarters in Riyadh. The GCC was formed as an initiative of King Abdullah of Saudi Arabia in response to the perceived threat that revolutionary Iran posed to the region. The war between Iran and Iraq (1980–8), which broke out after Saddam Hussein attempted to claim Iranian territory, was watched with concern in Riyadh and other capitals in the region. Indeed, Iran's post-1979 revolutionary zeal and Ayatollah Khomeini's message of mass revolt against US-friendly regimes had changed regional dynamics radically. The rise of revolutionary Iran forced a recalibration of regional alliances and, despite the history of a difficult relationship between Iraq and Saudi Arabia, presented Baghdad as the most credible bulwark against the Iranian threat for Riyadh. The formation of the GCC was, therefore, part of a broader anti-Iran push.

The end of the Iran–Iraq war and Iran's turn to pragmatism under the presidency of Hashemi Rafsanjani and Mohammad Khatami helped reduce tensions. While Saudi Arabia and many in other GCC capitals remained sceptical of Iran's regional ambitions, the toning down of revolutionary rhetoric in Tehran and the focus on reconstructing Iran's battered economy facilitated the expansion of trade and diplomatic relations across the Persian Gulf. The Emirate of Dubai, state of Qatar and the Sultanate of Oman took advantage of the opportunities offered by the new Iranian leadership, and there were general signs that regional tension was de-escalating. But the emergence of the popular revolts across the region in 2011 quickly reversed the dynamic.

The so-called Arab Spring, which led to the fall of the ruling regimes in Tunisia and Egypt in 2011 and the subsequent wars in Libya and Syria, changed the Middle East political landscape and reset relations between Iran and the GCC. Not all of the Arab sheikhdoms experienced popular uprisings. Bahrain witnessed the most visible case of an attempt at a popular push for political openness, while reports of street protests in the Shia-populated parts of Saudi Arabia trickled to the media. A prominent feature of the social convulsions in the Gulf was the presence of the Shia. In states that have been uncomfortable with recognizing diversity and suspicious of their Shia population, this was taken very seriously. At the same time, Iran had experienced a policy reversal under President Mahmoud Ahmadinejad and reverted back to its revolutionary rhetoric. From Tehran's perspective, the Arab Spring was nothing more than an Islamic Awakening, a belated attempt at emulating the Islamic revolution of Iran. The deterioration of relations between key GCC member states and Iran in the wake of the Arab Spring was due to a security assessment of, first, the risks Iran posed to the longevity of the ruling regimes and, second, Iran's capacity to expand its regional influence and project power beyond its borders.

This chapter examines the above dynamics with special attention to the smaller member states of the GCC, noting that these states have not had a uniform experience with Iran. Following a survey of relations in the first decades of the Iranian revolutionary regime, the analysis looks at the post-Arab Spring period, exploring the impact that President Hassan Rouhani has had on bilateral and multilateral relations. The chapter concludes by analysing the implications of the historic 2015 nuclear deal.

A complex picture

The 1979 Iranian revolution set the tone of relations between Iran and its Arab neighbours. Ayatollah Khomeini, the leader of the Islamic revolution in Iran who became the Supreme Leader of the new regime, held the ruling regimes in Iran's neighbourhood with disdain. To Khomeini, the Muslim world was being subjugated by the United States through US-friendly regimes that were more concerned with their own power and survival than Islam and the interests of their Muslim populations. Khomeini initially focused his ideological proclamations on Iraq, where he had lived for most of his 14 years of exile, promising to free the Shia population from Saddam Hussein's yoke en route to liberating Jerusalem from Israeli occupation. But he reserved special venom for the al-Saud dynasty in Saudi Arabia, due to its role as the custodian of Islam's holy places: Mecca and Medina. Khomeini advocated open revolt against ruling regimes across the region, a call that is widely linked to unrest in the Shia-populated part of eastern Saudi Arabia in November 1979 (Wehrey, 2013). Saudi's rulers interpreted the seven-day uprising as proof of Iran's role as a force of instability and a threat to existing regimes. Iran's revolutionary leaders' repeated calls for other Muslims to follow the Saudi Shia's example hardened attitudes in the Saudi Kingdom and among its Arab sheikhdoms' allies. Iran's model of mixing Islam and democracy and advocacy of popular rule, however flawed, was perceived to threaten the ruling regimes that had built their power on a mix of patronage and religion. This sense of threat seemed to be amplified in states with a sizeable Shia population. Even though Iran did not make any direct references to the Shia population in the Gulf, the Shia were presumed to be the target audience for calls of rebellion. As will be explored further in the assessment of the post-Arab Spring experience, the Shia factor has continued to be a key consideration in relations between Iran and the GCC.

While many analysts and policymakers have observed that the GCC failed to generate a uniform position towards Iran, this was not from a lack of Saudi Arabian effort. As the most powerful member of the group, the Saudis engineered substantial financial support for Iraq (estimated to be as high as US $65 billion) to sustain its war efforts against Iran (Crist, 2009). The International Monetary Fund (IMF) estimated that the Gulf War cost Saudi Arabia US $55 billion alone (Freedman, 1998). Soon after its formation, the GCC established the 'Peninsula Shield Force' to counter regional security threats associated with the Iranian menace. Saudi Arabia played host to the 5,000 Shield troops, although the Force did not see much action until the Bahrain uprising of 2012 (Shaheen, 2011). The clear anti-Iran orientation of the GCC during the Iran–Iraq war proved costly for the region as Iran broadened the Tanker War to target Iraq's backers in the Persian Gulf, also threatening to block the strategically important Hormuz Straight (Cordesman and Wagner, 2003). It is estimated that Iran attacked 190 container ships flying the flags of 31 different countries in the eight-year war (Crist, 2009).

For Saudi Arabia and many other members of the GCC, the Iran threat also manifested domestically. Saudi Arabia, Bahrain, Kuwait and the United Arab Emirates (UAE) have difficult relationships with their Shia populations, and have at times of crisis questioned the loyalty of their Shia subjects. This securitization of sectarian relations in the wake of the 1979 Iranian revolution and Khomeini's calls for popular revolts in the region implied that local Shia populations were a potential Iranian fifth column. Bahrain and Kuwait have substantial Shia populations, estimated to be 60 per cent and 30 per cent respectively (Shanahan, 2008). The UAE by contrast has a smaller Shia population (15 per cent), which is well integrated economically, but has Persian origins and strong ties to Iran (Majidyar, 2013). According to one analyst:

> Kuwait became a battleground during the Iran–Iraq war. . . . bomb attacks, an airplane hijacking and even an assassination attempt on Prince Jabir were carried out by dissident Iraqi and Lebanese Shia to retaliate against Kuwait's support of Saddam Hussein.
>
> *(Al-Marashi, 2015)*

Following a series of bomb attacks in 1987, 12 Kuwaiti Shia were arrested, signalling a serious deterioration of domestic sectarian relations. A similar pattern was evident elsewhere. In 1981 the Iranian-backed Shia Islamic Front for the Liberation of Bahrain sought to overthrow the government (Mabon, 2012). Such incidents gave credence to accusations that Iran was a source of instability and justified Saudi policy on containing the Islamic Republic.

The policy of containment, however, was not applied uniformly by all GCC member states. Gerd Nonneman has noted that, even during the Iran–Iraq war, a number of the sheikhdoms retreated 'into actual or semi-neutrality' with the Islamic Republic (Nonneman, 2004, p. 168). This was confirmed years later by Abu Dhabi's Crown Prince Mohammed bin Zayed, who privately told US officials in 2009 that the GCC had failed to form and implement a coherent foreign policy, most poignantly in relation to Iran (WikiLeaks, 2009a). This assessment of failure over the life of the GCC led Crown Prince Zayed to question the future of the body. This is a significant shortcoming given that containing the threat posed by Iran was a key concern for the formation of the GCC; one that continues to impact the organization. As noted by Wagner and Cafiero (2015), and will be explored later in the context of the Arab Spring, 'the most significant current source of division among the GCC states relates to Iran's role in the Middle East's evolving geopolitical order'.

Obvious divergence from the Saudi position on Iran was evident in emerging trade and diplomatic relations between Iran and a number of small sheikhdoms in the GCC, Oman, Dubai and Qatar. Clearly, geography proved to be an important factor. The shared maritime boundaries have lubricated good relations, partly due to a risk assessment in the sheikhdoms. As noted bluntly by Sultan Qaboos of Oman, 'Iran is a big country with muscles and we must deal with it' (*The Guardian*, 2008). This pragmatic assessment has allowed Oman and Qatar – who both share important gas fields with Iran – to ride the waves of regional discord that have engulfed the region. Furthermore, these small sheikhdoms have not experienced major domestic unrest with their Shia populations, a significant factor that has adversely affected relations between Bahrain, Saudi Arabia and Iran.

Oman has shared responsibility over navigation through the strategically important Hormuz Straight with Iran. Twenty per cent of the world's petroleum is shipped through the 3.2-kilometre straight, winning it the nickname 'the choke point'. Relations between Iran and Oman remained cordial even at the height of the Iran–Iraq war, with Oman attempting to mediate an end to the war and negotiate the release of Iranian crewmen, who were detained by US Marines for laying mines in the Persian Gulf in 1987 (Ross, 1987). Oman's mediation averted a major international show-down at a very tense period. Oman also shares the Buka/Hengam gas field with Iran, providing important economic incentives for close bilateral relations. The two states have moved collaboratively to utilize their shared interests, including forming a 2008 agreement to develop Iran's Kish gas field (Reuters, 2008). Plans for Oman to purchase Iranian gas was initially tabled in 2007 and finally ratified in 2015 (Press TV, 2015).

Shared interests in natural resources have also played an important role in bilateral relations between Iran and Qatar. As early as 1992, Qatar negotiated with Iran to import fresh water. While this plan did not come into force due to a local Iranian protest centring on the environmental impact of the deal, relations between the two has remained business-like (Islamic Republic News Agency, 2015). The two states jointly operate the South Pars/North Dome gas field, claimed to be the largest gas field in the world. Maintaining a working relationship with Iran over shared resources has been a key concern for Qatar. According to a leaked US diplomatic cable, Qatar's close relationship with Iran:

> [s]hould also be seen as an expression of Qatar's strong desire for a stable strategic environment and for a working relationship with Iran that ensures Qatar's continued freedom to exploit the two countries' shared gas field, the largest non-associated gas field in the world.
>
> *(WikiLeaks, 2009b)*

All indications suggest that Iran shared the same concerns, despite its revolutionary gestures. Relations between Iran and Qatar remained cordial even after the sheikhdom became host to the US Central Command Forward Headquarters (2002) at the height of the war on terror, which saw the US substantially increase its military presence in the region and regularly imply the possibility for regime change in Iran. Both Qatar and Iran deliberately worked around these controversial issues to insulate their relationship. While sitting on the UN Security Council between 2006 and 2007, Qatar expressed dismay at US efforts to isolate Iran and invited President Mahmoud Ahmadinejad to the 2007 GCC Summit (Cooper and Momani, 2011). This was a controversial move that implied that Qatar was seeking to chart an independent policy from Saudi Arabia, but was warmly welcomed by Ahmadinejad as a 'new chapter' in relations between Iran and the GCC (Al-Jazeera, 2007b). As might be expected, not everyone shared this optimism. Yet, Qatar was one of the first countries to congratulate Ahmadinejad after his controversial electoral victory in 2009, while Oman's Sultan Qaboos travelled to Tehran to meet the re-elected President (Katzman, 2016). A leaked US cable suggests that, 'Qatar has been one of the most highly public supporters of President Ahmadinejad in the aftermath of the Iranian election' (WikiLeaks, 2009b). Soon after Ahmadinejad's re-election, Qatar signed a security pact with Iran in 2010 (Fars News Agency, 2014). In contrast to the tune of warm bilateral relations, however, some observers remained more cynical. The former US ambassador to Qatar, Patrick Theros, for example, questioned the rationale for such closeness: 'Qatar definitely practices the maxim of holding your friends close, and your enemies even closer' (Al-Jazeera, 2008). It is noteworthy that Iran has also signed a security pact with Oman. The Iran–Oman agreement was signed in August 2009, committing the two countries to holding joint military exercises (Katzman, 2016).

But Iran's relations with other GCC member states have been more constrained. Iran has been locked in a territorial dispute with the UAE over three islands in the Persian Gulf ever since Iran occupied them in 1971 following the British withdrawal, which also coincided with the formation of the UAE. The newly formed state has contested the Iranian claim on Abu Musa and the two Tunb islands in international forums, ensuring that it is raised at every opportunity. The UAE Foreign Minister Sheikh Abdullah bin Zayed al-Nahyan has protested the Iranian occupation at successive annual UN General Assembly sessions. In 2015, al-Nahyan expressed his displeasure by stressing 'that all actions and measures carried out by the Iranian authorities are contrary to international law and all norms and common values' (United States Institute of Peace, 2015). Yet, Iran's response to UAE protests has simply been dismissive. In 2012 President Ahmadinejad inflamed tensions by visiting the islands (Erdbrink, 2012). It was the first time that an Iranian president had set foot on this disputed soil and demonstrated that time had not softened Iran's position on the matter. This has remained the case even under the presidency of Hassan Rouhani, despite early hopes for a policy change. When the newly appointed Foreign Minister Javad Zarif expressed a willingness to 'talk to UAE to remove any misunderstanding about the Islands' in 2013 (Mehr News, 2013), he was quickly rebuffed by Major General Mohammad Jafari from the Islamic Revolutionary Guards Corps, who asserted that this was a matter of national security and not open for negotiation (Theodoulou, 2013).

Notwithstanding this territorial dispute, and the formal UAE unhappiness with Iran, Tehran has managed to build very close trade ties with the Emirate of Dubai, allowing it to mitigate the impact of a harsh international environment. Even during the Iran–Iraq war and in the following decade, trade between the two countries expanded unabated, making Iran integral to Dubai's economic success (Marschall, 2003). Trade ties developed exponentially in the 1990s, with Dubai importing US $107 million in goods from Iran within a year, and re-exporting US $188 million of Iranian produce to third countries. Within five years, exports doubled and re-exports tripled, making Iran the largest trade partner for Dubai in the 1990s (Gueraiche, 2016). The imposition of sanctions on Iran in 2006 threatened to curb the booming trade, raising concern in Dubai and Tehran. But many Dubai traders actively contravened the sanctions regime while the Dubai government looked the other way, offering an important economic buffer for Iran to militate the impact of international sanctions. This was an obvious divergence with the formal position of the government of UAE (based in Abu Dhabi) and its international obligations, and was eventually stopped. The removal of sanctions following the 2015 nuclear deal, however, is very likely to revive a booming trade. The IMF estimates the resumption of Dubai–Tehran trade to add US $13 billion to the UAE economy (Bouyamourn, 2015).

Developing economic and trade relations with Arab sheikhdoms served two important objectives for Iran. It allowed Iran to mitigate its international isolation as well as drive a wedge in the GCC, undermining Saudi efforts to use the organization as a coherent anti-Iran tool. But Iran faced obvious limitations, especially in regard to states that had uncomfortable relations with their own Shia population. Bahrain stood out in that regard. Repeated claims by mid-ranking Iranian officials, including members of the parliament, about Iranian sovereignty over Bahrain and a history of Shia agitation in Bahrain against the ruling al-Khalifa family had made the Bahraini government suspicious of Iranian meddling and the loyalty of its Shia subjects. Nonetheless Iran did try to advance economic relations, as it had done with other GCC states. In 2007 the two states signed a deal for Bahrain to import 28 million cubic metres of gas per day from Iran (Al-Jazeera, 2007a). But the deal was soon derailed (2009) after the conservative daily *Kayhan,* with close ties to the Iranian Supreme Leader Khamenei, suggested that 'Bahrain was a part of Iran's territory until 46 years ago' (Mabon, 2012). The deal was formally annulled at the height of bilateral tensions during the Arab Spring.

Iran's relations with Kuwait have also remained tentative, generally due to Kuwait's suspicion of Iranian interference. As with other Gulf States, Iran shares a gas field with Kuwait (Dorra/Arash), but the field remains unexploited due to disagreements over extracting rights. As recently as August 2015, Kuwait summoned Tehran's Envoy to object to Iran's decision to circulate a brochure outlining investment opportunities in the Iran-controlled Arash side of the field (Reuters, 2015b). President Ahmadinejad visited Kuwait twice during his term in office, becoming the first Iranian president to visit Kuwait. However, his attempts at improving relations proved unsuccessful, with Kuwait's Emir refusing to travel to Tehran even in the context of the Non-Aligned Movement Summit in Tehran in 2012 (BBC Persian, 2012).

Iran's difficulty in stealing Bahrain, Kuwait and the UAE from the Saudi orbit, at least in economic terms, had as much to do with the political orientation of the ruling families, who found the revolutionary convulsion of Iran threatening, as their suspicion of their own Shia population. The fear that Iran would use the cover of economic ties and trade to entice local Shia populations to its revolutionary ideology and plot revolts or acts of terror against the ruling families was a significant barrier to close relations. As a result, it appeared that the Saudi line had sway over a number, but not all, of the GCC member states. In that regard, Riyadh was a beneficiary of pronounced sectarian suspicions in Bahrain, Kuwait and the UAE, a feature that it shared and promoted both in Saudi Arabia and the region.

Concern with Iran's sectarian agenda was heightened following the removal of Saddam Hussein from power in Iraq. The 2003 US invasion of Iraq removed the most ardent counterweight to Iran in the region and led to the ascendancy of Iran-friendly Shia political players in Iraq. Although this was of course not the expected outcome for the United States and its Arab allies, the unintended consequence of the war in Iraq was to open it to Iranian influence and its subsequent descent into sectarian strife. Iranian authorities took heart from the new opportunities in the first decade of the 21st century and grew more assertive in the Levant. The consolidation of ties with the Assad regime in Syria, and Hezbollah in Lebanon, on the back of a rising Shia power in Iraq offered Iran a land connection to the Levant, leading King Abdullah of Jordan to warn of an emerging Shia Crescent. For the Iranian leadership, this was an affirmation of Iran's revolutionary ideology, and President Ahmadinejad was only too eager to claim credit for building an 'axis of resistance' against Israel. The 2006 Israeli attack on Hezbollah failed to destroy this paramilitary organization, and was therefore hailed in Iran as a victory and testimony to Iran's role in propping up Hezbollah. Iran's growing regional assertiveness, simmering sectarian tensions and the mounting unease in Saudi Arabia and many other Arab sheikhdoms about Iran's reach into their territories provided the backdrop to subsequent deterioration of relations in the wake of the Arab Spring.

Arab Spring

The wave of popular protest that swept across the Arab world reached the Arab sheikhdoms in 2011, many of which were already grappling with a pronounced fear of Shia dissent. The fall of President Hosni Mubarak in Egypt, a close ally of Saudi Arabia, was a shock to many observers in the Gulf. Yet Iran welcomed the popular revolt as an 'Islamic Awakening', openly suggesting that the Arab masses were following the example of the Islamic revolution in Iran (Lutz, 2011). The Iranian Supreme Leader left no doubt that he expected the so-called Islamic Awakening to spread across the Arab world. This message was reinforced by President Ahmadinejad, who claimed that Iran was the role model for the Arab world. 'Egyptian and Tunisian uprisings', he claimed, 'were inspired by Iran's defiance against western powers' (Molavi, 2011). Seeking to assert a position of leadership over the fast-paced events, Iran convened an international conference under the rubric of 'Islamic Awakening' in September 2011 (The World Forum for Proximity of Islamic Schools of Thought, 2011). The following year, Iran hosted the newly elected President of Egypt and leader of the Muslim Brotherhood Mohammad Morsi to push the same message. However, by this time, the popular revolution had reached Syria and Bahrain, giving the crisis a decidedly sectarian flavour, which fundamentally changed regional dynamics.

Tension between Iran and Saudi Arabia, Bahrain and, by extension, the GCC escalated significantly in the wake of the Saudi decision to utilize the Peninsula Shield Force to put down the Bahraini uprising in March 2011. Iran was accused of masterminding the uprising and plotting to topple the rule of the al-Khalifa family. Iran responded no less aggressively by accusing the ruling family of shedding the blood of innocent people. President Ahmadinejad condemned the security crackdown as unjustified and a violation of people's rights: 'What has happened is bad, unjustifiable and irreparable' (Chulov, 2011). Iran was openly hostile to the Saudi intervention, labelling it an 'invasion' and 'occupation' of Bahrain (Bronner and Slackman, 2011). This free fall in relations was to be expected. Bahrain's Foreign Minister, Sheikh Khalid bin Ahmed bin Mohammed al-Khalifa, announced that the long-awaited plan 'to import Iranian gas is currently halted because of the blatant Iranian interference', adding that, 'the repeated provocative statements from Tehran would no doubt be an obstacle to any agreement between the two parties' (Carlisle, 2011). The GCC formally endorsed the Bahraini position and condemned Iran's meddling in the internal affairs of Bahrain. In April 2011, the GCC Secretary General slammed Iran's behaviour and accused it of threatening the 'security and stability in the region' (Al-Arabiya, 2011). The UAE Foreign Minister

Sheikh Abdullah bin Zayed al-Nahyan added his voice to the anti-Iran chorus and warned of collective action against Iran, to ensure 'the security and stability of the GCC' (Al-Arabiya, 2011). That same month, Kuwait announced that it had uncovered a decade-old spy ring linked to Tehran, prompting it to expel Iranian diplomats, recall the Kuwaiti Ambassador to Iran and sentence a number of Kuwaiti citizens to death. The Kuwaiti Foreign Minister Mohammed al-Sabah announced that 'there is a conspiracy network linked to official sides in the Islamic republic . . . . As a result we have set up a foreign ministry crisis cell and recalled our ambassador' (Al-Jazeera, 2011).

The spread of the Arab Spring to Bahrain amplified festering sectarian tensions and distrust of Iranian intensions in the region. According to a Chatham House study, the Bahrain conflict inflamed domestic sectarian tensions across the GCC (Chatham House, 2012). The years following the Bahrain uprising were therefore characterized by countless sheikhdom claims of Iranian conspiracies within their borders, leading to the revival of the image of Iran as a regional spoiler and source of instability. While Iran denied this charge and sought to shift the blame to the United States, Israel and US-friendly monarchies in the region for sowing the seeds of discord among Muslims, its image as regional troublemaker grew larger as the Arab Spring morphed into open sectarian warfare (Al-Jazeera, 2011).

Ironically, Iran used the same charge of external interference in describing anti-Assad protests in Syria. Protestors were labelled as terrorists in the pay of foreign powers. Popular protest against the Assad regime, whose anti-Israel credentials were immaculate, was unthinkable for the Iranian leadership. The close alliance between Iran and Syria went back to the 1980s, when Syria was the only Arab state to actively support Iran's efforts against Iraq during the eight-year war. It also facilitated Iran's expansion into Lebanon, which helped with the emergence of Hezbollah and its consolidation as a formidable paramilitary force. Iran could not afford to see Bashar al-Assad share the fate of Hosni Mubarak, which would put Iran at loggerheads with Saudi Arabia, Turkey and Qatar, all of which had heavily invested in Assad's removal from power. By 2013, Qatar was estimated to have spent US $3 billion in support of anti-Assad rebel groups (Khalaf and Smith, 2013). This was consistent with Qatar's growing assertiveness in the region and charting a foreign policy that was distinct from that of Saudi Arabia. Doha's support for the Muslim Brotherhood in Egypt, for example, caused a rift with Riyadh, and later Abu Dhabi, who both endorsed the military coup by General Abdel Fattah al-Sisi in 2013 which overthrew the Brotherhood. Tension between Qatar and the trio of Saudi Arabia, Bahrain and the UAE escalated further in March 2014 when the latter withdrew their ambassadors from Qatar in protest to Doha's proactive policies (BBC News, 2014). This was a rare case of serious discord in the GCC, one that Iran has been keen to exploit. While Qatar and Iran support opposing players in Syria, relations have not suffered as many observers expected. Both Qatar and Iran see value in not allowing their differences to adversely affect their bilateral relations. According to the Qatari Foreign Minister Khalid al-Attiyah, 'we do differ strongly from Iran over Syria . . . [but] Qatar does not consider Iran as an enemy' (Black,

2013). Putting the Syria issue aside, the Iranians see close ties with Qatar to be an important asset in undermining the Saudi hegemony over the GCC. Reflecting the same theme, Hassan Hani Zadeh has argued that Saudi hostility to Qatar's foreign policy activism could in fact push Qatar even closer to Iran (Hanizadeh, 2014).

Rouhani era

When Hassan Rouhani came to office (July 2013), Iran's reputation among many of its Arab neighbours was very poor. The Rouhani government was aware of the trust deficit and was keen to address that as part of the broader agenda to bring Iran out of isolation. President Rouhani sought to correct Iran's confrontational relationship with its neighbours, and Foreign Minister Zarif toured the Gulf States to personally deliver the message (Erdbrink, 2013). Earlier Zarif (2013) had penned an opinion piece for *Asharq al-Awsat* to assure Iran's neighbours about the policy change. Titled appropriately as 'our neighbours are our priority', he argued that Iran:

> [r]ecognize[s] that we cannot promote our interests at the expense of others. This is particularly the case in relation to counterparts so close to us that their security and stability are intertwined with ours .... We extend our hand in friendship and Islamic solidarity to our neighbors, assuring them that they can count on us as a reliable partner.

Rouhani's inauguration was warmly welcomed by Qatar and Oman, and generated a buzz in other capital cities. The Qatari Emir Sheikh Tamim bin Hamad bin Khalifa al-Thani attended Rouhani's swearing-in ceremony, and extended an invitation to Rouhani to visit Qatar in the same year (Rouhani, 2013). Qatar signed a security agreement with Iran in October 2015 to fight crime in their shared waters (Mamouri, 2015). A month after Rouhani's inauguration, Sultan Qaboos of Oman visited Iran to sign a US $60 billion gas deal (*The Guardian*, 2013). Shortly after, Oman and Iran were engaged in negotiation with India over an undersea gas pipeline project (Jacob, 2014).

The GCC response was also cautiously optimistic, with the members at a summit welcoming 'the new orientation by the Iranian leadership towards the Gulf Cooperation Council and hope it will be followed by concrete measures that would positively impact regional peace' (Gulf News, 2013). Subsequently the Kuwaiti Emir Sabah Al-Ahmad Al-Jaber Al-Sabah made his first visit to Iran, signing a number of cooperation agreements during his visit. But such gestures of good will were short lived (Al-Arabiya, 2014). The raging civil war in Syria and Iran's uncompromising position in relation to Assad, the rise of the Islamic State of Iraq and Syria (known by its Arabic acronym as Daesh), which many in Iran linked to the Wahhabi foundations of Saudi Arabia, and the escalation of political violence in Yemen forced a difficult agenda on Iran–GCC relations and effectively cut short the Rouhani–Zarif charm offensive.

In September 2014 the Houthi militia staged a coup in Yemen and deposed President Abd Rabbuh Mansur Hadi. Saudi Arabia and many other GCC states accused Iran of orchestrating the coup and soon committed themselves to reinstating Hadi. This eventually saw Saudi Arabia engage in an expansive military operation. What followed was a rapid deterioration of relations between Iran and the GCC, with many GCC statesmen reminding the world that Iran, even under the presidency of Rouhani, has not given up its regional ambitions. A piece in the *Al-Arabiya*, penned by a prominent UAE businessman, argued that 'most of this region's troubles are rooted in Iran's thirst for hegemony' (Al-Habtoor, 2015). This captured the mood in most GCC states, who saw the escalation of regional conflicts and sectarian disputes as evidence of Iranian meddling. The UAE Foreign Minister al-Nahyan was blunt in his appraisal of Iran:

> Iran is not carrying out this activity only in Yemen, it is conducting the same activity in Lebanon, in Syria, Iraq, Afghanistan and in Pakistan .... Someone might say that the information provided by Yemen is not accurate, but there is systematic action that has been going for years on the idea of exporting the (Iranian) revolution.
>
> *(Aboudi, 2015)*

He further added that 'Iran is not giving its partners in the region this hope (for a normalization of relations) .... Each time we try to come close to Iran it starts spoiling the region, making (matters) difficult for our countries' (Aboudi, 2015). The same sentiment was expressed by the Bahraini Foreign Minister al-Khalifa, who tweeted at the Iranian Foreign Minister: 'My brother Javad Zarif, stop exporting the weapons that have caused wars and sedition, and do not use the Daesh argument. We are capable of defeating them' (Toumi, 2015).

Iran's nuclear deal with the five permanent members of the UN Security Council and Germany (dubbed the P5+1) was signed against this backdrop of mistrust and acrimony. It must be noted that Oman and Qatar sounded a different chord from the rest of the GCC, applauding the deal (Alaan TV, 2015). Qatar's Emir was generous in his appraisal, looking 'forward with hope that this nuclear deal contributes to maintaining security and stability in our region' (United States Institute of Peace, 2015). Rouhani reciprocated, declaring that 'after this agreement, developing relations with our neighbours like Qatar as our brother and friend is our top priority' (The Official Site of the President of The Islamic Republic of Iran, 2015). It also emerged that Oman had played a key role in negotiations, holding secret talks with the United States and Iran in 2012, as a precursor to formal multilateral talks (Lakshmanan, 2015).

But Saudi Arabia and the other Arab sheikhdoms were much more sceptical. Indeed they worried that the removal of international sanctions would provide Iran with a *carte blanche* to pursue its regional ambitions unhindered. The Saudi position, subscribed by its regional allies, was that the removal of sanctions would offer Iran significant economic and financial resources to pursue its disruptive regional policies. There was nothing in Iranian statements to suggest otherwise, as Iran continued to become increasingly involved in the Syrian war and reconfirmed its commitment to Hezbollah. In the months that followed the deal, the UAE became a vocal opponent, articulating widespread concern in the GCC. The UAE dismissed suggestions that regional harmony would be a proposed consequence of the nuclear deal, by stating that the EU foreign policy chief, Federica Mogherini lacked the 'context and understanding of Iran's regional and aggressive policy and sectarian overtones that have polarized the Middle East' (Wagner and Cafiero, 2015). Subsequently, the UAE Foreign Minister al-Nahyan presented his formal rebuttal of Iran's role in the region at the UN General Assembly, concluding that 'the UAE stands firm with the Kingdom of Saudi Arabia against any Iranian attempts to interfere in the internal affairs of the Arab States' (United States Institute of Peace, 2015).

This sentiment was echoed by the Bahraini Foreign Minister al-Khalifa, who asserted that the nuclear deal 'does not address all sources of tension [between Tehran and the GCC states] . . . . In fact, the deal will lift sanctions on certain Iranian companies and figures who are linked to terrorism' (Abu Najm, 2015). Shortly after (October 2015), Bahrain recalled its ambassador from Iran and expelled the Iranian ambassador for 'continuing interference by Iran in the affairs of the kingdom . . . [and for fomenting] confessional sedition' (Al-Jazeera, 2015). The Bahraini Ministry of Foreign Affairs accused Iran of supporting domestic 'sabotage and terrorism' and for creating and arming terrorist groups on Bahraini soil after discovering 1.5 tonnes of C4 explosives as well as weapons in a house in a Shia town, with the perpetrators allegedly linked to Iran (Al-Jazeera, 2015). Bahraini Foreign Minister al-Khalifa later asked, 'Do you know the amount of explosive material smuggled into Bahrain? It was sufficient to obliterate Manama from existence' (Abu Najm, 2015). A similar scenario was played out in Kuwait. The discovery of a large cache of heavy weapons buried under houses near the Iraqi border led to accusations of an Iranian plot. According to government sources 'the suspects have disclosed that there is a direct Iranian line in supplying weapons to Kuwait by sea' (Reuters, 2015a).

President Rouhani may have hoped that his charm offensive and securing a nuclear deal with world powers would help advance his agenda of bringing Iran out of the cold and mending fences with its Arab neighbours. Instead, Iran's strategic commitment to Syria and Hezbollah, as well as the sporadic pronunciation of Shia opposition to the Saud monarchy by some Iranian members of parliament and the hard-line press affiliated with the Islamic Revolutionary Guard Corps (IRGC), ensured that GCC concerns with Iran's intensions remained unchecked. The nuclear deal, rather than offering hope, was seen by Saudi Arabia and its allies as offering Iran unprecedented resources to advance its hegemonic drive, effectively with no US objection. Indeed, the deal is generally seen as a precursor to the US disengagement from the region (Kinninmont, 2015). As a consequence, Saudi Arabia sees itself as the only state willing to counter Iranian influence, which explains the decision to increase its defence spending by 27 per cent by 2020 (Kerr, 2015).

Conclusion

Iran has had a very poor image among the GCC states. For the most part, Iran has provided fodder to regional sceptics by advocating revolt against ruling families in its early days, a message that grew more audible once again under the presidency of the firebrand President Ahmadinejad. The Iranian assessment of the Arab Spring as an Islamic Awakening and a move by Arab masses to follow the Iranian model was delusional and badly missed the mark. It reinforced the image of Iran as a pariah state bent on sowing discord and instability. Furthermore, the rapid descent of Syria into a sectarian war, the suppression of the popular revolt in Bahrain and the Houthi attempt at a political takeover of Yemen, put Iran and Saudi Arabia on a serious collision course, often called a proxy war by observers. But this is not simply a matter of inter-state rivalry. Given that each represent a very different version of Islam and both claim to be the guardian of all Muslims, the Saudi–Iran rivalry has taken on very pronounced sectarian characteristics which are transferable to many other GCC states. The recent break-down in diplomatic relations (January 2016) between the two, as well as the decision by Bahrain and Kuwait to recall their diplomats from Tehran in the wake of the mob attacks on the Saudi Embassy in Tehran and the Consulate in Mashhad, demonstrated the depth of distrust.

Iran's relationship with the small member states of the GCC takes place under the shadow of Saudi Arabia. Yet, Iran is aware of the importance of economic factors for all concerned and has pursued trade and economic ties with small sheikhdoms, a strategy that has proven successful in relation to Qatar, Oman and Dubai. It may be simplistic to argue that such economic interests have pulled these sheikhdoms away from the Saudi line, but it is clear that states with the greatest level of trade and engagement with Iran have proven most resilient to the Saudi's antagonistic line on Iran. Qatar is a special case in this regard as it has managed to maintain its close relations with Iran, even though it is actively engaged in efforts to topple Iran's ally in Syria.

Iran's obvious limitation in its relationship with the GCC is its Shia religion. Riyadh has accused Iran of seeking to use its Shia identity to subvert the Shia population in Saudi Arabia and has cracked down on Shia activists domestically. The same applies to Bahrain and Kuwait, which remain watchful of their own Shia population. The 2011 popular revolt in Bahrain, which was put down by Saudi forces, continues to serve as evidence of Iranian meddling and interference through the local Shia population. The state's fear of its own Shia population, therefore, extends onto external relations and affects attitudes towards Iran. Given this backdrop, it is not surprising that powerful players in the GCC have reacted so negatively towards Iran's nuclear deal with P5+1 and the prospects of sanctions removal. The fear that Iran seeks to exert hegemony over the region has been amplified by the prospect of significant resources at Tehran's disposal, making it even more assertive.

Note

1 The author wishes to thank Dara Conduit for her resourcefulness and diligence in researching this topic.

References

Aboudi, S. (2015, April 8). UAE says sees systematic Iranian meddling in Yemen, region. Reuters. Retrieved from www.reuters.com/article/2015/04/08/us-yemen-crisis-uae-iran-idUSKBN0MZ1P520150408#52rbqp7ByCAt6I83.97 (accessed 24 August 2016).

Abu Najm, M. (2015, September 10). Bahrain FM: Iran nuclear deal "does not address" all sources of tension with Tehran. Asharq al-Awsat. Retrieved from http://english.aawsat.com/2015/09/article55345077/bahrain-fm-iran-nuclear-deal-does-not-address-all-sources-of-tension-with-tehran (accessed 24 August 2016).

Alaan TV (2015, August 4). Qatar: Iran nuclear deal makes the region more secure. Retrieved from www.alaan.tv/news/world-news/135784/qatar-iran-nuclear-deal-makes-region-more-secure-safe (accessed 24 August 2016).

Al-Arabiya (2011, April 3). Gulf Arab states reject Iran "interference". Retrieved from www.alarabiya.net/articles/2011/04/03/144037.html (accessed 24 August 2016).

Al-Arabiya (2014, June 1). Kuwait's emir makes landmark visit to Iran. Retrieved from http://english.alarabiya.net/en/News/2014/06/01/Kuwait-s-emir-makes-landmark-visit-to-Iran.html (accessed 24 August 2016).

Al-Habtoor, K.A. (2015, August 19). Hezbollah sleeping cells in Kuwait are a wake-up call. Al-Arabiya. Retrieved from http://english.alarabiya.net/en/views/news/middle-east/2015/08/19/Hezbollah-sleeping-cells-in-Kuwait-are-a-wake-up-call.html (accessed 24 August 2016).

Al-Jazeera (2007a, November 18). Ahmadinejad boosts Bahrain ties. Retrieved from www.aljazeera.com/news/middleeast/2007/11/200852512238205149.html (accessed 24 August 2016).

Al-Jazeera (2007b, December 3). Ahmadinejad arrives for Gulf summit. Retrieved from www.aljazeera.com/news/middleeast/2007/12/200852514309702795.html (accessed 24 August 2016).

Al-Jazeera (2008, July 21). Qatar is a diplomatic heavy hitter. Retrieved from www.aljazeera.com/focus/2008/07/200872164735567644.html (accessed 24 August 2016).

Al-Jazeera (2011, April 1). Iran rejects Kuwait spy allegation. Retrieved from www.aljazeera.com/news/middleeast/2011/03/201133123525225240.html (accessed 24 August 2016).

Al-Jazeera (2015, October 2). Bahrain recalls ambassador from Iran over 'meddling'. Retrieved from www.aljazeera.com/news/2015/10/bahrain-recalls-ambassador-iran-meddling-151002032510372.html (accessed 24 August 2016).

Al-Marashi, I. (2015, June 30). Shattering the myths about Kuwaiti Shia. Al-Jazeera. Retrieved from www.aljazeera.com/indepth/opinion/2015/06/shattering-myths-kuwaiti-shia-150629081723864.html (accessed 24 August 2016).

BBC News (2014, March 5). Gulf ambassadors pulled from Qatar over 'interference'. Retrieved from www.bbc.com/news/world-middle-east-26447914 (accessed 24 August 2016).

BBC Persian (2012, October 16). Retrieved from www.bbc.com/persian/iran/2012/10/121016_l23_iran_kuwait_island_persian_gulf_ahmadinejad_visit.shtml (accessed 24 August 2016).
Black, I. (2013, December 4). Political solution to Syrian war does not interest Assad, says Qatari minister. *The Guardian*. Retrieved from www.theguardian.com/world/2013/dec/04/political-solution-syrian-war-assad-qatari-minister (accessed 24 August 2016).
Bouyamourn, A. (2015, August 6). UAE economy to gain $13bn from lifting of Iran sanctions, IMF predicts. *The National*. Retrieved from www.thenational.ae/business/economy/uae-economy-to-gain-13bn-from-lifting-of-iran-sanctions-imf-predicts (accessed 24 August 2016).
Bronner, E. and Slackman, M. (2011, March 15). Saudi troops enter Bahrain to help put down unrest. *The New York Times*. Retrieved from www.nytimes.com/2011/03/15/world/middleeast/15bahrain.html?pagewanted=all&_r=0 (accessed 24 August 2016).
Carlisle, T. (2011, May 23). Iran-Bahrain gas project off again. *The National*. Retrieved from www.thenational.ae/business/energy/iran-bahrain-gas-project-off-again (accessed 24 August 2016).
Chatham House (2012). Kuwait Study Group: Identity, citizenship and sectarianism in the GCC. *Workshop Summary*. Retrieved from www.chathamhouse.org/sites/files/chathamhouse/public/Research/Middle%20East/0212kuwaitsummary_identity.pdf (accessed 24 August 2016).
Chulov, M. (2011, March 16). Bahrain unleashes force on protesters' camp. *The Guardian*. Retrieved from www.theguardian.com/world/2011/mar/16/bahrain-protesters-military-operation-manama (accessed 24 August 2016).
Cooper, A.F. and Momani, B. (2011). Qatar and expanded contours of small state diplomacy. *International Spectator: Italian Journal of International Affairs*, Vol 46. Retrieved from www.arts.uwaterloo.ca/~bmomani/Documents/IS-%20qatar.pdf (accessed 24 August 2016).
Cordesman, A.H. and Wagner A. (2003). *The lessons of modern war: The Iran–Iraq War*. Vol. 2. New York: Westview Press.
Crist, D.B. (2009). Gulf of conflict: A history of U.S.–Iranian confrontation at sea. Policy Focus No. 95, Washington Institute. Retrieved from www.washingtoninstitute.org/uploads/Documents/pubs/PolicyFocus95.pdf (accessed 24 August 2016).
Erdbrink, T. (2012, April 30). A tiny island is where Iran makes a stand. *The New York Times*. Retrieved from www.nytimes.com/2012/05/01/world/middleeast/dispute-over-island-of-abu-musa-unites-iran.html?_r=0 (accessed 24 August 2016).
Erdbrink, T. (2013, December 4). Iran takes charm offensive to the Persian Gulf. *The New York Times*. Retrieved from www.nytimes.com/2013/12/05/world/middleeast/iran-takes-charm-offensive-to-the-persian-gulf.html?_r=0 (accessed 24 August 2016).
Fars News Agency (2014, April 15). Iran, Qatar discuss implementation of security pact. Retrieved from http://en.farsnews.com/newstext.aspx?nn=13930126000748 (accessed 24 August 2016).
Freedman, R.O. (1998). *The Middle East and the peace process: The impact of the Oslo accords*. Gainesville, FL: University Press of Florida.
Gueraiche, W. (2016). The UAE and Iran: the different layers of a complex security issue. In Shahram Akbarzadeh and Dara Conduit (eds.), *Iran in the world: President Rouhani's foreign policy*, New York: Palgrave Macmillan, pp. 75–92.
Gulf News (AFP). (2013, December 11). GCC Summit: Gulf states hail Iran's 'new orientation'. Retrieved from http://m.gulfnews.com/news/gulf/kuwait/gcc-summit-gulf-states-hail-iran-s-new-orientation-1.1265862 (accessed 24 August 2016).

Hanizadeh, H. (2014). The new foreign policy of Qatar in the Middle East. International Peace Studies Centre. Retrieved from http://peace-ipsc.org/fa/ (accessed 24 August 2016).

Islamic Republic News Agency (2015, April 15). Official: Iran pursues expansion of ties with Persian Arab neighbours. Retrieved from www.irna.ir/en/News/81124301/Politic/Official__Iran_pursues_expansion_of_ties_with_Persian_Gulf_Arab_neighbors (accessed 24 August 2016).

Jacob, J. (2014, February 28). India, Iran, Oman to start discussing gas pipeline. *Hindustan Times*. Retrieved from www.hindustantimes.com/business/india-iran-oman-to-start-discussing-gas-pipeline/story-6KS1sO1pR4TrQt3RiFfMSI.html (accessed 24 August 2016).

Katzman, K. (2016, April 26). Oman: Reform, security, and U.S. policy. Congressional Research Service. Retrieved from http://fas.org/sgp/crs/mideast/RS21534.pdf (accessed 24 August 2016).

Kerr, S. (2015, June 2). Saudi Arabia to boost defence spending by 27% over five years. *Financial Times*. Retrieved from www.ft.com/cms/s/0/4f3b5708-0903-11e5-b643-00144feabdc0.html#axzz3cRvGATqV (accessed 24 August 2016).

Khalaf, R. and Smith, A.F. (2013, May 16). Qatar bankrolls Syrian revolt with cash and arms. *Financial Times*. Retrieved from www.ft.com/intl/cms/s/0/86e3f28e-be3a-11e2-bb35-00144feab7de.html (accessed 24 August 2016).

Kinninmont, J. (2015). Iran and the GCC: Unnecessary insecurity. Chatham House. Retrieved from www.chathamhouse.org/sites/files/chathamhouse/field/field_document/20150703IranGCCKinninmont.pdf (accessed 24 August 2016).

Lakshmanan, I.A.R. (2015, September 25). If you can't do the deal . . . . Go back to Tehran. *Politico*. Retrieved from www.politico.com/magazine/story/2015/09/iran-deal-inside-story-213187 (accessed 24 August 2016).

Lutz, M. (2011, February 4). Iran's supreme leader calls uprisings an 'Islamic awakening'. *Los Angeles Times*. Retrieved from http://articles.latimes.com/2011/feb/04/world/la-fg-khamenei-iran-egypt-20110205 (accessed 24 August 2016).

Mabon, S. (2012). The battle for Bahrain: Iranian-Saudi rivalry. *Middle East Policy*, Vol. 19, No. 2, pp. 84–97.

Majidyar, A.K. (2013). Is sectarian balance in the United Arab Emirates, Oman, and Qatar at risk? American Enterprise Institute. Retrieved from www.aei.org/publication/is-sectarian-balance-in-the-united-arab-emirates-oman-and-qatar-at-risk/ (accessed 24 August 2016).

Mamouri, A. (2015, November 4). Is Qatar Iran's door to the Gulf? Al-Monitor. Retrieved from www.al-monitor.com/pulse/originals/2015/11/iran-qatar-rapprochement-middle-east.html#ixzz3sMQuySFD (accessed 24 August 2016).

Marschall, C. (2003). *Iran's Persian Gulf policy: From Khomeini to Khatami*. Routledge Carzon: London.

Mehr News (2013, September 2). Dialogue on Abu Musa; country's 'normal position,' Zarif says. Retrieved from http://en.mehrnews.com/news/100921/Dialogue-on-Abu-Musa-country-s-normal-position-Zarif-says (accessed 24 August 2016).

Molavi, A. (2011, April 6). Invoking the Arab Spring, Iran rewrites its own history. *The National*. Retrieved from www.thenational.ae/thenationalconversation/comment/invoking-the-arab-spring-iran-rewrites-its-own-history (accessed 24 August 2016).

Nonneman, G. (2004). The Gulf States and the Iran–Iraq War: Pattern shifts and continuities. In Lawrence G. Potter and Gary G. Sick (eds), *Iran, Iraq and the legacies of war*, New York: Palgrave Macmillan, pp. 167–92.

Press TV (2015, September 21). Iran inks gas deal as Omani minister visits. Retrieved from www.payvand.com/news/15/sep/1128.html (accessed 24 August 2016).
Reuters (2008, September 12). Oman and Iran will complete Kish gas field development by 2012. Retrieved from http://gulfnews.com/business/oman-and-iran-will-complete-kish-gas-field-development-by-2012-1.131034 (accessed 24 August 2016).
Reuters (2015a, August 16). Arms seized in Kuwait came from Iran: Kuwaiti newspapers. Retrieved from www.reuters.com/article/2015/08/16/us-kuwait-security-iran-idUSKCN0QL0CV20150816#BpPazCTXhpPLJi97.97 (accessed 24 August 2016).
Reuters (2015b, August 26). Kuwait summons Iran envoy over disputed gas field reports: KUNA. Retrieved from www.reuters.com/article/2015/08/26/us-energy-kuwait-iran-idUSKCN0QV0JI20150826 (accessed 24 August 2016).
Ross, M. (1987, September 25). U.S., Iran agree on repatriation of captured crew. *LA Times*. Retrieved from http://articles.latimes.com/1987-09-25/news/mn-6708_1_supply-ship (accessed 24 August 2016).
Rouhani, H. (2013). Twitter. Retrieved from https://twitter.com/HassanRouhani/status/390057247885119488 (accessed 24 August 2016).
Shaheen, K. (2011, March 16). Defensive shield for the Gulf since 1982. *The National*. Retrieved from www.thenational.ae/news/uae-news/defensive-shield-for-the-gulf-since-1982 (accessed 24 August 2016).
Shanahan, R. (2008). Bad moon not rising: The myth of the Gulf Shi'a crescent. Lowy Institute for International Policy. Retrieved from www.lowyinstitute.org/files/pubfiles/Shanahan,_Bad_moon__web.pdf (accessed 24 August 2016).
The Guardian (2008, March 1). US Embassy cables: Oman Sultan resists Iranian charm offensive. Retrieved from www.theguardian.com/world/us-embassy-cables-documents/143790 (accessed 24 August 2016).
The Guardian (2013, August 30). Oman's Sultan's Iran visit sparks hope of progress in nuclear standoff. Retrieved from www.theguardian.com/world/iran-blog/2013/aug/30/iran-oman-nuclear-negotiations (accessed 24 August 2016).
Theodoulou, M. (2013, December 11). Iran's hardliners tell Zarif to steer clear of military issues. *The National*. Retrieved from www.thenational.ae/world/middle-east/irans-hardliners-tell-zarif-to-steer-clear-of-military-issues (accessed 24 August 2016).
The Official Site of the President of The Islamic Republic of Iran (2015, July 18). Retrieved from www.president.ir/fa/88210 (accessed 24 August 2016).
The World Forum for Proximity of Islamic Schools of Thought (2011). Islamic Awakening Conference final communiqué. Retrieved from https://web.archive.org/web/20131015210932/http://www.taqrib.info/english/index.php?option=com_content&view=article&id=385:islamic-awakening-conference-final-communique-&catid=35:2009-08-31-05-01-28&Itemid=63 (accessed 24 August 2016).
Toumi, H. (2015, August 10). Iran uses Daesh as pretext to meddle in region. Gulf News. Retrieved from http://m.gulfnews.com/news/gulf/bahrain/iran-uses-daesh-as-pretext-to-meddle-in-region-1.1563956 (accessed 24 August 2016).
United States Institute of Peace (2015, October 2). Regional leaders at UNGA: On Iran. Retrieved from http://iranprimer.usip.org/blog/2015/oct/02/regional-leaders-unga-iran (accessed 24 August 2016).
Wagner, D. and Cafiero, G. (2015, September 11). Iran exposes myth of GCC unity. Huffington Post. Retrieved from www.huffingtonpost.com/daniel-wagner/iran-exposes-the-myth-of-_b_8102532.html?ir=Australia (accessed 24 August 2016).

Wehrey, F. (2013). The forgotten uprising in eastern Saudi Arabia. Carnegie Endowment for International Peace. Retrieved from http://carnegieendowment.org/files/eastern_saudi_uprising.pdf (accessed 24 August 2016).

WikiLeaks (2009a). US State Department Abu Dhabi. Strong words in private from MBZ at IDEX – Bashes Iran, Qatar, Russia. Retrieved from https://wikileaks.org/plusd/cables/09ABUDHABI193_a.html (accessed 24 August 2016).

WikiLeaks (2009b). US State Department Doha. Qatar: Balancing geographic interests with Iran, strategic interests with U.S. Retrieved from https://wikileaks.org/plusd/cables/09DOHA442_a.html (accessed 6 September 2016).

Zarif, M.J. (2013, November 21). Opinion: Our neighbors are our priority. Asharq al-Awsat. Retrieved from http://english.aawsat.com/2013/11/article55323055. (Accessed 24 August 2016).

7
OMAN'S INDEPENDENT FOREIGN POLICY

Abdullah Baabood

Introduction

Oman has been characterized as having an independent and unique foreign policy. Many analysts have attempted to understand the nature of foreign policy-making in Oman and explain its dynamics. The fact that foreign policy-making in Oman is highly personalized and often carried out through quiet and sometimes secret diplomacy has made the task harder for observers to explain and understand its determinants and processes. Indeed, the nature of Oman's foreign policy-making is not too dissimilar to other members of the Cooperation Council of the Arab Gulf States (Gulf Cooperation Council, GCC) of which Oman is a member. The GCC monarchies, with their family rule systems, have developed a highly personalized and secretive system of foreign policy-making, with very little, if any, popular or institutional input (Baabood, 2005).

Moreover, the GCC as a regional organization, which aims to coordinate the foreign policies of its member states, especially on issues affecting the region, has found it, at times, hard to align or even coordinate its member states' foreign policies let alone formulate a regional common foreign policy. Although it is not the only member that tends to follow an independent foreign policy, Oman seems to have made a number of foreign policy decisions that have not only diverged from, but at times contradicted with the policies of its fellow GCC members. However, because of its skillful diplomacy, it has managed to remain an integral part of the GCC mechanism and managed to maintain its relationship with its member states.

Oman's independent foreign policy-making is self-evident at the regional level. For example, since the formation of the GCC, Oman has supported the Egyptian–Israeli Peace Accord in 1980 and the subsequent Peace Accord between Israel and Jordan in 1994. Despite its good relations with the Shah of Iran, largely due to his military assistance in helping to quell the Dhofar Revolution, Oman has managed to conduct pragmatic cooperative relations with the Islamic Republic of Iran that overthrew the Shah in 1979. Oman also followed a neutral line in the Iran–Iraq War 1980–8, while other GCC member states sided with Iraq, and Oman played a meditating role in an effort to end the war. Following the conclusion of the war, Oman also signed a number of cooperation agreements with Iran and stepped up its relations with it on many levels. Oman, moreover, used its good relations with Iran to free a number of American hostages. Unlike other GCC states, Oman did not withdraw its ambassador from Baghdad following the election of what was considered by other GCC states as a sectarian government in Iraq. Oman also decided not be included in the GCC monetary union and the common currency and, more recently, it stood firmly against the formation of the GCC Union that was proposed by the late King of Saudi Arabia, King Abdullah. Even more bluntly, Oman facilitated and conducted secret negotiations between Iran and the United States of America (U.S.) that opened the door to the nuclear negotiations between Iran and the P5+1, and which subsequently led to the historic nuclear deal "The Joint Comprehensive Plan of Action" that was struck between Iran and the P5+1 in Vienna on July 14, 2015.

This chapter aims to examine and explain the nature of Oman's foreign policy. In doing so, it will apply three levels of foreign policy analysis, including the societal level, the state level, and the system level. The societal level will examine Oman's society and political culture (e.g., Ibadism), while focusing mainly on the perception of its leadership, which has contributed to the development of a unique nature of foreign decision-making in Oman. At the state level, the chapter argues that Oman's foreign policy-making is largely driven by its overwhelming desire for regime/state security within a tough and conflict-ridden region. Finally, the system level would explain Oman's unrelenting quest to maintain the balance of power between the main actors in the region. In order to pursue this argument, the chapter is divided into three main parts. The first part will provide an overview of Oman's geography, history, society, and political culture (including leadership perception). The second part will look at the state level; focusing mainly on the state's politics and economics. The third part will examine Oman's geopolitical position within the region and its balancing policy, mainly how Oman's relations with the GCC and Iran are directly related to its quest for security and regional balance.

Overview of Oman's history

During the 1920s, Oman was in the process of forming a nation-state. The formation of the national political units was not only a process of defining the national boundaries; instead, it was a more complex and dynamic process mainly due to the role played by oil revenues. In the aftermath of the Second World War, Oman was divided between the power of Sayyid Taimur along the coast and the Ibadi imamate in the interior. The post-war period was marked by an economic stagnation and the dissolution of the Ibadi imamate due to the election of Muhammad al-Khalili after the assassination of Imam al-Kharusi. In 1929, the British replaced Sayyid Taimur with his son Said, who was directing his efforts to enhance Oman's financial situation. Said was not able to exert full control over Oman due to the power of the tribal forces in the interior. As a result, Said attempted to build alliances with the different tribes through tribal diplomacy. Additionally, Said appointed several Ibadi ulama into clerical positions in order to co-opt them. These measures, while assisting Said in exerting a stronger grip on power, did not provide him with political legitimacy. The political situation in Oman was dominated by rulers' vulnerability and the rise of Ibadi imamate from time to time. However, there were four main events that brought tremendous changes to Omani politics. The first event was the oil concession of 1937, which saw the foundation of the British oil company "Petroleum Development Oman" (PDO) and altered Oman's tribal politics as well as Oman-Saudi relations due to border disputes. The second event was the Jebel Akhdar rebellion, which erupted in 1954 and again in 1957 in Oman, as an effort by Imam Ghalib bin Ali Al Hinai to protect the imamate of Oman proper from Sultan Said bin Taimur. The war continued until 1959, when British armed forces were involved in aiding the Sultan and winning the war, thus unifying the country under the Sultan's rule. The third event was the Dhofar Revolution that began in the mid-1960s, which played a great role in shaping Oman's current political reality. Sultan Said did not put much effort into initiating economic and political reform despite the fact that the country started receiving the oil revenues. He kept the country isolated and pursued an extensive reliance on foreigners, which alienated Omanis and contributed to the emergence of the revolution in Dhofar. The rebellion started to grow rapidly, taking hold of most of the Dhofar region in the south and, in 1970, it threatened to reach northern parts of Oman. The fourth event was the bloodless coup by Sultan Qaboos, the son of Sultan Said, against his reclusive father in 1970 that initiated intensive and wide-ranging political, economic, and social development and managed to counter the revolution effectively. The Shah of Iran, as well as other Gulf states, supported this coup since all of them were concerned by the potential threat Dhofar's revolution may have had if it had succeeded. The Dhofar Revolution was considered a leftist social revolution and was viewed as part of the Cold War. The coup was followed by a political vacuum since those who planned it did not give enough thought to what would be the next step. Townsend (1977, p. 78) claims that "the position of the British government was simply that the old Sultan's arch conservatism and intransigence was causing it no little embarrassment and was putting at risk the proposed withdrawal from the Persian Gulf at the end of 1971." However, the aftermath of the coup did not only contribute in countering the revolution, but further resulted in a radical change of Oman's foreign policy.

The coup was followed by a gradual development of Oman's economy and its foreign policy. Kechichian (1995b) has argued that, since Sultan Qaboos came to power, the foreign policy-making of Oman has passed through four main periods. The first phase, from 1970 to 1975, was characterized by focusing on regional and domestic aspects. Regionally, Oman was trying to enhance its relations with other Arab and international countries in order to enforce its independence. During this period Oman became a member of the Arab League and the United Nations, and tried to gain regional and international recognition. On the domestic level, the Sultan was trying to achieve internal unity and enhance the living conditions of his people after the revolution in Dhofar was declared over. The period from 1975 to 1980 marked the second phase, which witnessed an increased focus on domestic politics. The attempts to solve internal issues brought Oman into closer relations with the other Gulf states due to the financial assistance it was receiving from them. Moreover, Oman was able to preserve these ties despite its public support for the Egyptian peace efforts with Israel. During the same period, Oman made the first deal with the United States in the region, signing the 1980 Facilities Access Agreement. The following year, Qaboos helped in establishing the GCC, which was founded in order to enhance the security of the six Gulf states, particularly during the Iran–Iraq War. This step marked the beginning of the maturation period that lasted until 1985. Although Oman was part of several security activities due to its GCC membership, it did not take any side in the Iran–Iraq War. Since then, Qaboos started to become a regional figure on security matters. "After Iraq invaded Kuwait in 1990, Omani forces participated in the UN liberation effort, and Oman granted the United States access to prepositioned supplies and facilities in Oman via the Facilities Access Agreement (renewed in 1990)" (Kechichian, 1995b). Peterson labels this period as the progress period (1986–94). This period witnessed several Omani attempts to restore stability in the region that did not necessarily align with the other Gulf states' policies. First, Qaboos was trying to bring Iran and Iraq to the negotiating table after the war. Also, Qaboos, after the Oslo Agreement, welcomed the Israeli Prime Minister to Oman; the first time for an Israeli figure to publicly visit a Gulf state.

The following decades continued to witness growing distinctiveness in Omani foreign policy. Lefebvre states, "Oman opposed the use of military action to force Iraq to submit to inspections of its weapons capabilities by the UN Special Commission (UNSCOM)" (Lefebvre, 2010, p. 101). Since the 1997–8 UN–Iraq crisis, Oman's relationship with Iran has demonstrated the salient foreign policy that the Sultanate has followed. The call for regime change in Tehran that appeared in the renewal and modification of the Iran Sanctions Act in 2006 was overlooked by Oman. Despite the growing concerns about Iran's regional role, the Sultanate continued to have trade and diplomatic relations with Iran, a neighboring country that shares the strategic waterway of the Strait of Hormuz and which is globally important for the international oil shipments from the rich Gulf region.

Oman's troubled history and its strategic geographical location has played a large part in shaping its foreign policy outlook and its orientation. The stability of the country and conflict avoidance has been the prime reason for conducting a peaceful foreign policy with its neighbors, including Iran, which shares the Strait of Hormuz waterway and which, under the Shah, helped Oman to win the war against the Dhofar Revolution.

Oman's society, political culture, and economy

Foreign policy-making in Oman has also been impacted by domestic factors. While aspects such as desire for regime security and state stability have determined the direction of the Omani foreign policy, factors such as the Omani society, political culture, leadership perception, and economic endowments have formed the foundation of this independent foreign policy.

Omani society has mainly been shaped by Ibadism, a sect of Islam that is neither Sunni nor Shia. Ibadism has a history of tolerance and conservatism, and is based on just rule and tolerance. Moreover, acceptance of the other and peaceful compromises with opponents has contributed to shaping Ibadi thought. Such principles, coupled with Oman's turbulent history, have caused Omani society to drift away from political violence, producing an atmosphere of peaceful coexistence. Also, such religious and political culture has prevented the society from growing any tendencies toward religious extremism. Despite the fact that al-Qaeda in the Arabian Peninsula and the Islamic State of Iraq and the Levant are active in both Yemen and Saudi Arabia, they have almost zero presence in Oman. Lefebvre (2010) asserts, "Al-Qaeda apparently has not established an organizational presence in Oman, and no Omanis are known to have joined (or have been caught in) any radical religious-based terrorist group" (p. 111). This nature of tolerance and having no enemies is clearly reflected in Omani foreign policy-making. The peaceful principles followed by Omani society determine the foreign policy behavior of the Sultanate and shape its borders. However, this all was mainly put in context through the person of Sultan Qaboos himself. His main objective was to reverse his father's isolationist policy and reestablish Oman's role as a regional player. As a result, the Omani political culture was shaped by the tolerant nature of the society, which has been crafted mainly through the person of the Sultan.

Since the early 1970s, Qaboos was putting more efforts into the crafting of an independent Omani foreign policy. Therefore, Oman's foreign policy-making tends to be highly personalized by the direct involvement of Sultan Qaboos, who holds also the position of the Prime Minister and the Minister of Foreign Affairs among other senior posts. The nature of the Omani political system, which is based mainly on the person of the Sultan, has contributed in the production of an independent Omani foreign policy. This policy has been following a different approach since the rise of Sultan Qaboos to power. He has engaged in a pragmatic diplomacy that aims to engage in peaceful relations with different players in the region. In his first days, Qaboos was not able to dedicate much effort toward Oman's development due to the revolution in Dhofar. Qaboos, who was born in 1940, returned to Oman in 1964 after completing his military education and training in Europe. Moreover, his father isolated him by restricting his contact with the people; therefore he was unknown to the people of Oman. Qaboos knew only a small number of Omanis, which led him to rely on the British assistance and consultation in his early days. This resulted in the emergence of a unique relationship between Britain and Oman, which has lasted until today. Marc Valeri (2009, p. 71) states that the

Sultan's "room for maneuver with regard to the British was reduced to a minimum, and so was his legitimacy vis-à-vis the Omani population." Although during the initial period of his power, Qaboos did not enjoy much popular support, he gradually started to develop a vision to unify Oman through centralizing power around his personality. According to an observer, "much like Charles de Gaulle, who has a certain idea of France, Qaboos set out to reinvent Oman" (Kechichian, 1995a, p. 37). The Dhofar Revolution and its aftermath of state-building efforts played a significant role in unifying Oman around his sovereignty. The Sultan was personally involved in the Dhofar military campaign. This has enabled him to initiate a form of communication between Qaboos and the Omani people. However, the first attempt to officially personalize his authority was first established through the royal decree number 26/75 issued in 1975, which states that the Sultan is *masdar al-qawanin* (the source of all laws). Valeri (2015, p. 5) argues that "since then all Omani legislation has been promulgated through royal decrees, including the basic law of the state which was issued in November 1996." Qaboos wanted to keep control and exert authority over all state matters. This was done through the extreme centralization of power in the Diwan of the Royal Court:

> The Diwan has the role of filtering all cases coming before the ruler, while managing those national and private affairs which do not concern any other department but do not require the Sultan's personal intervention. As such, the Diwan has slowly become a super ministry above all the other Cabinet departments.
>
> *(Valeri, 2013a, p. 180)*

In addition, Qaboos started to expand his network of allies through forming different personal ties with the Omani population instead of allying with a single force. Thanks to the oil rent, the Sultan was able to lead the Omani state toward economic and social development that was unknown during the eras of previous Sultans and Sayyids. The main objective for Qaboos was to unify the Omani people around something else rather than tribalism. Joel Migdal states: "state leaders and their agencies have sought ways to change those they rule from disconnected subjects of state rule to some other status that would connect their personal identities to the continued existence and vitality of the state" (Migdal, 2001, p. 257). And state rulers have sought to establish this connection while remaining the ultimate authority and arbitrator, standing in a continuing object-subject relationship with them. In this view, Qaboos was able to replace the rivalry that existed between Oman's different parts, as well as the tribalism and clannism (*asabiyaat*), by establishing himself as the sole authority. As a result, all the old trends of identifying the Omani people were abolished and replaced by the reinvention of the Omani identity, leading to a process of national unification that evolved around the person of the Sultan. The control policy that was adopted by Qaboos constituted of two main pillars. First, the Sultan's ability to resolve the issues related to the state boundaries and Omani identity. Second, Qaboos was able to use oil revenues to consolidate his power through the redistribution system as in other Gulf states. The state monopoly of oil assisted Qaboos to co-opt different social actors such as ethnic groups, tribes, and regional actors into the state system.

Oil revenues were used to consolidate Qaboos's power during the early period of his leadership; however, oil revenues in Oman are neither the biggest in the region, nor infinite. Therefore, economic diversification has been an integral part of the Oman five-year plans series that started since 1970s. Sultan Qaboos early realized the necessity of diversification and the importance of finding alternatives for oil and gas revenues. To this end, Oman started to invest massively in agriculture, industry, fisheries, and tourism, as well as other sectors.

Unfortunately, this did not put an end to the dependence on oil and gas. Oil in Oman accounts for 50 per cent of its GDP and it is estimated to constitute around 70 per cent of the export earnings, as well as the government's receipts. Despite the fact that Oman is not a member of OPEC (Organization for Petroleum Exporting Countries), its policies are almost similar to those who are part of OPEC. Omani natural gas and oil reserves have a limited time horizon, around 24 years and 15 years respectively. Moreover, dependency on oil and gas is associated with the volatile energy markets which constitute a key risk to the Omani economy. A quick reading of the Omani budget for 2015 demonstrates that it is still dependent on oil revenues. Given the limited supply of its natural resources, along with the current decline of oil prices, Oman's economy is put under significant challenges. In addition, the high rate of unemployment (24 per cent) and the dominance of non-nationals in the private sector are also key obstacles to the Omani economy. Oman's limited economic capabilities have led it to pursue a diplomatic behavior that would not impact its economy negatively. First, Oman's relation with Iran and the geopolitics of the Strait of Hormuz illustrate Omani behavior. While Oman's relation with Iran has historical factors, economy is at the heart of it. Moreover, the mediation role that Oman has historically played, in which it has never been part of nor accepted a military action, demonstrate the limitations of its resources. While some may argue that economic instability may lead to foreign policy compromises, the Omani case is slightly different. The consistency in the Omani foreign policy and its silent diplomatic behavior illustrate that its economy was a motivation more than an obstacle.

Oman as a mediator

Oman has a long history of mediation in the region; this has stemmed from the way in which the country perceives regional political stability. Given its economic capabilities as well, Oman has a perception of internal vulnerability that should be dealt with in a pragmatic way. As a result, Oman started to sponsor consensus-oriented solutions. This mindset is not something new to the Omani foreign policy-making. In 1987, Oman was the first Arab country to support the Camp David agreement between Egypt and Israel, when the Arab region was against it. Later on, when the Arab States decided to expel Egypt from the Arab League, Oman was the sole opponent of that decision. In a relevant note, it should be noted that Oman and

Israel since the early 1990s have been engaged in direct but not official relations, which is not different from its Gulf peers. In 1985, Oman took the initiative to mediate between Pakistan and India. The following year, Oman mediated between Bahrain and Qatar, when the Qatari troops landed in Debil, and declared it as a restricted zone. Its mediation with other Gulf states helped to establish a framework agreement between the two states, as well as the removal of the Qatari troops (Asal *et al.*, 2007). Although this was carried out with other Gulf states, when Iraq invaded Kuwait Oman took a different stance. First, it did not cut its relations with Iraq, and it disagreed to a military solution; despite the fact that it viewed the Iraqi invasion as a violation of international law. Following that, in 1994, Oman was able to host the two sides of the Yemeni conflict in Salalah; such an effort is directly related to maintaining the stability of the Dhofar region.

Oman's mediating role when it comes to Iran is a significant one and was carried on a regular basis throughout history, given the hostility of the region toward Iran and its perception of Iran as well. After the 1979 Islamic Revolution, Oman did not break its diplomatic relations with Tehran. A decade later, the representative of Sultan Qaboos mediated between Iran and Iraq after the war; moreover, Oman succeeded in persuading Tehran to approve the UN resolution, which resulted in ending the war. In the same year, 1987, Oman attempted to improve the relations between the United States and Iran. The same effort was led to restore the diplomatic relations between Iran and Saudi Arabia in 1992.

Just recently, Oman was able to declare that it has negotiated the release of a British citizen, three Saudis, and two Americans who were held hostage by the Houthi rebels in Yemen (Gambrell and Schrek, 2015). Although there are no details about the term of their release or how the negotiation process was pursued, it demonstrates how Oman's role as a mediator is a constant and regular one. During the time of writing this chapter, the Libyan Constitution Drafting Assembly, which is sponsored by the UN, met in Salalah to discuss the process of drafting the constitution. Mostly, meetings related to constitution drafting take place in the country that seeks drafting a constitution; however, considering the circumstances of Libya such a process might be difficult. In that sense, Oman was considered to be a neutral place where those meetings could be held, giving its historical role in mediation. Due to its geographic location, as well as its limited economic resources, Oman had almost no other choice but to adopt a pragmatic diplomacy in order to maintain its stability. Moreover, this diplomatic role, due to its long history, becomes an integral part of the Omani foreign policy-making. It could be argued that there is no crisis in the region that has not seen Oman as a mediator or offering the will to do so. Most importantly, the success of most of its mediation roles shows the rational policy that Oman is trying to adopt and its awareness of the underlying geostrategic realities.

A desire for regime security

Oman's foreign policy- and decision-making stemmed mainly from Sultan Qaboos's desire for regime stability. There is a considerable difference between Oman and other

Gulf states in terms of the decision-making process due to Oman's worries about its national security. Domestically, Oman has emphasized developing its national political institutions that are directly linked with internal security and stability. The first action that Sultan Qaboos took when he came to power was to increase defense expenditures by up to 50 per cent of the whole state budget. The threat that the Dhofar Revolution created was one of the main factors behind this policy change. In addition, the Sultan's objective to establish long-term stability was another significant factor that transformed Oman's internal policy. A key element of regime security was the nation-building process that Qaboos started to implement in the 1970s. The main objective of nation-building was not only to achieve social and economic development, but also to refer this development to Qaboos solely. Valeri argues that:

> the nation-building process implemented since 1970, . . . links the country's economic and social development to the modernizing state (as the administrator of the oil rent), on the one hand, and to the person of the Sultan who embodies the state and has become the subject of a personality cult, on the other.
>
> *(2013b, p. 267)*

Another step implemented by Qaboos in order to enhance the stability of the regime was relying on various allies. As mentioned earlier, Qaboos was unknown to Omanis, and most of his consultants were foreigners. Consequently, in order to gain the confidence of the Omani people, Qaboos started to appoint individuals from different social groups into various political positions, including those previously involved with the Dhofar Revolution. Unlike the rest of the Gulf states, the Omani government is not fully controlled by a major tribe or a ruling family. Qaboos's royal family members do not hold many political positions. Moreover, sensitive positions were filled by some members of the Busa'idi tribe, such as Hamud bin Faisal al-Busa'idi holding the position of the Minster for the Interior. Another example is the Minister Responsible for Defense Affairs position, which is held by Said Badr bin Saud al-Busa'idi. Sultan Qaboos has also relied on merchant elites, a common practice among the Gulf states, to consolidate power. One reason was due to the fact that Qaboos was not able to rely on his small family when he first came to power. Second, the merchant elites were essential to help Qaboos to finance his nation-building projects. Consequently, some members of the merchant elites' families were given political decision-making positions. Although the oil revenues started to change the equation, this did not really influence the stability of the state. According to Valeri,

> The oil rent has at the same time profoundly changed the boundaries between politics and the economy, as many ministers whose families were not active in the economy before have become personally rich. This process has not been questioned by the ruler, as it has increased both the elites' dependency on the state and the stability of his rule.
>
> *(2013c, p. 21)*

The second pillar for regime stability was based on Oman's regional policy. In contrast to its regional partners, Oman had developed a strong relationship with Iran during the time of the Shah, as well as after the Islamic Revolution. For other Gulf states, the fear of Iran's regional expansion started to increase particularly after the revolution. A fear of a revolution spillover effect was common among the Gulf states. However, Oman thought that by cooperating with Iran it would be able to contain any threat from Iran. Kechichian asserts:

> Muscat did not accept the premise that the revolution would spill over into the lower Gulf, arguing that conservative Arab Gulf monarchies ought to engage Iran on their side, not only to ensure the safety of the straits but more important, not to isolate Iran from the affairs of the region.
>
> *(1995a, p. 59)*

By following this approach, Oman seemed to adopt a pragmatic foreign policy that aimed not only to preserve its regional independence but also to ensure its regime stability. Another important regional policy that was taken by Qaboos to enhance regime security was Oman's relationship with Yemen. Enhancing its relationship with Yemen during the early 1980s, and holding the first formal contacts with the Soviet Union, was essential to ensure stability in the Dhofar region. Although Qaboos directed this step for regime security reasons, it also demonstrated the independence of his policy in relation to the other Gulf states. Moreover, due to the fear from the regional reaction toward the revolution in Iran, and later the Iran–Iraq War's impact on the domestic stability of Oman, Qaboos welcomed and encouraged the creation of the GCC. His desire to preserve the economic development of his country led him to reaffirm his neutrality during the Iran–Iraq War, since any destabilizing of relations may have impacted on the oil tankers that use the Straits of Hormuz as a passage.

Oman–Iran's active relationship

The Omani–Iranian relationship illustrates Oman's different perception of the Iranian regional role, and the balance with other regional powers, as well as the Omani mediation efforts. Oman's relationship with Iran is based on three main elements; Iranian support during the Dhofar Revolution, Sultan Qaboos's concept of Omani-balancing, and Oman's belief that Iran is essential to guaranteeing regional security. Despite the support of the British and the expansion of the Sultan's armed forces, Qaboos was not able to crush the rebellion in Dhofar. As a result, in late 1973 Iran's Shah, at the request of Oman, decided to dispatch around 1,500 soldiers, who were backed by fighter aircraft, artillery, and helicopter troop-carriers. The Iranian support was able to defend major strategic positions and hold the territory, although it was not suitable for small-unit counterinsurgency operations. Ladwig III argues that the main objective behind the heavy Iranian support was that "the Shah of Iran had no desire to see a revolutionary government controlling the other side of the Strait of Hormuz" (2008, p. 76). The Iranian role was as important as the British role, resulting in enhanced relations between Oman and Iran despite regional fear over Iranian influence. During the 1970s Sultan Qaboos was still in a period of power consolidation, and he acknowledged the Shah's regional preeminence. The Shah's territorial claim over the islands belonging to the United Arab Emirates (UAE) demonstrated his hegemonic aspirations in the region. At that time, Oman was occupied by the Dhofar Revolution and it did not have enough capacity to deal with it, therefore, Qaboos thought of Iranian assistance as a means of countering the rebellion and protecting Oman from the Shah's hegemonic claims:

> By offering the Shah the explicit support of an Arab Gulf ruler and direct involvement in quelling Omani instability that could spill over into Iran, Qaboos secured a border agreement, essential aid, and the stature associated with being treated as an equal by the region's then most powerful country.
> *(Kechichian, 1995b, para. 8)*

Omani–Iranian relations started to become more consolidated due to Qaboos's regional strategy. Since his first years in power, Qaboos started to develop a strategy that would ensure his country's economic and social development through countering internal and external threats to the Omani state. This was illustrated through keeping the established Omani–Iranian relations in place even after Iran's Islamic Revolution. The main objective was to protect the Strait of Hormuz, to prevent possible aggression. Qaboos proposed a $100 million plan for the protection of it, thus maintaining the stability of Omani–Iranian relations and the strait as well. The concept of Omani-balancing was illustrated again during the Iran–Iraq War. In order to avoid the implications of the war, Qaboos preferred to stay neutral. After the end of the war, Qaboos also tried to bring Iraq and Iran into negotiations, illustrating Oman's role as a mediator and its aspiration toward preserving regional security.

The most historic move was Oman's recent mediation between the United States and Iran. In September 2011 Oman was successful in persuading the Iranians to return the three American hikers who were jailed on espionage charges in Iran. This move increased the level of confidence within the United States about Oman's role in facilitating the rapprochement between the United States and Iran. In the same year, John Kerry met with Qaboos secretly. The meeting included talks about the U.S. aim for direct discussions with Iran, which Qaboos encouraged. The direct outcome of the meeting was placing Oman as a main player in the subsequent nuclear deal. In July 2012, the first meeting between the Americans and the Iranians was held in the Omani capital, Muscat. Some argue that, as the discussions intensified, Qaboos continued to hold the meetings between the two parties, sometimes at his private residences. The talks continued throughout 2013 and 2014, although such a move would have several implications on Oman's position within the GCC, especially since the talks were held in a confidential manner. However, this demonstrates the secrecy of Oman's diplomacy and the manner in which its foreign policy is built. In the same regard, Valeri (2014) argues that such moves "can be understood within a recent history of conciliatory efforts intended to promote negotiated solutions to regional crises." Furthermore, Oman delivered secret messages that contained significant issues related to the negotiations between Iran and the United States. Even after the P5+1 talks ramped up, President Obama called Qaboos to discuss the nuclear deal. Oman has played a significant role in facilitating the relations between both parties, which is considered as a main factor in the success of the deal:

> Most of U.S. foreign policy in the Gulf has been dominated by Saudi Arabia due to its economic, geographic, and ideological influence in the region. However, Oman has proven that it has greater credibility in working cooperatively with the United States to further mutual policy goals in a productive manner.
>
> *(Gupta, 2015)*

Oman's role in the nuclear talks emerged from its belief that Iran is a core variable in the security equation of the region. A former U.S. ambassador to Oman, David Dunford, stated that, despite Oman's relationship with the United States, it was able to maintain its relationship with Tehran. He points out that "given Iran's size, population, and proximity, the Omanis believe there can be no genuine security in the Gulf until Iran becomes part of the solution" (Dunford, 1995, p. 63). Consequently, from the perspective of the pragmatism of Oman's foreign policy, such a move could be interpreted as another Omani effort to preserve regional stability, since any political insecurity in the region would result in a serious threat for Oman's internal stability. Furthermore, Oman has constantly believed that regional security could only be maintained by the inclusion of all regional powers, which includes Iran. The Omani proposal to include Iran in future regional security arrangements has been met with opposition from other Gulf states, particularly Saudi Arabia, and has added to the misperception of Oman's role among its partners in the GCC.

Oman and the GCC

Out of tune

Historically, Oman's relations with the other Gulf states were guided mainly by maintaining Oman's role as the gatekeeper of the Gulf. When Qaboos came to power, he was interested in protecting the Sultanate's borders with Yemen, the UAE, Saudi Arabia, and Iran. Moreover, Qaboos believed that there was no option but to develop solid ties with the region, particularly in economic terms, since Oman's future was linked to the stability of the region. Thus, the period from 1970 to 1975 was occupied by Oman's strategic focus on the Gulf region. This period witnessed a reverse of the isolationism policy that was adopted by his father, Said bin Taimur. The main shared objective that led to increased cooperation between Oman and the other Gulf states was their shared desire to protect their monarchies. Oman's attempts to recover from the rebellion in Dhofar contributed to enhancing its relations with neighboring Gulf states. Muscat received financial help from Kuwait as well as Saudi Arabia in order to develop its post-Dhofar War economy. Relations between Oman and Saudi Arabia in particular have improved because of the perceived Soviet-inspired threat that was taking place in Oman.

The focus that was devoted to develop Oman's internal policies during the first decade of Qaboos's rule influenced Oman's foreign policy positively later on:

> When the world community was caught off guard in the aftermath of the 1974 oil embargo, by upheavals in Iran and Afghanistan in 1979, and by a war between Iran and Iraq starting in 1980, Muscat's vital role was duly noted. To some extent, Oman succeeded because it managed to put its internal affairs in order.
>
> *(Kechichian, 1995a, p. 61)*

By the 1980s, Oman has already established a clear perspective of its foreign policy interests. At the Abu Dhabi summit, which established the GCC in 1981, Oman restated its proposal for close security cooperation between the Gulf states. The collaboration would be based on a close partnership with the United States, but would not be an anti-Iran bloc. This was a remark of how Oman was developing a foreign policy that is different than its Gulf neighbors. Qaboos was also convinced that the internal stability of Oman would not be impacted due to his pragmatic foreign policy. The Iraqi invasion of Kuwait is another example where Qaboos reacted independently vis-à-vis the actions of Saudi Arabia. Although Oman had disapproved of the Iraqi invasion as a violation of international law, it did not terminate Omani–Iraqi relations. Furthermore, in contrast to other Gulf states, Oman constantly called for removing the sanctions that were imposed on Iraq. Although the Omani–Saudi relations were never challenged by major disagreements, mainly due to Saudi's financial aid to Oman, relations with Saudi Arabia have fluctuated since the 1970s due to the unstable regional climate. However, during the Yemeni civil war, Saudi Arabia and Kuwait backed the southern leaders who were against the government of Sanaa, which strained Oman's relations with the Gulf states. It could be argued that the developments that occurred from the mid-1980s to the mid-1990s significantly impacted upon Omani–Saudi relations as well as Oman's general relations with the wider Gulf.

More recently, several developments have portrayed Oman's outlier foreign policy vis-à-vis the GCC. Although Oman's refusal to join the GCC Union was expected, the decisiveness of the Omani position was surprising. According to Al-Rasheed (2013), "Omani Foreign Minister Youssef bin Alawi surprised the audience when he bluntly declared that his country is against the union and will withdraw from the new body if it sees the light" (para. 2). This was not the first time that Oman refused the proposal for moving the GCC toward unity. In 2011, Oman also rejected the Saudi proposal. She further argues that, "Alawi's statement shattered the illusion of cooperation and the chances of Gulf unity at a time when Saudi Arabia is desperate to rein its stature, at least among its Gulf neighbors"

(Al-Rasheed, 2013, para. 2). Oman is keen to develop the mechanisms of the GCC states and to see the implementations of the decisions of the Supreme Council leading to further gradual regional integration and cooperation. However, it is against the quick transformation of the GCC into a political union because it believes that the integration process is still slow and has not reached a sufficient level that could lead to a union. The rejection of the Gulf Union proposal could be attributed to several reasons. As al-Rasheed mentioned, Omani concerns stem from their acknowledgment of Saudi influence. Oman has several reservations when it comes to Saudi's influence in the region, which carries with it Salafi ideas, and its potential impacts. Oman's fear that the creation of such a union would increase confrontation with Iran is another reason for its rejection. The proposal for the formation of a Gulf Union has come at a time where the perceived threat from Iran has reached its peak because of the Arab Spring and perceived and actual Iranian intervention in some Arab countries. On the other hand, Oman believes that instead of continuing hostility toward Iran, the Gulf states should turn it into an ally if they aim to increase the stability of the region. Oman, moreover, called for the inclusion of Iran in Gulf-wide security architecture.

The Yemeni crisis is another prominent example that illustrates Oman's unique foreign policy. Oman's government has refused to participate in the Saudi-led coalition that has intervened in Yemen. Paradoxically, Sultan Qaboos has called for noninterference, in addition to providing for talks to seek a political solution. In May 2015, Iranian Foreign Minister Javad Zarif visited Oman to discuss and sign navigation agreements. During that visit, Zarif met with Houthi representatives, who were based in Oman. Purportedly, the Houthi representatives have met with Saudi-led coalition representatives and U.S. officials in order to discuss the possibility of a political compromise. Regardless of Oman's growing role as a good-faith broker and a neutral mediator, its stance contradicts its Gulf neighbors' political will. From a geopolitical point of view, prolonged conflict in Yemen would have severe impacts on the stability of Oman. As Roby Barrett (2015) points out:

> [t]he history of neglect and the diverging Sunni and tribal culture of the southern mountain and coastal regions of Oman created a situation in which the South Yemen-based People's Front for the Liberation of Oman and the Arabian Gulf (PFLOAG) insurgency almost succeeded.
>
> *(para. 5)*

Furthermore, given the history of Oman's decision-making process, internal stability and long-term security interests were its main pillars. The current health situation of Sultan Qaboos, accompanied by the decline of oil revenues, threatens both factors. In order to ensure long-term stability in Oman's southern region, Yemen's stability should be guaranteed and a peaceful resolution of the military conflict should be arrived at soon to alleviate the suffering of the Yemeni people. The Omani position on the Yemen war has added to the out-of-sync policies with the other GCC states that supported the Saudi-led military intervention in the country.

Conclusion

Oman's foreign independent policy has raised several questions. The debate about Oman being an outlier player within the GCC has intensified, particularly during the nuclear talks and the Yemeni crisis. Certainly, Oman practices a different and independent foreign policy in regard to the other Gulf states; however, this is not something that has emerged recently, as evidence discussed throughout this chapter shows. Oman's foreign policy-making started to develop once Sultan Qaboos came to power. Since the early periods of his reign, divergence between Oman and the Gulf has occurred frequently, and Oman has always demonstrated that it is holding a different vision toward regional issues.

Oman is a monarchy like the other Gulf states; however, the personalization of power is clearly demonstrated in the Omani case. This has played a significant factor in shaping Oman's foreign policy and response toward most of the developments that have occurred with its neighbors as well as the wider region. The perception of its leadership has contributed to the development of a unique nature of foreign policy decision-making in Oman. In addition, the internal conflicts and particularly the Dhofar War, which was the first challenge facing Sultan Qaboos, helped in shaping a second significant pillar in Oman's foreign policy. Oman's desires for internal security and regime stability constitute a major part of its foreign policy-making. Regional issues as well as its relationship with Iran demonstrate how Oman's foreign policy is based on its national interest, and how the Sultanate aims to consolidate its position within the region. Moreover, Oman's relations with the Gulf, particularly with Saudi Arabia and Iran, are part of an Omani tactic to maintain the balance of power in the region.

In fact, the adoption of a different foreign policy in Oman is not unique in the Gulf region. Saudi Arabia, Qatar, and the UAE have also demonstrated coherence in their foreign policies as well as conflicts of interest. Therefore, arguing that Oman is an outlier overlooks the fact that there is no common Gulf foreign policy. However, the uniqueness of Oman's foreign policy lies mainly in its positive neutrality, and the consistency of its regional positions. Moreover, throughout the last decades, Oman was able to achieve its main goals from pursuing an independent foreign policy, which are regime security and internal stability. While it could be argued that Sultan Qaboos was the main pillar behind this success, it raises the question about the future of its foreign policy-making. The fact that Qaboos has no apparent successor puts his neutrality, opposition to armed interventions, different perception of the regional balance of power, mediation skill, and other aspects of the Omani foreign policy at stake. It could not be guaranteed that the successor would be able to follow the same direction of Sultan Qaboos. Furthermore, the regional and internal developments such as the Dhofar Revolution, oil revenues, the Iranian Revolution, and the Gulf War have assisted Qaboos in a way, and helped him consolidate his internal position, as well developing his foreign policy. However, the current regional climate, the war in Yemen, extensive rivalry between Saudi Arabia and Iran, as well as the decline in oil prices, would give the coming successor real challenges. Although Qaboos was able to deal with the regional developments in a neutral manner and uses them for Oman's advantage, only the future will determine whether the successor will be able to do so. However, the determinants of Oman's political culture, the realities of its economic structure, and its geostrategic location are expected to continue to determine its foreign policy-making and its orientation after Qaboos regardless of the personality of the successor.

References

Al-Rasheed, M. (2013). Omani rejection of GCC union adds insult to injury for Saudi Arabia – Al-Monitor: The pulse of the Middle East. Retrieved April 24, 2016, from www.al-monitor.com/pulse/originals/2013/12/oman-rejects-gcc-union-insults-saudi-arabia.html#ixzz3tqxdbgR3.

Asal, V., Quinn, D., Wilkenfeld, J., Young, K., Young, K., & Msn, R.N. (2007). *Mediating international crises*. London and New York: Routledge.

Baabood, A. (2005). Dynamics and determinants of the GCC state's foreign policy, with special reference to the EU, in Nonneman, Gerd (ed.), *Analyzing Middle East foreign policies and the relationship with Europe*, London and New York: Routledge, pp. 254–82.

Barrett, R. (2015). Oman's balancing act in the Yemen conflict. Retrieved April 24, 2016, from www.mei.edu/content/at/oman's-balancing-act-yemen-conflict.

Dunford, D. (1995). The US and Oman: An enduring partnership. *Middle East Insight*, 12, 62–4.

Gambrell, J., & Schreck, A. (2015, September 21). Oman, again the Mideast mediator, helps free Yemen hostages. Retrieved April 24, 2016, from www.businessinsider.com/ap-oman-again-the-mideast-mediator-helps-free-yemen-hostages-2015-9.

Gupta, S. (2015). Oman: The unsung hero of the Iranian nuclear deal. *Foreign Policy Journal*. Retrieved April 24, 2016, from www.foreignpolicyjournal.com/2015/07/23/oman-the-unsung-hero-of-the-iranian-nuclear-deal/.

Kechichian, J.A. (1995a). *Oman and the world: The emergence of an independent foreign policy*. Santa Monica, CA: Rand Corporation.

Kechichian, J.A. (1995b). Oman: A unique foreign policy produces a key player in Middle Eastern and global diplomacy. Retrieved April 24, 2016, from www.rand.org/pubs/research_briefs/RB2501.html.

Ladwig III, W.C. (2008). Supporting allies in counterinsurgency: Britain and the Dhofar Rebellion. *Small Wars & Insurgencies*, 19(1), 62–88.

Lefebvre, J.A. (2010). Oman's foreign policy in the twenty-first century. *Middle East Policy*, 17(1), 99–114.

Migdal, J.S. (2001). *State in society: Studying how states and societies transform and constitute one another*. Cambridge: Cambridge University Press.

Townsend, J. (1977). *Oman: The making of a modern state*. London: Taylor & Francis.

Valeri, M. (2009). *Oman: Politics and society in the Qaboos state*. London: Hurst.

Valeri, M. (2013a). Oman: Politics and Society in the Qaboos States. New York: Oxford University Press.

Valeri, M. (2013b). Domesticating local elites: Sheikhs, Walis and state-building under Sultan Qaboos, in Wippel, S. (ed.), *Regionalizing Oman: Political, economic and social dynamics*. Dordrecht: Springer Science+Business Media, pp. 267–77.

Valeri, M. (2013c). Oligarchy vs. Oligarchy: Business and Politics of Reform in Bahrain and Oman, in Hertog, S., Luciani, G. & Valeri, M. (eds), *Business politics in the Middle East*. London: Hurst and Company, pp. 17–42.

Valeri, M. (2014). Oman's mediatory efforts in regional crises, Norwegian Peacebuilding Resource Centre (NOREF). Retrieved August 31, 2016, from www.peacebuilding.no/Regions/Middle-East-and-North-Africa/The-Gulf/Publications/Oman-s-mediatory-efforts-in-regional-crises/(language)/eng-US.

Valeri, M. (2015). *Simmering Unrest and Succession Challenges in Oman*. Washington DC: Carnegie Endowment for International Peace.

8

EVOLVING FOREIGN AND SECURITY POLICIES

A comparative study of Qatar and the United Arab Emirates

Emma Soubrier

Introduction

The Arab Spring set deep forces of change in motion throughout the Middle East and North Africa (MENA) region. Evolutions occurred not only where the political order was directly confronted or overthrown, but also in countries which felt that the reshaping of the regional context called a redefinition of their own rules of engagement within it. This was particularly the case of the Gulf Cooperation Council (GCC) states.

This chapter focuses more specifically on Qatar and the United Arab Emirates (UAE) and examines their foreign and security policies in the face of new regional dynamics. This allows one to test hypotheses regarding the adequate theoretical framework to apply in order to understand where their strategies come from – and where they might head to next.

Amidst the profuse literature on Gulf security issues, few publications focus on the GCC countries' own perception of their strategic environment. Most of them rather analyse the regional complex through the lens of Western priorities and primarily commercial interests. Yet, these monarchies' decision-making processes are highly personalized, which calls for a focus on the perception of the individuals in power.

Moreover, it has been noted that the rise of Qatar and the UAE has challenged the existing academic literature on the role of small states in comparative politics and international relations (Ulrichsen 2012: 2). Today, there is a need for scholars to update the theoretical framework of small states' strategies and Gulf case studies might just be the perfect way to do this.

This chapter offers a comparative study of Qatari and Emirati policies prior to and after the Arab Spring. First, the author seeks to build an analytical framework of their contrasted policies up until 2011. The chapter then turns to the new ins and outs of their strategies in the face of the Arab Spring and their consequences on the emergence of a new regional security order.

Contrasted policies of Qatar and the UAE

Building an analysis framework

Confronting Qatar and the UAE with the theoretical framework of small states' strategies calls for a definition of what this taxonomy implies. Not only is there no consensus among scholars regarding this classification, but the two monarchies under scrutiny seem to escape each and every attempt to capture the essence of what a small state is in the International Relations (IR) and Comparative Politics (CP) notional worlds.

Qatar and the UAE perfectly illustrate the idea that one state may be weak in one area while strong in another. Both are small in geography and demography but big in GDP terms. Hence, they do not necessarily consider themselves as 'small', and they shaped their strategies towards the world accordingly, using this economic power to carve themselves the role of what would be better qualified as medium states or middle powers. This is not surprising since 'foreign policy choices are made by actual political leaders [so] it is their perceptions of relative power that matter, not simply relative quantities of physical resources or forces in being' (Rose 1998: 147). Size is, to a great extent, a matter of self-perception. This first part aims at building a theoretical framework for Qatari and Emirati policies, following the stages advocated by neoclassical realists – namely, a primary focus on structural determinants supplemented by intervening variables at the domestic level.[1]

This paper adopts the dynamic definition of small states through their relation to power (Goetschel 1998; Archer *et al.* 2014). One should note that Qatari and Emirati policies are articulated in relation to the *global* distribution of power but also, primarily, to the *regional* balance of power. The first section defines the specificities of their position in both regional and international systems, the superposition of which helps understanding their policies. The second section further anchors the two case studies in neoclassical realism, showing how these structural factors have influenced their policies through their perception at the domestic level. The third section uses this theoretical framework to explore the contrasted policies of Qatar and the UAE, labelled 'Prince States', up until 2011.

Security policies of the small Gulf states

Where global order meets regional anarchy

Small-states literature argues that the security dilemma of these actors is based on a dichotomy between autonomy and influence. Should they decide to favour the former, their preference would go to a neutral and defensive strategy. Should they choose to maximize the latter, they would adopt a cooperative strategy, relying on alliances which could follow either balancing or band-wagoning logics, depending on whether they would rather ally against or with the threats (Rickli 2008; Mouritzen 1997; Walt 1985). In any case, it is assumed that small states cannot combine both autonomy and influence due to lack of resources, this offensive strategy being restricted to great powers which are the only ones with 'the power to influence the structure of the international system while guaranteeing their security' (Reiter 1996: 65).

Qatar and the UAE, however, challenge these assumptions on small states' security options. Through the adoption of a hedging strategy, they achieved a combination of influence and relative autonomy by making the most of their security constellation, and particularly of the interplay across their global and regional contexts (Rickli 2016b).

In 1990, the end of the Cold War led to the emergence of a unipolar global environment. For small states everywhere, it increased the incentives to adopt a cooperative strategy through an alliance with the United States (US) which had become the sole global superpower. For European small states, this even rendered any other security policy almost unrealistic since their regional environment had evolved into a situation of 'mature anarchy' (Rickli 2008: 315).

Small Gulf states, however, still found themselves confronted with a regional context defined by 'immature anarchy', power struggles between Saudi Arabia, Iraq and Iran, and conventional threats, as the 1990 invasion of Kuwait showed. Hence, it is logical that their strategy differed from their European counterparts. While European small states were arguably no longer concerned with direct regional security incentives, the small Gulf states continued to illustrate the fact that the regional level is the crucial one for security analysis. The relative autonomy of security features at the level of regions 'was revealed by the ending of the Cold War, when enmities such as that between . . . Iraq and the Gulf Arab states easily survived the demise of a superpower rivalry that had supported, but not generated, them' (Buzan and Waever 2003: 47). The arguments developed here rely on the Regional Security Complex Theory (RSCT). RSCT serves as a useful framework to organize the empirical study of Gulf security since it not only specifies different levels of analysis, but also points to the interaction of these levels,[2] allowing a deeper understanding of multi-level strategies such as those of Qatar and the UAE. RSCT can logically be articulated with the neoclassical realist approach of this paper since both frameworks emphasize the need to reconcile all levels of analysis rather than apprehending IR along either-or choices. This section addresses the articulation of Qatari and Emirati strategies with the global and regional contexts, while the following section brings the domestic level into the equation.

For the small Gulf states, 1990 represented a consolidation of the 'regional security complex', defined through 'the degree to which certain geographically grouped states spend most of their time and effort worrying about each other and not other states' (Buzan 1991; Gause 2009: 3–4). Ten years after the Iranian revolution and the Iran–Iraq War – the first threats which led them to ally within the GCC under the leadership of Saudi Arabia in 1981 – the small Gulf monarchies had a blunt reality check as they realized this attempted cooperative strategy proved a failure: they could not rely on the Saudi umbrella, let alone on themselves, to ensure their security. Consequently, Qatar and the UAE readjusted their strategy, mixing various degrees of band-wagoning and balancing approaches at the regional and global levels.

At the regional level, being part of the GCC meant that Qatar and the UAE band-wagoned with Saudi Arabia to balance the Iraqi and Iranian threats. They also tacitly relied on the US, by virtue of the security arrangements between Saudi Arabia and the US. The US thus represented the main security guarantee of an apparent cooperative strategy. However, Qatar and the UAE also decided to ally more directly with the American power to overcome their own security dilemma within the Arabian Peninsula. They signed bilateral defence cooperation agreements with the US in 1992 and 1994 which served the purpose of balancing another perceived threat, this time coming from Saudi Arabia.[3] While band-wagoning with Saudi Arabia under a common American military umbrella within the GCC, they used the same global strategic partner to achieve a goal of relative autonomy regarding the Saudi power. Thus, the opposition between influence and autonomy might only be apparent.

As it turns out, moving on to the global level, Qatar and the UAE managed to defend a relative autonomy within the multi-level cooperative strategy they built with the US itself. This has to do with the means used to implement their alliance with the US, namely the enlarged 'oil for security' pact. According to this paradigm, not only did the Gulf states provide cheaper oil to the US, but they also invested billions in the American defence industrial base through huge arms purchases[4] in exchange for a security guarantee. Qatar and the UAE did not merely enter a dependency relation with the US but rather engaged in a mutually (though not equally) dependent partnership which allowed them to feel relatively autonomous regarding their great ally. Moreover, in the 1990s, the Gulf became a key destination for the US to maintain its industrial base precisely because of the huge drop in military orders coming from NATO countries associated with the end of the Cold War. Well aware of their strategic importance for their American ally, and hence of a relative leverage on them, Qatar and the UAE balanced too strong a dependence towards the US by signing bilateral defence-cooperation agreements and purchasing major arms contracts with two other Western countries: France and the United Kingdom (UK).[5]

Qatar and the UAE somehow escaped assumptions on small states' security options since they managed to articulate a mix of cooperative and defensive approaches tailored to their needs of relative autonomy within their regional and international contexts. This peculiar hedging strategy was rendered possible by the emergence of the US as the world's only superpower, although Qatar and the UAE also sought to balance this relation with the US through a diversification of strategic partnerships. In fact, their security choices can be visualized as an addition of concentric circles of 'balanced opposition', the heart of which is regime survival.

This chapter will try and theorize these dynamics against the international–domestic nexus before exploring the contrasted Qatari and Emirati strategies (prior to the Arab Spring).

Theorizing regime-centred strategies amidst international–domestic entanglements

The theoretical puzzle of international–domestic entanglements has been thoroughly addressed by scholars. While previous works distinguished between external and internal determinants of state behaviour (Waltz 1959; Singer 1961), one of the first to bring attention to 'linkage politics' was James Rosenau (Rosenau 1969). Later on, milestone works focused on foreign economic policy stated that decision-makers were *simultaneously* pressured by domestic and international incentives (Katzenstein 1976; Krasner 1978). Against this background, Robert Putnam initiated the 'two-level games' literature and noted the need to take into account entanglements between the IR and CP notional worlds (Putnam 1988: 459). From then on, a scholars' dispute (Elman 1995) opposed neo-realists who argued that systemic/structural factors overrule domestic determinants in shaping foreign policies (Waltz 1979; Posen 1984; Miller 1992) and those insisting on the need to bring back the domestic level of analysis into foreign policy studies, hence effectively bridging IR and CP through what was labelled 'neoclassical realism' (Snyder 1991; Bueno de Mesquita and Lalman 1992; Fearon 1998).

The idea that this latter approach is the most relevant to analyse small Gulf states' policies can be tested through the following empirical comparison. Were structural factors enough to explain their choices of strategy, one could expect to find common policies in Qatar and the UAE, but also in Kuwait, Bahrain and Oman. However, this is far from reality: confronted with similar regional incentives, they adopted very different strategies. From this, it can be assumed that their contrasts are at least partly linked to domestic factors – but which?

To understand the way states interpret and respond to their external environment, 'one must analyze how systemic pressures are translated through unit-level intervening variables such as decision-makers' perceptions and domestic state structure' (Rose 1998: 152). This chapter argues that the most important factor shaping Qatar's and the UAE's responses to their external environment is their leaders' perception. Among the smaller Gulf states, those two are the ones which have the most similar domestic environments and state structure – which leads one to explain their differences of strategy through the other unit-level intervening variable identified by neoclassical realists. Following Elman's idea that if we can show that the domestic level matters '*even in these instances where we would expect that it should not* [namely in small states], then we will have provided the strongest possible support for domestic level theorizing' (Elman 1995: 172), showing that small Gulf states' strategies differ *even in instances where we would expect that they should not*, namely when both external and internal incentives are alike, provides the best argument that the overruling factor in shaping their strategies is the leaders' perception of their entangled international and domestic determinants. It has been argued that 'leaders, not states, choose actions' – 'alas, leaders seem to be motivated by their *own* well-being and not by the welfare of the state' (Bueno de Mesquita 2002: 4). Focusing on leaders' individual choices seems more relevant than state-centred studies. Conclusively, a comparative approach of Qatari and Emirati Prince-States' strategies represents a valuable contribution to both small states and neoclassical realist literature. Coming back to the concentric circles of 'balanced opposition' illustrating the multi-level security policies of Qatar and the UAE, one could say they echo a perception of enmity drawn from the 'Middle East's tribal DNA', notably the Arab saying 'Me against my brother, me and my brother against my cousin; me, my brother, and my cousin against the world' (Salzman 2008), and that the heart of their strategy is the regime in power rather that the state or the nation. They share this particularity with all GCC monarchies. The very creation of this regional entity arguably represented a collective survival strategy to protect their monarchical system against the perceived ideological threat coming from the revolution in Iran more than their territorial integrity against a conventional threat coming from Teheran.[6]

In the wake of the Iraqi invasion of Kuwait, the GCC even considered that Iran had reacted responsibly in the face of the crisis and consequently, for a short period, thought of Teheran as a viable security partner. GCC–Iranian relations improved tremendously during most of 1991 and 1992 (Bahgat 1995: 59). This shows just how important leaders' perception of systemic pressures is when it comes to understanding Gulf actors' policies.

Within the GCC, Qatar and the UAE have the most analogous domestic environments and state structure in addition to similar regional incentives. Both became independent in 1971, have a highly concentrated decision-making structure, and small territory and population. More importantly, they are the only 'national-minority states' – 'countries where nationals (citizens holding nationality) are a minority among the population' (Horinuki 2011: 41) – in the world, with Kuwait, where this factor ought to be less salient since nationals represent some 30 per cent of the population, while they account for possibly less than 10 per cent in Qatar and the UAE.[7]

When it comes to their security, the most salient determinant of Qatar and the UAE is their lack of human resources, which qualifies them as 'micro-states' – in that they reach 'a threshold below which a state may not be able to function as fully or efficiently as normal sized states' (Peterson 2006: 735) – in this area. In the face of the entanglements between this domestic weakness and the security incentives of their regional environment, leaders of both countries articulated the peculiar strategy previously mentioned. The implementation of this strategy was rendered possible by the use of their one true power, economic power, and led to the interrelation of their foreign and security policies to such a point that they can be considered as 'merged'.

Their military procurement has for example long been considered as a political act towards their allies and protectors more than an actual way to increase their capabilities of self-defence (Samaan 2013: 53). Hence, arms purchases serve as an instrument of foreign policy, providing more security but only indirectly, through the protection guarantee it buys from strategic partners. It has been argued that 'defense manufacturers were able to sell virtually what they wanted in the Gulf region, often taking advantage of, and profiting from, their clients' lack of knowledge' (Hasbani 2006: 81). But one could suggest that their clients' *indifference* be a better explanation than 'lack of knowledge' since procurement met their 'foreign policy mission'.

Defensive realism, which sees foreign policy activity as the record of rational states reacting properly to clear systemic incentives, could also be deemed a good theoretical framework with which to analyse Qatari and Emirati policies. However, defensive realism is misguided because 'its emphasis on countries' responses to threats overlooks the fact that one's perceptions of threat are partly shaped by one's relative material power' (Rose 1998: 150). While Qatar and the UAE could have decided to put their security in the hands of the US only, thus acknowledging their impossibility to develop efficient defence capabilities, they did not do that. Not only did they choose to foster relative autonomy from the US by allying with other powers, but they also decided to develop capabilities of their own. Moreover, the articulation of their strategy had everything to do with their economic power. Relative material power and leaders' perception of the status they could accordingly claim on the international stage being at the heart of their behaviour, neoclassical realism appears to be the most relevant theoretical framework to use.

Exploring two small Gulf Prince-States' contrasted strategies

Beyond their seemingly similar security policies, there are contrasts between Qatar's and the UAE's behaviours. Their differences lie in a choice between favouring the development of their *hard-power* or *soft-power* capabilities. Abu Dhabi's preference was for the former, while Doha opted for the latter. Their survival strategies relied on the different priorities of their leaders: while the Emiratis defended an idea of *credibility* with a focus on state-building, turned towards the domestic front, the Qataris defended an idea of *legitimacy* with a focus on state-branding, turned towards the international front. One should also note that their policies eventually combine all aspects (hard power–soft power, credibility–legitimacy, state-building–state-branding). Hence, the UAE and Qatar ultimately end up in some sort of competition in different areas. For the UAE, the 1990s marked the beginning of the modernization of their armed forces. The Emirati defence apparatus significantly improved in terms of technology and overall quality through the introduction of sophisticated weapon systems and military equipment. Moreover, a special effort was undertaken in terms of agency and training of the armed forces. Finally, the UAE elaborated a military policy similar to what can be labelled 'armed neutrality', relying on a 'two-tier military doctrine composed of dissuasion and territorial defence' (Rickli 2008: 310–12). UAE leaders mainly organized their security policy around the idea of *credibility*. Their will to be regarded as credible players within the international order is reflected in their participation in peacekeeping operations, which enhances their prestige and '[increases] the political cost of violating their neutrality, which in turn [strengthens] their own security' (Sundelius 1989: 110). This dynamic of *credibility* was confirmed in the late 2000s with the attempted development of a local defence industry. Thus, the UAE implemented a strategic culture[8] based on a priority given to (relative) autonomy and a defensive strategy.

Qatar's strategic culture seems to have been based on a priority given to influence and a cooperative strategy. For its national security, Qatar has relied on the US through the aforementioned multi-level band-wagoning approach. This dynamic was reinforced in the 2000s. One important event in this regard was the American transfer from the Prince Sultan Air Base in Saudi Arabia to al-Udeid, in Qatar. Contrary to the UAE, which still developed hard-power capabilities of their own, Qatari leaders seem to have decided that deterrence provided by the US and too strong a dependence on the US being balanced through a strategic partnership with France were enough. Hence, they did not develop their armed forces much, nor did they articulate a military policy beyond this. Instead, their survival strategy was articulated on distinctive soft-power capabilities, which contribute to maintaining security in two ways. 'First, by fostering an attractive brand to draw attention and investment whilst contributing to Qatar's deterrence. Second, through creating a web of international allies to enhance security through "safety in numbers"' (Roberts 2009: 246). Much of the country's foreign policy in fact appears to be part of its survival strategy 'aimed at ensuring the security of the ruling Al Thanis' (Kamrava 2011: 556). While the UAE put an emphasis on credibility, which can be formulated as security through hard-power dissuasion, Qatar seems to have aimed at *legitimacy*, visibility (state-branding) on the international stage and security through a logic of 'being friends with everyone'.

Given how similar external and internal incentives are in the UAE and Qatar, how can one explain these dissimilarities in their strategies? First, while both countries fit the description of 'small states', one can note that Qatar has a micro territory and population compared with those of the UAE,[9] which could be one reason why the former did not try to develop domestic deterrence capabilities in addition to the protection offered by the US, whereas the latter did. Another difference between their 'unit-levels' is that while Qatar is formed of a homogeneous territory and population, the UAE is formed of seven emirates, each of which has its given history, territory and population. Hence, developing the armed forces was part of a larger goal: the centralization of power. 'The main objective of this rationalization [came] from the state's necessity to assert its authority on all [its] territory and populations. Thus, the armed forces [aimed] at state-building' (Gervais 2011: 109). Lastly, their differences in strategies were linked to their *leaders'* perception of their entangled external and domestic environment, and to their interests. Regarding the UAE, Victor Gervais explains how state-building strategies evolved in the 1990s, as rules of the political game and actors at the head of state were renewed. Thus, Sheikh Zayed put sovereign functions of the state linked to external and internal security in the hands of the '*Bani Fatima*',[10] which put them at the forefront of their efforts to strengthen the role of Abu Dhabi in the federal system of the UAE and its position in the regional game. At the top of the military institution, Sheikh Mohammed bin Zayed tried to use the modernization of the armed forces to his advantage against his older step-brother, Sheikh Khalifa bin Zayed. 'These motivations contributed in putting the armed forces at the center of state-building strategies deployed in Abu Dhabi by certain members of the ruling family who used them as a springboard for their private ambitions' (Gervais 2011: 110–11).

In addition to this, we would like to offer a story accounting for personal-level theorizing of the UAE's chosen strategy. The backdrop of it is 'unconfirmed reports from the UAE and Oman published by *The Times* on December 5, 1977 [claiming] that troops from both countries had moved to the disputed area' (Al-Sayegh 2002: 132) between Oman and the Ras-al-Khaimah emirate. Faced with the threat coming from the Sultanate, Sheikh Zayed allegedly decided not to give way to conflict escalation, declared that no Emirati blood shall be spilled on his watch and that the Sultan may take the territory he wanted – which eventually led to the Sultan drawing back his troops. The story goes that young Mohammed bin Zayed was infuriated with his father's decision and would have liked to actually confront Omani troops. This frustration in youth is often reported as one of the personal reasons for him to have developed a firm military policy focused on territorial defence.[11]

When it comes to explaining Qatar's survival strategy focused on the development of soft-power capabilities, analyses are not short of 'lovely stories' accounting for personal-level theorizing either. It is indeed often argued that it is linked to international–domestic entanglements as perceived by the decision-makers of the country, namely the Emir Hamad bin Khalifa – with the help of his Prime Minister, Hamad bin Jassem, from 1995 onwards. As the story goes, Hamad bin Khalifa's will to 'put Qatar on the map' also finds root in a youth's frustration: the first time he travelled to the UK, an airport employee would have looked at his passport with surprise and declared he had never heard of a country called 'Qatar' . . . . Years later, thanks to state-branding, there is barely anyone in the world who has not heard of the tiny Qatari peninsula. This was acknowledged by the new Emir since 2013, Tamim bin Hamad, who praised his father for having transformed Qatar 'from a state that *some people could barely locate on a map* into a major player in politics, economy, media, culture, and sport worldwide' (Al-Thani 2013).

By assessing how crucial the domestic level of analysis as well as the personal dimensions are in understanding Qatari and Emirati policies, this section not only tried to anchor their study in neoclassical realism, but paved the way to a new concept in IR and CP: the 'Prince State', which echoes the idea that, in these two countries, 'individuals have not just replaced institutions. They have become institutions. If Louis XIV were alive today, he would have felt at home in Qatari [and Emirati] politics' (Kamrava 2013: 104).

In fact, an overview of the entangled foreign and security policies of Qatar and the UAE would not be complete without a quick word on the competition that plays between them – an issue which easily relates to ego-centred – hence, personal – dynamics. This is linked to the fact that their policies combine all the aforementioned aspects (hard power–soft power, credibility–legitimacy, state-building–state-branding).

Although Qatar put an emphasis on soft power, it did purchase high-technology military equipment throughout the years, along what has been labelled as the 'glitter factor competition';[12] and although the UAE put an emphasis on hard power, it did engage in a state-branding competition with other small Gulf states. The competition arising between the two small Prince States can be understood in sociological terms, and be related to the Freudian concept of the 'narcissism of small differences', that is 'the phenomenon that it is precisely communities with adjoining territories, and related to each other in other ways as well, who are engaged in constant feuds and in ridiculing each other' (Freud 1961: 61). Although there are contrasts in the strategies developed by Qatar and the UAE, it can thus be said that their goal in the end remains to keep the world interested in them in order to survive.

New ins and outs associated with the Arab Spring and its consequences

The Arab Spring opened a new chapter in the history of the MENA region. The revolts in Egypt, Libya and Syria led to a temporary vacuum of power. Added to the weakness of Iraq since the downfall of Saddam Hussein as a result of the Anglo-American invasion in 2003, not only did this somehow transform the Gulf as the 'centre of gravity' of the Arab world, but it also intensified the competition among its members to take the leadership within this new geostrategic environment. This phenomenon is also linked to their having enhanced their international status by rescuing Western struggling economies through their sovereign wealth funds, in light of the 2008 financial crisis.

Not least of the fuelled antagonisms associated with the reshaping of the region, the rivalry between Iran and Saudi Arabia has led commentators to talk about a 'regional Cold War' undertaken through proxies, particularly in Syria. Amidst the regional disorder and the apparent radicalization of the Gulf region's 'immature anarchy', it is important to examine the chosen strategies of Qatar and the UAE to test previous hypotheses on the logics of their policies. Running through the new ins and outs of their strategies, this section questions whether and how their traditional logics evolved. We first examine the external security incentives associated with the reshaping of the regional context and assess how the policies undertaken by Qatar and the UAE can be seen as a rupture. Pointing to the different perception and interests of their decision-makers facing the regional events, and linking the discussion to previous findings on domestic- and personal-level theorizing, we then argue that there might be a lot more continuity than meets the eye in the Qatari and Emirati choices. Specifically, we analyse two case studies: their involvement in

Libya and Egypt. The emergence of a new regional security order is measured in a last section which focuses on the impact of these two small Prince-States' policies on the regional and sub-regional dynamics over the past five years.

Reshaping of the regional security context

A rupture in Qatari and Emirati strategies?

There is a double dimension in the GCC states' security concerns: their regimes try to maintain national security against conventional or asymmetric regional threats and to preserve their domestic monarchical stability and legitimacy against transnational ideological challenges (Soubrier 2014a: 67). The events of the Arab Spring had an impact on both aspects: their national security could be endangered by the regional disorder, which fuelled the development of armed groups and terrorism, and their regimes' stability was particularly shaken when the wave of popular uprisings hit the shores of Bahrain and, to a lesser extent, Oman. Finally, at the crossroads of these two dimensions lies Iran: leaders of the Arabian Peninsula feared that the regional turmoil presented Teheran with the opportunity to destabilize them internally and to adopt a more offensive stance towards them. The oil monarchs' fears were also heightened by the fact that the security dynamics of the region, particularly the 'oil for security' paradigm ensuring that the US remain the chief security guarantor of the Gulf, are possibly changing. American announcements of a shift in focus towards the Asia-Pacific region and of efforts to become as independent as possible from foreign sources of energy supply make GCC leaders wonder whether the US will give the same strategic priority to the Gulf region in the future – and the recent US–Iran rapprochement did nothing to soothe their concerns.

The 'regrouping' of the Gulf monarchies within the GCC against too-immediate security challenges and too-dramatic changes, as well as the reassertion of Saudi leadership within it, have been regarded as some of the key changes brought by recent events to the GCC's collective foreign policy (Kamrava 2012: 98; Soubrier 2014b: 6). It is important to examine the specific strategies of Qatar and the UAE against this background. Going back to the Bahraini uprising, while both of them, as members of the GCC, officially supported the military intervention in the tiny kingdom on 14 March 2011 under the clout of the 'Peninsula Shield', the UAE alone sent troops alongside the Saudis to put an end to the popular movement. This example serves as a starting point to assess the *rupture* commentators identified in Qatari and Emirati policies.

With regard to the UAE, it has been observed that their military policy prior to 2011 resembled one of 'armed neutrality' which, by definition, implied no projection of forces except for the occasional peacekeeping operations. However, in the face of the regional turmoil, the Emirati strategy seems to have shifted to an actual projection of hard-power capabilities along specific interests which no longer reflect neutrality. Illustrations of this are to be found in Bahrain, which qualifies as a 'law enforcement' operation rather than peacekeeping, in Libya, and more recently in Yemen. One can also argue that a shift in Emirati rules of engagement within the MENA region be reflected in their proactive use of economic diplomacy in Egypt, where the federation proved non-neutral. While the UAE, following the fall of Mubarak, had announced, in October 2011, that it would provide $3 billion to Egypt in the form of loans, deposits and grants, it then did not take any real step to fulfil this promise, leading some to talk about 'empty promises'. As it happened, this had much to do with the Muslim Brotherhood being in power at that time. A certain economic activism of the Emiratis – and the Saudis – towards Egypt is to be noted since the return of the army to power: in addition to a $1 billion grant to Egypt and a $2 billion loan in the form of an interest-free deposit with the Egyptian Central Bank in July 2013, the UAE announced an extra $3.9 billion in aid to this country in October 2013 (Soubrier 2014c).

As for Qatar, the evolution of its foreign and security policies in light of the Arab Spring was allegedly even more striking. As has been observed, these relied chiefly on soft power with a focus on neutrality through mediation. However, when the Arab uprisings started to occur throughout the MENA region, Qatar took cause for one party, that is the forces of change within the countries where the political order was confronted or overthrown, which 'involved a drastic shift away from its previous focus on diplomatic mediation in favour of actual intervention and picking sides in regional conflicts' (Ulrichsen 2012: 12). This translated in the coverage Al Jazeera's English and Arabic channels offered of the Arab uprisings. In addition, Qatar also deployed hard-power capabilities to back its support of Arab uprisings. Similar to the UAE, this translated in two ways: projection of forces in Libya and a more proactive *riyal politik* – that is, the use of oil money as a foreign policy tool. This was the case in Tunisia, Libya and Egypt. For instance, a Qatari bank deposit of $500 million was given to Tunisia and deals amounting to $8 billion were signed between Qatar and Libya after the fall of Gaddhafi (Ragab 2012: 16). As for Egypt, Qatari authorities offered $7 billion in aid to the country during the year Mohamed Morsi spent in power before being ousted in June 2013.

In both countries, the external security incentives seem to have provoked an evolution of their strategies. However, as was observed, Qatari and Emirati policies shall not be read in relation to systemic/structural determinants only, but rather in light of their regime's perception of international–domestic entanglements. Focusing our attention on this may lead us to argue that there is actually a lot more continuity than meets the eye in their strategic choices.

Perceptions, (mis)perceptions and the permanence of interests

Two case studies

The dissimilar approaches Qatar and the UAE developed in the new regional context associated with the Arab Spring are linked to the different interpretation their leaders had of various issues such as Iran, the rising of the Muslim Brotherhood or the relevance of band-wagoning with Saudi Arabia and the GCC collective survival strategy. The saliency of each of them in the eyes of the Qatari and Emirati regimes depends on the way they echo domestic incentives felt as security challenges and on the personal dynamic given to their policies.

In Libya, both Qatar and the UAE intervened alongside the Western coalition, which helped the rebels and eventually led to Muammar Gaddhafi's downfall (Rickli 2016a; Ulrichsen 2016). Two main reasons have been identified to explain Arab, and specifically Qatari and Emirati, involvement in Libya. First, the more international and local media focuses on Libya, the less it focuses on other simmering conflicts around the region,

> Moreover, at a time of ferment throughout much of the [MENA] region, it may be considered opportune and useful for leaders, wary for their own sake, to show that they are aware of the prevailing mood and will 'combat injustice' when they see it.
>
> *(Roberts 2011)*

The decision of Doha and Abu Dhabi to lead the Arab response to Libya also echoed the will of their leaders to boost their international status and to show that their countries could truly be counted on within the reshaping of the MENA region. However, it seems that the motivations of Qatar and the UAE slightly differed from one another.

It can be assumed that the Emirati participation in air operations was easier to understand than that of Qatar given the previous development of their hard-power capabilities and their possible will to move further with the build-up of a trained and effective, *credible* military might. In this sense, the involvement of the UAE in Libya, sometimes deemed a shift away from its traditional – and neutral – foreign policy, could in fact be read as the logical continuity of the regime's chosen survival strategy relying on *credibility* and focused on state-building exercise. It is also necessary to underline the weight of legitimacy concerns in the Emirati leadership's decision to send forces to Libya. Indeed, the UAE did not prove entirely immune to the winds of change blowing throughout the MENA region and its leaders faced opposition at home, a 'youth and intellectual-led activism in the UAE inspired by the Arab uprisings of 2011' adding up to 'political Islamist movements linked to the Muslim Brotherhood – particularly a UAE affiliate of the Brotherhood called Islah (Reform)' (Katzman 2013: 3; 6). Hence, it can be said that UAE activism, notably in Libya, aimed at securing legitimacy within the country itself.

While it appears that *credibility* remains a driving factor of Emirati policies, one can, however, point to a shift in priorities, from territorial defence to internal security. Some argue today that the UAE moved from a strategy relying on *regime security* to a main concern for *state security*. Considering our latest remarks, such an argument may seem somewhat doubtful. The UAE prompt reaction to the Bahraini uprisings along Saudi Arabia points to similar concerns towards a possibly contagious crisis of legitimacy within the Gulf. Interestingly enough, Abu Dhabi leaders precisely linked their intervention in Libya to the Bahraini issue. Indeed, the Emiratis promptly threatened to withdraw from the coalition being assembled to support a NATO-led strike against Gaddhafi 'and quickly named their price for staying on board: Mrs. Clinton must issue a statement that pulled back from any criticism of the Bahrain operation' (Cooper and Worth 2012). A similar argument can be made for Abu Dhabi's intervention in Yemen to stop the Houthis' influence and to send a strong signal to Teheran.

As for Qatar, participating in the Libyan intervention may have appeared surprising in light of its quasi-sole development of soft-power capabilities until then and the fact that this represented a shift away from traditional neutrality and mediation. However, if one considers that the most salient determinant of the Qatari leadership has always been to acquire as much visibility as possible on the international stage and to distinguish itself from Saudi Arabia, engaging in an active support for forces of change throughout the MENA region can be regarded as an illustration of a continuity of interests merely adapting to the evolution of context. One should also stress the fact that the Qatari leaders could 'afford' to adopt such a stance because they were much freer from any domestic incentives than the UAE, which allowed them to conduct such policies without fearing that it compromise their domestic stability. While every country has dissenters,

> the majority of Qataris seem pleased that their little country, previously known for little more than being unknown, is today known around the wider region and world for mostly positive reasons. (. . .) The Qatari elite, therefore, has an almost entirely free hand when it comes to foreign affairs.
> *(Roberts 2013: 10)*

Finally, it can be noted that while Qatar did shift away from diplomatic neutrality, there was consistency in its attitude towards the events of the Arab Spring, as it not only fought for the rebels in Libya but also supported change in Egypt, which was not the case of the UAE.

In Egypt, Qatar and the UAE undertook a particularly proactive economic diplomacy which somewhat marked a rupture from previous policies. This time, they did not, however, fight the same battle. This had to do with the difference of interests and domestic security incentives associated (or not) with post-Mubarak Egypt, particularly the rise of the Muslim Brotherhood. While concerns that the Egyptian Brotherhood could 'export the revolution' to them were allegedly the highest in the UAE, which 'deals with the Muslim Brotherhood as an advocacy group, *Da'weia*, and refuses to allow it to practice any political activity' (Ragab 2012: 15), there were none in Qatar. 'Given that Qatar does not see the Muslim Brotherhood as a threat, it has broadened its support to them as a channel through which Qatar can control the path of change in these countries' (Ragab 2012: 16). However, the active support from Doha to the Brotherhood has been repeatedly presented as a risky move. First, because, much like in Tunisia and Libya, the Egyptian public was not particularly keen on what was viewed as 'Qatari intervention'.[13]

Second, because such an open support to the Brotherhood antagonized other GCC states – antagonisms which reached a new level in March 2014, when Saudi Arabia, the UAE and Bahrain pulled their ambassadors from Qatar over this issue: 'The other Gulf states see Qatar as this extremely rich child that has got all this money and all these big toys and wants to play but doesn't know how to do it'.[14]

If anything, this possibly 'adventurous' foreign policy of Doha appears to validate the theoretical assumption that 'small states may engage in risky foreign-policy behaviour because of their inability to monitor developing international situations as thoroughly as larger states' (East 1973: 558–60). However, the policies chosen by the Qataris were consistent with at least two traditional dynamics of their survival strategy: trying to step out of the shadow of its Saudi neighbour, and seeking alliances with powerful entities to counter basic security concerns. Hence, supporting the Brotherhood in Egypt may have been a calculated risk rather than a hazardous policy. And while observers reading regional events through the prism 'Saudi Arabia vs. Qatar' may be tempted to say that the latter lost its 'advantage' in Egypt, it also appears that Qatar has not voiced its last say in terms of supporting Islamist groups – and trying to capitalize on it to continue playing with 'the big guys on the block'.[15]

The UAE, on the other hand, views the Brotherhood as such a security challenge that the chief of the Dubai Police, Lieutenant-General Dhahi Khalfan, declared at a conference held in Bahrain in January 2012 that this threat to Gulf security 'is equivalent in importance to the Iranian threat' (Ragab 2012: 14). Interestingly, this threat perception appears to have suspended the antagonisms and competition that traditionally defined Emirati relations to Saudi Arabia. Certainly, both countries have conducted rather aligned policies for a while. It leads one to wonder whether UAE leaders might have decided that band-wagoning with the kingdom could be a suitable solution after all, regardless of previous history.

In addition to Dhahi Khalfan's declarations, Sheikh Abdullah bin Zayed, the UAE Foreign Minister, criticized the Muslim Brotherhood for not respecting national boundaries and accused them of plotting to 'undermine states' sovereignty', calling upon all the GCC to cooperate to confront this threat (*Gulf Times* 2012). This may stand as a sign that the UAE, faced with too-critical a security challenge – at least in the eyes of its leaders – might decide to go for the Saudi project of a Gulf Union. In many ways, the foreign and security policies that Qatar and the UAE adopted after the Arab Spring account for the fact that domestic- and personal-level theorizing is at least as important as a relevant interpretation of implications of the evolving systemic/structural factors in the attempt to understand where Qatari and Emirati policies come from and where they might head next. However, it is just as crucial to understand how much of an impact these policies have, in turn, on regional and sub-regional dynamics.

Assessing the possible emergence of a new regional security order

The reshaping of the MENA region led Qatar and the UAE to rethink their rules of engagement within it. This evolving context offers new depth with which to capture the logics of these two small Gulf states, which is very useful to recalibrate theoretical frameworks mobilized in scholarly analyses. More importantly, it allowed the emergence of a new matrix of regional roles within which Qatar and the UAE play an enhanced part. This is why it is more important than ever to try and anticipate future developments of Qatari and Emirati policies. However, doing so is rendered difficult by the eminently personalized nature of these policies.

This section discusses how the state- or rather regime-centric strategies of Qatar and the UAE and their new avatars after the Arab Spring might paradoxically fuel security challenges rather than soothe them. Then, we question the feasibility and viability of a more integrated GCC entity in this light. 'The continuing relevance of state-centric approaches as the dominant frame of reference in the GCC states [leads to] myriad cross-cutting obstacles to regional and global governance' (Baabood 2005: 148).[16] It is important to assess whether and how the reshaping of the security environment affected this reality.

The newly proactive policy of the Gulf states within the MENA region in the face of the Arab Spring may have a destabilizing effect through two dynamics. A first risk factor lies in the divergence of interests that these countries so actively defend. And while they are rather aligned when it comes to preventing Iran to expand its influence and power in the region, a second risk factor lies in the rhetoric and action they deploy in this regard. In the case of Qatar and the UAE, their policies which can be considered as having fuelled security challenges were always very much linked to Saudi Arabia, in one way or another. When it comes to the aforementioned divergence of interests, the competition between Qatar and Saudi Arabia has become an important risk factor for the broader region. As for countering a perceived 'comeback' of Iran on the regional stage representing a certain risk factor for the stability of the region, a telling example can be seen in the Emirati intervention in Bahrain alongside the Saudis.

Starting with Qatar, its competition with Saudi Arabia and the negative effects it had were particularly visible in Egypt, but also in Syria, where the two GCC neighbours both supported forces against Bashar al-Assad, but not the same groups. Sadly, the phenomenon whereby the battle of interests in which international powers engage through proxy groups on an outside field generally ends up in a deteriorated situation which local populations are the first to suffer from is all too well-known. ... Not only did the avatars of this Qatari–Saudi competition add tensions to the regional turmoil, but they created new domestic threats at the national level by magnifying internal GCC divisions, as was made clear in March 2014. All in all, one can see how much the divergence of interests among the Gulf states today, in a context where their actions have actual consequences on the reshaping of their geostrategic environment, has the potential to create new security challenges for everyone.

The same can be said of Gulf leaders' hard-line rhetoric against Iran and of their actions to counter an alleged and demonized 'Iranian invisible hand' in events they perceive as challenges for their legitimacy and stability. One example of this is to be found in the Bahrain operation conducted by Saudi Arabia and the UAE under the banner of the GCC: 'Saudi and GCC intervention in Bahrain [is] almost certain to create added tension between KSA's dominant Sunni puritans and its Shi'ites' (Cordesman 2011: 15). This is all the more true as the operation was precisely justified in the Saudi discourse by the assumption that Iran was using the Shia community there to revive its regional hegemony by destabilizing the 'weakest link' of the GCC countries, which could lead to a domino effect onto the rest of the Arabian Peninsula. Using such rhetoric, Gulf states fuel – and possibly instrumentalize (Matthiesen 2013) – the sectarian divide between Sunni and Shia communities, which can be deemed one of the greatest dangers for the MENA region and international stability in the long run. A similar process can be observed in the Saudi-led intervention in Yemen. Since this benefits no one and paradoxically heightens the concerns of the small Gulf states themselves about their survivability, it seems important to assess the relevance and feasibility of a greater degree of integration within the GCC and an increased alignment in their foreign and security policies.

The fact that the GCC witnessed little progression from the time it was created in 1981 until the Iraqi invasion of Kuwait lends weight to the idea that the regional entity is kept together by the shared security challenges of its member states. The Arab Spring proved this trend: as it represented new security incentives, a 'regrouping' of GCC members was witnessed at first. However, the subsequent unfolding of events revived antagonisms and rivalries among them which had temporarily been soothed by the immediacy of the challenges perceived by the regimes of the Peninsula. With regards to the 'myriad cross-cutting obstacles to regional and global governance' (Baabood 2005: 148), it is interesting to note that the temporary suspension of antagonisms might have been explained by the fact that GCC leaders had a reflex of sticking together as authoritarian regimes, regardless of their rivalries. As discussed, the biggest threat brought about by the Arab uprisings in the Gulf was to regime stability rather than to state security. On this note, Qatar appears to be much more impermeable to a potential crisis of legitimacy than the UAE. This might be the reason why the UAE is still seemingly more dedicated to further integration within the GCC than Qatar is. The same can be said about Bahrain, for that matter.

Considering at least some rivalries linked to state-centric approaches emerged again recently, shall it be concluded that the GCC remains a first and foremost 'grand idea' with little empirical potential? It has been repeatedly argued that the GCC has the potential to become a far more effective security structure. But it does require the GCC countries to act upon it: 'There is no future in relying on deterrence and defense by declaration, conference, or *Diwaniya*' (Cordesman 2013: iii; Soubrier 2014b: 22). Beyond this, there is also a lack of unanimity on the idea that Saudi Arabia should take on the leadership mantle. 'Upstart Qatar and perhaps also the UAE are unlikely to be content to let Saudi Arabia take a GCC leadership role in regional affairs, especially once the dust of the Arab Spring is settled' (Kamrava 2012: 104).[17]

As long as the competition between the Gulf states remains, the establishment of a truly integrated GCC will be difficult. For now, a multiplication of bilateral agreements and 'special relations' with traditional allies is most likely to remain the chief survival strategy of the GCC individual leaders, particularly in the small states of Qatar and the UAE. It is, however, important to underline that many unresolved regional issues such as the Syrian crisis, the rise of the Islamic State of Iraq and Syria or the agreement on the Iran nuclear programme may accelerate, in the foreseeable future, shifts in their foreign and security policies.

Notes

1 'Structural considerations provide a useful point from which to begin the analysis of international politics rather than a place at which to end it. Even if one acknowledges that structures exist and are important, there is still the question of how statesmen grasp their contours from the inside, so to speak' (Friedberg 1988: 8).
2 'To understand [the] unusually convoluted RSC [of the Middle East], one has to see its full constellation as an interplay across the domestic, regional, and global levels' (Buzan and Waever 2003: 218).
3 'Some of the smaller GCC states have even identified Saudi Arabia as a threat because of its size and increasing assertiveness within the GCC' (Kostiner 2011: 116–17). 'The smaller Gulf states have now found a new patron and protector, the US, which allows them (if they want it) a bit of room to maneuver within the Saudi orbit' (Gause 2009: 7).
4 In 1992, 'the total values of the arms transfer agreements of Taiwan, Saudi Arabia, and Kuwait with the US were $6.4 billion, $4.2 billion and $1.1 billion, respectively. These agreements collectively constituted 86 per cent of all US arms transfer agreements with the Third World' (Grimmett 1993: 7).
5 Chronologically, their bilateral defence cooperation agreements were signed as follows: Qatar–France in 1994, UAE–France in 1995, UAE–UK in 1996, Qatar–UK in 2006.
6 'The GCC (. . .) is as much a means of reinforcing the domestic security of a set of anachronistic monarchical regimes as an alliance against external threats'(Buzan and Waever 2003: 197).
7 Interviews in Abu Dhabi and Doha between March 2013 and May 2014 – the most frequent estimations state that Emirati nationals account for 9.5 per cent and Qatari nationals for 7.5 per cent of the total population.
8 'A nation's tradition, values, attitudes, pattern of behaviour, habits, symbols, achievements and particular way of adapting to the environment and solving problems with respect to the threat and use of force' (Booth 1990: 121).
9 The Qatari peninsula is 11,571 km^2, while the territory of the UAE is 82,880 km^2. As for their population, in 2014, the Qatari nationals were believed to be around 250,000 while the Emirati nationals were believed to be around 1,000,000.
10 Name given to the group composed of the six sons Sheikh Zayed had with Fatima Bint Mubarak Al-Ketbi.
11 Interviews in Abu Dhabi and Muscat in 2013–14.
12 That is, the 'competition to buy the most advanced weapons system possible regardless of mission priority and the ability to operate and sustain an integrated mix of systems and forces in combat' (Cordesman 2013: 48).
13 For instance, a protest was organized in January 2012 by the General Coalition of Popular Committees against Doha's policies in the country, demanding the suspension of Qatar as a member in the Arab league.
14 M. Stephens, quoted in Kirkpatrick, 2014.
15 The development of events during the second part of 2014 calls analysts to reconsider this assumption. In a move that has sometimes been read as giving in to the pressures coming from other GCC countries, Qatar has asked several prominent Muslim Brotherhood leaders to leave the country. However, the author would still argue that this is too soon to determine whether this means that GCC unity prevails.

16 This chapter transformed this assumption to make it more 'regime-centric' than 'state-centric'.
17 The military operation led by Saudi Arabia in Yemen from March 2015 onwards tends to challenge this assumption, but it is still too soon to tell whether this trend is sustainable in the long run.

Bibliography

Abo-Alabbas, B. (2012) 'Empty Promises? Ahram Online Investigates Aid Pledges Made to Egypt Since Uprising', *Ahram Online*, 20 August. Retrieved from http://english.ahram.org.eg/NewsContent/3/12/50807/Business/Economy/Empty-promises-Ahram-Online-investigates-aid-pledg.aspx (accessed on 30 August 2016).
Al-Sayegh, F. (2002) 'The UAE and Oman: Opportunities and Challenges in the Twenty-First Century', *Middle East Policy*, 9 (3): 124–37.
Al-Thani, Sheikh Tamim bin Hamad (2013) 'First Speech of Qatar's Emir Sheikh Tamim bin Hamad Al-Thani' (in Arabic), 26 June. Retrieved from www.youtube.com/watch?v=rMsrQpi7D9g (accessed on 30 August 2016).
Archer, C., Bailes, A.J.K. and Wivel, A. (2014) *Small States and International Security: Europe and Beyond*, London: Routledge.
Baabood, A. (2005) 'Dynamics and Determinants of the GCC States' Foreign Policy, with Special Reference to the EU', in G. Nonneman (ed) *Analyzing Middle Eastern Foreign Policies*, London: Routledge, pp. 145–73.
Bahgat, G. (1995) 'Military Security and Political Stability in the Gulf', *Arab Studies Quarterly*, 17 (4): 55–70.
Booth, K. (1990) 'The Concept of Strategic Culture Affirmed' in C.G. Jacobsen (ed) *Strategic Power: USA/USSR*, New York: St Martin's Press, pp. 121–8.
Bueno de Mesquita, B. (2002) 'Domestic Politics and International Relations', *International Studies Quarterly*, 46 (1): 1–9.
Bueno de Mesquita, B. and Lalman, D. (1992) *War and Reason: Domestic and International Imperatives*, New Haven: Yale University Press.
Buzan, B. (1991) *People, States and Fears*, Boulder, CO: Lynne Rienner.
Buzan, B. and Waever, O. (2003) *Regions and Powers, The Structure of International Security*, Cambridge: Cambridge University Press.
Cooper, H. and Worth R.F. (2012) 'In Arab Spring, Obama Finds a Sharp Test', *The New York Times*, September 24.
Cordesman, A. (2011) *Saudi Stability in a Time of Change*, Washington: Center for Strategic and International Studies (CSIS).
Cordesman, A. (2013) *Securing the Gulf: Key Threats and Options for Enhanced Cooperation*, Washington: Center for Strategic and International Studies (CSIS).
East, M.A. (1973) 'Size and Foreign Policy Behavior: A Test of Two Models', *World Politics*, 25 (4): 558–560.
Elman, M.F. (1995) 'The Foreign Policies of Small States: Challenging Neorealism in Its Own Backyard', *British Journal of Political Science*, 25 (2): 171–217.
Fearon, J.D. (1998) 'Domestic Politics, Foreign Policy, and Theories of International Relations', *Annual Review of Political Science*, 1: 289–313.
Freud, S. (1961) *Civilization and its Discontents*, New York: W. W. Norton.
Friedberg, A.L. (1988) *The Weary Titan: Britain and the Experience of Relative Decline, 1895–1905*, Princeton: Princeton University Press.

Gause, G. III (2009) *The International Relations of the Persian Gulf*, Cambridge: Cambridge University Press.

Gervais, V. (2011) *Du pétrole à l'armée: les stratégies de construction de l'Etat aux Emirats arabes unis*, Paris: Institut de Recherche Stratégique de l'Ecole Militaire (IRSEM).

Goetschel, L. (1998) 'The Foreign and Security Policy Interests of Small States in Today's Europe', in L. Goetschel (ed) *Small States Inside and Outside the European Union*, Dordrecht: Kluwer Academic Publishers, pp. 13–31.

Grimmett, R.F. (1993) 'Conventional Arms Transfers to the Third World, 1985–1992', Washington: Congressional Research Service (CRS).

Gulf Times (2012, 9 October) 'UAE: Gulf States must Stop Plotters'.

Hasbani, N. (2006) 'The Geopolitics of Weapons Procurement in the Gulf States', *Defense & Security Analysis*, 22 (1): 73–88.

Horinuki, K. (2011) 'Controversies over Labour Naturalisation Policy and Its Dilemmas: 40 Years of Emiratisation in the United Arab Emirates', *Kyoto Bulletin of Islamic Area Studies*, 4 (1–2): 41–61.

Kamrava, M. (2011) 'Mediation and Qatari Foreign Policy', *Middle East Journal*, 65 (4): 539–56.

Kamrava, M. (2012) 'The Arab Spring and the Saudi-Led Counterrevolution', *Orbis*, 56 (1): 96–104.

Kamrava, M. (2013) *Qatar: Small State, Big Politics*, Ithaca, NY: Cornell University Press.

Katzenstein, P.J. (1976) 'International Relations and Domestic Structures: Foreign Economic Policies of Advanced Industrial States', *International Organization*, 30 (1): 1–45.

Katzman, K. (2013) 'The United Arab Emirates (UAE): Issues for U.S. Policy', Washington: CRS.

Kirkpatrick, D.D. (2014) '3 Gulf Countries Pull Ambassadors from Qatar over Its Support of Islamists', *The New York Times*, 5 March.

Kostiner, J. (2011) 'Perceptions of Collective Security in the Post-Saddam Era', in M. Kamrava (ed) *International Politics of the Persian Gulf*, Syracuse: Syracuse University Press, pp. 94–119.

Krasner, S.D. (1978) *Defending the National Interest: Raw Materials Investments and U.S. Foreign Policy*, Princeton, NJ: Princeton University Press.

Matthiesen, T. (2013) *Sectarian Gulf: Bahrain, Saudi Arabia, and the Arab Spring that Wasn't*, Stanford: Stanford University Press.

Miller, B. (1992) 'Explaining Great Power Cooperation in Conflict Management', *World Politics*, 45 (1): 1–46.

Mouritzen, H. (1997) *External Danger and Democracy: Old Nordic Lessons and New European Challenges*, Aldershot, UK: Ashgate.

Peterson, J.E. (2006) 'Qatar and the World: Branding for a Micro-State', *Middle East Journal*, 60 (4): 732–48.

Posen, B.R. (1984) *The Sources of Military Doctrine: France, Britain, and Germany Between the World Wars*, Ithaca, NY: Cornell University Press.

Putnam, R.D. (1988) 'Diplomacy and Domestic Politics: The Logic of Two-Level Game', *International Organization*, 42 (3): 427–60.

Ragab, E. (2012) 'A Formative Stage: Relations between GCC and North African Countries after the Arab Spring', in S. Colombo, K.C. Ulrichsen, S. Ghabra, S. Hamid and E. Ragab (eds) *The GCC in the Mediterranean in Light of the Arab Spring*, Washington: The German Marshall Fund (GMF), pp. 9–20.

Reiter, D. (1996) *Crucible of Beliefs: Learning, Alliances, and World Wars*, Cornell: Cornell University Press.

Rickli, J.-M. (2008) 'European Small States' Military Policies after the Cold War: From Territorial to Niche Strategies', *Cambridge Review of International Affairs*, 21 (3): 307–25.

Rickli, J.-M. (2016a) 'The Political Rationale and Implications of the United Arab Emirates' Military Involvement in Libya', in Dag Henriksen and Ann Karin Larssen (eds) *Political Rationale and International Consequences of the War in Libya*, Oxford: Oxford University Press, pp. 134–54.

Rickli, J.-M. (2016b) 'New Alliances Dynamics and Their Impact on Small GCC states', *Third World Thematic (Thematic issue of Third World Quarterly)*, 1 (1): 1–19.

Roberts, D. (2009) 'Qatar's Search for Security', *Proceedings of the Plymouth Postgraduate Symposium*. Plymouth, UK: Plymouth University.

Roberts, D. (2011) 'Arab Involvement in the Libyan Intervention', Commentary for RUSI.org (Royal United Services Institute), 23 March. Retrieved from https://rusi.org/commentary/arabo-involvement-libyan-intervention (accessed on 18 October 2016).

Roberts, D. (2013) 'Qatar: Domestic Quietism, Elite Adventurism', in F. Ayub (ed) *What Does the Gulf Think about the Arab Awakening?* London: European Council on Foreign Relations (ECFR), pp. 9–11.

Rose, G. (1998) 'Neoclassical Realism and Theories of Foreign Policy', *World Politics*, 51(1): 144–72.

Rosenau, J. (1969) 'Toward the Study of National–International Linkages', in J. Rosenau (ed) *Linkage Politics: Essays on the Convergence of National and International Systems*, New York: Free Press, pp. 44–63.

Salzman, P.C. (2008) 'The Middle East's Tribal DNA', *Middle East Quarterly*, 15 (1): 23–33.

Samaan, J.-L. (2013) 'Les Monarchies du Golfe: Un Marché d'Armement sans Armées?', *Moyen-Orient*, 17: 48–53.

Singer, J.D. (1961) 'The Level of Analysis Problem in International Relations', *World Politics*, 14 (1): 77–92.

Snyder, J. (1991) *Myths of Empire: Domestic Politics and International Ambitions*, Ithaca, NY: Cornell University Press.

Soubrier, E. (2014a) 'Sécurité des Monarchies du Golfe: De Nouvelles Règles du Jeu?', *Moyen-Orient*, 23: 66–71.

Soubrier, E. (2014b) *Regional Disorder and New Geo-economic Order: Saudi Security Strategies in a Reshaped Middle East*, Geneva: Gulf Research Center (GRC).

Soubrier, E. (2014c) 'La Diplomatie Économique des Pays du Golfe à l'Aune du Printemps Arabe: Du Rayonnement à la Puissance', in F. Charillon and A. Dieckhoff (eds) *Annuaire Afrique du Nord Moyen-Orient 2014–2015*, Paris: La Documentation Française, pp. 123–36.

Sundelius, B. (1989) 'National Security Dilemmas and Strategies for the European Neutrals', in M.H. Haltzel and J. Kruzel (eds) *Between the Blocs: Problems and Prospects for Europe's Neutral and Nonaligned States*, Cambridge, UK: Cambridge University Press, pp. 98–121.

Ulrichsen, K.C. (2012) 'Small States with a Big Role: Qatar and the United Arab Emirates in the Wake of the Arab Spring', Durham University, *HH Sheikh Nasser al Mohammad al Sabah Publication Series*, 3.

Ulrichsen, K.C. (2016) 'The Rationale and Implications of Qatar's Intervention in Libya,' in Dag Henriksen and Ann Karin Larssen (eds) *Political Rationale and International Consequences of the War in Libya*, Oxford: Oxford University Press, pp. 118–35.

Walt, S. (1985) 'Alliance Formation and the Balance of World Power', *International Security*, 9 (4): 3–43.

Waltz, K.N. (1959) *Man, the State and War: A Theoretical Analysis*, New York: Columbia University Press.

Waltz, K.N. (1979) *Theory of International Politics*, Reading, UK: Addison-Wesley.

9
RISK DIVERSIFICATION AND THE UNITED ARAB EMIRATES' FOREIGN POLICY

Leah Sherwood

Introduction

Geography makes the United Arab Emirates (UAE) a small state, but it also makes the UAE influential. The UAE leverages the power of economy and energy to exert power and employ risk-diversification strategies typically incompatible with small states. Yet, the classic small-state strategies of band-wagoning and alliance-forming are salient features of the UAE's foreign policy track record. The UAE does not always conform to typical small-state strategic behaviour, nor is it – as a case study – a perfect match with existing theory on small-state security strategy. Little is known about how the security strategies are chosen for small states such as the UAE that vacillate between proactive and defensive security postures, being powerful and weak simultaneously. But, it is known that the UAE adopts distinctive strategies in different areas, and analysing this general strategy through a small-state lens represents a new area of academic investigation.

One of the most enduring challenges for scholars of international relations has been the elusive definition of power. There is no consensus and this plagues small-states studies because analysis of a state behaviour is linked to the possession of power. The problem is 'not that the term has no meaning, but that it has too many meanings' (Claude, 1962, p.13). Arguably, the nature and location of power is shifting, but to what degree remains a subject of intense debate. Thus, classifying levels of power and capability can be problematic. The UAE illustrates the tension quite well as it is a wealthy, resource-rich nation capable of exerting power, but on balance its power is issue-specific. Ultimately, the UAE's foreign policy record shows that, despite evidence of power and capability, it is the weaker party within its asymmetrical relationships.

The aim of this chapter is not to attempt to contribute to the literature defining small states nor to develop another approach to studies of power. The objective is to identify what the UAE's strategies are and how are they chosen. The purpose is to argue that, from a relational standpoint on power, the UAE's possession of it or the reverse largely dictates its risk-diversification strategies and foreign policy. This article will assess the last decade of the UAE's risk-diversification strategies within the context of the effect of economic globalization in the Arabian Gulf, the political ramifications of the 'Arab Spring', the rise of Iranian influence, wars in Yemen, Libya, Syria, Iraq and Afghanistan, shifting US geostrategic priorities, and the ascension of China and India as new 'global players'. From a relational power perspective, the UAE's reaction to these events in foreign policy terms sheds light on its risk-diversification strategies and adds to the literature on small states' security strategies.

The first section briefly reviews the challenge of defining power and then moves onto power as it pertains to small states, suggesting it is better understood from a relative power perspective because it attributes influence and power in terms of capabilities *and* relationships. Its utility stems from its capacity to weigh the UAE's relative strengths and weaknesses separately, unlike analyses from traditional international relations theory. The next section provides a series of examples that demonstrate that the UAE possesses dimensions of power from a relational point of view and suggests this explains its foreign policy activism, or defensive foreign policy, which is aimed at diversifying its security risks. The UAE also adopts the proactive strategy of band-wagoning as a tactic to diversify threats. Thus, it either adopts defensive policies that provide autonomy or co-operative foreign policies centred upon alliance formation at the expense of its autonomy. At times, it hedges by using both strategies simultaneously. Flexibility, pragmatism and innovation are hallmarks of small states. Through an artful, nimble balancing of risk and opportunity, the UAE's leadership capitalizes on its strengths and mitigates its weaknesses.

Small states and the power problem

The debate on power focuses on whether it is generated from resources or relationships. Realists posit that the goal of any state is to maximize power relative to another or produce a 'balance of power' (Morgenthau, 1948, p. 167). They claim power is based on material resources such as the military, wealth and geography (Mattern, 2015). Small states were traditionally thought to be irrelevant (Maass, 2014) and today they still tend to be understood in relation to capabilities such as military spending, GDP and population, which relate to power possession. Waltz emphasized different capabilities, but integrated them into a single assessment, claiming 'economic, military, and other capabilities of nations cannot be sectored and separately weighed' (Waltz, 1979, p. 131). He asserted that states': 'rank depends on how they score on *all* of the following items: size of population and territory, resource endowment, economic capability, military strength, political stability' (p. 131). Despite these categories, neo-realists such as Walt assert small states are at best somewhat significant in power brokering and ultimately extraneous in absolute outcomes.

The assertion that small states cannot exert power is flawed from a relational perspective. They can exert types of power. The rigidity of traditional power constructs fail to explain the security strategies for states such as the UAE. A different conceptual tool is needed and it is postulated that analysing the UAE's security strategy though its foreign policy choices from a relational point of view is more pragmatic because it allows for the inclusion of different aspects of its 'power portfolio', which can be viewed separately. This relational perspective can explain both the risk-diversification strategies and the rationale for using them. A relational power shifts power analyses from 'power-as-resources' concepts (Lasswell and Kaplan, 1950) to power as 'a relationship (actual or potential) in which the behaviour of actor A influences the behavior of actor B' (Baldwin, 2013, p. 274).

The relational power perspective views power as multidimensional and allows one dimension of power to decrease while another increases, and this gives more room for 'scoring' power capabilities. Table 8.1 illustrates the dimensions of power.

Thorhallsson and Wivel claim that being a small state is linked to a 'spatio-temporal context' that defines the nature of its challenges and opportunities (2006, p. 654) and leave it 'struck with the . . . power configuration and its institutional expression' (Mouritzen and Wivel, 2005, p. 4). This can be conceptually linked to power defined in terms of scope, domain and means (Baldwin, 2013). Smallness is thus relational and power can be understood in the context of environment and relationships, which means that resource endowment, economic strengths, Islamic cultural identity, ethno-anthropological history and political stability are sources of power. Admittedly, the multidimensionality of power from a relational perspective makes it hard to add up power dimensions to arrive at a total power assessment. The same is true for pinning down the measurements for a balance of power. This is the power *problematique*. The UAE demonstrates capacity in various dimensions, but it is difficult to definitively declare what it adds up to in the end. It is clear, however, that the UAE is changing and diversifying risk in new ways.

TABLE 8.1 Power dimensions

Indicator	Analytical questions
Scope	Where is the power? E.g. Japan's is economic and North Korea's is military (Baldwin, 2013, p. 275).
Domain	How many are affected by the power? How big is B and how many Bs are there? E.g. Russia today vs the USSR (Dahl, 1957, p. 215).
Weight	How credible is the actualization of the 'threat'? E.g. Does state A have a 30 per cent or a 90 per cent chance of achieving its aim in negotiations?
Costs	How 'cheap' is it for state A to exert power? How easy is it? (Harsanyi, 1962).
Means	How many of the means of power (economic, symbolic, military and diplomatic) are available to the state? (Baldwin, 2002).

In the last decade, the UAE has simultaneously pursued seemingly contradictory security strategies. Based on power in the realms of *domain, weight, cost* and *economic means,* it has advanced more defensive security strategies and more independent foreign policies. This neutrality-based, defensive security strategy has included diversifying security partners, asserting regional influence, leveraging financial resources and contributing to the dispersal of old geo-economic and geo-political centres of power. This is all influencing its increased level of internationalization and reducing its dependency on the US. These neutrality-based strategies individually and collectively represent UAE manoeuvres to diversify risk. However, the UAE's political and security architecture is layered and complex, much like the Gulf region, which, based on its power calculation in terms of *scope* and military *means,* is why it has also continued to invest in co-operative, alliance-based security policies. So, while it diversifies risk in new ways, it is also maintains traditional, productive band-wagoning security policies. This strategy also includes a robust commitment to international organizations and regional alliances. The parallel pursuit of the two types of small-state security options is unusual, but interestingly reflects actions typical of them in that it represents a display of versatility, pragmatism and innovation.

UAE foreign policy from a relational power perspective

Historically, UAE foreign policy is aimed at the Gulf, the Arab world, the Muslim world and the world at large. As small states typically prefer the 'community method' of decision-making (Keating *et al.*, 2014) and 'buy in' power by joining alliances (Archer, 2013), the UAE consistently engages with various co-operative entities and was a founding member of the Gulf Cooperation Council (GCC). Beyond Arab partners, the UAE co-operates on the world at large with the United Nations, for example. Since 1991, the UAE has strengthened bilateral relationships with Western states – the US, UK and France in particular. In 2004, the UAE joined NATO's Istanbul Cooperation Initiative (ICI) as a partner (not member) (de Santis, 2004). Constructive engagement has always been key to the UAE's success in dealing with its biggest foreign policy challenges, which at different times means the UAE's leadership uses different tactics, ranging from compromises, direct negotiations and reasonable propositions to, above all, valuing the preservation of the regional balance of power (Al Mashat, 2010, p. 458). This pragmatic response to security dilemmas may also be viewed as co-operative security. It is a small-state strategic choice that mirrors what is termed a 'proactive posture', which involves utilizing different co-operative schemes such as international partnerships, organizational affiliation and regional activism to seek both fundamental protection and expanded influence (Rickli, 2008). Therefore, foreign policy decisions in the UAE necessarily revolve around a 'smart policy': a mix of hard and soft powers based on an objective analysis of a situation and its prevalent circumstances (Al-Suwaidi, 2011). In small-state studies, this is considered typical behaviour because it is an indigenous strategy designed to cope with vulnerability and a limited ability to exert influence (Prasad, 2009, p. 43).

UAE foreign policy from 2004 to 2016 illustrates what the UAE considers to be risks and its strategies to mitigate them. That decade also locates the UAE's national nodes of power to diversify risks and reveals how and when they are leveraged. UAE security and foreign policies are either as a reaction to a perception (or reality) of external circumstances or an opportunistic act to gain influence, power and prestige while reducing risk levels and/or shifting the risk types to gain strategic ground. The discussion below shows that the UAE intermittently or simultaneously adopts different strategies to meet different ends. The security strategies are either co-operative or defensive. UAE–Iranian relations will be used as a case study to illustrate this two-pronged and seemingly contradictory approach to its security and foreign policy. The UAE's relationship with Iran illustrates the UAE's modern constructive engagement policies simultaneously using defensive and proactive security policies. Dubai, host to the globe's biggest Iranian diaspora community (Sadjadpour, 2011), is a fertile source of intelligence on Iran. In the context of US–UAE relations, the UAE capitalizes on Dubai's informational assets, allowing the US to use it as a 'staging ground to observe and interpret Iran's internal political and popular dynamics' (Sadjadpour, 2011, p. 4). Some scholars argue that a small state's foreign policy may include compensatory informational assets disproportionate to their physical size (Lemass, 1971), and it can be a leveller between great and small powers. It is an intriguing capability associated with the *means* dimension of power. The UAE leverages intelligence to gain political power: money and diplomatic influence. For instance, sanctions prevent big international airlines from direct flights into Iran and the Emirates airline flies roughly 200 flights per week. Further, Dubai's lightly regulated ports support significant Iranian trade despite US pressure and UN sanctions. UAE–Iran trade ties have grown steadily over the last decade and bilateral trade was officially worth over USD8.5 billion in 2010, although unofficial estimates are much higher (Yousef, 2011). In the same year, the UAE imported or re-exported over USD9 billion worth of goods to Iran (Sadjadpour, 2011). The *Khaleej Times* reports that in 2014 the UAE, Iran's fourth-largest trading partner, recorded a rise in trade exchange with Iran to USD17 billion, but this remains lower than the record USD23 billion recorded in 2011 before sanctions had a noticeable effect. Most of the above trade comes from Dubai, where a 400,000-strong Iranian community operates a business network (John, 2015).

In 2011, it was reported in Abu Dhabi's *The National*, that much of Iranian–Chinese bilateral commercial and energy trade – estimated at $15 billion – was conducted through the UAE (Kane, 2011). Dubai is Tehran's main connection to the global economy. Small states also commonly use economic strategies to advance their causes (Baldacchino, 2006) and the UAE–Iran relationship heavily weighs in the UAE's favour (Briguglio *et al*., 2006, p. 20). UAE risk diversification on Iran is innovative and contributes to its autonomy.

Beyond capitalizing on opportunity, Abu Dhabi is responding to Iran by fortifying its strategic alliance with the US (and exercising restraint over Dubai to preserve internal stability). Its concerns have made it one of the US, biggest export markets for sophisticated and expensive weaponry. Its consistent investment ensures the US security umbrella remains intact and the UAE has state-of-the art technology. In 2013, Abu Dhabi was forecasted to spend 'up to $12.9 billion per year on defence over the next three years, compared with $9.3 billion in 2011', (David Reeths, quoted in Reuters, 2013). Although mutually beneficial, the level of defence spending in US industry represents asymmetric power in the US–UAE relationship. For the US, the UAE has become an important source of political support for its policies in the Middle East. This is coupled with the value of UAE military bases to US operations.

What makes the UAE–US–Iran example so fascinating is the complexity and display of innovation. The UAE has deep commercial, historical and social networks with Iran (Dubai) and simultaneously maintains a close strategic relationship with Washington (Abu Dhabi). This mix of economic and political policies is an example of an indigenous strategy often employed by small states (Prasad, 2003; 2004), which are well-known innovators because they have different modes of agency available to them (Cooper and Shaw, 2009: 5). The UAE is the primary benefactor in the US–UAE–Iran nexus in terms of gains in economy and security. This clever engineering illustrates UAE pragmatism. The UAE's two-pronged, 'smart policy' approach is constructive and ultimately reduces risks facing it by leveraging the *scope* and diplomatic *means* of its power to compensate for its weakness in military *means*. This example illustrates that small states such as the UAE are capable of pushing the boundaries on what their security strategy can look like for small states and where influence can be sourced.

The last decade of the UAE's foreign policy illustrates that its posture is transforming while the region is at the same time destabilizing. In response to the political events of the Arab Spring, the UAE (and other Gulf states) developed regional policies that shed light on what risk-diversification strategies look like in practice. In the face of regional revolutions, one risk-diversification strategy used by the UAE was to provide massive financial (and political) support to internally stabilize the monarchical regimes in Bahrain, Oman, Jordan and Morocco (Friedman, 2012) demonstrating power in the realms of *domain, cost* and *weight*. This mixture of economic and political approaches can be conceptually anchored to a small-state strategy to cope with vulnerability by 'buying' stability (Prasad, 2009, p. 43). The UAE leadership has referred to this adaptive approach as a 'smart policy' as mentioned earlier and it attempted to use it in Libya, Yemen, Syria and Egypt.

Egypt highlights what the UAE considers its strategic interests to be and shows how power in *scope, cost, weight* and economic *means* can influence the direction of change. This demonstrates a level of power not commonly attributed to small states. To illustrate this point, the UAE held up aid to Egypt when the Muslim Brotherhood's Mohamed Morsi came to power (*Buenos Aires Herald*, 2013a; El Dahan, 2013), and when he was removed '[it] offered a USD 1 billion grant and a USD 2 billion no-interest loan to Egypt' (*Buenos Aires Herald*, 2013b). The UAE joined Saudi Arabia to curb Salafi jihadism and ensure the Muslim Brotherhood's regional influence fades (Watanabe, 2014). The UAE's effort to influence outcomes by tying aid to political streams rather than outcomes such as good governance is also influencing wider change, perhaps marking a regional departure from the Western-centric normative foundations towards a multipolar power structure with different normative perspectives (Ulrichsen, 2013). Desire to weaken Iran's influence *vis-à-vis* the Muslim Brotherhood reveals the UAE's strategy to use economic power to diversify risk. This plan does not appear to include a direct US role; this evolution in practice is noteworthy. The UAE is more influential in Egypt than an ordinary small state, leveraging diplomatic, economic and symbolic *means* of power in terms of *scope, domain* and *weight*. This proactive security policy of band-wagoning with Saudi Arabia represents a new approach to an old policy.

The UAE also participated in joint Egyptian–Emirati air strikes against Islamist militias in Libya in August 2014 (Kingsley *et al.*, 2014) without the knowledge or consent of US officials (Chandrasekaran, 2014). The assertiveness can be attributed to the UAE's risk perception and serves as evidence that new alliances are forming, even if only due to the merging of a shared interest. Earlier, the UAE took on a leadership role within the GCC on Libya. It lobbied the Arab League to endorse an air campaign, coupled with a UN mandate, which led to NATO-backed military action. Militarily, the UAE and Qatar represented Gulf contributions. They deployed special operations forces on the ground and these forces helped to arm and train the rebels before they advanced into Tripoli (Larrabee, 2013, p. 5). They sent six F-16s and six Mirage fighters to participate in the NATO-led no-fly zone enforcement, supported ground target strike operations and also participated directly in the air strikes on Colonel Qadhafi's forces (unpublished conference paper by S. Larrabee, 2013). Beyond its military contributions, the UAE formally accepted the Benghazi-based Transitional National Council as the single representative of Libya and guaranteed financial backing to it. In March 2012, it transferred '58 aging Mirage 2000 combat aircraft to the fledgling post-Qadhafi government' (Katzman, 2013, p. 19). This type of political, military, diplomatic and economic engagement – from beginning to end – is unconventional for a small state. The UAE approach to Libya was initially more multilateral than the more recent bilateral effort. Regarding the former, the UAE recognized there was no Arab League equivalent to NATO and without (multilateral) action the Islamist security threat would grow to dangerous levels (Almezaini, 2011). Pragmatism seems to have guided the UAE's proactive risk-diversification strategy on Islamist insurgency. The UAE's behind-the-scenes bilateral effort in Libya without the US diplomatic 'stamp of approval' indeed marks a watershed moment.

The UAE supported the Al Khalifa regime in Bahrain, by sending '500 UAE police to join a 1,000 troop Saudi force to Bahrain' (Al Arabiya, 2011), and left its security personnel afterwards to provide additional support (*Khaleej Times*, 2014). The military intervention was the first strong unilateral action out of step with the US, which discouraged a military response (Sanger and Schmitt, 2011). It symbolically showed that the UAE was willing to diverge with the US on policy matters and this defensive policy was linked to a wider Gulf narrative framed by changing perceptions of the US. Yet, the need for a uniform response to Iran's multidimensional security threat motivates continued co-operation. This tension between the

UAE's proactive and defence foreign security policies is significant. The main trend, however, is towards more 'Gulf policy' and less band-wagoning, which highlights UAE perception that it needs to be responsible for more of its own security. This development extends to all the Gulf states, which agreed to ramp up efforts to form a joint GCC military command (not a unified military force) in Riyadh based on the NATO military structure model (Amos, 2014). A joint military command will 'help coordinate at the operational level the different forces of the GCC countries against military threats . . . [and] at the moment, we are witnessing a new spirit' (Vela, 2014). This initiative was then broadened to include a coalition of Arab states to counter terrorism under the impetus of Saudi Arabia in December 2015.

Although the UAE–US alliance remains central to the UAE's defence policy, it is changing. The UAE is developing its own policies as seen in Bahrain, Libya, Egypt and Yemen, where it is substantively contributing to the Saudi-led coalition intervention in Yemen to restore ousted President Hadi to power. Its contributions included direct counter-insurgency efforts on the ground, air support, land mine clearance, military hardware provisions, aid and intelligence. The fifth of September 2015, a day dubbed 'the UAE's Pearl Harbor moment', marked an unprecedented loss of 52 Emirati soldiers, the most since the nation was founded in 1971 when Iranian-backed Houthi militias stormed their camp (Qassemi, 2015). UAE leadership views it necessary to stand hand-in-hand with Saudi Arabia. It claims any threat to the kingdom is a direct threat to the UAE (Zarooni, 2015). Gargash stated: 'The Emirati political and military stand in supporting Saudi and Gulf security is progressive . . . [and] our goal is to succeed in returning security to Yemen and to protect the security of the Gulf through Yemen' (Salem, 2015). This stands in contrast to Iraq, where the GCC was reluctant to openly confront the US or challenge Iran on its political gains (Friedman, 2012). The ability of the UAE (and other GCC leaders) to pivot towards GCC-centric governance is a result of growing capacity and intention expressed in policy terms – a relative power underscored by various capabilities. The UAE's new-found decisiveness is earning it a reputation as a regional player, power conferred under the *domain* dimension. This defensive security policy defies conventional small-state decision-making patterns. UAE assertiveness also represents an evolution in the applicability of relational power as a vantage point to evaluate security and foreign policy.

The UAE in the global economy

Since 2004 the UAE has gradually become more assertive and leveraged the benefits conferred by its geography – natural resources, central location and trade – to create tangible forms of power. The UAE has been more active regionally and internationally in the last few years than during its first three decades combined. The shift is visible in the very content as well as the approach the UAE is using to address external opportunities and challenges. Foreign policy in the Arabian Gulf is highly linked to the personalities of elite decision-makers, in contrast to most other countries, where state apparatuses are more institutionalized (Kamrava, 2011, p. 81).

After Sheikh Zayed's death, his son Sheikh Khalifa bin Zayed Al Nahyan (among others) began pursuing a more ambitious, 'global' and deliberately more 'realistic foreign policy', expanding existing policy, not replacing it (Abdulla, 2012), beyond the four circles that UAE foreign policy runs in – the Gulf, the Arab world, the Muslim world and the world at large. In the last decade new pillars have grown within these circles, which can be conceptually pegged to issues of security, economy and identity. The Sheikh suggests that the UAE is advancing a tripartite foreign policy: 'the Arab world for identity, the West for security and most recently Asia for the economy', and among these the economic pillar anchors its heavily realistic approach to international politics (Abdulla, 2012). From the perspective of relational power, leveraging its vast financial resources gives power through *means*, which includes cultural symbolism, diplomatic and political influence, but also power according to the measurements of *costs, domain* and *scope*.

In general, globalization processes have modified small states' external environment, facilitating political innovation and domestic restructuring to exploit opportunity for economic growth and technological development – conferring dimensions of power. Some small states have been able to transition in part from being strictly security consumers to security producers, by contributing to the production of other types of security than military defence – namely economic security (Steinmetz and Wivel, 2010, p. 8); and its translation into power has allowed them to create new security strategies. During the oil price hike between 2002 and 2006, the UAE nearly doubled its annual oil revenue average to approximately USD 327 billion per year (Bi-me.com, 2009). This capital boosted the UAE's capacity to use its economic resources as a tool at the international level. This dimension of the UAE's national profile is the biggest challenge to its 'smallness' and it is leveraging the power card to maximize influence. Truly globalized views on capital accumulation, the means of production and economic integration would suggest a transformation has taken place in in the global system. From a relational power approach, this represents a change of the very nature of global security and power.

More than population, military resources or land, money constitutes power in relationships if goals are defined in terms of *scope* and *domain*. Abu Dhabi did both when it announced it wants to be a regional power with an international reach (Al-Suwaidi, 2011). Money as power relates to influence when it can get others to change their behaviour and as such it is an important aspect of risk diversification (Baldwin, 2013). But, to designate a state 'asset' such as money as a power resource also implies a judgement about its utility in the context of the value system it exists within and the capability of others. Analytically, the questions associated with the UAE's wealth and subsequent power are: What power does it have to get whom to do what? Can money buy security? What kind of security? This leads to the issue of 'fungibility' in power analysis, which refers to the ease with which a resource's usage can transfer. Some scholars suggest 'the fungibility of power assets increase in tandem with the volume of cash' (Art, 1996; Waltz, 2000).

The evolution of the UAE's risk-diversification policies over the last decade contribute to developments that would shift future geo-economic patterns. The UAE's foreign and security policies exist in a setting of economic globalization and the aftermath of the 2007–8 financial crisis. Its massive capital resources are positioning it (and other Gulf states) as a pivot around which modifications in the global balance of power are occurring. At a macro level, Gulf countries were not impacted by the 2007–8 crisis as negatively as others, which allowed them to tap global trade flows and contribute to developments that would shift future geo-economic patterns. The power of energy and trade were combined with investment policy-making decisions to exploit opportunity for (growing) influence in the global economy. The fungibility of UAE financial resources is arguably clearest when evaluating the potential stemming from the world's second-largest sovereign wealth fund (SWF): the Abu Dhabi Investment Authority (ADIA) (Sovereign Wealth Fund Institute, 2014). Abu Dhabi's ADIA served as lifeblood to financial markets during the 2007–8 global crisis along with other Gulf-based SWFs (Al-Bishi, 2014). Gulf-based SWFs provided liquidity to US firms such as Merrill Lynch and Citigroup at the onset of the crisis and later accounted for a third of the emergency funding to European governments to avert financial collapse in the fall of 2008 (Youngs, 2009, p. 1). Post-2008, SWFs such as ADIA are predicted to play a major role in shaping future global investment (Al-Bishi, 2014). The art of survival for small states includes rigorous efforts to broaden influence globally. The UAE engaged as an 'equal player' alongside larger states. It was a rare moment.

Importantly, the financial resources provided were tied to conditions outlining reform of global governance structures, which poorly represent emerging economies (Ulrichsen, 2012). The UAE wanted the International Monetary Fund (IMF) reform to better reflect its weight in the global economy in exchange for financial backing. Nasser Al-Suwaidi, Governor of the UAE Central Bank, offered a blunt statement: 'If . . . given more voice then they [Gulf states] will provide money maybe . . . . They will not be providing funds without extra voice and extra recognition' (Gerlach and Jones 2008). Aid and loans tied to conditions produce a form of security not unlike the powerful conditionalities associated with World Bank and IMF loans (Craze, 2008). As a result of influence in exchange for money, the UAE has become more integrated into in the global system of power, politics and policy-making. The two principal areas reformed were oversight of international financial institutions and energy governance (Ulrichsen, 2013). The remodelling went so far as to affect the politics of the relative positions regarding the global debate on climate change (Ulrichsen, 2011a). It is an innovative way to constructively promote security. Small states commonly use membership in organizations as a means of exerting influence, and the IMF is one example. International governance frameworks are significant power *domains*, and money facilitated UAE inclusion. As Robert Keohane suggests, the governance of globalization is more likely to occur through inter-state co-operation and trans-national networks (Keohane, 2002, p. 325). As a result, GCC policymakers have become contributors in real-world measures related to the governance of globalization. In this light, the UAE is contributing to the creation of new contours in global governance and the governance of globalization (Ulrichsen, 2011b). This is a potent, long-term policy to diversify risk.

The UAE is shifting towards being a 'player' in co-operative security schemes. It (and other Gulf states) supported US strategic interests by co-operating with the US on energy policy, which permitted it 'to weather the second largest economic crisis in the past century with its global influence more or less intact' (Barrett, 2014). Another part of the UAE's formula for success lies in its co-operation with emerging economies to fashion 'coalitions of convenience'. These increasingly powerful coalitions are working to rearticulate international governance structures. It is a practical strategy. Foreign Affairs Minister Abdulla bin Zayed said: 'The UAE looks forward to bolstering our relations with the fast growing countries, such as India, Russia, China, Brazil and South Africa' (The Business Year, 2012). These alliances represent strategic partnerships. In particular, it gives the UAE a presence in major international forums and therefore a voice in global affairs. Establishing economic and in some cases security ties with emerging economies is itself a way of engraining the UAE into the new multipolar world order. Leveraging financial resources and diplomacy are part of the UAE's wider risk-diversification strategy. In effect, the UAE is contributing to the redirection of old geo-economic power configurations, (Grether and Mathys, 2010) which can be conceptually understood as the 'world economic centre of gravity', empirical proof of the location of today's global economic 'hot spots' (Quah, 2011).

As of 2012, the UAE makes up a third of all trade between China and the Gulf states, which amounts to $100 billion; and nearly 70 per cent of Chinese exports to the UAE are re-exported, making it a major hub (ECSSR, 2012a). Further, the UAE anticipated a 30 per cent increase in bilateral trade with China from $46 billion in 2013 to $60 billion by 2015 (Dasgupta, 2014). Economic co-operation is expanding into areas such as renewable energy and telecommunications. The broadening relationship reflects deepening political ties (Bardsley, 2010). The importance of the bilateral relationship is clear to Abu Dhabi and Beijing. China's economy continues to grow and it is the world's second-largest oil consumer. It also holds a permanent seat at the UN Security Council. The constructive engagement thread of UAE foreign policy runs into its trade relations, too. It is noteworthy that the UAE's improved relations with emerging Asian powers have not undermined relations with traditional allies. The volume of non-oil US–UAE trade in 2011 was approximately $20 billion, up 44 per cent from 2010 (ECSSR, 2012b). Moreover, despite the global financial crisis, trade relations with the European Union (EU) have seen similar improvement. The UAE has successfully established strong relations with various international powers, which has allowed it to apply its diplomacy with increased vigour and success. Over the last five years, the UAE's trade diplomacy has expanded to new regions such as South and Central America, Africa, Central Asia and the Pacific, where several embassies and consulates are now established (UAE Ministry of Foreign Affairs, 2014). Therefore, it is adding influence, not 'swapping' it, and this should be understood as a risk-diversification strategy.

Another way to leverage finance is though humanitarian projects to gain security through *scope, domain, weight, costs* and symbolic *means*. In 2010, the UAE gave AED 2.81 billion globally in grants and loans to development, humanitarian and charity programmes. In addition, UAE donors committed another AED 2.2 billion to development programmes beyond 2010 (Al-Awadhi, 2010). Diplomacy is an important tool for small states. Aid-based diplomacy enables a state to build institutional friends such as the United Nations (Archer, 2010) and test its capabilities in terms of political diplomacy (Badrakhan, 2013). However, aid disbursement must also been viewed as a security strategy especially when tied to military forces or given in the context of conflict and/or conflict resolution (O'Hanlon, 1994, p. 14). The Arab Spring demonstrated how aid has political and military dimensions. Further, aid distribution enables access to the global political stage, which can balance internal and external pressures (Archer, 2010). In another example, the UAE used economic investment as a tool to garner support and direct it. For example, the UAE gave a $3 billion line of credit to the Serbian government to help it avoid default, but the money was tied to a commitment. Serbia was required to support UAE defence, food and aviation interests (Karasik, 2013). Food security in the UAE remains a key strategic security consideration (Bailey and Willoughby, 2013). These examples illustrate that the UAE has a real-world strategy allowing it to play a role in regional and global politics, and is benefiting from that involvement. It also has a productive risk-diversification policy.

Risk diversification, security policy and a classic small state

The UAE, as a small state, employs more proactive than defensive risk-diversification strategies at times as a result of capability it has accumulated in some power domains. Yet, the UAE is ultimately bound to act and react in accordance with its vulnerabilities. This means at other times it is forced to use another set of strategies to diversify risks because it occupies the weaker position in asymmetrical security relationships. The UAE adopts far more co-operative strategies when it cannot capitalize on its innovative energies for relative gains in its status, standing and security. The following analysis will illustrate that the UAE is rather skilful at minimizing the extent of encroachment upon its autonomy as it band-wagons. Indeed, the UAE has band-wagoned with the US since 1991 and small-state literature reveals this comes with the risk of entrapment in the security hegemon's wars. This is an observable price the UAE has paid for the US security umbrella. The UAE Embassy in Washington, DC, reports that 'the UAE is only one of three countries and the only Arab nation to participate in all five US coalition actions over the last 20 years: Afghanistan, Libya, Somalia, Bosnia–Kosovo, and the 1990 Gulf War' (The Embassy of the United Arab Emirates in Washington, 2014). As of 2015, the UAE has been involved in counter-insurgency coalitions fighting against rebel extremists in Libya, Yemen, Syria and Iraq. The list is considerable indeed and reveals a security-policy pattern that remains unchanged.

In exchange for a US-backed security guarantee, the UAE supported US operations in Iraq (1991); although it did not openly support the intervention in 2003, it consistently granted the US permission to use its military facilities, pre-position in ports and access Jebel Ali airport. It also allowed the US to refuel at Al Dhafra airbase and enforce the no-fly zone above Iraq in 2003. This reflects a continuous current of support and provides evidence of the UAE behaving like a small state in terms of its risk calculation. The UAE's small-state obligation also explains its participation in the International Security Assistance Force (ISAF) in Afghanistan. As in Iraq, the UAE was drawn into the conflict and expected to contribute to the US effort. The UAE supported initiatives by providing the UN, US, EU and NATO forces unprecedented access to ports and territory, over-flight clearances and other critical and important logistical assistance. The UAE kept a contingent of 250 UAE troops in Afghanistan from 2003 (Makahleh, 2011) until the end of the mission in December 2014. The UAE gave unwavering support for the military missions more connected to US interests than its own; but, a closer look at the UAE's involvement reveals important cleavages in the view of the UAE as a powerless small state with limited ability to devise its own security and foreign policies.

While in lockstep with the US, the UAE also employed indigenous strategies to contribute to the regional security challenge in ways that serve its domestic interests. In Afghanistan, the bulk of UAE contributions have been in recovery and stabilization activities such as education and training. The UAE has built '11 schools, 6 medical clinics, 38 mosques, 160 wells, a general public library, and Zayed University, Afghanistan, which serves over 6,400 students per year' (Presidential Guard, 2014). Since 2009, the UAE's financial aid to the country reached $1.5 billion (Al Awadhi, 2012). This humanitarian strategy is similar in Iraq. Between 2003 and 2007, the UAE donated $215 million to the reconstruction of schools and hospitals (Sharp and Blanchard, 2007, p. 16). Bilateral trade is estimated at about $5 billion, and 'Dubai's direct exports to Iraq posted AED 1.17 billion while the total Free Zone exports were valued at AED 13.37 billion in 2010' (Middle East Events, 2011). In July 2008, the UAE wrote off $7 billion (including interest) in Iraqi debt (Katzman, 2013, p. 18). These sorts of activities build up symbolic *means* and scope of power in an Islamic light, which is becoming increasingly important to regional politics and security.

Innovation is another face of constructive engagement regardless of nuance and represents part of the UAE's risk-diversification policies. The strategy has worked. John Chipman said: 'The US, UK, France see in the UAE an Arab state that thinks strategically, and one with which they can co-operate.' He continued: 'The contribution of UAE Special Forces to Afghanistan and air assets to the coalition effort in Libya demonstrated that the UAE had no strategic aversion to direct co-operation with Western militaries when strategic perspectives and aims were aligned.' He added: 'This case by case, but unemotional, strategic co-operation is likely to continue' (Fenton, 2011). The UAE's participation in US-led military missions benefited the UAE because it gained operational experience, training and practice in combat missions, a valuable asset to UAE air and armed forces. Further, it increased the UAE's prestige as a 'player' and gave it the ability to showcase its impressive array of technological military hardware. Security imperatives coupled with pragmatism led to a balancing of internal and external pressures.

At times, UAE and US interests merge. The Islamic State of Iraq and the Levant's (ISIL) insurgency in Iraq and Syria is an example of a common agenda, and stands as an increasingly rare example of favourably viewed US foreign policy in the Arab world. Survey findings show that 85 per cent of the Arab sample of 5,100 participants hold negative opinions of ISIL to varying degrees (Arab Center for Research and Policy Studies, 2014). In this case, the band-wagoning enhances regime security. UAE citizens support UAE–US military co-operation and missions in Syria, for instance. Al-Dhafra base is the UAE's key contribution to the US (and allies) effort to combat ISIL (Amos, 2014). For example, the base's two runways have launched more strike aircraft – including the Air Force's most sophisticated warplane, the F-22 Raptor – than any other military facility in the region (Chandrasekaran, 2014). It is important to clarify that this example of co-operation is more complex than a small state caught up in a hegemon's war. The UAE's keenness to attack ISIL is tied to its zero-tolerance policy towards Islamic militancy. Home-grown extremist groups do not pose a direct threat to the UAE due to its far-reaching and considerably aggressive internal security service, but Emirati officials are concerned about future spillover from Syria, Iraq, Libya and Yemen that can threaten its stability and prosperity. 'We can't be a stable house if there is a brush fire around us', said Anwar Gargash, the UAE Minister of State for Foreign Affairs (Chandrasekaran, 2014).

The underlying security framework in the Arabian Gulf is also changing. One stream relates to views on the shifting role of the US in the region's future. Despite change, the US is not withdrawing commitments; its footprint will remain. On one level, US foreign policies in the region and its two unpopular wars fed changing views on the UAE's strategic relationship with the US. On another level, UAE perception of the so-called US 'pivot to Asia' and its shifting strategic priorities as well as the impact of sequestration produced negative views on the US medium- to long-term security commitment. The US has significantly reduced its defence spending and announced it is less willing to play a leadership role, especially in the Middle East. Many US policymakers connect this development to 'Little America' foreign policy, which is marked by conservative approaches to deep involvement in foreign crises. Libya, Egypt and Yemen were examples of the US for having little involvement (Barrett, 2014). The issue around defence spending areas and figures is deeper than the policies of the current US President and arguably the aftermath of the global financial crisis as well. On a macro level, the US is reacting to a new external environment and on the micro level it is contending with limitations produced by decades of overspending. In January 2014, as one example, an additional $52 billion was sliced from the US defence budget after more than $1 trillion in cuts (Kyl and Lieberman, 2013). The UAE's concerns about US defence spending cuts on its regional footprint are substantiated by its modified military commitments (Kagan, 2013). In the short term, these decisions undermine US military capability in the Gulf by reducing its readiness and operational effectiveness (Kagan, 2013), which concerns Emirati leadership.

US reductions in Gulf defence capability are part of the US new neo-isolationist foreign policy (Haass, 2013) that will gradually reorient US military commitments with the logic that the US does not need to be the dominant power in the Gulf protecting eastward transit of its oil supplies towards rising powers (Kahwaji, 2013). This is coupled with US recognition that it cannot be everywhere at once, and its resources should be used closer to home. This neo-isolationist school of thought transfers responsibility for the UAE's security more towards the UAE. The UAE's view of the US as a form of security insurance is being reduced. Yet it is concerned about the security vacuum if the US continues to progressively withdraw. This strikes at the core of its security and reflects an awareness of its vulnerability as well as an acknowledgement it cannot defend itself. It also explains its rigorous efforts to fill in security gaps.

The UAE's risk-diversification strategy in response to this evolving arrangement is to layer and diversify. The tripartite policy seeks to preserve the intact parts of the UAE–US military relationship and reach out to others while bolstering its own defence industry. For example, the UAE asked for a French military presence on its territory in exchange for a USD 6 billion deal with France on civilian nuclear activities in 2008 (Ira, 2009). This layers security provisions, similar to its NATO partnership through the ICI in 2004. UAE foreign policy is also shifting towards Asia – China, South Korea and the other Asian tigers – for economy, energy and security (Abdulla, 2012). These are clearly risk-diversification policies. The visible surge in business diplomacy through large contracts and partnerships represents a strategic choice. For instance, the UAE strengthened ties with Seoul after it awarded it a contract worth nearly $40 billion to build four nuclear reactors in Abu Dhabi by 2020. It signals the UAE effort to establish diplomatic capital where it previously had little influence (Miller, 2012). Also, in a tactical light it is the Eastern powers that rely on oil and gas from the Gulf region, and perhaps the UAE calculates they would protect it if a threat arose. Although the US is the only state with the ability to truly project power in the Arabian Gulf, China and India are also building powerful navies, which will significantly enhance their power projection capabilities in a decade and potentially offer an alternative strategic alliance concept to the UAE. In short, UAE defence co-operation has taken on numerous dimensions.

The UAE is also diversifying traditional sources for defence and security capabilities from the US, UK, France, China, Russia and Germany (Louth et al., 2013, p. 3). In 2010, it established defence agreements with Brazil to buy military equipment, conduct training and deepen defence co-operation, for example (Al Lawati, 2010). A new armament strategy of diversification deepens ties and reinforces new strategic relations. HH Sheikh Mohammed bin Rashid Al Maktoum said 'Weapons are, in themselves, a strategic commodity' (Al Khaleeji, 2003). As the UAE diversifies its sources of arms, it diversifies its strategic relationship design through activities such as ammunition, repair, replacement part, training and modernization, which spill over into other areas of co-operation. If power is resource-based, the UAE remains small and weak. Small states typically aim to guarantee their military and security survival by 'adopting pragmatic policies responding to the agenda set by near-by powers and external developments' rather than carving out their own unique strategic goals (Steinmetz and Wivel, 2010, p. 9).

Beyond new defence ties, the UAE relies on US weapons, technology and expertise, which to date remain hallmarks of the UAE's defence strategy (Awad et al., 2013). But, efforts to transition away from this include heavy investment in the domestic defence sector and leveraging of off-set programmes. At the International Defence Exhibition and Conference (IDEX) in 2013, the UAE spent more than 70 per cent of AED 14 billion on weapons from local companies (Al Makahleh, 2013). It wants its defence industry to be globally competitive (Al Makahleh, 2013) and self-sufficient (United Press International, 2013). To do so, it is linking its domestic defence sector with global defence manufacturers and has gained cutting-edge defence industrial knowledge through access to the global defence bazaar (Saab, 2014b, p. 2). In the last decade, the UAE has been the leader of this type of activity in the Gulf Security Council (United Press International, 2013). It has developed a new capability in manufacturing and modernizing military vehicles, communication systems, aerial drones and more. It has also significantly improved its ability to maintain, repair, and retrofit aircraft (Saab, 2014a). Despite its achievements, the UAE is still far from being self-sufficient and must rely on US military technology and training. Defence sector autonomy is not challenging the asymmetrical defence relationships and, in terms of small-state studies, this point is crucial.

Conclusion

In the end, it is worth returning to the central questions of this article. Namely, what are the risk-diversification policies small states choose? And how do they choose them? The UAE is an exciting case study as it embodies classic small-state traits that guide many of its policy decisions yet paradoxically challenge core assumptions of what roles small states play and how they are often strategically understood in the international arena. In 42 years, the UAE has transformed into to a wealthy, modern state with an increasingly diversified economy, which at times provides enough capacity for the Emirati leadership to pursue its distinctive and independent foreign policy. The Arab Spring gave opportunity for the UAE to be more assertive and even influence some transformation through indigenous risk-diversification policies. It addressed threats with constructive, pragmatic and assertive policies that earned it a reputation as a new regional 'player'. But, this must be contextualized against the UAE's visible discomfort with political changes within Arab states and the changing US role in the region. It has layered security and built up domestic capacity in the defence sector. Innovative strategies shield it from risk and prevent exposure to a threatening security environment. From a small-state study, relational power perspective, the UAE risk-diversification strategies and capacities are fascinating.

While the regional environment presented new risks, the international system opened up opportunity. The economic globalization of the Gulf region has deepened and expanded the UAE's involvement on the global stage – most importantly in the reform of global financial and energy frameworks. This new influence stems partially from its support to Western nations after the 2007–8 financial crises as well as power being increasingly refracted through new and old intersections of regional, national and global governance mechanisms. At the core, there are transformations in global geo-economic and geo-political power, which represent a systemic pivot and which confer benefits to the UAE. It is being enmeshed in the global environment in the form of new influence through complex interdependencies that enable its participation in global frameworks of governance opening up new space to develop inventive security policies. Economic power is a dimension of power and the UAE leveraged it to essentially buy influence and form coalitions with the 'global south' to lobby for a bigger voice within international institutional governance frameworks. It used the same power in Egypt to influence political change. This suggests that the UAE holds a valuable type of transferrable, flexible power to diversify risk, which challenges small-states theory. The combination of more international presence through financial and energy policy, itself a form of risk diversification, changing US roles and opportunity to assert itself in the political aftermath of the Arab Spring, all produced new contours in the spectrum of UAE foreign and defence policy options. This assertiveness buttresses and is buttressed by the economic globalization of the Gulf, which has opened up opportunity for greater inclusion in new global political, economic and even security contexts.

The UAE's use of its wealth, political stability and resource endowment to influence global governance, international institutions and politics in the Gulf, Middle East and North Africa, and beyond is significant. Indeed, at times the UAE pursues its own foreign policy (Al-Suwaidi, 2011). In this context, it is exerting influence far outmatching its size, and this challenges small-state studies, which are nearly always marred by a lack of clarity in terms of what defines small states. Some scholars question why small states matter, while others claim they play a more important role in international relations now than ever (Hey, 2003, p. 1; Knudsen, 2002). There is considerable complexity associated with labelling a state 'small' due to an elusive definition of power in political science. Agreement does not exist on how to ultimately define a small state or how to measure power and influence; but, power remains a pivotal concept in small-state theory and a state's smallness is inherently linked to a power analysis. Although there is little analytical precision regarding small states and power, the end of the Cold War created a unipolar world, which gave all states a smallish hue in their inability to affect power politics. As the world becomes increasingly multipolar and economically globalized, small states are able to manage their own security affairs more independently than they should, theoretically. The reality is that they represent the majority of states in the world now and hold membership in influential international organizations such as the UN, EU, OECD (Organization for Economic Cooperation and Development), OPEC (Organization for Petroleum Exporting Countries) and NATO, in many cases based on democratic principles. Based on material, relational or normative resources, if the ability of a small state to design and implement its own security and foreign policies is directly associated with its power levels (Rickli, 2008), then the UAE is a remarkable case study of defiance. If a relational notion of power is taken as a conceptual perspective, then the UAE has some interesting capacity to diversify its risk despite some noteworthy constraints on what it can achieve.

Power is diffusing and the need for co-operation is increasing. Since the number of small states has grown, it is clear that power politics and zero-sum games are mostly tempered by institutions, alliances, trade and other forms of capacity such as wealth and workforce capability. The evolution of power from World War II to the Cold War until today is marked by the reconfiguration of power in international relations. Military capabilities will always matter. The essential question is to what extent they matter now. In terms of power, context matters. Policymakers, as practical people, are likely to understand this more readily than academics. It is foolish to continuously associate the same elements of power as 'high cards' in an international card game, because it implies there is only one kind of card game in international politics. Policymakers and states such as the UAE have more or less power to diversify risk depending on their cards, what game is being played and who is playing. To evaluate a state's power, it is necessary to identify more than the means – the ends are key. They inform policymakers which power dimensions are best applied to meet an objective. The US 'big war' approach to 'small wars' in Iraq and Afghanistan are excellent illustrations of this point. Small risk-diversification strategies can meet big objectives. It is essential, therefore, that the small-state scholarship does not equate smallness to power deficits. It defies conventional realist and neo-realist logic to suggest that strengths coexist with weaknesses, but they can. This is the thematic core of resilience in recent small-state research and the key to understanding what the UAE's risk-diversification strategies are and how they are selected.

References

Abdulla, A. (2012). New assertiveness in UAE foreign policy. *Gulf News*. [online] Available at: http://gulfnews.com/opinion/thinkers/new-assertiveness-in-uae-foreign-policy-1.1086667. [Accessed 31 Oct. 2015].

Al Arabiya (2011). GCC troops dispatched to Bahrain to maintain order. [online] Available at: www.alarabiya.net/articles/2011/03/14/141445.html. [Accessed 29 Oct. 2015].

Al-Awadhi, A. (2010). The fundamentals of the UAE foreign policy. The Emirates Center for Strategic Studies and Research. [online] Available at: www.ecssr.ac.ae/ECSSR/print/ft.jsp?lang=en&ftId=/FeatureTopic/Abdullah_AlAwadhi/FeatureTopic_1342.xml. [Accessed 29 Oct. 2015].

Al-Awadhi, A. (2012). The humanitarian aspect of the UAE foreign policy. Abu Dhabi: The Emirates Center for Strategic Security and Research. [online] Available at: www.ecssr.ae/ECSSR/print/ft.jsp?lang=en&ftId=/FeatureTopic/Abdullah_AlAwadhi/FeatureTopic_1576.xml. [Accessed 1 Nov. 2015].

Al-Bishi, M. (2014). Abu Dhabi's sovereign wealth fund is world's second largest. *Asharq Al-Awsat*. [online] Available at: http://english.aawsat.com/2014/01/article55328255. [Accessed 31 Oct. 2015].

Al Khaleeji, A. (2003). Unification of armed forces significant. [online] Available at: www.sheikhmohammed.co.ae/vgn-exttemplating/v/index.jsp?vgnextoid=2eb7600c3a384110VgnVCM1000003f140a0aRCRD&vgnextchannel=9b834c8631cb4110VgnVCM100000b0140a0aRCRD&vgnextfmt=mediaPublication&date=1052046562633&mediatype=INTERVIEW. [Accessed 15 Oct. 2015].

Al Lawati, A. (2010). UAE and Brazil to sign defence agreement. *Gulf News*. [online] Available at: http://gulfnews.com/news/uae/government/uae-and-brazil-to-sign-defence-agreement-1.686015. [Accessed 1 Nov. 2015].

Al Makahleh, S. (2013). UAE defence industries show significant progress. *Gulf News*. [online] Available at: http://m.gulfnews.com/business/uae-defence-industries-show-significant-progress-1.1149170. [Accessed 1 Nov. 2015].

Al Mashat, A. (2010). Politics of constructive engagement: The foreign policy of the United Arab Emirates. In: B. Korany and A. Hallil Dessouki, eds, *The foreign policies of Arab States: The challenge of globalization*.Cairo:The American University in Cairo Press, pp. 457–80.

Almezaini, K. (2011). Bold foreign policy of the UAE brings benefits for GCC. *The National*. [online] Available at: www.thenational.ae/thenationalconversation/comment/bold-foreign-policy-ofthe-uae-brings-benefits-for-gcc. [Accessed 29 Oct. 2015].

Al-Suwaidi, A. (2011). UAE 40th National Day: Effective and balanced foreign policy. Abu Dhabi: Emirates Center for Strategic Security and Research. [online] Available at: www.ecssr.ac.ae/ECSSR/appmanager/portal/ecssr?_nfls=false&_nfpb=true&lang=en&_pageLabel=featuredTopicsPage&_event=viewFeaturedTopic&ftId=/FeatureTopic/ECSSR/FeatureTopic_1480.xml. [Accessed 29 Oct. 2015].

Amos, D. (2014). Facing threats from ISIS and Iran, Gulf States set to join forces. NPR.org. [online] Available at: www.npr.org/sections/parallels/2014/12/08/369374722/facing-threats-from-isis-and-iran-gulf-states-set-to-join-forces. [Accessed 29 Oct. 2015].

Arab Center for Research and Policy Studies (2014). The military campaign against the Islamic State in Iraq and the Levant: Arab public opinion. Doha, Qatar. [online] Available at: http://english.dohainstitute.org/file/Get/40ebdf12-8960-4d18-8088-7c8a077e522e. [Accessed 1 Nov. 2015].

Archer, C. (2010). Small states and European security and defence policy. In: R. Steinmetz and A. Wivel, eds, *Small states in Europe: Challenges and opportunities*. Farnham, Surrey, UK: Ashgate, pp. 55–6.

Archer, C. (2013). Small state security in Europe: The Nordic states. In: A. Wivel, A. Bailes and C. Archer, eds, *Small states and international security: Europe and beyond*. New York: Routledge, pp. 95–112.

Art, R. (1996). American foreign policy and the fungibility of force. *Security Studies*, 5(4), pp. 7–42.

Awad, M., Mehta, A., Chuter, A. and Tran, P. (2013). US bid delays Qatar jet competition: UAE fighter contest is also up for grabs. *Defence News*. [online] Available at: www.defensenews.com/article/20131110/DEFREG04/311100014/US-Bid-Delays-Qatar-Jet-Competition. [Accessed 1 Nov. 2015].

Badrakhan, A. (2013). UAE's foreign policy: A model of balance and efficiency. Abu Dhabi: The Emirates Center for Strategic Security and Research. [online] Available at: www.ecssr.ac.ae/ECSSR/print/ft.jsp?lang=en&ftId=/FeatureTopic/Abdel_Wahab_Badrakhan/FeatureTopic_1741.xml. [Accessed 1 Nov. 2015].

Bailey, R. and Willoughby, R. (2013). *Edible oil: Food security in the Gulf*. EER Briefing Paper 2013/03. Chatham House, pp. 2–5. [online] Available at: www.chathamhouse.org/publications/papers/view/195281. [Accessed 1 Nov. 2015].

Baldacchino, G. (2006). Innovative development strategies from non-sovereign island jurisdictions? A global review of economic policy and governance practices. *World Development*, 34(5), pp. 852–67.

Baldwin, D. (2002). Power and international relations. In: W. Carlsnaes, T. Risse and B. Simmons, eds, *Handbook of international relations*. London: SAGE, pp. 177–92.

Baldwin, D. (2013). Power and international relations. In: W. Carlsnaes, T. Risse and B. Simmons, eds, *Handbook of international relations*, 2nd edn. Thousand Oaks, CA: SAGE, pp. 273–97.

Bardsley, D. (2010). UAE–China economic ties 'to expand beyond oil industry'. *The National*. [online] Available at: www.thenational.ae/news/world/asia-pacific/uae-china-economic-ties-to-expand-beyond-oil-industry. [Accessed 1 Nov. 2015].

Barrett, R. (2014). Obama: The anti-Bush. MEI Scholar Series. Washington: Middle East Institute. [online] Available at: www.mei.edu/content/article/obama-anti-bush. [Accessed 1 Nov. 2015].

Bi-me.com (2009). Gulf economies must diversify to weather crisis, says Carnegie report – *Business Intelligence Middle East* – bi-me.com – News, analysis, reports. [online] Available at: www.bi-me.com/main.php?id=33584&t=1. [Accessed 31 Oct. 2015].

Briguglio, L., Cordina, G. and Kisangga, E. (2006). *Building the economic resilience of small states*. Malta and London: Islands and Small States Institute.

Buenos Aires Herald (2013a). Egypt names new PM. [online] Available at: www.buenosairesherald.com/article/135664/egypt-names-new-pm. [Accessed 29 Oct. 2015].

Buenos Aires Herald (2013b). New regime gets Gulf money in show of support for army. [online] Available at: www.buenosairesherald.com/article/135665/new-regime-gets-gulf-money-in-show-of-support-for-army. [Accessed 29 Oct. 2015].

Chandrasekaran, R. (2014). In the UAE, the United States has a quiet, potent ally nicknamed a 'Little Sparta'. *The Washington Post*. [online] Available at: www.washingtonpost.com/world/national-security/in-the-uae-the-united-states-has-a-quiet-potent-ally-nicknamed-little-sparta/2014/11/08/3fc6a50c-643a-11e4-836c-83bc4f26eb67_story.html. [Accessed 1 Nov. 2015].

Claude, I. (1962). *Power and international relations*. New York: Random House.

Cooper, A. and Shaw, T. (2009). The diplomacies of small states at the start of 21st century: How vulnerable? How resilient? In: A. Cooper and T. Shaw, eds, *The diplomacies of small states: Between vulnerability and resilience*. Basingstoke: Palgrave Macmillan, pp. 1–19.

Craze, J. (ed) (2008). *World Bank conditionalities: Poor deal for poor countries*. The Netherlands: A SEED Europe, supported by Oxfam Novib, p. 7.

Dahl, R. (1957). The concept of power. *Behavioral Science*, 2(3), pp. 201–15.

Dasgupta, S. (2014). UAE envoy sees 30 per cent jump in China trade. *Khaleej Times*. [online] Available at: www.khaleejtimes.com/article/20140607/ARTICLE/306079873/1037. [Accessed 1 Nov. 2015].

de Santis, N. (2004). Nato review. Nato.int. [online] Available at: www.nato.int/docu/review/2004/issue3/english/art4.html. [Accessed 29 Oct. 2015].

ECSSR (2012a). The UAE and China: A strategic partnership. Abu Dhabi: The Emirates Centre for Strategic Studies and Research. [online] Available at: www.ecssr.ac.ae/ECSSR/print/ft.jsp?lang=en&ftId=/FeatureTopic/ECSSR/FeatureTopic_1500.xml. [Accessed 1 Nov. 2015].

ECSSR (2012b). UAE foreign policy: Dynamic activities and effective roles. The Emirates Center for Strategic Security and Research. [online] Available at: www.ecssr.ae/ECSSR/print/ft.jsp?lang=en&ftId=/FeatureTopic/ECSSR/FeatureTopic_1513.xml. [Accessed 1 Nov. 2015].

El Dahan, M. (2013). UAE signs $4.9 billion aid package to Egypt. Reuters. [online] Available at: www.reuters.com/article/2013/10/26/us-uae-egypt-idUSBRE99P07F20131026. [Accessed 29 Oct. 2015].

Fenton, J. (2011). Libya. Wordpress.com. [online] Available at: https://jeniferfenton.wordpress.com/tag/libya/. [Accessed 1 Nov. 2015].

Friedman, B. (2012). Battle for Bahrain: What one uprising meant for the Gulf States and Iran. *World Affairs*. (March/April). [online] Available at: www.worldaffairsjournal.org/article/battle-bahrain-what-one-uprising-meant-gulf-states-and-iran. [Accessed 29 Oct. 2015].

Gerlach, M. and Jones, M. (2008). Interview–UAE central bank chief says dollar peg stays. Reuters. [online] Available at: http://in.reuters.com/article/uae-central-bank-idINLL23994820081121. [Accessed 31 Aug. 2016].

Grether, J. and Mathys, N. (2010). Is the world's economic centre of gravity already in Asia? *Area*, 42(1), pp. 47–50.

Haass, R. (2013). How the shutdown weakens U.S. foreign policy. [online] Available at: www.cfr.org/budget-debt-and-deficits/shutdown-weakens-us-foreign-policy/p31534. [Accessed 30 Aug. 2016].

Harsanyi, J. (1962). Measurement of social power, opportunity costs, and the theory of two-person bargaining games. *Systems Research and Behavioral Science*, 7(1), pp. 67–80.

Hey, J. (2003). Introducing small state foreign policy. In: J. Hey, ed, *Small states in world politics: Explaining foreign policy behavior*. Boulder: Lynne Rienner, pp. 1–13.

Ira, K. (2009). France opens first permanent military base in the Persian Gulf – World Socialist Web Site. [online] Available at: www.wsws.org/en/articles/2009/06/base-j15.html. [Accessed 1 Nov. 2015].

John, I. (2015). Boost for UAE–Iran trade. *Khaleej Times*. [online] Available at: www.khaleejtimes.com/business/economy/boost-for-uae-iran-trade [Accessed 31 Aug. 2016].

Kagan, F. (2013). The peril of sequestration. *National Review Online*. [online] Available at: www.nationalreview.com/nrd/articles/345942/peril-sequestration. [Accessed 1 Nov. 2015].

Kahwaji, R. (2013). Sequestration, new US foreign policy priorities and the likely impact on the Middle East. *Arabian Aerospace*. [online] Available at: www.arabianaerospace.aero/sequestration-new-us-foreign-policy-priorities-andthe-likely-impact-on-the-middle-east. [Accessed 1 Nov. 2015].

Kamrava, M. (2011). *International politics of the Persian Gulf*. Syracuse, NY: Syracuse University Press.

Kane, F. (2011). Trade ties with Iran at the crossroads. *The National*. [online] Available at: www.thenational.ae/business/industry-insights/economics/trade-ties-with-iran-at-the-crossroads. [Accessed 29 Oct. 2015].

Karasik, T. (2013). Gate to the Balkans: UAE and Serbia strengthen ties. Al Arabiya News. [online] Available at: http://english.alarabiya.net/en/views/news/world/2013/12/18/Gate-to-the-Balkans-the-growing-relationship-between-the-UAE-and-Serbia.html. [Accessed 1 Nov. 2015].

Katzman, K. (2013). The United Arab Emirates (UAE): Issues for U.S. policy. Congressional Research Service Report for Congress. [online] Available at: www.fas.org/sgp/crs/mideast/RS21852.pdf. [Accessed 29 Oct. 2015].

Keating, M., McEwen, N. and Harvey, M. (2014). *The role of small states in the European Union: Lessons for Scotland*. Scottish Parliament written submission. Edinburgh: Economic Social Research Council, Scottish Centre on Constitutional Change.

Keohane, R. (2002). Governance in a partially globalized world. In: A. McGrew and D. Held, eds, *Governing globalization: Power, authority and global governance*. Cambridge, UK: Polity, pp. 325–47.

Khaleej Times (2014). Emirati police officer among three dead in Bahrain blast. [online] Available at: www.khaleejtimes.com/article/20140304/ARTICLE/303049992/1011. [Accessed 29 Oct. 2015].

Kingsley, P., Stephen, C. and Roberts, D. (2014). UAE and Egypt behind bombing raids against Libyan militias, say US officials. *The Guardian*. [online] Available at: www.theguardian.com/world/2014/aug/26/united-arab-emirates-bombing-raids-libyan-militias. [Accessed 29 Oct. 2015].

Knudsen, O. (2002). Small states, latent and extant: Towards a general perspective. *Journal of International Relations and Development*. 5(2), pp. 182–98.

Kyl, J. and Lieberman, J. (2013). Too much crisis, too little defense. American Enterprise Institute. [online] Available at: www.aei.org/publication/too-much-crisis-too-little-defense/. [Accessed 1 Nov. 2015].

Larrabee, S. (2013). NATO'S role in the Middle East and Gulf. In *NATO'S approach to Gulf cooperation: Lessons learned and future challenges conference*, Dubai, 22 October, p. 5.

Lasswell, H. and Kaplan, A. (1950). *Power and society: a framework for political inquiry*. New Haven: Yale University Press.

Lemass, S. (1971). Small states in international organizations. In: A. Schou and A. Brundtland, eds, *Small states in international relations*. Stockholm: Almqvist & Wiksell, pp. 115–21.

Louth, J., Bontems, P., Carlier, B. and Pilottin, A. (2013). *Defence industry and the reinvigorated UK–UAE security relationship*. Occasional Paper, June 2013. London, UK: The Royal United Services Institute (RUSI).

Maass, M. (2014). Small states: Survival and proliferation. *International Politics*, 51(6), pp. 709–28.

Makahleh, S. (2011). UAE troops spare no effort to bring peace to Afghanistan. *Gulf News*. [online] Available at: http://uae-troops-spare-no-effort-to-bring-peace-to-afghanistan-1.856240. [Accessed 1 Nov. 2015].

Mattern, J. (2015). The concept of power and the (un)discipline of international relations. In: C. Reus-Smit and D. Snidal, eds, *The Oxford handbook of international relations*. Oxford, UK: Oxford University, pp. 691–7.

Middle East Events (2011, 10 December) Dubai Exports & Foreign Direct Investment Host Iraqi Officials From Federation Of Kurdistan Chambers Of Commerce And Industry. [online] Available at: www.middleeastevents.com/news/page/dubai-exports--foreign-direct-investment-host-iraqi-officials-from-federation-of-kurdistan-chambers-of-commerce-and-industry/14684#.WCMqAfl97IV. [Accessed 11 Nov. 2016].

Miller, J. (2012). With UAE nuclear partnership, South Korea gains Mideast traction. Worldpoliticsreview.com. [online] Available at: www.worldpoliticsreview.com/articles/12211/with-uae-nuclear-partnership-south-korea-gains-mideast-traction. [Accessed 1 Nov. 2015].

Morgenthau, H. (1948). *Politics among nations: The struggle for power and peace*. New York: Knopf.

Mouritzen, H. and Wivel, A. (2005). *The geopolitics of Euro-Atlantic integration*. London: Routledge.

O'Hanlon, M. (1994). *Enhancing U.S. security through foreign aid*. Washington, DC: Congress of the United States Congressional Budget Office.

Prasad, N. (2003). Small islands' quest for economic development. *Asia-Pacific Development Journal*, 10(1), pp. 47–67.

Prasad, N. (2004). Escaping regulation, escaping convention: Development strategies in small economies. *World Economics*, 5(1), pp. 41–65.

Prasad, N. (2009). Small but smart: Small states in the global system. In: A. Cooper and T. Shaw, eds, *The diplomacies of small states: Between vulnerability and resilience*. Houndmills, Basingstoke, UK: Palgrave, pp. 41–64.

Presidential Guard (2014). Mission: Winds of goodness–UAE contributions. [online] Available at: www.uaeafghanistan.ae/en/UAE-contributions.php. [Accessed 1 Nov. 2015].

Qassemi, S. (2013). What intervention in Yemen means for UAE's national identity. Time.com. [online] Available at: http://time.com/4040220/uae-intervention-in-yemen/. [Accessed 10 Nov. 2015].

Quah, D. (2011). The global economy's shifting centre of gravity. *Global Policy*, 2(1), pp. 3–9.

Reuters (2013). UAE leads Gulf Arab push to build up domestic defence industry. [online] Available at: www.reuters.com/article/2013/02/19/uae-defenceidUSL6N0BJ73020130219. [Accessed 29 Oct. 2015].

Rickli, J.-M. (2008). European small states' military policies after the Cold War: From territorial to niche strategies. *Cambridge Review of International Affairs*, 21(3), pp. 307–25.

Saab, B. (2014a). Arms and influence in the Gulf Riyadh and Abu Dhabi get to work. *World Affairs Journal*. Foreign Affairs. [online] Available at: www.worldaffairsjournal.org/content/arms-and-influence-gulf-riyadh-and-abu-dhabi-get-work. [Accessed 1 Nov. 2015].

Saab, B. (2014b). The Gulf rising: Defense industrialization in Saudi Arabia and the UAE. The Atlantic Council: Brent Scowcroft Center on International Security. [online] Available at: www.atlanticcouncil.org/publications/reports/the-gulf-rising-defense-industrialization-in-saudi-arabia-and-the-uae. [Accessed 1 Nov. 2015].

Sadjadpour, K. (2011). *The Battle of Dubai: The United Arab Emirates and the US–Iran Cold War*. Washington, DC: Carnegie Endowment for International Peace, pp. 1–46.

Salem, O. (2015). UAE military intervention in Yemen was 'inevitable'. *The National: UAE*. [online] Available at: www.thenational.ae/uae/uae-military-intervention-in-yemen-was-inevitable. [Accessed 10 Nov. 2015].

Sanger, D. and Schmitt, E. (2011). U.S.–Saudi tensions intensify with Mideast turmoil. *The New York Times*. [online] Available at: www.nytimes.com/2011/03/15/world/middleeast/15saudi.html?_r=0. [Accessed 29 Oct. 2015].

Sharp, J. and Blanchard, C. (2007). *Post-war Iraq: Foreign contributions to training, peacekeeping, and reconstruction*. Washington, DC: Congressional Research Service: Foreign Affairs, Defense, and Trade Division.

Sovereign Wealth Fund Institute (2014). Source on sovereign wealth funds, pensions, endowments, superannuation funds, central banks and public funds. [online] Available at: www.swfinstitute.org/fund-rankings. [Accessed 31 Oct. 2015].

Steinmetz, R. and Wivel, A. (2010). Introduction. In: R. Steinmetz and A. Wivel, eds, *Small states in Europe challenges and opportunities*. Farnham, UK: Ashgate, pp. 1–14.

The Business Year (2012). A vision true. [online] Available at: www.thebusinessyear.com/uae-dubai-2012/a-vision-true/review. [Accessed 1 Nov. 2015].

The Embassy of the United Arab Emirates in Washington (2014). UAE–US security relationship. The Embassy of the United Arab Emirates in Washington. [online] Available at: www.uae-embassy.org/uae-us-relations/key-areas-bilateral-cooperation/uae-us-security-relationship. [Accessed 1 Nov. 2015].

Thorhallsson, B. and Wivel, A. (2006). Small states in the European Union: What do we know and what would we like to know? *Cambridge Review of International Affairs*, 19(4), pp. 651–68.

UAE Ministry of Foreign Affairs (2014). Foreign policy. [online] Available at: www.mofa.gov.ae/EN/Pages/default.aspx. [Accessed 1 Nov. 2015].

Ulrichsen, K. (2011a). Rebalancing global governance: Gulf States' perspectives on the governance of globalisation. *Global Policy*, 2(1), pp. 65–74.

Ulrichsen, K. (2011b). Repositioning the GCC states in the changing global order. *Journal of Arabian Studies*, 1(2), pp. 231–47.

Ulrichsen, K. (2012). *Small states with a big role: Qatar and the United Arab Emirates in the wake of the Arab Spring*. Number 3. Durham University, UK: HH Sheikh Nasser al Mohammad al Sabah Publication Series.

Ulrichsen, K. (2013). The Gulf goes Global: The evolving role of Gulf countries in the Middle East and North Africa and beyond. No. 121. FRIDE and HIVOS. [online] Available at: http://fride.org/descarga/WP_121_The_Gulf_Goes_Global.pdf. [Accessed 29 Oct. 2015].

United Press International (2013). Emirates builds its own defense industry. UPI. [online] Available at: www.upi.com/Business_News/Security-Industry/2013/03/18/Emirates-builds-its-own-defense-industry/UPI-77731363633569/. [Accessed 1 Nov. 2015].

Vela, J. (2014). GCC to set up regional police force based in Abu Dhabi. *The National*. [online] Available at: www.thenational.ae/world/gcc/gcc-to-set-up-regional-police-force-based-in-abu-dhabi. [Accessed 29 Oct. 2015].

Waltz, K. (1979). *Theory of international politics*. London: Addison-Wesley, p. 131.

Waltz, K. (2000). Structural realism after the Cold War. *International Security*, 25(1), pp. 5–41.

Watanabe, L. (2014). Qatar and the UAE in a changing Middle East. ETH Zurich. [online] Available at: www.isn.ethz.ch/Digital-Library/Articles/Detail/?ots591=4888caa0-b3db-1461-98b9-e20e7b9c13d4&lng=en&id=184991. [Accessed 29 Oct. 2015].

Youngs, R. (2009). *Impasse in Euro-Gulf relations*. Working Paper 80. Madrid: FRIDE.

Yousef, D. (2011). Iran sanctions pinch carpet sellers. *Gulf News*. [online] Available at: http://gulfnews.com/business/sectors/retail/iran-sanctions-pinch-carpet-sellers-1.855697. [Accessed 29 Oct. 2015].

Zarooni, M. (2015). 8 reasons why UAE has to liberate Yemen. *Khaleej Times*. [online] Available at: www.khaleejtimes.com/nation/general/8-reasons-whyuae-has-to-liberate-yemen. [Accessed 10 Nov. 2015].

10
GULF STATES' ENGAGEMENT IN NORTH AFRICA

The role of foreign aid

Lisa Watanabe

Introduction

Against the odds, small states have found means of affecting their regional and international environments. While the Gulf states do not immediately appear as small states, due to their tremendous hydrocarbon resources, they do find themselves in asymmetric relations that they cannot easily change on their own. This can even be said for Saudi Arabia in relation to the United States (US). Despite this being so, they have found means of impacting on regional and international environments to their advantage. Moreover, the Arab uprisings and their aftermath have pushed Saudi Arabia, Qatar, and the United Arab Emirates (UAE) in particular to adopt more assertive and interventionist foreign policies—something that their status as small states, if defined in terms of relative power, would not lead us to expect. Foreign aid has constituted an important dimension of their engagement in North Africa. Indeed, Saudi Arabia, the UAE, and, until recently, Qatar constitute the biggest foreign aid donors to North Africa since 2011. The particular characteristics of Gulf states as foreign aid donors have enabled them to play a significant role in the transitions, which at least at present outweighs that of many bigger external actors, including the US and the European Union (EU). Yet, despite the importance of foreign aid as a foreign policy instrument of many Gulf states, it has received relatively little scholarly attention. This chapter analyses the role of foreign aid in the foreign policy responses of Gulf states, specifically focusing on Qatar, Saudi Arabia, and the UAE as generous aid donors that have taken a more interventionist stance, to the uprisings and transitions in North Africa. It also examines the impact of foreign aid on the transition states in North Africa, with a particular focus on Egypt, since it has been the largest recipient of foreign aid and financial assistance from the three Gulf states under consideration here. It concludes that Qatar, Saudi Arabia, and the UAE have had a significant influence on the uprisings and subsequent transitions in North African countries, with the UAE and Saudi Arabia being particularly important in Egypt since the July 2013 ouster of Mohamed Morsi. Qatar, by contrast, became a less significant external actor in Egypt after this date, due to its more sympathetic stance toward the Muslim Brotherhood, which has been severely repressed and classified as a terrorist organization since.

The Gulf states as small states

There is no agreed definition of small states (Keohane, 1971). However, many analyses of small states have tended to focus on material resources, such as population size, economic wealth, and military strength, leading to a focus on material resources as the bases of state power, as well as the source of threats to state security (Wivel et al., 2014: 6). Clearly if such a definition were adopted, most Gulf states would not qualify as small states, given their enormous hydrocarbon resources, wealth, and in some cases, high level of military spending. Yet, despite their significant material resources they are, nevertheless, unable to guarantee their own security by relying solely on their own capabilities. This suggests that a relational definition of power may be more helpful in capturing the nature of their weakness. Anders Wivel, Alyson J. K. Bailes, and Clive Archer, for example, define a small state as "the weaker part in an asymmetric relationship, which is unable to change the nature or the functioning of the relationship on its own" (Wivel et al., 2014: 9). This definition captures the sense in which small states, whether defined in terms of absolute or relative power, are unlikely to have the kind of assets that have endowed some states within the international system with significant power and influence in the global arena. However, this does not mean that small states do not possess other assets that can serve the interests of bigger states, such as natural resources, wealth, strategic location, or allegiance. How they deploy these assets to maintain their autonomy, national identity, and to exert influence is important in explaining their foreign and security policies.

Being informed by realism, the early literature on small states viewed states as self-interested actors and security as zero-sum in an anarchic international system. Consequently, the focus was on survival, and alignment policy was examined as a means employed by small states to guarantee their security. In such a system, small states could only ensure their survival by seeking the protection of a larger state or by "bandwagoning," through joining coalitions and alliances with bigger states, or by "balancing," through allying with more modest actors to achieve a balance of power (Neumann and Gstöhl, 2006: 10). Most Gulf states have opted for a cooperative strategy or an alliance, either bilaterally or multilaterally to ensure their security. Yet, their foreign and security policy choices are not only responses to systemic constraints. Domestic factors, as more recent literature on small states has pointed out, also play an important role in shaping the policy choices and behavior of small states (Hey, 2003). The interrelationship between regional dynamics and domestic stability and regime survival is especially important in explaining the foreign and security policies of Gulf states, as well as accounting for behavior that defies the expectations of these states as small states.

Alliances are not the sole means that Gulf states have at their disposal to either maintain their autonomy or exert influence. They have also employed foreign aid assistance as an important foreign policy tool. Looking at foreign aid as a foreign policy instrument illustrates how domestic factors and regional dynamics interact to inform their foreign policies. It allows Gulf states to react to regional developments that may have an impact on domestic stability and regime survival. It constitutes a particularly effective instrument in this regard, given the significant resources of many of these states, as well as the relative autonomy of small circles of decision-makers around key members of ruling families which allows them to react and to do so rapidly. Foreign aid can also be used as a means of boosting their prestige in regional and international spheres. Yet, despite the fact that Gulf states are particularly generous donors in global terms, studies of small states as aid donors have tended to focus on Organisation for Economic Co-operation and Development (OECD) donors. Gulf states may, indeed, merit study as a particular category of small-state aid donors. Their specific characteristics affect, for example, their range of recipients and fluctuations in foreign aid assistance, as well as the types of foreign aid they give. Moreover, when considering the motivations of Gulf states as aid donors, the interrelationship between domestic factors and regional dynamics is likely to be more important than for OECD small-state aid donors given the political economies of many Gulf states.

Foreign aid as a foreign policy tool

With the nationalization of domestic oil industries in the 1960s, oil-producing Arab states accrued a large amount of national wealth in a short time frame (Momami and Ennis, 2012: 608). From the 1970s, the Gulf states emerged as major foreign aid donors against the backdrop of the oil boom (Shushan and Marcoux, 2011: 2). Saudi Arabia, Qatar, Kuwait, and the UAE are among the non-OECD Development Assistance Committee (DAC) aid donors that emerged during this period (Almezaini, 2012: 10). Gulf foreign aid assistance as a percentage of GDP is often higher than that of OECD-DAC aid donors (Davidson, 2013: 81). Indeed, they are also recognized as the largest per capita foreign aid donors in the world (Momami and Ennis, 2012: 615). Apart from being especially generous aid donors, another specific feature of Gulf aid is that changes in the levels of aid have been linked to oil-price fluctuations. The high levels of aid in the 1970s that reflected high oil prices were equally matched by decreases in aid in the 1980s and 1990s as oil revenues declined. With oil prices increasing again toward the latter part of the 1990s and the 2000s, Gulf states' foreign aid began to modestly grow again (Momami and Ennis, 2012: 606, 608). Bessma Momani and Crystal Ennis suggest that, while the impact of the financial crisis and declining oil revenues is not yet clear, "It appears that times may have changed for the Gulf states, likely as a result of their stronger interest in channeling their surplus capital towards projects (domestic and international) that are deemed of interest to strategic objectives" (Momami and Ennis, 2012: 615). That said, much may depend on regional developments, as noticeably increased aid levels to North Africa since 2011 demonstrate.

In broad terms, foreign aid may be defined as the transfer of resources and the provision of concessional loans and grants from rich to poor countries. However, given the lack of financial reporting until fairly recently, the lack of definitional coherence, and the difficulty of discerning official from unofficial forms of aid, adopting a very rigid definition of foreign aid would exclude too much from the analysis of Gulf foreign aid assistance. These very same factors also render the study of Gulf states' foreign aid assistance challenging. Of particular difficulty is discerning the significance of aid when states rely heavily on unreported transfers. Saudi Arabia, for example, is thought to make major contributions that are not reported, which are channeled through the Ministry of Finance rather than through its national aid agency, the Saudi Fund for Development. The difficulty of distinguishing between public and private wealth and donations can also render assessing and tracking foreign aid assistance difficult (Shushan and Marcoux, 2011: 3).

Foreign aid assistance has been provided bilaterally by the Gulf region's major donors, Saudi Arabia, Kuwait, and the UAE (World Bank, 2010a: 10). Reported foreign aid assistance is generally channeled through national aid agencies, such as the Saudi Fund for Development, the Kuwait Fund for Arab Economic Development (KFAED), and the Abu Dhabi Fund for Development. These national aid agencies are largely devoted to administering project funding, as well as to some extent debt rescheduling. Project funding takes the form of concessional, untied loans that are usually accompanied by a grant dimension. The Saudi Fund for Development has also issued export credits to recipients to promote the export of Saudi goods (Momami and Ennis, 2012: 619; Almezaini, 2012: 53). Kuwait channels most of its foreign aid through the KFAED, whereas Saudi Arabia and the UAE also make direct bilateral transfers to aid recipients through their ministries of finance and foreign affairs, with Saudi Arabia, as mentioned, thought to administer a greater part of its foreign aid through the Ministry of Finance. Qatar's foreign aid is, by contrast, primarily channeled through the Ministry of Foreign Affairs' Department of International Development (World Bank, 2010a: 18; Momami and Ennis, 2012: 619). Besides official state contributions, Gulf rulers often actively donate funds through charitable foundations, making it difficult to discern what is public and private (family) money (Momami and Ennis, 2012: 620).

In addition to bilateral aid, Gulf states also provide foreign aid assistance to multilateral forums. The five main regional funds are the Arab Fund for Economic and Social Development (AFESD), Arab Bank for Economic Development in Africa (BADEA), Islamic Development Bank (IsDB), OPEC Fund for International Development (OFID), and the Arab Monetary Fund. While the IsDB and OFID are not exclusively funded by Arab states, they do provide the majority of their funds. In addition, the Arab Gulf Program for United Nations Development Organizations (AGFUND) finances technical cooperation and humanitarian assistance through its support of specialized UN agencies (World Bank, 2010b: 2). In contrast to national aid agencies, multilateral regional aid and development institutions exclusively provide low-interest loans and guarantees, but very few grants (Almezaini, 2012: 73). Gulf states have also become increasingly involved in humanitarian aid, contributing to the Arab Red Crescent and Red Cross Societies (World Bank, 2010a: 18–19).

Bilateral aid, which has been shown to be fairly steady since the late 1980s, constitutes the largest part of Gulf foreign aid. While multilateral aid has been increasing over the same period, the levels of bilateral aid still remain higher than those of multilateral aid (Shushan and Marcoux, 2011: 92). This stands in contrast to small OECD-DAC aid donors that give comparatively more multilateral aid. This appears to reflect the type of role that foreign aid plays in the foreign policies of Gulf states, particularly its use for political purposes, such as reacting to regional developments, as well as the political economies of Gulf states that allow financial transfers to occur without the approval of foreign ministries, making foreign aid a particularly effective tool for promoting the interests of the ruling elite. Bilateral aid also offers greater flexibility and rapidity of delivery, particularly when administered through the ministries rather than national aid agencies, though the rulers of Gulf states often have considerable influence over the decision-making mechanisms of national aid agencies, in any case.

In addition to being predominantly bilateral, another distinguishing factor of Gulf foreign aid is that it is untied aid. Gulf states have a tradition of providing unconditional aid, in the sense of an absence of specified policy conditions in return for aid granted. This method of aid delivery is believed to generate good relations and a sense of local ownership for projects undertaken with foreign aid assistance. Indeed, it reflects a general preference of Arab aid for non-interference in recipient countries' policies, at least at the formal level. This characteristic of Gulf states' aid stands in contrast to the major forms of OCED-DAC small-states' foreign aid, which is multilateral and, for the most part, conditional.

The motivations for foreign aid of course vary from country to country and may be dependent on international and regional developments. However, Gulf states' foreign aid has generally been used to promote Arab solidarity and, to a lesser extent, Islam (Watanabe, 2014: 40). These factors partly explain the limited geographic range of Gulf aid that is expected of small-state aid donors, as well as the precise geographic area. As Khalid Almezaini points out, just as Arabism and Islamism are important factors in understanding the Middle East, they are equally significant motivating factors behind Gulf states' foreign aid contributions. Indeed, Arab and Muslim states have tended to take a higher priority in foreign aid disbursements from Gulf states than non-Arab, non-Muslim nations (Almezaini, 2012: 17–18; Momami and Ennis, 2012: 614). However, this appeared to have declined since the 1990s, with higher proportions of aid being channeled to Sub-Saharan Africa, Asia, and Latin America. Nevertheless, in 2010 Arab aid to Middle East and North Africa (MENA) countries still constituted 75 per cent of all Arab overseas development aid (World Bank, 2010a: 12–13). And, one would expect this percentage to be slightly higher following the Arab uprisings. To this end, the geographic range of recipients of Gulf states' aid is restricted largely to the MENA region and ideational factors are important in understanding that geographic range (Neumayer, 2003).

In addition to ideational factors, political considerations also help to determine foreign aid flows from Gulf states. Eric Neumayer, for example, found a positive bias toward states voting similarly to the donors in the UN General Assembly to leverage their influence, as well as some evidence supporting Afro-Arab solidarity and political factors such as not maintaining diplomatic relations with Israel (Neumayer, 2003: 144). Gulf states appear also to use foreign aid to react to regional developments. Almezaini, for example, notes that the UAE has used aid as a tool to react to regional changes, such as the 1967 and 1973 wars (Almezaini, 2012: 59). Against the backdrop of unrest and transitions in the MENA region, there has been an increase in intraregional aid since 2011 (Momami and Ennis, 2012: 606). Part of the motivation for dramatically increasing foreign aid to North African countries in transition in particular appears to be influencing the transition processes in such a way as to support the maintenance of the status quo regionally and domestically, as well as to increase prestige. Moreover, the Arab uprisings and transitions appear to have prompted Saudi Arabia, the UAE, and Qatar to favor more direct forms of action in which foreign aid plays an important role (Khatib, 2013).

Gulf foreign aid and the Arab uprisings

The altered geopolitical balance in North Africa, its linkage to shifts in the Middle East, and concerns about the consequences of a US pivot to Asia have prompted several Gulf states to reinforce their engagement in the sub-region, and encouraged them to adopt a more assertive and interventionist stance in North Africa. In part, this is related to the inability of Syria, Egypt, and Iraq to play their traditionally dominant roles in the MENA region, as well as the difficulties of the EU, and to a lesser extent the US, to act decisively and effectively, which has created a window of opportunity for some Gulf states to play a greater regional role. However, their increased engagement in North Africa should also be understood as efforts to maintain the balance between regional and domestic stability within the Gulf States most heavily engaged, notably Saudi Arabia, the UAE, and, until Morsi's ouster, Qatar (Watanabe, 2014: 38). Indeed, their involvement needs to be understood against the backdrop of the political landscape of the transitions in North Africa and its relationship to domestic stability, as well as their capacity to use substantial amounts of untied foreign aid assistance as a means to shape the transitions and the regional balance.

While Gulf states generally shared the aim of preventing contagion from the Arab uprisings, they adopted different approaches to the uprisings, largely linked to the relationship between regional and domestic security within each country. Divergent attitudes toward the Muslim Brotherhood movements in North Africa, in particular, have generated differing approaches among the Gulf states examined here, with Qatar supporting the Muslim Brotherhood in the region, and Saudi

Arabia and the UAE seeking to counter its rise. This reflects the degree of concern about the impact of the Muslim Brotherhood on domestic stability. The question of how to respond to non-Wahhabi Islamist groups has preoccupied the rulers of Gulf states since the 1970s, as Muslim Brothers fleeing persecution under former Egyptian President Gamal Abdel Nasser established similar reformist Islamist movements in the Gulf. However, the Arab uprisings have added a new urgency to these concerns. Saudi Arabia is home to Wahhabi Sunni Islam. The Wahhabis in Saudi Arabia have been traditionally accommodating of the Saudi state, making Saudi rulers nervous about forms of political Islam that accept participation in electoral politics as challengers to Wahhabism and the political status quo. The Muslim Brotherhood in Egypt is seen as a particular threat, due to Egypt's size and traditionally influential role in the MENA region (Watanabe, 2014: 39).

Like Saudi Arabia, the Emiratis had accommodated Muslim Brotherhood members fleeing Nasser's crackdown, though they were never permitted to establish a domestic branch of the movement in the UAE. A local Islamist Al-Islah (Reform) society, which was believed to have links with the Muslim Brotherhood organization, was founded in 1974 as a nongovernmental organization. It was closed down by the authorities in 1994, however. Following the Arab uprisings, members of the by-then clandestine Islah society were suspected of cooperating with more liberal pro-democracy activists in Abu Dhabi, although ultimately calls for political reform failed to gain momentum. Nevertheless, Emirati rulers, as well as their Saudi counterparts, have been concerned that the Muslim Brotherhood movements in North Africa could encourage their affiliates in the Arabian Gulf to generate domestic instability. The UAE's foreign policy stance has thus been largely in line with that of its larger ally, Saudi Arabia (Watanabe, 2014: 39–40).

While Qatar adheres to Wahhabism, it has been less uneasy about the Muslim Brotherhood than its neighbors, Saudi Arabia and the UAE. In part, this reflects the fact that Qatar has provided a haven, as well as financial support, for the Muslim Brotherhood movement for decades, and has promoted their cause through Al-Jazeera, rendering Qatar's relationship with the Muslim Brotherhood in Egypt and elsewhere in North Africa less concerning from the viewpoint of domestic stability. As such, it backed the Morsi government in Egypt, developed good relations with the Ennahdha-led government in Tunisia, and established a close relationship with the Muslim Brotherhood in Libya (Watanabe, 2014: 40). Qatar's different approach in part reflected the opportunities afforded to it by its previous role as a quasi-neutral mediator, which had generated linkages with the Muslim Brotherhood, which Qatar sought to use as a means of boosting its influence and autonomy following the uprisings. To this end, there appears to have been a shift in Qatari strategy in the first few years following the upheavals in the sub-region. Qatar's support for the Muslim Brotherhood indicated a departure from its previous role of neutral mediator and the adoption of a more partisan interventionist role, something that brought it into conflict with Saudi Arabia and the UAE. Despite its more assertive and independent role, Qatar appeared to refrain from crossing the line of what is acceptable to its larger ally, Saudi Arabia, which is indicative of the continued constraints it faces as small state.

Despite these differences in the relationship between regional and domestic stability, and the variations in foreign policy responses they have generated, common to the major Gulf state donors to North Africa examined here, namely Qatar between 2011 and 2013, Saudi Arabia, and the UAE, is the use of foreign aid to increase their influence in the countries where uprisings and regime change have occurred, and to reinforce their regional role in the early phase of the transitions. In addition to financial assistance in the form of cash and central bank depositions reaching into the billions and aid in the form of energy resources, these states' project funding to North Africa has also grown since the uprisings. In 2012, the greatest funds for such projects were pledged by Qatar, with infrastructural projects linked to natural resources and tourism in Egypt receiving the lion's share—some US $18 billion over a five-year period. US $2 billion were also allocated to infrastructural projects in the energy sphere in Tunisia. Saudi Arabia's commitments were more modest. It contributed US $200 million toward the construction of a high-speed railway network in Morocco, US $120 million for the expansion of electrical power plant capacities and US $85 million for natural gas transport networks in Tunisia, and US $170 million for agricultural infrastructure projects in Egypt. The UAE also committed US $84 million to North African countries, most of which was allocated to infrastructure projects (Watanabe, 2014: 40–1).

At the time of writing, figures for 2013 were available only for Saudi Arabia and the UAE. They indicate that the UAE had significantly increased its commitment to North African countries in general and in particular to Egypt in 2013. Approximately US $1.56 billion was allocated to projects linked to housing construction, healthcare, education, and agricultural projects in Egypt, which is a clear indication of the importance the UAE attaches to Egypt. Additionally, US $80.5 million was assigned to Morocco toward projects linked to healthcare, transport infrastructure, and energy, US $52.7 million was allotted to Algeria, US $5.8 million to Tunisia toward food distribution to the poor and projects connected to the health sector, and US $0.5 million to Libya for relief supplies, the construction of mosques, and Ramadan-related projects. In 2013, Saudi Arabia provided approximately US $150 million in loan agreements to Tunisia only for the construction of social housing (UAE Ministry of International Cooperation and Development, 2014: 37–41; Saudi Fund for Development, 2014).

While official figures for Gulf aid and credit lines alone are impressive in terms of their scale, as well as their unconditional nature, this does not capture the full extent of financial assistance they provide to North Africa. Not all loans and grants are made public. Financial assistance by Gulf states to political and social actors in the transition countries remain largely unknown and are difficult to track. It has been suggested that part of this assistance may go to Salafi political parties, while another part goes to religious outreach and social services provided by Salafi religious organizations. Both constitute additional sources of influence for Gulf states in North Africa, at least among some political and social actors. However, the extent of this influence is unclear. These bilateral sources of aid are also complemented by multilateral forms of foreign aid assistance, granted through institutions such as the AFESD (Watanabe, 2014: 41).

The ability of Qatar, Saudi Arabia, and the UAE to provide substantial amounts of rapid and untied aid and nonproject-related aid has been important in enabling them to significantly boost their regional role. Foreign aid assistance from these Gulf states has clearly provided a lifeline to Egypt in particular, largely due to the unconditional nature of rapid provision of credit lines aimed at boosting the country's foreign-exchange reserves and providing a fiscal stimulus. Saudi, Emirati, and Qatari credit lines have enabled outstanding debts to foreign companies, such as oil companies, to be paid, as well as public sector wages, and projects and services such as housing, education, and health to take place. The fiscal stimulus enabled by Gulf aid has helped to prevent Egypt from becoming insolvent, as well as to enable a slower implementation of politically costly reforms than would have been required by the International Monetary Fund. At least in the short term, then, Gulf aid, of which Saudi, Emirati, and Qatari (until 2013) aid was the most significant, has contributed to economic stabilization in Egypt. Some observers fear that Gulf aid could be a double-edged sword, if it results in the continual deferral of reforms necessary to create a sustainable recovery and to address fundamental socioeconomic grievances. However, this seems unlikely, since Gulf aid donors themselves are likely to press the Egyptian government to undertake difficult reforms, if their aid is to continue to flow. Indeed, the UAE is already actively doing so through the establishment of the so-called UAE–Egypt Task Force, which aims to facilitate the adoption of legislation, reforms, and other measures designed to attract investment in Egypt (Sons and Wiese, 2015: 34). Over the longer term, the greater priority given to project funding is an encouraging development, since it may have a positive impact on infrastructure modernization and possibly economic diversification. Indeed, Gulf states' experience in rapid infrastructural development could provide valuable knowledge of planning and development of such projects.

The untied nature of Saudi, Qatari, and Emirati foreign aid, especially the rapid delivery of cash transfers at critical moments, has also provided transition states with more options when faced with pressure from other international donors. As Kristian Coates Ulrichsen has noted, "For states in transition, this opens up new possibilities with regard to the political and economic choices facing new (or re-empowered) policy elites" (Ulrichsen, 2014). Indeed, when Egypt faced threats from international donors to withdraw financial assistance following the crackdown on supporters of the ousted former President Mohammed Morsi in 2013, Cairo was able to rely more heavily on Saudi, Emirati, and even Qatari aid. Saudi Arabia and the UAE collectively pledged US $8 billion in the form of cash, central bank deposits, and petroleum products (Galani, 2013). Qatar also transferred at least US $5 billion to Egypt, which included US $1 billion in the form of a grant and a deposit of US $4 billion to the Central Bank of Egypt, of which US $3.5 were to be converted into bonds. Following the failure to agree on that conversion, US $2 billion was returned to Qatar, though (Sons and Wiese, 2015: 41).

The ousting of Morsi and the subsequent crackdown on the Muslim Brotherhood by the military-led government in Egypt have enabled Saudi Arabia and the UAE to use their resources to their advantage. Both Gulf states, like the current military-backed government in Egypt, view the Muslim Brotherhood as an extremist group with an agenda that could destabilize the domestic status quo (Hamza, 2014). An Egypt in which the Muslim Brotherhood does not play an important role would certainly help both Saudi Arabia and the UAE maintain a balance between regional and domestic stability, although the need to curb the rise of so-called Islamic State may necessitate a softening of their position with regard to the Muslim Brotherhood in Egypt. The Egyptian army, in turn, is relying on backing from Saudi Arabia and the UAE in particular. In April 2014, Egypt was reported to be considering an arms deal with Russia for the purchase of 24 MiG-35 fighter jets, following a partial suspension of US military aid to Egypt in response to the military-led interim Egyptian government's crackdown on pro-Morsi protestors. Saudi Arabia announced that it would underwrite the purchase, partly to signal displeasure with the US decision (Shapir *et al.*, 2014; Schenker and Trager, 2014). This has since transpired into negotiations to purchase 46 such jets. Since Mohamed Morsi's overthrow, some UAE aid is also being managed by the Egyptian army. In March 2014, it was announced that UAE Arabtec Holdings had signed an agreement with the military for the construction of one million low-income housing units in 13 locations across the country. The contract was rumored to be worth approximately US $40 billion (Hammond and Wan, 2014; Sons and Wiese, 2015: 35). This greater expression of faith in the Egyptian military than the private sector, while perhaps aimed at demonstrating support for the military-backed government and bolstering its credibility, somewhat contradicts its efforts to boost confidence in the Egyptian economy, however.

Egypt's Salafist Nour Party was also reported to have received steady funding from Saudi Arabia in order to assist their candidates to win support in elections (Khalifa, 2014: 9), though such claims have proved hard to verify. Saudi support for Egyptian Salafis has also been devoted to nonpolitical *dawah* (preaching) networks. During the 2012 electoral campaigning, Salafi charity organizations were reported to have received funding from the Gulf to finance television channels and Internet websites (Elagati, 2013: 7). Two of Egypt's largest Salafi organizations—Gamey'ah Shar'iah and Ansar al-Sunna—both of which are registered with the Ministry of Social Solidarity and are engaged in charity work, including offering healthcare services and educational assistance to lower-class Egyptians, as well as in preaching activities and Quran recitation classes, are said to have received significant funding from Saudi Arabia (Lavizzari, 2013; WikiLeaks, 2011). While the motives for such aid are at least in part ideational, Saudi Arabia's aim of marginalizing the Muslim Brotherhood in Egypt as a movement that conflicts with its interests may also be served by such use of funding.

Despite Qatar's generous aid provision, even after the ousting of President Morsi, it has found itself marginalized in Egypt due to its previous support and relations with the Muslim Brotherhood. With criticism in Tunisia and Libya, too, for its support for the Muslim Brotherhood, Qatar has been less successful in increasing its regional influence as a result of its engagement in North Africa than Qataris may have hoped. This highlights the importance of the right constellation of factors coming together to enable small states to play a big role in the regional and international systems through adopting a more interventionist and assertive stance. Qatar has not only found itself relatively marginalized in Egypt, however. Its support for the Muslim Brotherhood has also generated tensions between Qatar and some of its Gulf neighbors, prompting Saudi Arabia, the UAE, and Bahrain to withdraw their ambassadors from Doha in March 2014. In addition, its departure from the role of a quasi-neutral mediator has also tarnished its image and exposed its relative weakness as a small state. Since late 2014, Qatar appears to be engaging in a more careful approach toward Egypt and rapprochement with the El-Sisi regime, although it is unlikely to become more economically engaged with the country in the absence of some sort of political reconciliation with the Muslim Brotherhood. It could even play the role of mediator in any future reconciliation between the El-Sisi regime and the Muslim Brotherhood (Sons and Wiese, 2015: 43–4). The Qatari elite also appear to recognize that multilateral efforts may be needed to address some of the region's problems, as well as the need to repair relations with its Gulf neighbors, as Qatar's participation in the Saudi-led intervention in Yemen in 2015 indicates. The extent to which it has taken an extremely proactive and interventionist stance in North Africa, often acting in ways that do not accord with the policies of Saudi Arabia, illustrates that small states do not always simply follow the policies of their larger allies. Yet, in Qatar's case, an absence of close relations with those actors that became major stakeholders ultimately exposed the limits of its capacity to act unilaterally and pursue an independent interventionist foreign and security policy.

Conclusion

This chapter has attempted to demonstrate the important role that foreign aid plays in the foreign policies of Qatar, Saudi Arabia, and the UAE. As the most significant foreign aid donors to North Africa since the uprisings in 2011, they have challenged the idea that small states cannot play an influential role in the international system. All three countries have taken on a more assertive and interventionist foreign policy stance with regards to the region, and they have used foreign aid assistance as an important foreign policy tool. Their special characteristics as resource-rich countries with highly concentrated decision-making processes, dominated by just a few individuals, have enabled them to have an impact beyond what one would expect from small states. Saudi Arabia and the UAE in particular are demonstrating a greater capacity to influence the trajectory of Egypt's transition than the EU or indeed the US, for example. Their capacity to provide large amounts of untied aid within the context of transition has placed these Gulf states in a rather unique position in relation to bigger external actors.

Indeed, the manner in which the Gulf states have been able to deploy their soft power has been critical in enabling at least Saudi Arabia and the UAE to play a comparatively significant role in the transitions, particularly in Egypt. Indeed, their more assertive engagement is revealing the weaknesses of other states' soft-power resources. However, the success with which Gulf states use their assets to their advantage will also depend to a great extent on permissive conditions within the transition states. Despite its generous funding, Qatar, for example, has not been able to build strong relations with the current Egyptian government and this will remain so long as the military continues to play a critical political role and the Muslim Brotherhood remains a pariah in the view of the Egyptian government. While its foreign policy response to the Arab uprisings demonstrated the extent to which it is willing to pursue policies that are at odds with its larger ally, Saudi Arabia, the move away from its previous role as neutral mediator has demonstrated the risk entailed in adopting an independent and interventionist strategy for a small state. Saudi Arabia, too, has also demonstrated a will to pursue policies that are at least to some extent at odds with those of its larger ally, the US. To this end, these Gulf states, particularly small states, are managing to deploy their power to meet their interests, and often in a more effective way than bigger actors in the international arena.

Bibliography

Almezaini, K.S. (2012) *The UAE and Foreign Policy: Foreign Aid, Identities and Interests*, Abingdon, UK: Routledge.

Davidson, C.M. (2013) *After the Sheikhs: The Coming Collapse of Gulf Monarchies*, London: Hurst and Company.

Elagati, M. (2013) "Foreign Funding in Egypt after the Revolution," Arab Forum for Alternatives/FRIDE/Hivos, available from http://fride.org/download/WP_EGYPT.pdf (accessed September 4, 2016).

Galani, U. (2013) "Breaking Views: Gulf Aid Helps Egypt Avoid Financial Collapse," *Reuters*, 10 July, available from http://en.aswatmasriya.com/analysis/view.aspx?id=950a6bb7-d529-45f6-831ee26af54e485d (accessed September 4, 2016).

Hammond, J. and Wan, J. (2014) "With Sisi Likely to Take Over, How Will Egypt's Military Economy Look Like?" *Al Bawaba Business*, 16 April, available from www.albawaba.com/business/egypt-economy-sisi-569557 (accessed October 19, 2016).

Hamza, Y. (2014) "Gulf Aid Helps Pull Egyptian State Back from the Brink," *The National*, 22 March, available from www.thenational.ae/world/egypt/gulf-aid-helps-pull-egyptian-state-back-from-the-brink#page1 (accessed September 4, 2016).

Hey, J.A.K. (2003) "Refining Our Understanding of Small State Foreign Policy," in Small States in J. A. K. Hey (ed.) *World Politics: Explaining Foreign Policy Behaviour*, Boulder; London: Lynne Rienner, pp. 185–95.

Keohane, R. (1971) "The Big Influence of Small Allies," *Foreign Policy* 2: 161–82.

Khalifa, Isaac S. (2014) "Explaining the Patterns of Gulf Monarchies' Assistance after the Arab Uprisings," *Mediterranean Politics* 19, 3: 413–30.

Khatib, L. (2013) "Qatar's Foreign Policy: The Limits of Pragmatism," *International Affairs* 89, 2: 417–31.

Lavizzari, A. (2013) "The Arab Spring and Funding of Salafism in the MENA Region," *International Security Observer*, 22 May, available from http://securityobserver.org/the-arab-spring-and-the-funding-of-salafism-in-the-mena-region/ (accessed October 19, 2016).

Liska, G. (1968) *Alliances and the Third World, Studies in International Affairs 5*, Baltimore: Johns Hopkins Press.

Momani, B. and Ennis, C.A. (2012) "Between Caution and Controversy: Lessons from the Gulf," *Cambridge Review of International Affairs* 25, 4: 605–27.

Neumann, I.B. and Gstöhl, S. (2006) "Introduction: Lilliputians in Gulliver's World?" in C. Ingebritsen, I. Neumann, S. Gstöhl and J. Beyer (eds.) *Small States in International Relations*, Seattle: Washington University Press/Reykjavik: University of Iceland Press, pp. 3–36.

Neumayer, E. (2003) "What Factors Determine the Allocation of Aid by Arab Countries and Multilateral Agencies?" *Journal of Development Studies* 39, 4: 134–47.

Osgood, R.E. (1968) *Alliances and American Foreign Policy*, Baltimore, MD: Johns Hopkins Press.

Racimora, W. (2013) "Salafist/Wahhabite Financial Support to Educational, Social and Religious Institutions," report requested by the Directorate-General for External Policies of the Union, European Parliament, Brussels.

Rieter, D. (1994) "Learning, Realism and Alliances: The Weight of the Shadow of the Past," *World Politics* 46, 4: 490–526.

Reiter, E. and Gärtner, H. (2001) (eds.) *Small States and Alliances*, Heidelberg; New York: Physica-Verlag.

Revkin, M. (2012) "Saudi Arabia, Qatar and the Arab Spring," *Al-Ahram Weekly Online*, available from http://weekly.ahram.org.eg/Archive/2012/1119/op6.htm (accessed September 4, 2016).

Rothstein, R.L. (1968) *Alliances and Small Powers*, New York: Columbia University Press.

Saudi Fund for Development (2014) "Annual Report 2013," Riyadh, Saudi Arabia: Saudi Fund for Development.

Schenker, D. and Trager, E. (2014) "Egypt's Arms Deal with Russia: Potential Strategic Costs," *Policy Analysis*, The Washington Institute, 4 March, available from www.washingtoninstitute.org/policy-analysis/view/egypts-arms-deal-with-russia-potential-strategic-cost (accessed September 4, 2016).

Shapir, Y., Magen, Z. and Perel, G. (2014) "MiG-35s for Egypt: A Veritable Change of Direction?" *INSS Insight* 544, 1 May, available from www.inss.org.il/index.aspx?id=4538&articleid=6946 (accessed September 4, 2016).

Shushan, D. and. Marcoux, C. (2011) "Arab Aid Allocation in the Oil Era," AidData, Brief 2.

Sons, S. and Wiese, I. (2015) "The Engagement of Arab States in Egypt and Tunisia since 2011—Rational and Impact," *DGAP Analyse*, 9, available from https://dgap.org/en/think-tank/publications/dgapanalysis/engagement-arab-gulf-states-egypt-and-tunisia-2011 (accessed October 19, 2016).

The Economist (2012) "Egypt's Salafists: Dogma and Purity v Worldly Politics," *The Economist*, 20 October 2012, available from www.economist.com/news/middle-east-and-africa/21564911-will-egypt%E2%80%99s-salafists-manage-evolve-party-practical-politics (accessed September 4, 2016).

Ulrichsen, K. (2014) "The Changing Face of Gulf Aid," *The Majjalla*, 14 May, available from www.majalla.com/eng/2014/05/article55249941 (accessed September 4, 2016).

United Arab Emirates Ministry of International Cooperation and Development (MICAD) (2014) "United Arab Emirates Foreign Aid 2013," Abu Dhabi: UAE MICAD.

Vital, D. (1971) *The Survival of Small States: Studies in Small Power/Great Power Conflict*, Oxford: Oxford University Press.

Walt, S.M. (1987) *The Origins of Alliances*, Ithaca; New York: Cornell University Press.

Watanabe, L. (2014) "Sinking in Shifting Sands: The EU in North Africa," in O. Thränert and M. Zapfe (eds.) *Strategic Trends 2014: Key Developments in Global Affairs*, Zurich: Center for Security Studies, ETHZ, pp. 31–48.

WikiLeaks (2011) "Salafism on the Rise in Egypt," passed to *The Telegraph* from WikiLeaks, 15 February 2011, available from www.telegraph.co.uk/news/wikileaks-files/egypt-wikileaks-cables/8327088/SALAFISM-ON-THE-RISE-IN-EGYPT-CAIRO-00000202-001.2-OF-004.html (accessed September 4, 2016).

Wivel, A., Bailes, A.J.K. and Archer, C. (2014) "Setting the Scene: Small States and International Security," in C. Archer, A. J. K. Bailes and A. Wivel (eds.) *Small States and International Security: Europe and Beyond*, London/New York: Routledge, pp. 3–35.

World Bank (2010a) "Arab Development Assistance, Four Decades of Cooperation," Middle East and North Africa Region, Concessional Finance and Global Partnerships Vice Presidency, June.

World Bank (2010b) "Arab Development Assistance, Four Decades of Cooperation," Quick Notes Series 28, August.

11

THE FOREIGN POLICIES OF THE SMALL GULF STATES

An exception in small states' behaviours?

Khalid Almezaini and Jean-Marc Rickli

The foreign and security policies of the small states in the Gulf can be seen as a product of the Middle East and North Africa (MENA) regional system's political and security dynamics. The changes in the behaviour of these states exhibit many characteristics that are unusual for small states over the past ten years. Proponents of neo-realism argue that small states will balance or band-wagon, while the current behaviour of the Gulf Cooperation Council (GCC) small states indicates a more complex behaviour in their foreign and security policies. The formation of regional alliances and bilateral relations with great powers, while maintaining some autonomy and sometimes even using military power unilaterally to counter the rise of security challenges at the domestic and regional levels, is per se very unusual for small states. The small Gulf states are using every opportunity to maintain their autonomy while trying to influence their immediate environment by resorting to hedging strategies and sometimes even extending their reach in declining regional powers.

The different contributions in this book each shed a different light on the policies of the small Gulf states. This chapter captures this knowledge by first summarizing the main findings of the different chapters. It then discusses the emergence of the small Gulf states as small powers in the region and concludes by assessing the sustainability of the small Gulf states' foreign and security policies.

Theoretical analysis:

Are small states in the Gulf an anomaly?

The second chapter, by Jean-Marc Rickli and Khalid Almezaini, sets the theoretical framework that contributes to enhancing our understanding of small states' foreign and security policies, particularly with reference to small states in the Gulf. These evolve along a spectrum of autonomy and influence, and should be understood as a product of systemic and domestic pressures and opportunities. The international and regional systems define the scope of possible actions, while the domestic systems characterized by monarchies supported by tribal allegiances act as lenses that interpret threat perceptions and provide the boundaries of acceptable actions.

David Goldfischer's chapter defines the structural parameters that constrain the small Gulf states' foreign and security policies. The author argues that the US pursued a realpolitik approach towards the Middle East in general and the Gulf in particular even after the end of Cold War, when there was an evolution from realism towards liberalism in US foreign policy in other parts of the world. The rise of Islamic extremism and anti-Americanism in the Middle East since 2001 changed US foreign policy, however, from its dual containment of Iran and Iraq towards neoconservative policies bolstering the general case for war against enemy regimes, which 'had galvanized the belief that only the democratic transformation of the Middle East could uproot the anti-U.S. hatred—and terrorism—emanating from the region' (this volume, p. 70). The US invasion of Iraq in 2003 was the concrete application of this policy but was perceived as a dual betrayal by the Gulf monarchies on the grounds that it posed a threat to their monarchical rule and facilitated the prospects of increased influence of Iran in the region.

The Obama Administration's oscillation between realist and liberal approaches of foreign policy culminated in a reactive incrementalism that has confused the US Gulf partners, failed to address threats to regional and global security, and contributed to an incoherent debate over future policy. Indeed, Obama's liberal pivot in Egypt against Mubarak and his realist-based non-interventionism in Syria undermined the credibility of US commitments in the region in the eyes of the Gulf states. Given the shortcomings of the US approaches in the Middle East over the past decades, Goldfischer underlines liberal institutionalism as a compelling, near-term strategic necessity requiring political leadership.

Similar to Goldfischer, Krieg argues for the necessity of a liberal normative security approach, one that allows for the inclusion of individual security in the conduct of small states' foreign and security policies. Using the cases of Qatar and Bahrain, the chapter explains the different security approaches employed by the two monarchies – particularly in the wake of the 2011 Arab Spring. The latter has exacerbated the political identity tensions of Bahrain. The small emirate is indeed caught between Sunni and Shi'a influences. Manama relies on the continuous support and protection of Riyadh, while Tehran tries to intervene in its domestic politics.

Qatar's homogenous society, with the majority of Qataris subscribing to Wahhabi interpretation of Sunni Islam, plays a significant role in the country's domestic stability. The latter, however, is due not only to the homogenous society, it is argued, but also to the socioeconomic stability the Qataris enjoy in comparison with the Bahraini. Krieg argues then that the provision of public security to Qatari citizens has indeed allowed Doha to divert its attention towards a more proactive policy at the regional level, something that is impossible for Bahrain, which battles Iranian influence on its territory and has limited financial capabilities.

Iran is the second regional structuring factor of the small Gulf states' foreign and security policies. Shahram Akbarzadeh's chapter examines Iran–GCC relations since the 1979 Iranian Revolution. Following the US invasion of Iraq in 2003, Tehran found an opportunity to extend its influence towards the Levant as Baghdad was neutralized and became an ally of Iran with the pro-Shia government of Nouri al-Maliki. This growing influence contributed to strengthen sectarianism in the region.

With the election of President Rouhani in 2013, the mood about Iran among the GCC countries was 'cautiously optimistic'. Yet, the continued confrontation through proxies in Syria as well as the Saudi-led intervention in Yemen rendered this optimism short lived. It is worth noting, however, that there has been no unified policy by the GCC states against Iran, as the Gulf states' reaction towards the agreement demonstrated. Qatar's idea to invite Iran to a GCC meeting did not find support in the organization. Thus, the author concludes that the regional developments and increased sectarianism have facilitated Saudi–Iranian rivalry and therefore have shaped, to a certain extent, Iran–GCC relations.

After having established the structural and domestic factors that constrain the foreign and security policies of the small Gulf states, the other chapters have provided specific case studies. Thus, Victor Gervais argues that the traditional way that the small Gulf states guarantee their security and survival is by adopting a hedging strategy that prioritizes both protection and a degree of regional autonomy. They chose to co-operate at the regional level through the GCC, but only to address internal security threats while at the same time offsetting the influence of the regional power, that is, Saudi Arabia, by relying on an extra-regional protector, namely the US. The overarching goal of the small Gulf states has traditionally been to preserve the status quo and the stability of the ruling regimes. This security model, however, has been questioned since the start of the Arab Spring. Firstly, the ambivalence of the US commitment in the region has brought uncertainties into the implicit security guarantee provided by Washington. Secondly, the rise of the political activism of the small Gulf monarchies has increasingly exposed their divergence and their different interests, and consequently contributed to further undermine the smaller GCC states' alliance model. Similar to Gervais, Emma Soubrier argues that the small Gulf states have adopted hedging strategies to survive in the anarchical regional security complex that is the Gulf and the Middle East. To illustrate her point, she compares Qatar and UAE foreign and security policies prior to and after the Arab Spring. She argues that the UAE developed a security strategy based on credibility with a focus on state-building, while Qatar opted for state-branding in order to be perceived as a legitimate actor in regional and global politics. The UAE developed a strategic culture based on defensive strategy to guarantee its autonomy, while Qatar's quest for legitimacy through international visibility led the small emirate to develop a strategic culture based on influence and co-operation. Soubrier indeed argues that domestic factors in the form of leaders' perceptions and strategic culture based on their personal experience are key to understanding these two different strategic options. The reactions of these two countries to the Arab Spring built upon their internal constraints and strategic culture. Abu Dhabi's newly interventionist policy is interpreted as a continuity of the Emiratis' strategic culture aimed at being perceived as a credible actor, while Doha's interventions are considered in line with the Qataris' drive for visibility on the international stage. Soubrier also concludes that these internal divergences among the small Gulf states bear important risks for the stability of the region.

Leah Sherwood's chapter looks at the UAE's foreign policy as an example of risk-diversification strategy and argues that the UAE's behaviour defies small states' theoretical assumptions because the country exhibits both defensive policies as well as co-operative strategies based on alliance formation. The purpose of these hedging strategies is to balance risks and opportunities. The chapter demonstrates this argument by looking at the way the UAE exerts influence across the different dimensions of power. It argues that the UAE conducts a pragmatic policy dubbed 'smart policy' using different tactics ranging from compromises and direct negotiations to the preservation of the regional balance of power. In other words, the UAE uses both hard and soft power, depending on the situation at hand, by translating and leveraging different dimensions of power, such as financial power, into influence. Nonetheless, Sherwood acknowledges that the UAE's foreign policy record despite this risk-diversification strategy is the weaker party within its asymmetrical relations, demonstrating therefore the limitations of small states in exerting regional and global influence.

Oman's foreign policy is highly personalized through the leadership of Sultan Qaboos. Abdullah Baabood argues that Oman has adopted an independent foreign and security policy diverging from, and sometimes contradicting those of the other GCC members. Baaboob supports his argument by demonstrating that, unlike in the other Gulf states, Sultan Qaboos, after the Iranian Revolution, thought that co-operation with Iran would lead to the containment of any threat from Tehran and was therefore the best way to guarantee regime stability. Hence, Oman has adopted unique positions towards Iran, such as during the war in Yemen or its facilitation of US–Iran contacts prior to the negotiations on Iran nuclear capabilities. Oman's foreign and security policy, Baaboob argues, is a reflection of Sultan Qaboos' leadership and Muscat's pragmatic approach to regime security and stability.

The chapter by Lisa Watanabe looks at an important foreign policy instrument of the Gulf states: foreign aid. The chapter looks specifically at North Africa, following the 2011 uprisings, and Egypt as major aid recipients from the Gulf states. Foreign aid delivered from the main Gulf donors played a significant role during the Arab Spring. Qatar, the UAE and Saudi Arabia used foreign aid differently, however, in order to support their regional allies. This, in turn, contributed to intra-GCC conflicts. Thus, for instance, Doha's support of the Morsi government and the Muslim Brotherhood alienated Qatar's neighbours and contributed to deepen the internal crisis of the GCC. Nonetheless, foreign aid has contributed to make the small Gulf states play an unusual influential role at the regional level.

The different contributions of this book demonstrate that the foreign and security policies of the small Gulf states have unique characteristics. Almost all small Gulf states have adopted hybrid approaches focusing on hedging strategies. The massive wealth increase due to oil revenues has provided these states with the unique ability to influence weak and even declining regional powers. The next section develops these points further.

The small Gulf states' foreign and security policies

Emergence of small powers?

Since the emergence of the small Gulf states, power and hegemony were always in the hands of larger regional states, which include Iraq, Syria, Egypt, Saudi Arabia and Iran. The small Gulf states were marginalized and played minimum roles in the changing dynamics of the Middle East from the 1970s until the late 1990s. Due to their limited capabilities, the main tool of the foreign and security policies of the small Gulf states was foreign aid until the end of the 20th century. The other tools and mechanisms were fairly limited, such as weak militaries, limited media influence and developing economies. One is therefore left to wonder: How did the small Gulf states manage to survive the hostile environment in the region and the centrifugal dynamics unleashed by the Arab Spring?

The security dynamics in the Middle East and the Gulf have in fact rather strengthened the positions of the small Gulf states. While these states were developing and maturing politically, power in the region started to shift to the Gulf. This was due to dramatic changes over the past forty years in the MENA region, such as the Iraq–Iran war, the Iraqi invasion of Kuwait, the US invasion of Iraq in 2003 and the Arab Spring. These events led to the decline of the Arab republics and the rise of the Gulf monarchies. This has been even more evident since the Arab Spring, when popular uprisings led to the decline of many of the Arab republics' role in the region and provided new opportunities for some small states.

The rise of the small states in the Gulf is thus a direct consequence of the decline of the traditional powers in the Middle East such as Egypt, Syria and Iraq. While these states have been busy trying to resolve their own domestic instabilities, the GCC small states took this opportunity to play a significant role in their domestic politics by supporting groups in Syria, Iraq and Egypt. For instance, Qatar has been very active in its support of the Muslim Brotherhood in Egypt and was the most important financial supporter of the Morsi government (Roberts 2014). The UAE, in contrast, has adopted a rather secular foreign policy by supporting anti-Muslim Brotherhood leaders such as General Sisi in Egypt and Haftar in Libya (Roberts 2016; Zayed 2014). This total opposition led, incidentally, these two states to confront each other indirectly.

The engagement of the small Gulf states has also reached a new level of confidence through their first-time use of military force in North Africa, as well as their military contribution in Yemen to fight the Houthis. Both Qatar and the UAE used their air forces in Libya and provided military support for different groups. The UAE also used similar forces in Yemen. The UAE's military contribution is unmatched for a small state. This led it to play a co-leading role with Saudi Arabia in Yemen by providing up to thirty fighter jets and by playing the leading role in recapturing Aden with ground troops (Knights and Mello 2015).

The foreign policy changes of the small Gulf states, especially those of Qatar and the UAE, have been, to a great extent, linked to sudden additional revenues coming from a hike in oil and gas prices, which saw the oil price jump from $20 a barrel in 2001 up to $145 in July 2008 (Hamilton 2009). This has been a major enabler of more interventionist foreign and security policies. The fungibility of small states' power to exert influence has never been as clear as in the Gulf (Art 2004; Khan 2006). The relative strong economies of the small Gulf states in comparison to other states in the MENA region brought these states to the forefront of foreign policy activism. Indeed, as Ulrichsen points out, the increase in energy and commodity prices that started near the start of the 21st century allowed small resource-rich states to vastly increase their wealth, while at the same time providing them with an asymmetrical advantage in foreign policy (2012).

Qatar relied on existing tools of influence such as Al Jazeera to become a strong voice in the Arab world and of the Arab world globally. During the Arab Spring, Qatar could rely on its TV channel to provide an echo chamber to the social movements proliferating in the Arab world. It also used its global reach to become one of the world's most proactive mediators (Kamrava 2011). Qatar's mediation policy has traditionally relied on an extensive network of connections in the Islamic world, which gives Doha access to many actors that sometimes the international community is reluctant to talk to. The surge in the wealth of the small emirate contributed to increase its capacity to host mediations for lengthy periods of times despite the difficulties and complications surrounding the different negotiations. In three of the most notable cases in which Qatar was involved – Lebanon, Sudan and Yemen – Doha has proven to be a capable mediator in reducing tensions but not, crucially, in resolving these conflicts (Kamrava 2011: 21). The UAE, while competing with Qatar, has also used its financial power through direct financial and infrastructure investments to support its Arab allies in the region. For instance, in 2013 the UAE provided $4.9 billion in Egypt to support the Sisi government (El Dahan 2013).

The investments of Qatar, the UAE, Kuwait and Saudi Arabia in many Arab countries should be seen not only as a political but also as a security investment to diversify their security partners. The struggle for influence in Egypt is a case in point. Yet, the policies of the UAE and Qatar regarding the governance of Egypt have also highlighted their diametrically opposed vision and magnified the acute tensions between the two Gulf monarchies.

Unlike the UAE and Qatar, Oman has been very cautious in taking similar steps to the two other monarchies. Oman is relatively larger in size but not as economically strong as the two other GCC states. Oman has traditionally been very reluctant to engage in any conflict, since the creation of the country forty-five years ago. This is due to its history, when foreign powers waged wars on its territory, but also due to its proximity to Iran. Thus, Oman has played a rather neutral role within the GCC, opting out of any military decisions, as well as within the region.

The different interests within the GCC have contributed to make any progress towards more political integration impossible. To the contrary, the different policies conducted by the UAE and Qatar almost led to the implosion of the organization in 2014, when the UAE, Bahrain and Saudi Arabia withdrew their ambassadors from Doha. The conflict was only resolved when King Abdallah of Saudi Arabia put pressure on Doha and Abu Dhabi to settle their differences after he realized the worsening of the crisis could lead to the end of the GCC and therefore the political vehicle of Saudi influence in the region.

The development of the new 'small powers' in the MENA region paralleled, and sometimes contributed, to produce dramatic shifts in the political dynamics in the region. Yet, a legitimate question to ask is whether the small Gulf states' foreign and security policies are sustainable. As mentioned previously, the rise of power of these states can be mainly attributed to two structural developments: the dramatic rise of oil prices which gave these states new economic resources and the decline of traditional regional powers following the outbreak of the Arab Spring. Yet, this one factor has changed: the oil prices have collapsed since July 2014, dropping from $114 a barrel to $30 at the time of writing. It is not clear whether the decline of oil prices will force these small powers to step back and return to more restrained foreign and security policies. The next section, therefore, examines the future of the small Gulf states' foreign policy and security behaviours.

The sustainability of the small Gulf states' foreign and security policies

The cost of the financial and political activism of the small Gulf states in the last ten years has created new responsibilities towards many states in the MENA region. Therefore one can legitimately raise the question of the sustainability of such policies when the oil prices are less than a third of what they were when these policies were initiated. In addition, domestic structural reforms to move from an oil-based towards a knowledge-based economy, as well as the war in Yemen are additional factors that impose financial pressure on these states' budgets and hence on their capacity to project influence.

The GCC countries are still spending large amounts of money in Yemen, providing financial support to different groups in Syria, financing Egyptian economy and increasing support to Jordan and Morocco. However, the relationship with these countries is starting to change. With oil prices having dropped at some point to $30 per barrel, the small Gulf states are not as active as before. Since 2015, the only foreign aid that has been provided is humanitarian aid to people in Syria and Yemen. In general, the volume of aid from the Gulf seems to be decreasing. For instance, the UAE and Kuwait's grants to Egypt in 2016 are much less important than in 2013. Saudi Arabia decided to cancel $4 billion in aid to Lebanon: $3 billion in aid to the Lebanese army and a further $1 billion for security services (Al-Rasheed 2016).

The decline of oil prices and the desire to maintain their current external behaviour have forced most of these states to take serious steps towards stabilizing their economies. Budget deficits as well as very lavish domestic expenses have forced these states to get rid of many subsidies that their citizens used to benefit from. For instance, petrol prices in Qatar were raised by 30 per cent in January 2016. This was due to the announcement of the government's budget deficit of 46.5 billion riyals ($12.8 billion) in 2015, as its first deficit in 15 years (Gulf News 2016). Qatar followed in the footsteps of its neighbours. The UAE raised gasoline prices in August 2015, while Saudi Arabia did so in December 2015, followed by Oman, Bahrain and Kuwait (Gulf News 2016). These measures, aimed at compensating for the budget deficit due to low oil prices, also include the freezing of many economic and infrastructural projects in these countries as well as in the other Arab states, such as the financial support of the UAE and Saudi Arabia in Egypt for instance. This clearly indicates that these states are significantly affected by the oil prices and that their foreign and security policies are changing accordingly. It follows that one can cast strong doubt about the sustainability of the rise of the small Gulf states' political activism which was directly supported by the revenues generated by high oil prices.

The near future will demonstrate the extent to which oil can force small states in the Gulf to behave differently. With limited budgets, it will be riskier for the small Gulf states to continue the pursuit of such active foreign and security policies. Reduced financial power will translate into less foreign influence, though one should not overstate this decline. The small Gulf states have built strong foundations and have become dominant media, social and economic players over the past ten years. Yet, it is likely that the small Gulf states will exhibit more traditional small states' strategies through alignment. The rise of Saudi activism under King Salman, which aims at unifying Sunni Arab states, is also a contributing factor towards more aligned foreign and security policies.

This pressure towards alignment and common position, spearheaded by Saudi Arabia, which can already be seen in Yemen, for instance, does not mean the end of different interests, however. Yemen still demonstrates that Oman conducts a different policy than its fellows within the GCC. Qatar and the UAE still have different interests and conduct different policies when it comes to Libya, Syria or Egypt. The decrease in oil prices and the concomitant loss of financial power means that the small Gulf states are more vulnerable towards regional hegemonic states and that they are more likely to adopt common positions in the future, while their lingering different interests will remain.

Conclusion

As the different chapters have demonstrated, the foreign and security policies of the small Gulf states have dramatically evolved over the last ten years. For instance, the use of foreign aid in the foreign policies of the small Gulf states evolved from being a tool to provide support for countries in need to a tool of influence and change. This allowed them to pursue their own interests without the support of larger regional powers by notably gaining visibility and influence over traditional powers in the MENA region. This evolution has been the result of the changing economic and geopolitical situation. With oil prices skyrocketing, the small Gulf states were suddenly endowed with huge financial resources. They converted them into political influence abroad. While this policy seems to contradict the theories of small states' foreign and security policies, it is, however, a product of an exceptional situation. By being granted so much financial power, the small Gulf states managed to extricate themselves from their small states' security dilemma. However, the dramatic fall of the oil prices since 2014 demonstrates that the structural pressure of smallness has not disappeared. These small states have since then adopted policies that are much more in line with small states' alignment strategies. These, however, are likely to evolve as the changing policy of the US in the region, the rise of radical non-state actors and the increased hostility between Iran and Saudi Arabia will force these small states to find a new security equilibrium to guarantee their survival and their security.

References

Al-Rasheed, M. (2016). 'Why did Riyadh cancel $4 billion in aid to Lebanon?', Al-Monitor, 26 Feb. Available at: www.al-monitor.com/pulse/originals/2016/02/saudi-arabia-lebanon-withdraw-aid-military-iran.html, accessed 6 Sept. 2016.

Art, R. (2004). 'The fungibility of force', in Art, Robert J. and Waltz, Kenneth N. (eds) *The use of force: Military power and international politics*. Lanham, MD: Rowman & Littlefield, 6th edn, pp. 3–33.

El Dahan, M. (2013). 'UAE signs $4.9 billion aid package to Egypt', Reuters, 26 Oct. Available at: www.reuters.com/article/2013/10/26/us-uae-egypt-idUSBRE99P07F20131026, accessed 29 Oct. 2015.

Gulf News (2016). '30% spike in Qatar petrol prices from Friday', Gulf News, 24 Jan. Available at: http://gulfnews.com/business/sectors/energy/30-spike-in-qatar-petrol-prices-from-friday-1.1654059, accessed 6 Sept. 2016.

Hamilton, J.D. (2009). *Causes and consequences of the oil shock of 2007–08*, Washington DC: Brookings Institute.

Kamrava, M. (2011). 'Mediation and Qatari foreign policy', *Middle East Journal*, 65(4): 539–56.

Khan, I. (2006). 'Fungibility of military power and imperatives for small nations', *Bangladesh Institute of International and Strategic Studies Journal*, 27(1): 1–20.

Knights, M. and Mello, A. (2015, 10 August). 'The Saudi–UAE war effort in Yemen (Part 2): The air campaign', The Washington Institute. Available at: www.washingtoninstitute.org/policy-analysis/view/the-saudi-uae-war-effort-in-yemen-part-1-operation-golden-arrow-in-aden, accessed 18 Oct. 2016.

Roberts, D. (2014). 'Qatar and the Muslim Brotherhood', *Middle East Policy*, 21(3): 84–94.

Roberts, D. (2016, 18 March). 'Mosque and state: The United Arab Emirates' Secular foreign policy', Foreign Affairs. Available at: www.foreignaffairs.com/articles/united-arab-emirates/2016-03-18/mosque-and-state, accessed 6 Sept. 2016.

Ulrichsen, K.C. (2012). 'Small states with a big role: Qatar and the United Arab Emirates in the wake of the Arab Spring', Discussion Paper. Durham, UK: Durham University, HH Sheikh Nasser al-Mohammed al-Sabah Programme.

Zayed, A. (2014). 'HH Sheikh Abdullah bin Zayed gives interview to Bret Baier of US TV Channel Fox News', UAE Ministry of Foreign Affairs, 22 Nov. Available at: www.mofa.gov.ae/mofa_english/portal/bf96f3d4-38b7-4a96-b902-e39faf416bf4.aspx, accessed 6 Sept. 2016.

BIBLIOGRAPHY

Abdulla, A. (2012, 9 October). New assertiveness in UAE foreign policy. Gulf News. Available at http://gulfnews.com/opinion/thinkers/new-assertiveness-in-uae-foreign-policy-1.1086667 (accessed 31 October 2015).

Aboudi, S. (2015, 8 April). UAE says sees systematic Iranian meddling in Yemen, region. Reuters. Available at www.reuters.com/article/us-yemen-crisis-uae-iran-idUSKBN0MZ1P520150408 (accessed 6 September 2016).

Abraham, G. (2008, 21 July). Qatar is a diplomatic heavy hitter. Al-Jazeera. Available at www.aljazeera.com/focus/2008/07/200872164735567644.html (accessed 1 September 2016).

Abu Najm, M. (2015, 10 September). Bahrain FM: Iran nuclear deal 'does not address' all sources of tension with Tehran. Asharq al-Awsat. Available at http://english.aawsat.com/2015/09/article55345077/bahrain-fm-iran-nuclear-deal-does-not-address-all-sources-of-tension-with-tehran (accessed 24 August 2016).

Adib-Moghaddam, A. (2006). *The international politics of the Persian Gulf: A cultural genealogy*. London: Routledge.

Agence France-Presse (AFP). (2015, 2 October). Bahrain recalls ambassador from Iran over 'meddling'. Al-Jazeera. Available at www.aljazeera.com/news/2015/10/bahrain-recalls-ambassador-iran-meddling-151002032510372.html (accessed 1 September 2016).

Agius, C. and Devine, K. (2011). Neutrality: A really dead concept? A Reprise, *Cooperation and Conflict*, 46(3): 263–84.

Ajami, F. (2014). *In this Arab time: The pursuit of deliverance*. Stanford, CA: Hoover Institution Press.

Alaan TV (2015, 4 August). Qatar: Iran nuclear deal makes the region more secure. Available at www.alaan.tv/news/world-news/135784/qatar-iran-nuclear-deal-makes-region-more-secure-safe (accessed 6 September 2016).

Al-Akim, H.H. (2011). *Dynamics of Arab foreign policy-making in the twenty-first century: Domestic constraints and external challenges*. London: SAQI.

Al Arabiya (2011a, 14 March). GCC troops dispatched to Bahrain to maintain order. Available at www.alarabiya.net/articles/2011/03/14/141445.html (accessed 29 October 2015).

Al Arabiya (2011b, 3 April). Gulf Arab states reject Iran 'interference'. Available at www.alarabiya.net/articles/2011/04/03/144037.html (accessed 6 September 2016).

Bibliography

Al Arabiya (2014, 1 June). Kuwait's emir makes landmark visit to Iran. Available at http://english.alarabiya.net/en/News/2014/06/01/Kuwait-s-emir-makes-landmark-visit-to-Iran.html (accessed 6 September 2016).

Al-Awadhi, A. (2010, 21 October). The fundamentals of the UAE foreign policy. ECSSR. Available at www.ecssr.ac.ae/ECSSR/print/ft.jsp?lang=en&ftId=/FeatureTopic/Abdullah_AlAwadhi/FeatureTopic_1342.xml (accessed 29 October 2015).

Al-Awadhi, A. (2012, 19 July). The humanitarian aspect of the UAE Foreign policy. Abu Dhabi: The Emirates Center for Strategic Security and Research. Available at www.ecssr.ae/ECSSR/print/ft.jsp?lang=en&ftId=/FeatureTopic/Abdullah_AlAwadhi/FeatureTopic_1576.xml (accessed 1 November 2015).

Al-Bishi, M. (2014, 30 January). Abu Dhabi's sovereign wealth fund is world's second largest. Asharq Al-Awsat. Available at http://english.aawsat.com/2014/01/article55328255 (accessed 31 October 2015).

Alden, C. and Aran, A. (2012). Foreign policy analysis: New approaches. Abingdon, UK: Routledge.

Al-Ebraheem, H.A. (1984). *Kuwait and the Gulf: Small states and the international system.* Washington, DC: Center for Contemporary Arab Studies.

Al-Habtoor, K.A. (2015, 19 August). Hezbollah sleeping cells in Kuwait are a wake-up call. Al-Arabiya. Available at http://english.alarabiya.net/en/views/news/middle-east/2015/08/19/Hezbollah-sleeping-cells-in-Kuwait-are-a-wake-up-call.html (accessed 6 September 2016).

Al-Jazeera (2007, 18 November). Ahmadinejad boosts Bahrain ties. Available at www.aljazeera.com/news/middleeast/2007/11/200852512238205149.html (accessed 6 September 2016).

Al-Jazeera (2007, 3 December). Ahmadinejad arrives for Gulf summit. Available at www.aljazeera.com/news/middleeast/2007/12/200852514309702795.html (accessed 6 September 2016).

Al-Jazeera (2008, July 21). Qatar is a diplomatic heavy hitter. Retrieved from www.aljazeera.com/focus/2008/07/200872164735567644.html (accessed 24 August 2016).

Al-Jazeera (2011, 1 April). Iran rejects Kuwait spy allegation. Available at www.aljazeera.com/news/middleeast/2011/03/201133123525225240.html (accessed 6 September 2016).

Al-Jazeera (2013, 21 October). Qatari court upholds poet's jail sentence. Al-Jazeera. Available at www.aljazeera.com/news/middleeast/2013/10/qatar-court-upholds-sentence-against-poet-20131021123723850815.html (accessed 19 August 2016).

Al-Jazeera (2015, October 2). Bahrain recalls ambassador from Iran over 'meddling'. Retrieved from www.aljazeera.com/news/2015/10/bahrain-recalls-ambassador-iran-meddling-151002032510372.html (accessed 24 August 2016).

Al Khaleeji, A. (2003, 5 May). Unification of armed forces significant. Available at www.sheikhmohammed.co.ae/vgn-ext-templating/v/index.jsp?vgnextoid=2eb7600c3a384110VgnVCM1000003f140a0aRCRD&vgnextchannel=9b834c8631cb4110VgnVCM100000b0140a0aRCRD&vgnextfmt=mediaPublication&date=1052046562633&mediatype=INTERVIEW (accessed 15 October 2015).

Al Lawati, A. (2010, 23 September). UAE and Brazil to sign defence agreement. Gulf News. Available at http://gulfnews.com/news/uae/government/uae-and-brazil-to-sign-defence-agreement-1.686015 (accessed 1 November 2015).

Allison, G.T. (1971). *Essence of decision: Explaining the Cuban Missile Crisis*, 2nd edn. Boston, MA: Little, Brown.

Al Makahleh, S. (2013, 21 February). UAE defence industries show significant progress. Gulf News. Available at http://m.gulfnews.com/business/uae-defence-industries-show-significant-progress-1.1149170 (accessed 1 November 2015).

Al-Marashi, I. (2015, 30 June). Shattering the myths about Kuwaiti Shia. Al-Jazeera. Available at www.aljazeera.com/indepth/opinion/2015/06/shattering-myths-kuwaiti-shia-150629081723864.html (accessed 24 August 2016).

Al-Mashat, A.-M. (2008). Politics of constructive engagement: The foreign policy of the United Arab Emirates, in Bahgat Korany and Ali E. Hillal Dessouki (eds), *The foreign policies of Arab States: The challenge of globalization*. Cairo: The American University in Cairo Press, pp. 457–80.

Almezaini, K. (2011, 15 December). Bold foreign policy of the UAE brings benefits for GCC. *The National*. Available at www.thenational.ae/thenationalconversation/comment/bold-foreign-policy-of-the-uae-brings-benefits-for-gcc (accessed 29 October 2015).

Almezaini, K.S. (2012). *The UAE and foreign policy: Foreign aid, identities and interests*. Abingdon, UK: Routledge.

Al-Rasheed, M. (2013, 9 December). Omani rejection of GCC union adds insult to injury for Saudi Arabia. Al-Monitor: The Pulse of the Middle East. Available at from www.al-monitor.com/pulse/originals/2013/12/oman-rejects-gcc-union-insults-saudi-arabia.html#ixzz3tqxdbgR3 (accessed 24 April 2016).

Al-Rumaihi, M.G. (1975). *Bahrain: A study on social and political changes since the First World War*. Kuwait: University of Kuwait.

Al-Sayegh, F. (2002). The UAE and Oman: Opportunities and challenges in the twenty-first century, *Middle East Policy*, 9 (3): 124–37.

Al Shayji, A. (2013, 27 October). Gulf allies losing faith in their allies, *Gulf News*.

Al Suwaidi, A. (2011, 8 December). UAE 40th National Day: Effective and balanced foreign policy. Abu Dhabi: Emirates Center for Strategic Security and Research. Available at www.ecssr.ac.ae/ECSSR/appmanager/portal/ecssr?_nfls=false&_nfpb=true&lang=en&_pageLabel=featuredTopicsPage&_event=viewFeaturedTopic&ftId=/FeatureTopic/ECSSR/FeatureTopic_1480.xml (accessed 29 October 2015).

Alterman, J.B. (2004). The information revolution and the Middle East, in Nora Bensahel and Daniel L. Byman (eds), *The future security environment in the Middle East: Conflict, stability, and political change*. Santa Monica, CA: RAND, pp. 227–51.

Amos, D. (2014, 8 December). Facing threats from ISIS and Iran, Gulf States set to join forces. NPR.org. Available at www.npr.org/sections/parallels/2014/12/08/369374722/facing-threats-from-isis-and-iran-gulf-states-set-to-join-forces (accessed 29 October 2015).

Anderson, J.W. (2003). The Internet and Islam's new interpreters, in D. F. Eickelman and Jon W. Anderson (eds), *New media in the Muslim world – The emerging public sphere*. Indianapolis, IN: Indiana University Press, pp. 45–61.

Arab Center for Research and Policy Studies (2014, 11 November). The military campaign against the Islamic State in Iraq and the Levant: Arab public opinion. Doha, Qatar. Available at http://english.dohainstitute.org/file/Get/40ebdf12-8960-4d18-8088-7c8a077e522e (accessed 1 November 2015).

Arab Human Development Report (2009). *Challenges to human security in the Arab countries*. New York: UN Development Program.

Arango, T. (2016, 13 February). Sunni resentment muddles prospect of reunifying Iraq after ISIS. *The New York Times*. Available at www.nytimes.com/2016/02/13/world/middleeast/sunni-resentment-muddles-prospect-of-reunifying-iraq-after-isis.html?_r=0 (accessed 18 February 2016).

Archer, C. (2010). Small states and European security and defence policy, in Robert Steinmetz (ed), *Small states in Europe: Challenges and opportunities*. London: Ashgate, pp. 47–64.

Archer, C. (2013). Small state security in Europe: The Nordic states, in A. Wivel, A. Bailes and C. Archer, (eds), *Small states and international security: Europe and beyond*. New York: Routledge, pp. 95–112.

Archer, C., Bailes, A. and Wivel, A. (2014). *Small states and international security: Europe and beyond*. London: Routledge,.

Art, R. (1996). American foreign policy and the fungibility of force, *Security Studies*, 5(4): 7–42.

Art, R. (2004). The fungibility of force, in Robert J. Art and Kenneth N. Waltz (eds), *The use of force: Military power and international politics* 6th edn. Lanham, MD: Rowman & Littlefield, pp. 3–33.

Asal, V., Quinn, D., Wilkenfeld, J., Young, K. and Msn, R.N. (2007). *Mediating international crises*. London and New York; Routledge.

Awad, M., Mehta, A., Chuter, A. and Tran, P. (2013, 11 November). US bid delays Qatar jet competition: UAE fighter contest is also up for grabs. Defence News. Available at www.defensenews.com/article/20131110/DEFREG04/311100014/US-Bid-Delays-Qatar-Jet-Competition (accessed 1 November 2015).

Axelrod, R. (1976). *Structure of decision: The cognitive maps of political elites*. Princeton, NJ: Princeton University Press.

Ayish, M.I. (2009). *The new Arab public sphere*. Berlin: Frank & Timme.

Ayubi, M. (1996). *The Third World security predicament: State making, regional conflict, and the international system*. Boulder, CO: Lynne Rienner.

Baabood, A. (2005). Dynamics and determinants of the GCC states' foreign policy, with special reference to the EU, in Gerd Nonneman (ed), *Analyzing Middle East foreign policies and the relationship with Europe*. London: Routledge, pp. 145–73.

Badrakhan, A. (2013, 13 November). UAE's foreign policy: A model of balance and efficiency. Abu Dhabi: The Emirates Center for Strategic Security and Research. Available at www.ecssr.ac.ae/ECSSR/print/ft.jsp?lang=en&ftId=/FeatureTopic/Abdel_Wahab_Badrakhan/FeatureTopic_1741.xml (accessed 1 November 2015).

Baehr, P.R. (1975). Small states: A tool for analysis?, *World Politics*, 27(3): 456–66.

Bahgat, G. (1995). Military security and political stability in the Gulf, *Arab Studies Quarterly*, 17(4): 55–70.

Bailes, A. and Thorhallsson, B. (2014). Instrumentalising the European Union in small states' strategies, *Journal of European Integration*, 35(2): 99–115.

Bailes, A., Rickli, J.-M. and Thorhallsson, B. (2014). Small states, survival and strategy, in Clive Archer, Alyson Bailes and Anders Wivel (eds), *Small states and international security: Europe and beyond*. London: Routledge, pp. 26–45.

Bailey, R. and Willoughby, R. (2013). Edible oil: Food security in the Gulf. EER Briefing Paper 2013/03. Chatham House pp. 2–5. Available at www.chathamhouse.org/publications/papers/view/195281 (accessed 1 November 2015).

Baillie, S. (1998). A theory of small state influence in the European Union, *Journal of International Relations and Development*, 1(3–4): 195–219.

Baker Fox, A. (1969). Small states in the international system: 1919–1969, *International Journal*, 24(4): 751–64.

Baldacchino, G. (2006). Innovative development strategies from non-sovereign island jurisdictions? A global review of economic policy and governance practices, *World Development*, 34(5): 852–67.

Baldwin, D. (2002). Power and international relations, in W. Carlsnaes, T. Risse and B. Simmons (eds), *Handbook of international relations*. London: SAGE, pp. 177–92.

Baldwin, D. (2013). Power and international relations, in W. Carlsnaes, T. Risse and B. Simmons (eds), *Handbook of international relations*, 2nd edn. Thousand Oaks, CA: SAGE, pp. 273–97.

Bardsley, D. (2010, 22 October). UAE-China economic ties 'to expand beyond oil industry'. *The National*. Available at www.thenational.ae/news/world/asia-pacific/uae-china-economic-ties-to-expand-beyond-oil-industry (accessed 1 November 2015).

Barnett, M.N. (1993). Institutions, roles and disorder: The case of the Arab States system, *International Studies Quarterly*, 37(3): 271–96.

Barnett, M. (1996–7). Regional security after the Gulf War, *Political Science Quarterly*, 111(4): 597–618.

Barnett, M.N. (1998). *Dialogues in Arab politics: Negotiations in regional order*. New York: Columbia University Press.

Barnett, M. (1999). Culture, strategy and foreign policy change: Israel's road to Oslo, *European Journal of International Relations*, 5(1): 5–36.

Barnett, M.N. and Gause, F.G. III (1998). Caravans in opposite directions: Society, state, and the development of community in the GCC, in E. Adler and M. Barnett (eds), *Security communities*. Cambridge, UK: Cambridge University Press, pp. 161–97.

Barnett, M.N. and Telhami, S. (2002). *Identity and foreign policy in the Middle East*. Ithaca, NY: Cornell University Press.

Barrett, R. (2014). Obama: The Anti-Bush. MEI Scholar Series. Washington, DC: Middle East Institute. Available at www.mei.edu/content/article/obama-anti-bush (accessed 1 November 2015).

Barrett, R. (2015). Oman's balancing act in the Yemen conflict. Available at www.mei.edu/content/at/oman's-balancing-act-yemen-conflict (accessed 24 April 2016).

Basrur, R.M. (2006). Decentralizing theory: Regional international politics, *International Studies*, 43(4): 419–24.

Bassiouni, M.C., Rodley, N., Al-Awadhi, B., Kirsch, P. and Arsanjani, M.H. (2011a). *Report of the Bahrain Independent Commission of Inquiry*. Chapter IV: Narrative of Events of February and March 2011, pp. 65–170.

Bassiouni, M.C., Rodley, N., Al-Awadhi, B., Kirsch, P. and Arsanjani, M.H. (2011b). *Report of the Bahrain Independent Commission of Inquiry*. Chapter VI: Allegations of human rights violations against the person. Manama: BICI, pp. 219–317.

BBC News (2014, 5 March). Gulf ambassadors pulled from Qatar over 'interference'. Available at www.bbc.com/news/world-middle-east-26447914 (accessed 6 September 2016).

BBC Persian (2012, 16 October). Kuwait criticism of Iran over the three islands on the eve of Ahmadinejad's trip. Available at www.bbc.com/persian/iran/2012/10/121016_l23_iran_kuwait_island_persian_gulf_ahmadinejad_visit.shtml (accessed 6 September 2016).

Belfer, M. (2014). *Small state, dangerous regions. A strategic assessment of Bahrain*. Frankfurt: Peter Land.

Bellin, E. (2012). Reconsidering the robustness of authoritarianism in the Middle East. Lessons from the Arab Spring, *Comparative Politics*, 44(2): 127–49.

Bensahel, N. and Byman, D. (2004). *The future security environment in the Middle East: Conflict, stability, and political change*. Santa Monica, CA: RAND.

Beyer, J.L. and Hofmann, S.C. (2011). Varieties of neutrality: Norm revision and decline, *Cooperation and Conflict*, 46(3): 285–311.

Bill, J.A. and Springborg, R. (1999). *Politics in the Middle East*, 5th edn. New York: Addison Wesley Longman.

Bi-me.com (2009). Gulf economies must diversify to weather crisis, says Carnegie report – Business Intelligence Middle East – bi-me.com – News, analysis, reports. Available at www.bi-me.com/main.php?id=33584&t=1 (accessed 31 October 2015).

Bindschedler, R.L. (1976). Neutralitätspolitik und Sicherheitspolitik, *Österreichische Zeitschrift für Aussenpolitik*, 6: 339–54.

Bjerga, K.I. and Haaland, T.L. (2010). Development of military doctrine: The particular case of small states, *Journal of Strategic Studies*, 33(4): 505–33.

Björkdahl, A. (2008). Norm advocacy: A small state strategy to influence the EU, *Journal of European Public Policy*, 15(1): 135–54.

Björkdahl, A. (2013). Ideas and norms in Swedish peace policy, *Swiss Political Science Review*, 19(3): 322–37.

Black, A. (2001). *The history of Islamic political thought – From the Prophet to the present.* Edinburgh, UK: Edinburgh University Press.

Black, I. (2013, 4 December). Political solution to Syrian war does not interest Assad, says Qatari minister. *The Guardian.* Available at www.theguardian.com/world/2013/dec/04/political-solution-syrian-war-assad-qatari-minister (accessed 4 September 2016).

Booth, K. (1990). The concept of strategic culture affirmed, in Carl G. Jacobsen (ed), *Strategic power: USA/USSR.* London: Macmillan, pp. 121–8.

Bouyamourn, A. (2015, 6 August). UAE economy to gain $13bn from lifting of Iran sanctions, IMF predicts. *The National.* Available at www.thenational.ae/business/economy/uae-economy-to-gain-13bn-from-lifting-of-iran-sanctions-imf-predicts (accessed 4 September 2016).

Boyes R. and Watson R. (2013, 22 November). Saudi Arabia turns up the heat on the West over possible Iran nuclear deal. *The Times.* Available at www.thetimes.co.uk/tto/news/world/middleeast/article3929509.ece (accessed 20 February 2016).

Briguglio, L., Cordina, G. and Kisangga, E. (2006). *Building the economic resilience of small states.* Malta and London: Islands and Small States Institute, Commonwealth Secretariat.

Bromley, S. (1994). *Rethinking Middle East politics.* Austin, TX: University of Texas Press.

Bronner, E. and Slackman, M. (2011, 15 March). Saudi troops enter Bahrain to help put down unrest. *The New York Times.* Available at www.nytimes.com/2011/03/15/world/middleeast/15bahrain.html?pagewanted=all&_r=0 (accessed 6 September 2016).

Bronson, R. (2006). *Thicker than oil: America's uneasy partnership with Saudi Arabia*, 1st edn. Oxford: Oxford University Press.

Brooks, R. (2004). Civil–military relations in the Middle East, in Nora Bensahel and Daniel L. Byman (eds), *The future security environment in the Middle East – Conflict, stability, and political change.* Santa Monica, CA: RAND, pp. 129–35.

Bueno de Mesquita, B. (2002). Domestic politics and international relations, *International Studies Quarterly*, 46(1): 1–9.

Bueno de Mesquita, B. and Lalman, D. (1992). *War and reason: Domestic and international imperatives.* New Haven: Yale University Press.

Buenos Aires Herald (2013a, 10 July). Egypt names new PM. Available at www.buenosairesherald.com/article/135664/egypt-names-new-pm (accessed 29 October 2015).

Buenos Aires Herald (2013b, 10 July). New regime gets Gulf money in show of support for Army. Available at www.buenosairesherald.com/article/135665/new-regime-gets-gulf-money-in-show-of-support-for-army (accessed 29 October 2015).

Buzan, B. (1991). *People, states and fear: An agenda for international security studies in the post-Cold War era.* Boulder, CO: Lynne Rienner.

Buzan, B. and Waever, O. (2003). *Regions and powers: The structure of international security.* Cambridge, UK: Cambridge University Press.

Buzan, B., Waever, O. and Wilde, J. de (1998). *Security: A new framework for analysis.* Boulder, CO: Lynne Rienner.

Caldwell, Dan (1977). Bureaucratic foreign policy-making, *American Behavioral Scientist,* 21(1): 87–110.

Campbell, J.C. (1958). *Defense of the Middle East: Problems of American policy.* New York: Council on Foreign Relations. Cited by Hudson, M. (2005). The United States in the Middle East, in Fawcett, L. *International relations of the Middle East.* Oxford: Oxford University Press, p. 285.

Carlisle, T. (2011, 23 May). Iran–Bahrain gas project off again. *The National.* Available at www.thenational.ae/business/energy/iran-bahrain-gas-project-off-again (accessed 4 September 2016.

Carlsnaes, W. (1992). The Agency–structure problem in foreign policy analysis, *International Studies Quarterly,* 36(3): 245–70.

Chandrasekaran, R. (2014, 9 November). In the UAE, the United States has a quiet, potent ally nicknamed a 'Little Sparta'. *The Washington Post.* Available at www.washingtonpost.com/world/national-security/in-the-uae-the-united-states-has-a-quiet-potent-ally-nicknamed-little-sparta/2014/11/08/3fc6a50c-643a-11e4-836c-83bc4f26eb67_story.html (accessed 1 November 2015).

Chatham House (2012, February). Kuwait Study Group: Identity, citizenship and sectarianism in the GCC. Workshop Summary. Available at www.chathamhouse.org/sites/files/chathamhouse/public/Research/Middle%20East/0212kuwaitsummary_identity.pdf (accessed 4 September 2016).

Cheng-Chwee, K. (2008). The essence of hedging: Malaysia and Singapore's response to rising China, *Contemporary Southeast Asia,* 30(2): 159–85.

Chulov, M. (2011, 16 March). Bahrain unleashes force on protesters' camp. *The Guardian.* Available at www.theguardian.com/world/2011/mar/16/bahrain-protesters-military-operation-manama (accessed 4 September 2016).

Claude, I. (1962). *Power and international relations.* New York: Random House.

Cohen, R. (2016, 8 February). America's Syrian shame, *The New York Times.* Available at www.nytimes.com/2016/02/09/opinion/americas-syrian-shame.html (accessed 22 February 2016).

Commonwealth Secretariat (1997). *A future for small states: Overcoming vulnerabilities.* London: Commonwealth Secretariat.

Cooper, A. (ed) (1997). *Niche diplomacy: Middle powers after the Cold War.* New York: Macmillan.

Cooper, A.F. and Momani, B. (2011, 29 September). Qatar and expanded contours of small state diplomacy. *International Spectator: Italian Journal of International Affairs,* 46. Available at www.arts.uwaterloo.ca/~bmomani/Documents/IS-%20qatar.pdf (accessed 4 September 2016).

Cooper, A. and Shaw, T. (2009a). The diplomacies of small states at the start of 21st century: How vulnerable? How resilient?, in A. Cooper and T. Shaw (eds), *The diplomacies of small states: Between vulnerability and resilence.* Basingstoke, UK: Palgrave Macmillan, pp. 1–19.

Cooper, A.F. and Shaw, T. (eds) (2009b). *The diplomacies of small states.* Basingstoke, UK: Palgrave Macmillan.

Cooper, S. (2003). State-centric balance-of-threat theory: Explaining the misunderstood GCC, *Security Studies,* 13(2): 306–49.

Cordesman, A. (2011). *Saudi stability in a time of change.* Washington, DC: Center for Strategic and International Studies (CSIS).

Cordesman, A. (2013). *Securing the Gulf: Key threats and options for enhanced cooperation.* Washington, DC: CSIS.

Cordesman, A.H. and Wagner, A. (2003). *The lessons of modern war: The Iran–Iraq War*, Vol. 2. New York: Westview Press.

Crandall, M. and Allan, C. (2015). Small states and big ideas: Estonia's battle for cybersecurity norms, *Contemporary Security Policy*, 36(2): 346–68.

Craze, J. (ed) (2008). *World Bank conditionalities: Poor deal for poor countries.* The Netherlands: A SEED Europe, supported by Oxfam Novib.

Crist, D.B. (2009, June). Gulf of conflict: A history of U.S.–Iranian confrontation at sea. Policy Focus No. 95, Washington Institute. Available at www.washingtoninstitute.org/uploads/Documents/pubs/PolicyFocus95.pdf (accessed 24 August 2016).

Dahl, R. (1957). The concept of power, *Behavioral Science*, 2(3): 215.

Dahl, R. (1991). *Modern political analysis*, 5th edn. Englewood Cliffs: Prentice Hall.

Däniker, G. (1966). *Strategie des Kleinstaates*. Huber: Frauenfeld.

Daoud, K. (2015, 21 November). Saudi Arabia: An ISIS that has made it. *The New York Times*. Available at www.nytimes.com/2015/11/21/opinion/saudi-arabia-an-isis-that-has-made-it.html (accessed 19 February 2016).

Dasgupta, S. (2014, 8 June). UAE envoy sees 30 per cent jump in China trade. *Khaleej Times*. Available at www.khaleejtimes.com/article/20140607/ARTICLE/306079873/1037 (accessed 1 November 2015).

David, S.R. (1991). Explaining Third World alignment, *World Politics*, 42(2): 233–56.

Davidson, C. (2012). *After the Sheikhs: The coming collapse of the Gulf monarchies.* London: Hurst.

de Carvalho, B. and Neumann, I.B. (eds) (2015). *Small state status seeking: Norway's quest for international standing.* London: Routledge.

de Santis, N. (2004). *Nato Review*. Available at www.nato.int/docu/review/2004/issue3/english/art4.html (accessed 29 October 2015).

Diamond, L. (2010). Liberation technology, *Journal of Democracy*, 21(3): 69–83.

Donnelly, J. (2000). *Realism and international relations.* Cambridge, UK: Cambridge University Press.

Doran, M.S. (2011). The impact of new media – The revolution will be tweeted, in K. Pollack (ed), *The Arab awakening: America and the transformation of the Middle East.* Washington, DC: Brookings, pp. 39–46.

Drezner, D.W. (2000). Ideas, bureaucratic politics, and the crafting of foreign policy, *American Journal of Political Science*, 44(4): 733–49.

Duke, S. (2001). Small states and European security, in Erich Reiter and Heinz Gartner (eds), *Small states and alliances.* Heildelberg: Physica-Verlag, pp. 39–50.

Dunford, D. (1995). The US and Oman: An enduring partnership, *Middle East Insight*, 12(1): 62–4.

East, M.A. (1973). Size and foreign policy behaviour: A test of two models, *World Politics*, 25(4): 556–76.

Economist Intelligence Unit (EIU) (2011). Bahrain. *Country Report*, September 2011. London: EIU.

Ehteshami, A. (2007). *Globalization and geopolitics in the Middle East: Old games, new rules.* New York: Routledge.

Elagati, M. (2013). Foreign funding in Egypt after the revolution, Arab Forum for Alternatives/FRIDE/Hivos. Available at http://fride.org/download/WP_EGYPT.pdf (accessed 4 September 2016).

El Dahan, M. (2013). UAE signs $4.9 billion aid package to Egypt. Reuters. Available at www.reuters.com/article/2013/10/26/us-uae-egypt-idUSBRE99P07F20131026 (accessed 29 October 2015).

El-Din Haseeb, K. (2013). The Arab Spring revisited, in Khair El-Din Haseeb (ed), *The Arab Spring – Critical analyses*. London: Routledge, pp. 4–17.

Elman, M.F. (1995). The foreign policies of small states: Challenging neorealism in its own backyard, *British Journal of Political Science*, 25(2): 171–217.

Erdbrink, T. (2012, 30 April). A tiny island is when Iran makes a stand. *The New York Times*. Available at www.nytimes.com/2012/05/01/world/middleeast/dispute-over-island-of-abu-musa-unites-iran.html?_r=0 (accessed 6 September 2016).

Erdbrink, T. (2013, 4 December). Iran takes charm offensive to the Persian Gulf, *The New York Times*. Available at www.nytimes.com/2013/12/05/world/middleeast/iran-takes-charm-offensive-to-the-persian-gulf.html?_r=0 (accessed 6 September 2016).

Fars News Agency (2014, 15 April). Iran, Qatar discuss implementation of security pact. Available at http://en.farsnews.com/newstext.aspx?nn=13930126000748 (accessed 6 September 2016).

Fawcett, L. (2013). The Iraq War Ten Years On: Assessing the Fallout, *International Affairs*, 89(2), 325–43.

Fearon, J.D. (1998). Domestic politics, foreign policy, and theories of international relations, *Annual Review of Political Science*, 1: 289–313.

Fendius Elman, M. (1995). The foreign policies of small states: Challenging Neorealism in Its Own Backyard, *British Journal of Political Science*, 25(2): 171–217.

Fenton, J. (2011). Libya. Wordpress.com. Available at https://jeniferfenton.wordpress.com/tag/libya/ (accessed 1 November 2015).

Finnemore, M. and Sikkink, K. (1998). International norm dynamics and political change, *International Organization*, 52(4): 887–917.

Freedman, R.O. (1998). *The Middle East and the peace process: The impact of the Oslo accords*. Gainesville, FL: University Press of Florida.

Freud, S. (1961). *Civilization and its discontents*. New York: W.W. Norton.

Friedberg, A.L. (1988). *The weary Titan: Britain and the experience of relative decline, 1895–1905*. Princeton, NJ: Princeton University Press.

Friedersdorf, C. (2015, 28 September). How America's drone war in Yemen strengthens al-Qaeda. *The Atlantic*. Available at www.theatlantic.com/international/archive/2015/09/drone-war-yemen-al-qaeda/407599/ (accessed 17 February 2016).

Friedman, B. (2012, March/April). Battle for Bahrain: What one uprising meant for the Gulf States and Iran. *World Affairs*. Available at www.worldaffairsjournal.org/article/battle-bahrain-what-one-uprising-meant-gulf-states-and-iran (accessed 29 October 2015).

Friedman, T.L. (2015, 2 September). Our radical Islamic BFF Saudi Arabia. *The New York Times*. Available at www.nytimes.com/2015/09/02/opinion/thomas-friedman-our-radical-islamic-bff-saudi-arabia.html (accessed 21 February 2016).

Fromherz, A.K. (2013). *Qatar – A modern history*. London: I.B. Tauris.

Galani, U. (2013, 10 July). Breaking views: Gulf aid helps Egypt avoid financial collapse, Reuters. Available at http://en.aswatmasriya.com/analysis/view.aspx?id=950a6bb7-d529-45f6-831e-e26af54e485d (accessed 6 September 2016).

Galbreath, D. (2014). Western European armed forces and the modernisation agenda: Following or falling behind, *Defence Studies*, 14(4): 394–413.

Gambrell, J. and Schreck, A. (2015, 21 September). Oman, again the Mideast mediator, helps free Yemen hostages. Available at www.businessinsider.com/ap-oman-again-the-mideast-mediator-helps-free-yemen-hostages-2015-9 (accessed 24 April 2016).

Gärtner, H. (2001). Small states and alliances, in Erich Reiter and Heinz Gartner (eds), *Small states and alliances*. Heidelberg: Physica-Verlag, pp. 1–10.
Gates, R.M. (2014). *Duty: Memoirs of a Secretary at War*. London: WH Allen.
Gause, F.G. III (1994). *Oil monarchies: Domestic and security challenges in the Arab States*. New York: Council on Foreign Relations.
Gause, F.G. III (1997a). Arms supplies and military spending in the Gulf, *Middle East Report*, 204 (July to September), pp. 12–14.
Gause, F.G. III (1997b). The Political Economy of National Security in the GCC States, in Gary Sick and Lawrence Potter (eds), *The Persian Gulf at the Millennium: Essays in Politics, Economy, Security, and Religion*. New York: St. Martin's Press, pp. 61–84.
Gause, F.G. III (2000). The UAE: Between Pax Britannica and Pax Americana, in Joseph Kechichian (ed), *A century in thirty years: Sheikh Zayed and the United Arab Emirates*, Washington, DC: Middle East Policy Council, pp. 213–34.
Gause, F.G. III (2003). Balancing what? Threat perception and alliance choice in the Gulf, *Security Studies*, 13(2): 273–305.
Gause, F.G. III (2005). The international politics of the Gulf, in L. Fawcett (ed), *International relations of the Middle East*. Oxford: Oxford University Press, pp. 278–9.
Gause, F.G. III (2010). *The international relations of the Persian Gulf*. Cambridge, UK: Cambridge University Press.
Gause, F.G. III (2011). Why Middle East studies missed the Arab Spring – The myth of authoritarian stability, *Foreign Affairs*, 90(4): 81–90.
Gengler, J. (2011, 1 November). Qatar's ambivalent democratization. Foreign Policy. Available at http://foreignpolicy.com/2011/11/01/qatars-ambivalent-democratization/ (accessed 21 March 2014).
Gerner, D.J. (1995). The evolution of the study of foreign policy, in Laura Neack, Jeanne A.K. Hey and Patrick J. Haney (eds), *Foreign policy analysis: Continuity and change in its second generation*. Englewood Cliffs, NJ: Prentice Hall, pp. 17–32.
Gervais, V. (2011). *Du pétrole à l'armée: Les stratégies de construction de l'Etat aux Emirats arabes unis*. Paris: Institut de Recherche Stratégique de l'Ecole Militaire (IRSEM).
Gibbs, D.N. (2000, June). Afghanistan: The Soviet invasion in retrospect, *International Politics*, 37: 233–46. Available at: http://dgibbs.faculty.arizona.edu/sites/dgibbs.faculty.arizona.edu/files/afghan-ip.pdf (accessed 10 January 2016).
Gilpin, R. (1981). *War and change in world politics*. Cambridge, UK: Cambridge University Press.
Glenn, J. (2009). Realism versus strategic culture: Competition and collaboration?, *International Studies Review*, 11(3): 523–51.
Goetschel, L. (1998). The foreign and security policy interests of small states in today's Europe, in L. Goetschel (ed), *Small states inside and outside the European Union*. Dordrecht: Kluwer Academic, pp. 13–31.
Goetschel, L. (2000). *Small states and the common foreign and security policy of the EU: A comparative analysis*. Bern: Institut für Politikwissenschaften.
Goldberg, J. (2015, 5 November). Ashton Carter: Gulf Arabs need to get in the fight. *The Atlantic*. Available at www.theatlantic.com/international/archive/2015/11/ashton-carter-gulf-iran-isis/414591/Goldberg (accessed 21 February 2016).
Goldfischer, D. (2005). Prospects for a New World Order, in E. Andali and J. Rosenau (eds), *Globalization, security, and the nation-state: Paradigms in transition*. Albany, NY: State University of New York Press, pp. 199–219.
Gourevitch, P. (2002). Domestic politics and international relations, in Walter Carlsnaes, Thomas Risse and Beth Simmons (eds), *Handbook of international relations*. New York: SAGE, pp. 309–28.

Grether, J. and Mathys, N. (2010). Is the world's economic centre of gravity already in Asia?, *Area*, 42(1): 47–50.

Grimmett, R.F. (1993). *Conventional arms transfers to the Third World, 1985–1992*. Washington, DC: Congressional Research Service (CRS).

Gueraiche, W. (2016). The UAE and Iran: The different layers of a complex security issue, in Shahram Akbarzadeh and Dara Conduit (eds), *Iran in the world: President Rouhani's foreign policy*. New York: Palgrave Macmillan, pp. 75–92.

Gulf News (AFP). (2013, 11 December). GCC Summit: Gulf states hail Iran's 'new orientation'. Available at http://m.gulfnews.com/news/gulf/kuwait/gcc-summit-gulf-states-hail-iran-s-new-orientation-1.1265862 (accessed 6 September 2016).

Gupta, S. (2015, 23 July). Oman: The unsung hero of the Iranian nuclear deal. *Foreign Policy Journal*. Available at www.foreignpolicyjournal.com/2015/07/23/oman-the-unsung-hero-of-the-iranian-nuclear-deal/ (accessed 24 April 2016).

Gvalia, G., Siroky, D., Lebanidze, B. and Iashvili, Z. (2013). Thinking outside the bloc: Explaining the foreign policies of small states, *Security Studies*, 22(1): 98–131.

Haass, R. (interviewee) (2013, 2 October). How the shutdown weakens U.S. foreign policy. Council on Foreign Relations. Available at www.cfr.org/budget-debt-and-deficits/shutdown-weakens-us-foreign-policy/p31534 (accessed 5 September 2016).

Habermas, J. (1974). The public sphere: An encyclopedia article (1964), trans. Sara Lennox and Frank Lennox, *New German critique*, Vol. 3, pp. 49–50.

Hamilton, J.D. (2009). *Causes and consequences of the oil shock of 2007–08*. Washington DC: Brookings Institute.

Hammond, J. and Wan, J. (2014, 16 April). With Sisi likely to take over, how will Egypt's military economy look like?, *Al Bawaba Business*. Available at www.albawaba.com/business/egypt-economy-sisi-569557 (accessed 19 October 2016).

Hamza, Y. (2014, 22 March) Gulf aid helps pull Egyptian state back from the brink. *The National*. Available at www.thenational.ae/world/egypt/gulf-aid-helps-pull-egyptian-state-back-from-the-brink#page1 (accessed 6 September 2016).

Handel, M. (1990). *Weak states in the international system*. London: Cass.

Hanizadeh, H. (2014). The new foreign policy of Qatar in the Middle East. International Peace Studies Centre. Available at http://peace-ipsc.org/fa/ (accessed 6 September 2016).

Harsanyi, J. (1962). Measurement of social power, opportunity costs, and the theory of two-person bargaining games, *Systems Research and Behavioral Science*, 7(1): 67–80.

Hasbani, N. (2006). The geopolitics of weapons procurement in the Gulf States, *Defense & Security Analysis*, 22(1): 73–88.

Hawthorne, A. (2005). Is civil society the answer? in Thomas Carothers and Marina Ottaway (eds), *Uncharted journey: Promoting democracy in the Middle East*. New York: Carnegie Endowment for International Peace, pp. 81–114.

Held, D. and Ulrichsen, K. (2012). *The transformation of the Gulf politics, economics and the global order*. Abingdon, UK: Routledge.

Hellyer, P. (2001). The evolution of UAE foreign policy, in I.A. Abed and P. Hellyer (eds), *United Arab Emirates: A new perspective*. UAE: Trident Press, pp. 161–78.

Hertog, S. (2011). Rentier militaries in the Gulf States: The price of coup-proofing, *International Journal of Middle East Studies*, 43(3): 400–2.

Hey, J.A.K. (2003a). Introducing small state foreign policy, in J. Hey (ed), *Small states in world politics: Explaining foreign policy behavior*. Boulder, CO: Lynne Rienner pp. 1–13.

Hey, J.A.K. (2003b). Refining our understanding of small state foreign policy, in J.A.K. Hey (ed), *Small states in world politics: Explaining foreign policy behaviour*. Boulder, CO: Lynne Rienner, pp. 185–95.

Hey, J.A.K. (2003c). *Small states in world politics: Explaining foreign policy behavior*. Boulder, CO: Lynne Rienner.

Hill, C. (1993). *The changing politics of foreign policy*. Basingstoke, UK: Palgrave.

Hinnebusch, R.A. and Ehteshami, A. (2002). *The foreign policies of Middle East states*. Boulder, CO: Lynne Rienner.

Hobbes, T. (2004). *Leviathan*. Sioux Falls, SD: Nuvision Publications.

Holland S., Storey D. and Grenon, A. (eds) (2014, 7 October). Biden adds Saudi Arabia to his apology list over Islamic State. Reuters. Available at www.reuters.com/article/us-mideast-crisis-biden-idUSKCN0HW21M20141007 (accessed 20 February 2016).

Holsti, K.J. (1996). *The state, war, and the state of war*. Cambridge, UK: Cambridge University Press.

Horinuki, K. (2011). Controversies over Labour naturalisation policy and its dilemmas: 40 years of Emiratisation in the United Arab Emirates, *Kyoto Bulletin of Islamic Area Studies*, 4(1–2): 41–61.

Horovitz, J. (1930). Ibn Qutaiba's *Uyun al-Akhbar, Islamic Culture*, 4: 171–98.

Hourani, A.H. (2002). *A history of the Arab peoples*. Harvard, MA: Harvard University Press.

Human Rights Watch (HRW). (2013). *World Report 2013*. Qatar. New York: HRW.

Ignatius, D. (2016, 5 January). The costly blunders of Saudi Arabia's anxiety-ridden monarchy. *Washington Post*. Available at www.washingtonpost.com/opinions/the-glass-house-of-saud/2016/01/05/47583676-b3f0-11e5-9388-466021d971de_story.html (accessed 16 February 2016).

Inbar, E. and Sheffer, G. (1997). *The national security of small states in a changing world*. London: Frank Cass.

Ingebritsen, C. (2002). Norm entrepreneurs. Scandinavia's role in world politics, *Cooperation and Conflict*, 37(1): 11–23.

Ira, K. (2009, 15 June). France opens first permanent military base in the Persian Gulf – World Socialist Web Site. Available at www.wsws.org/en/articles/2009/06/base-j15.html (accessed 1 November 2015).

Isaacson, W. and Thomas, E. (1986). *The wise men: Six friends and the world they made: Acheson, Bohlen, Harriman, Kennan, Lovett, McCloy*. London: Faber and Faber.

Ishay, M. and Kretzmer, D. (2016). Reclaiming human rights: Alternative paths for an Israeli/Palestinian peace, in J. Ehrenberg and Y. Peled (eds), *Israel and Palestine: Alternative perspectives on statehood*, Lanham, MD: Rowman & Littlefield (in press).

Islamic Republic News Agency (2015, 16 April). Official: Iran pursues expansion of ties with Persian Arab neighbours. Available at www.irna.ir/en/News/81124301/Politic/Official__Iran_pursues_expansion_of_ties_with_Persian_Gulf_Arab_neighbors (accessed 6 September 2016).

Jacob, J. (2014, 28 February). India, Iran, Oman to start discussing gas pipeline. *Hindustan Times*. Available at www.hindustantimes.com/business/india-iran-oman-to-start-discussing-gas-pipeline/story-6KS1sO1pR4TrQt3RiFfMSI.html (accessed 6 September 2016).

Jazbec, M. (2001). *The diplomacies of new small states: The case of Slovenia with some comparison from the Baltics*. Aldershot, UK: Ashgate.

Jervis, R. (1976). *Perception and misperception in international politics*. Princeton, NJ: Princeton University Press.

Kaarbo, J. (2012). *Coalition politics and cabinet decision making: A comparative analysis of foreign policy choices*. Ann Arbor, MI: University of Michigan Press.

Kagan, F. (2013, 6 May). The peril of sequestration. National Review Online. Available at www.nationalreview.com/nrd/articles/345942/peril-sequestration (accessed 1 November 2015).

Kagan, R. (1998). The benevolent Empire, *Foreign Policy*, Summer, pp. 24–35.

Kahl, C., Gfoeller, M., Katz, M. and Kimmitt, M. (2014). U.S. commitments to the Gulf Arab States: Are they adequate?, *Middle East Policy*, 21(2): 1–33. Available at http://mepc.org/journal/middle-east-policy-archives/us-commitments-gulf-arab-states-are-they-adequate (accessed 20 February 2016).

Kahwaji, R. (2004). U.S.–Arab cooperation in the Gulf: Are both sides working from the same script?, *Middle East Policy*, 11(3): 52–62.

Kahwaji, R. (2013, 6 February). Sequestration, new US foreign policy priorities and the likely impact on the Middle East. Available at www.arabianaerospace.aero/sequestration-new-us-foreign-policy-priorities-and-the-likely-impact-on-the-middle-east (accessed 1 November 2015).

Kamrava, M. (ed) (2011a). *International politics of the Persian Gulf*. Syracuse, NY: Syracuse University Press.

Kamrava, M. (2011b). Mediation and Qatari foreign policy, *Middle East Journal*, 65(4): 539–56.

Kamrava, M. (2012). The Arab Spring and the Saudi-led counterrevolution, *Orbis*, 56(1): 96–104.

Kamrava, M. (2013). *Qatar: Small state, big politics*. New York: Cornell University Press.

Kane, F. (2011, 18 August). Trade ties with Iran at the crossroads. *The National*. Available at www.thenational.ae/business/industry-insights/economics/trade-ties-with-iran-at-the-crossroads (accessed 29 October 2015).

Karasik, T. (2013, 18 December). Gate to the Balkans: UAE and Serbia strengthen ties. Al Arabiya News. Available at http://english.alarabiya.net/en/views/news/world/2013/12/18/Gate-to-the-Balkans-the-growing-relationship-between-the-UAE-and-Serbia.html (accessed 1 November 2015).

Kassem, M. (2004). *Egyptian politics – The dynamics of authoritarian rule*. London: Lynne Rienner.

Katzenstein, P.J. (1976). International relations and domestic structures: Foreign economic policies of advanced industrial states, *International Organization*, 30(1): 1–45.

Katzman, K. (2005). *The United Arab Emirates (UAE): Issues for U.S. policy*. Congressional Research Service Report for Congress, Prepared for Members and Committees of Congress.

Katzman, K. (2013, 18 March). The United Arab Emirates (UAE): Issues for U.S. policy. Congressional Research Service Report for Congress. Available at www.fas.org/sgp/crs/mideast/RS21852.pdf (accessed 29 October 2015).

Katzman, K. (2016, 26 April). Oman: Reform, security, and U.S. policy. Congressional Research Service. Available at http://fas.org/sgp/crs/mideast/RS21534.pdf (accessed 24 August 2016).

Keating, M., McEwen, N. and Harvey, M. (2014). *The role of small states in the European Union: Lessons for Scotland*. Edinburgh, UK: Economic Social Research Council, Scottish Centre on Constitutional Change.

Kechichian, J.A. (1995a). *Oman and the world: The emergence of an independent foreign policy*. Santa Monica, CA: RAND.

Kechichian, J.A. (1995b, 1 January). Oman: A unique foreign policy produces a key player in Middle Eastern and global diplomacy. Available at www.rand.org/pubs/research_briefs/RB2501.html (accessed 24 April 2016).

Keohane, R.O. (1969). Lilliputians' dilemmas: Small states in international politics, *International Organization*, 23(2): 291–310.

Keohane, R. (1971). The big influence of small allies, *Foreign Policy*, 2: 161–82.

Keohane, R. (2002). Governance in a partially globalized world, in A. McGrew and D. Held (eds), *Governing globalization: Power, authority and global governance*. Cambridge, UK: Polity, pp. 325–47.

Keohane, R.O. and Martin, L. (1995). The promise of an institutional theory, *International Security*, 20(1): 39–51.

Keohane, R.O. and Nye, J.S. (1977). *Power and interdependence*. New York: Longman.

Kerr, S. (2015, 2 June). Saudi Arabia to boost defence spending by 27% over five years. *Financial Times*. Available at www.ft.com/cms/s/0/4f3b5708-0903-11e5-b643-00144fe-abdc0.html#axzz3cRvGATqV (accessed 24 August 2016).

Khalaf, R. and Smith, A.F. (2013, 16 May). Qatar bankrolls Syrian revolt with cash and arms. *Financial Times*. Available at www.ft.com/intl/cms/s/0/86e3f28e-be3a-11e2-bb35-00144feab7de.html (accessed 6 September 2016).

Khaldun, I. (1858). *Muqaddimah*, trans. by Franz Rosenthal. Paris: Benjamin Duprat.

Khaleej Times (2014, 4 March). Emirati police officer among three dead in Bahrain blast. Available at www.khaleejtimes.com/article/20140304/ARTICLE/303049992/1011 (accessed 29 October 2015).

Khalifa Isaac, S. (2014). Explaining the patterns of Gulf monarchies' assistance after the Arab uprisings, *Mediterranean Politics*, 19(3): 413–30.

Khan, I. (2006). Fungibility of military power and imperatives for small nations, *Bangladesh Institute of International and Strategic Studies Journal*, 27(1): 1–20.

Khatib, L. (2013). Qatar's foreign policy: The limits of pragmatism, *International Affairs*, 89(2): 417–31.

Kier, E. (1995). Culture and military doctrine – France between the wars, *International Security*, 19(4): 65–93.

Kingsley, P., Stephen, C. and Roberts, D. (2014, 26 August). UAE and Egypt behind bombing raids against Libyan militias, say US officials. *The Guardian*. Available at www.theguardian.com/world/2014/aug/26/united-arab-emirates-bombing-raids-libyan-militias (accessed 29 October 2015).

Kinninmont, J. (2011). Bahrain, in C. Davidson (ed), *Power and politics in the Persian Gulf monarchies*. London: Hurst, pp. 31–62.

Kinninmont, J. (2015, 3 July). Iran and the GCC: Unnecessary insecurity. Chatham House. Available at www.chathamhouse.org/sites/files/chathamhouse/field/field_document/20150703IranGCCKinninmont.pdf (accessed 6 September 2016).

Kinninmont, J. and Spencer, C. (2013). The Arab Spring: The changing dynamics of West–GCC cooperation, IAI report, in R. Alcaro and A. Dessì (eds), *The uneasy balance. Potential and challenges of the West's relations with the Gulf States*, IAI Research Papers no. 8, Chatham House, pp. 49–69. Available at www.iai.it/sites/default/files/iairp_08.pdf (accessed 15 July 2014).

Kirkpatrick, J. (1979, 1 November). Dictatorships and double standards. *Commentary*. Available at www.commentarymagazine.com/articles/dictatorships-double-standards/ (accessed 21 February 2016).

Kisangani, E.F. and Pickering, J. (2011). Democratic accountability and diversionary force: Regime types and the use of benevolent and hostile military force, *Journal of Conflict Resolution*, 55(6): 1021–46.

Kissinger, H. (1994). *Diplomacy*. New York: Simon & Schuster.

Knights, M. and Mello, A. (2015, 10 August). The Saudi–AE war effort in Yemen (Part 2): The air campaign. The Washington Institute. Available at www.washingtoninstitute.org/policy-analysis/view/the-saudi-uae-war-effort-in-yemen-part-1-operation-golden-arrow-in-aden (accessed 18 October 2016).

Knudsend, O. (2002). Small states, latent and extant: Towards a general perspective, *Journal of International Relations and Development*, 5(2): 182–98.
Knudsen, O. (ed) (2007). *Security strategies, power disparity and identity*. Aldershot, UK: Ashgate.
Koch, C. and Long, D.E. (2003). *Gulf security in the twenty-first century*. London: I.B. Tauris.
Korany, B. and Hillal Dessouki, A.E. (eds) (2008). *The foreign policies of Arab States: The challenge of globalization*. Cairo: American University in Cairo Press.
Kostiner, J. (2011). Perceptions of collective security in the post-Saddam era, in M. Kamrava (ed), *International politics of the Persian Gulf*. Syracuse, NY: Syracuse University Press, pp. 94–119.
Krasner, S.D. (1978). *Defending the national interest: Raw materials investments and U.S. foreign policy*. Princeton, NJ: Princeton University Press.
Krauthammer, C. (1986, 17 February). In defense of interventionism, *The New Republic*, 194(7): 14.
Kristof, N. (2015, 29 October). Sentenced to be crucified. *The New York Times*. Available at www.nytimes.com/2015/10/29/opinion/sentenced-to-be-crucified.html (accessed 20 February 2016).
Kyl, J. and Lieberman, J. (2013, 30 October). Too much crisis, too little defense. American Enterprise Institute. Available at www.aei.org/publication/too-much-crisis-too-little-defense/ (accessed 1 November 2015).
Lacey, R. (2010). *Inside the Kingdom: Kings, clerics, modernists, terrorists, and the struggle for Saudi Arabia*. London: Arrow Books.
Ladwig III, W.C. (2008). Supporting allies in counterinsurgency: Britain and the Dhofar Rebellion, *Small Wars & Insurgencies*, 19(1): 62–88.
Lakshmanan, I.A.R. (2015, 25 September). If you can't do the deal…. Go back to Tehran. *Politico*. Available at www.politico.com/magazine/story/2015/09/iran-deal-inside-story-213187 (accessed 6 September 2016).
Lambton, A.K.S. (1981). *State and Government in medieval Islam: an introduction to the study of Islamic political thought: The Jurists*. Oxford: Oxford University Press.
Larrabee, S. (2013). NATO's role in the Middle East and Gulf, unpublished paper from conference: *NATO's approach to Gulf cooperation: Lessons learned and future challenges conference*. p. 5.
Lasswell, H. and Kaplan, A. (1950). *Power and society. A framework for political inquiry*. New Haven: Yale University Press.
Lavizzari, A. (2013, 22 May). The Arab Spring and funding of Salafism in the MENA region, *International Security Observer*. Available at http://securityobserver.org/the-arab-spring-and-the-funding-of-salafism-in-the-mena-region/ (accessed 19 October 2016).
Lefebvre, J.A. (2010). Oman's foreign policy in the twenty-first century, *Middle East Policy*, 17(1): 99–114.
Legrenzi, M. (2011). *The GCC and the international relations of the Gulf: Diplomacy, security and economy coordination in a changing Middle East*. London: I.B. Tauris.
Legrenzi, M. (ed). (2013). *Security in the Gulf*. London: Routledge.
Lemass, S. (1971). Small states in international organizations, in A. Schou and A. Brundtland (eds), *Small states in international relations*. Stockholm: Almqvist & Wiksell/New York: Wiley Interscience, pp. 115–21.
Lewis, B. (2010). *Faith and power – Religion and politics in the Middle East*. Oxford: Oxford University Press.
Lim, D.J. and Cooper, Z. (2015). Reassessing hedging: The logic of alignment in East Asia, *Security Studies*, 24(4): 696–727.

Lippman, T. (2014, 26 April). The U.S. and the Gulf: A failure to communicate. LobeLog Foreign Policy (blog). Available at www.lobelog.com/the-u-s-and-the-gulf-a-failure-to-communicate/ (accessed 20 February 2016).

Lipton, E., Williams B. and Confessore, N. (2014, 6 September). Foreign powers buy influence at think tanks. *The New York Times*. Available at www.nytimes.com/2014/09/07/us/politics/foreign-powers-buy-influence-at-think-tanks.html (accessed 20 February 2016).

Liska, G. (1968). *Alliances and the Third World*, Studies in International Affairs 5. Baltimore: Johns Hopkins Press.

Locke, J. (1988). *The two treatises of government*, in Peter Laslett (ed), *Of the ends of political society and government*, Chapter IX. Cambridge, UK: Cambridge University Press, pp. 350–4.

Loo, B. (ed) (2009). *Military transformation and strategy: Revolutions in military affairs and small states*. London: Routledge.

Louth, J., Bontems, P., Carlier, B. and Pilottin, A. (2013). *Defence industry and the reinvigorated UK–UAE security relationship*. Occasional Paper, June 2013. London, UK: The Royal United Services Institute (RUSI).

LSE Middle East Centre (2015). *The new politics of intervention of Gulf Arab States*. London: LSE Middle East Centre. Collected Papers, Volume 1, April.

Lutterbeck, D. (2013). Arab uprisings, armed forces, and civil–military relations, *Armed Forces & Society*, 39(1): 28–52.

Lutz, M. (2011, 4 February). Iran's supreme leader calls uprisings an 'Islamic awakening'. *Los Angeles Times*. Available at http://articles.latimes.com/2011/feb/04/world/la-fg-khamenei-iran-egypt-20110205 (accessed 6 September 2016).

Lynch, M. (2007). *Voices of a new Arab public – Iraq, Al Jazeera, and Middle East politics today*. New York: Colombia University Press.

Maass, M. (2009). The elusive definition of the small state, *International Politics*, 46(1): 65–83.

Maass, M. (2014). Small states: Survival and proliferation, *International Politics*, 51(6): 709–28.

Mabon, S. (2012). The battle for Bahrain: Iranian–Saudi rivalry. *Middle East Policy*, 19(2): 84–97.

Macris, J.F. (2010). *The politics and security of the Gulf: Anglo-American hegemony and the shaping of a region*. London: Routledge.

Majidyar, A.K. (2013, 21 October). Is sectarian balance in the United Arab Emirates, Oman, and Qatar at risk? American Enterprise Institute. Available at www.aei.org/publication/is-sectarian-balance-in-the-united-arab-emirates-oman-and-qatar-at-risk/ (accessed 24 August 2016).

Makahleh, S. (2011, 24 August). UAE troops spare no effort to bring peace to Afghanistan. Gulf News. Available at http://uae-troops-spare-no-effort-to-bring-peace-to-afghanistan-1.856240 (accessed 1 November 2015).

Mamouri, A. (2015, 4 November). Is Qatar Iran's door to the Gulf? Al-Monitor. Available at www.al-monitor.com/pulse/originals/2015/11/iran-qatar-rapprochement-middle-east.html#ixzz3sMQuySFD (accessed 6 September 2016).

Männik, E. (2004). Small states: Invited to Nato – Able to contribute?, *Defense & Security Analysis*, 20(1): 21–37.

Marschall, C. (2003). *Iran's Persian Gulf policy: From Khomeini to Khatami*. Routledge Carzon: London.

Martin, L.G. (2011). *New frontiers in Middle East security*. London: Palgrave Macmillan.

Mattern, J. (2015). The concept of power and the (un)discipline of international relations, in C. Reus-Smit and D. Snidal (eds), *The Oxford handbook of international relations*. Oxford, UK: Oxford University Press, pp. 691–97.

Matthews, R. and Yan, N.Z. (2007). Small country 'total defence': A case study of Singapore, *Defence Studies*, 7(3): 376–95.
Matthiesen, T. (2013). *Sectarian Gulf: Bahrain, Saudi Arabia, and the Arab Spring that wasn't*. Stanford: Stanford University Press.
May, A.S. (2015, 15 May). Missile shield for Gulf to take years, and heavy U.S. commitment, Reuters. Available at www.reuters.com/article/us-usa-gulf-missiledefense-idUSKBN0O00C720150515 (accessed 19 February 2016).
Mehr News (2013, 2 December). Dialogue on Abu Musa; country's 'normal position', Zarif says. Available at http://en.mehrnews.com/news/100921/Dialogue-on-Abu-Musa-country-s-normal-position-Zarif-says (accessed 6 September 2016).
Middle East Events (2011, 10 December). Dubai Exports & Foreign Direct Investment Host Iraqi Officials From Federation Of Kurdistan Chambers Of Commerce And Industry. Available at: www.middleeastevents.com/news/page/dubai-exports--foreign-direct-investment-host-iraqi-officials-from-federation-of-kurdistan-chambers-of-commerce-and-industry/14684#.WCMqAfl97IV (accessed 11 November 2016).
Migdal, J. (2001). *State-in-society: Studying how states and societies transform and constitute one another*. Cambridge, UK: Cambridge University Press.
Miller, B. (1992). Explaining great power cooperation in conflict management, *World Politics*, 45(1): 1–46.
Miller, B. (2005). When and how regions become peaceful: Potential theoretical pathways to peace, *International Studies Review*, 7(2): 229–67.
Miller, J. (2012, 30 July). With UAE nuclear partnership, South Korea gains Mideast traction. Available at www.worldpoliticsreview.com/articles/12211/with-uae-nuclear-partner-ship-south-korea-gains-mideast-traction (accessed 1 November 2015).
Mofa.gov.ae (2014). *UAE Ministry of Foreign Affairs: Foreign Policy*. Available at. mofa.gov.ae/EN/Pages/default.aspx (accessed 1 November 2015).
Molavi, A. (2011, 6 April). Invoking the Arab Spring, Iran rewrites its own history. *The National*. Available at www.thenational.ae/thenationalconversation/comment/invoking-the-arab-spring-iran-rewrites-its-own-history (accessed 6 September 2016).
Molis, A. (2006). The role and interests of small states in developing European security and defence policy, *Baltic Security & Defence Review*, 8: 81–100.
Momani, B. and Ennis, C.A. (2012). Between caution and controversy: Lessons from the Gulf, *Cambridge Review of International Affairs*, 25(4): 605–27.
Morgenthau, H. (1948). *Politics among nations: The struggle for power and peace*. New York: Knopf.
Mouritzen, H. (1991). Tensions between the strong, and the strategies of the weak, *Journal of Peace Research*, 28(2): 217–30.
Mouritzen, H. (1997). *External danger and democracy: Old Nordic lessons and new European challenges*. Aldershot, UK: Ashgate
Mouritzen, H. and Wivel, A. (2005). *The geopolitics of Euro-Atlantic integration*. London: Routledge.
Müller, H. (2002). Security cooperation, in Walter Carlsnae, Thomas Risse and Beth A. Simmons (eds), *Handbook of international relations*. London: SAGE, pp. 369–91.
Nasr, V. (2006). *The Shia revival how conflicts within Islam will shape the future*. New York: W.W. Norton.
Nawar, I. (2003). *The state of the Arab Media: The fight for democracy*. Annual Report 2003. London: Arab Press Freedom Watch.

Neumann, I.B. and Gstöhl, S. (2004). *Lilliputians in Gulliver's world: Small states in international relations.* Working Paper 1–2004. Reykjavik: Centre for Small State Studies, University of Iceland Press.

Neumann, I.B. and Gstöhl, S. (2006). Introduction: Lilliputians in Gulliver's world? in C. Ingebritsen, I. Neumann, S. Gstöhl and J. Beyer (eds), *Small states in international relations.* Seattle, WA: University of Washington Press/Reykjavik: University of Iceland Press, pp. 3–36.

Neumayer, E. (2003). What factors determine the allocation of aid by Arab countries and multilateral agencies?, *Journal of Development Studies*, 39(4): 134–47.

Nonneman, G. (2004). The Gulf States and the Iran–Iraq War: Pattern shifts and continuities, in Lawrence G. Potter & Gary G. Sick (eds), *Iran, Iraq and the legacies of war.* New York: Palgrave Macmillan, pp. 167–92.

Nonneman, G. (2005). *Analyzing Middle East foreign policies and the relationship with Europe.* London: Routledge.

Norton, A.R. (1995). *Civil Society in the Middle East.* Leiden, NL: E.J. Brill.

Noueihed, L. & Warren, A. (2013). *The battle for the Arab Spring – Revolution, counter-revolution and the making of a new era.* New Haven: Yale University Press.

Nye, J. (2004). *Soft power: The means to success in world politics.* New York: Public Affairs.

Obama, B. (2014a, 28 May). Remarks by the President at the United States Military Academy Commencement Ceremony, The White House. Available at www.whitehouse.gov/the-press-office/2014/05/28/remarks-president-united-states-military-academy-commencement-ceremony (accessed 19 October 2016).

Obama, B. (2014b, 24 September). Remarks by President Obama in Address to the United Nations General Assembly, The White House. Available at www.whitehouse.gov/the-press-office/2014/09/24/remarks-president-obama-address-united-nations-general-assembly (accessed 19 October 2016).

O'Hanlon, M. (1994). *Enhancing U.S. security through foreign aid.* Washington, DC: The Congress of the United States Congressional Budget Office.

Osgood, R.E. (1968). *Alliances and American foreign policy.* Baltimore, MD: Johns Hopkins University Press

Otaiba, Y.A. (2015, 2 December). A vision for a moderate, modern Muslim world. *Foreign Policy.* Available at http://foreignpolicy.com/2015/12/02/a-vision-for-a-moderate-modern-muslim-world-uae-abu-dhabi-isis/ (accessed 18 February 2016).

Owen, R. (1992). *State, power and politics in the making of the modern Middle East.* London: Routledge.

Panke, D. (2010). *Small states in the European Union: Coping with structural disadvantages.* London: Routledge.

Panke, D. (2011). Small states in EU negotiations, political dwarfs or power-brokers?, *Cooperation and Conflict*, 46(2): 123–43.

Panke, D. (2012). Dwarfs in international negotiations: How small states make their voices heard, *Cambridge Review of International Affairs*, 25(3): 313–28.

Partrick, N. (2011). The GCC: Gulf State integration or leadership cooperation, Kuwait Programme on Globalisation, Governance and Development in the Gulf, London: London School of Economics & Political Science (LSE).

Partrick, N. (2012). Nationalism in the Gulf states, in D. Held and K. Ulrichsen (eds), *The transformation of the Gulf politics, economics and the global order.* Abingdon: Routledge, pp. 47–65.

Payne, A. (1993). The politics of small state security in the Pacific, *Journal of Commonwealth and Comparative Politics*, 31(2): 103–32.

Peterson, J.E. (2006). Qatar and the world: Branding for a micro-state, *Middle East Journal*, 60(4): 732–48.
Piscatori, J. (ed) (1983). *Islam in the political process*, Cambridge, UK: Cambridge University Press.
Pollack, K. (2002, 1 March). Next stop Baghdad. *Foreign Affairs*. Available at www.foreignaffairs.com/articles/iraq/2002-03-01/next-stop-baghdad (accessed 20 February 2016).
Poore, S. (2004). Strategic culture, in Stuart Poore (ed), *Neorealism versus strategic culture*. London: Ashgate, pp: 45–71.
Posen, B.R. (1984). *The sources of military doctrine: France, Britain, and Germany between the World Wars*. Ithaca, NY: Cornell University Press
Prasad, N. (2003). Small islands' quest for economic development, *Asia-Pacific Development Journal*, 10(1): 47–67.
Prasad, N. (2004). Escaping regulation, escaping convention: Development strategies in small economies, *World Economics*, 5(1): 41–65.
Prasad, N. (2009). Small but smart: Small states in the global system, in A. Cooper and T. Shaw (eds), *The diplomacies of small states: Between vulnerability and resilience*. Houndsmills, UK: Palgrave, pp. 41–64.
Presidential Guard (2014). Mission: Winds of goodness – UAE contributions. Available at www.uaeafghanistan.ae/en/UAE-contributions.php (accessed 1 November 2015).
Press TV (2015, 21 September). Iran inks gas deal as Omani minister visits. Available at www.payvand.com/news/15/sep/1128.html (accessed 4 September 2016).
Priess, D. (1996). Balance of threat theory and the genesis of the Gulf Cooperation Council: An interpretive case study, *Security Studies*, 5(4): 143–71.
Putnam, R.D. (1988). Diplomacy and domestic politics: The logic of two-level game, *International Organization*, 42(3): 427–60.
Qassemi, S. (2015, 22 September). What intervention in Yemen means for UAE's national identity. Available at http://time.com/4040220/uae-intervention-in-yemen/ (accessed 10 November 2015).
Quah, D. (2011). The global economy's shifting centre of gravity, *Global Policy*, 2(1): 3–9.
Quinlivan, J.T. (1999). Coup-proofing: Its practice and consequences in the Middle East, *International Security*, 24(2): 131–65.
Quinlivan, J.T. (2000). *Coup-proofing: Its practice and consequences in the Middle East*. Santa Monica, CA: RAND.
Racimora, W. (2013). *Salafist/Wahhabite financial support to educational, social and religious institutions*, report requested by the Directorate-General for External Policies of the Union, European Parliament, Brussels.
Ragab, E. (2012). North African countries after the Arab Spring, in S. Colombo, K.C. Ulrichsen, S. Ghabra, S. Hamid and E. Ragab (eds), *The GCC in the Mediterranean in light of the Arab Spring*. Washington, DC: The German Marshall Fund (GMF), pp. 41–64.
Ralston, J.W. (1969). *The defense of small states in the nuclear age*. PhD Dissertation: Graduate Institute of International Studies, University of Geneva.
Ramazani, R.K. (1988). *The Gulf Cooperation Council: Record and analysis*. Charlottesville, VA: University of Virginia Press.
Ratti, L. (2006). Post-Cold War Nato and international relations theory: The case for neoclassical realism, *Journal of Transatlantic Studies*, 4(1): 81–110.
Raymond, G.A. (1997). Neutrality norms and the balance of power, *Cooperation and Conflict*, 32(2): 123–46.
Regier, T. and Khalidi, M.A. (2009). The Arab Street: Tracking a Political Metaphor, *Middle East Journal*, 63(1): 11–29.

Reiter, D. (1994). Learning, Realism and Alliances: The Weight of the Shadow of the Past, *World Politics*, 46, 4: 490–526.

Reiter, D. (1996). *Crucible of beliefs: Learning, alliances, and world wars*. Cornell: Cornell University Press.

Reiter, E. and Gärtner, H. (eds) (2001). *Small states and alliances*. Heidelberg/New York: Physica-Verlag.

Reuters (2008, 12 September). Oman and Iran will complete Kish gas field development by 2012. Available at http://gulfnews.com/business/oman-and-iran-will-complete-kish-gas-field-development-by-2012-1.131034 (accessed 6 September 2016).

Reuters (2013, 19 February). UAE leads Gulf Arab push to build up domestic defence industry. Available at www.reuters.com/article/2013/02/19/uae-defence-idUSL6N0BJ73020130219 (accessed 29 October 2015).

Reuters (2015a, 16 August). Arms seized in Kuwait came from Iran: Kuwaiti newspapers. Available at www.reuters.com/article/2015/08/16/us-kuwait-security-iran-idUSKCN0QL0CV20150816#BpPazCTXhpPLJi97.97 (accessed 24 August 2016).

Reuters (2015b, 26 August). Kuwait summons Iran envoy over disputed gas field reports: KUNA. Available at www.reuters.com/article/2015/08/26/us-energy-kuwait-iran-idUSKCN0QV0JI20150826 (accessed 6 September 2016).

Revkin, M. (2012, 18–24 October). Saudi Arabia, Qatar and the Arab Spring, *Al-Ahram Weekly Online*. Available at http://weekly.ahram.org.eg/Archive/2012/1119/op6.htm (accessed 6 September 2016).

Rickli, J.-M. (2004). The Western influence on Swedish and Swiss policies of armed neutrality during the early Cold War, in René Schwok (ed), *Interactions Globales*. Geneva: Institut Européen de l'Université de Genève, pp. 117–34.

Rickli, J.-M. (2008). European small states' military policies after the Cold War: From territorial to niche strategies, *Cambridge Review of International Affairs*, 21(3): 307–25.

Rickli, J.-M. (2010a). *The evolution of the European neutral and non-allied states' military policies after the Cold War 1989–2004*. PhD Dissertation, University of Oxford.

Rickli, J.-M. (2010b). Neutrality inside and outside the EU: A comparison of the Austrian and Swiss security policies after the Cold War, in Robert Steinmetz, Baldur Thorhallson and Anders Wivel (eds), *Small states in Europe: Challenges and opportunities*. Aldershot, UK: Ashgate, pp. 181–98.

Rickli, J.-M. (2014). Clean energy as a niche strategy for small states to guarantee energy security. The example of the Gulf countries, in Giacomo Luciani and Rabia Ferroukhi (eds), *Political economy of energy reform: The clean energy–fossil fuel balance in the Gulf*. Berlin: Gerlach Press, pp. 265–88.

Rickli, J.-M. (2016a). The political rationale and implications of the United Arab Emirates' military involvement in Libya, in Dag Henriksen and Ann Karin Larssen (eds), *Political rationale and international consequences of the war in Libya*. Oxford: Oxford University Press, pp. 134–54.

Rickli, J.-M. (2016b). New alliances dynamics and their impact on small GCC states, *Third World Thematic* (Thematic issue of *Third World Quarterly*), 1(1): 1–19.

Ricks, T.E. (2006). *Fiasco: The American military adventure in Iraq*. New York: Penguin Press.

Risse-Kappen, T. (1991). Public opinion, domestic structure, and foreign policy in liberal democracies, *World Politics*, 43(4): 479–512.

Risse-Kappen, T. (ed) (1995). *Bringing transnationl relations back in: Non-state actors, domestic structures and international institutions*. Cambridge, UK: Cambridge University Press.

Roberts, D. (2009). Qatar's search for security, *Proceedings of the Plymouth Postgraduate Symposium*. Plymouth, UK: Plymouth University Press.

Roberts, D. (2011, 23 March). Arab Involvement in the Libyan Intervention, Commentary for RUSI.org (Royal United Services Institute). Available at https://rusi.org/commentary/arabo-involvement-libyan-intervention (accessed 18 October 2016).

Roberts, D. (2011b, 28 September). Behind Qatar's intervention in Libya. Why was Doha such as strong supporter of the rebels? *Foreign Affairs*. Available at www.foreignaffairs.com/articles/libya/2011-09-28/behind-qatars-intervention-libya (accessed 19 October 2016).

Roberts, D. (2011c). Kuwait, in Christopher Davidson (ed), *Power and politics in the Persian Gulf monarchies*. London: Hurst, pp. 89–112.

Roberts, D.B. (2012). Understanding Qatar's foreign policy objectives, *Mediterranean Politics*, 17(2): 233–9.

Roberts, D. (2013). Qatar: domestic quietism, elite adventurism, in F. Ayub (ed), *What does the Gulf think about the Arab awakening?* London: European Council on Foreign Relations (ECFR), pp. 9–11.

Roberts, D. (2014). Qatar and the Muslim Brotherhood, *Middle East Policy*, 21(3): 84–94.

Roberts, D. (2016, 18 March). Mosque and state: The United Arab Emirates' secular foreign policy. *Foreign Affairs*. Available at www.foreignaffairs.com/articles/united-arab-emirates/2016-03-18/mosque-and-state (accessed 6 September 2016).

Rogin, J. (2014, 14 June). America's allies are funding ISIS. *The Daily Beast*. Available at www.thedailybeast.com/articles/2014/06/14/america-s-allies-are-funding-isis.html (accessed 18 February 2016).

Roosevelt, F.D. (1941, 6 January). Four freedoms speech during Annual Message to Congress on the State of the Union. Franklin D. Roosevelt Presidential Library and Museum. Available at www.fdrlibrary.marist.edu/pdfs/fftext.pdf (accessed 20 February 2016).

Rose, Gideon (1998). Neoclassical realism and theories of foreign policy, *World Policy*, 51(1): 144–77.

Rosenau, J. (1966). Pre-theories and theories and foreign policy, in Barry Farrell (ed), *Approaches to comparative and international politics*. Evanston: Northwestern University Press, pp. 27–92.

Rosenau, J. (1969). Toward the study of national–international linkages, in J. Rosenau (ed), *Linkage politics: Essays on the convergence of national and international systems*. New York: Free Press, pp. 44–63.

Ross, M. (1987, 25 September). U.S., Iran agree on repatriation of captured crew. *LA Times*. Available at http://articles.latimes.com/1987-09-25/news/mn-6708_1_supply-ship (accessed 3 September 2016).

Rothstein, R.L. (1968). *Alliances and Small Powers*. New York: Columbia University Press.

Rouhani, H. (2013, 15 October). Twitter. Available at https://twitter.com/HassanRouhani/status/390057247885119488 (accessed 6 September 2016).

Rousseau, J.J. (1762/2003). *The social contract or principles of political right*. Translated by G.D.H. Cole. Mineola, NY: Courier Dover.

Roy, J. (1999) 'Polis' and 'Oikos' in Classical Athens, *Greece & Rome*, 46(1): 1.

Roy, O. (1999). Moyen-Orient: Faiblesse des etats, enracinement des nations, *Critique International*, 4: 79–104.

Rummel, R. (1995). Democracies are less warlike than other regimes, *European Journal of International Relations*, 1(4): 449–64.

Russell, J.A. (2007). *Regional threats and security strategy: The troubling case of today's Middle East*. Strategic Studies Institute, Carlisle: U.S. Army War College.

Russet, B.M. (1993). *Grasping the democratic peace: Principle for a post-Cold War world*. Princeton, NJ: Princeton University Press.

Saab, B. (2014a, 5 May). Arms and influence in the Gulf: Riyadh and Abu Dhabi get to work. *World Affairs Journal*. Foreign Affairs. Available at www.worldaffairsjournal.org/content/arms-and-influence-gulf-riyadh-and-abu-dhabi-get-work (accessed 1 November 2015).

Saab, B. (2014b, 7 May). The Gulf rising: Defense industrialization in Saudi Arabia and the UAE. The Atlantic Council: Brent Scowcroft Center on International Security. Available at www.atlanticcouncil.org/publications/reports/the-gulf-rising-defense-industrialization-in-saudi-arabia-and-the-uae (accessed 1 November 2015).

Sadjadpour, K. (2011). *The Battle of Dubai: The United Arab Emirates and the US–Iran Cold War*. Washington, DC: Carnegie Endowment for International Peace.

Salame, G. (1978). *Le développement du rôle régional et international de l'Arabie Saoudite*, Unpublished thesis, Paris: Université de Paris I (Panthéon–Sorbonne).

Salem, O. (2015). UAE military intervention in Yemen was 'inevitable'. *The National*. Available at www.thenational.ae/uae/uae-military-intervention-in-yemen-was-inevitable (accessed 10 November 2015).

Salem, P. (2008). The Middle East: Evolution of a broken regional order, *Carnegie Papers*. Available at http://carnegieendowment.org/files/cmec9_salem_broken_order_final.pdf (accessed 28 September 2016).

Salzman, P.C. (2008). The Middle East's tribal DNA, *Middle East Quarterly*, 15(1): 23–33.

Samaan, J.-L. (2013). Les monarchies du Golfe: Un marché d'armement sans armées?, *Moyen-Orient*, 17: 48–53.

Sanger, D. (2015, 13 May). Saudi Arabia promises to match Iran in nuclear capability. *The New York Times*. Available at www.nytimes.com/2015/05/14/world/middleeast/saudi-arabia-promises-to-match-iran-in-nuclear-capability.html?_r=0 (accessed 20 February 2016).

Sanger, D. and Schmitt, E. (2011, 14 March). U.S.–Saudi tensions intensify with Mideast turmoil. *The New York Times*. Available at www.nytimes.com/2011/03/15/world/middleeast/15saudi.html?_r=0 (accessed 29 October 2015).

Saouli, A. (2012). *The Arab state: Dilemmas of late formation*. London: Routledge.

Saudi Fund for Development (2014). Annual Report 2013, Saudi Fund for Development.

Schelling, T. (1984). *Choice and consequence: Perspectives of an errant economist*. Cambridge, MA: Harvard University Press.

Schenker, D. and Trager, E. (2014, 4 March). Egypt's arms deal with Russia: Potential strategic costs, policy analysis, The Washington Institute. Available at www.washingtoninstitute.org/policy-analysis/view/egypts-arms-deal-with-russia-potential-strategic-costs (accessed 6 September 2016).

Schindler, D. (1992). Changing conceptions of neutrality in Switzerland, *Austrian Journal of Public and International Law*, 44: 105–16.

Schweller, R. (1994). Bandwagoning for profit, *International Security*, 19(1): 72–107.

Setälä, M. (2004). *Small states and Nato: Influence and accommodations*. Helsinki: The Atlantic Council of Finland.

Shaheen, K. (2011, 16 March). Defensive shield for the Gulf since 1982. *The National*. Available at www.thenational.ae/news/uae-news/defensive-shield-for-the-gulf-since-1982 (accessed 6 September 2016).

Shalal, A. (2015, 15 May). Missile shield for Gulf to take years, and heavy U.S. commitment. Reuters. Available at www.reuters.com/article/us-usa-gulf-missiledefense-idUSKBN0O00C720150515 (accessed 21 February 2016).

Shanahan, R. (2008, 17 September). Bad moon not rising: The myth of the Gulf Shi'a crescent. Lowy Institute for International Policy. Available at www.lowyinstitute.org/files/pubfiles/Shanahan,_Bad_moon__web.pdf (accessed 6 September 2016).

Shanker, T. (2012, 8 August). U.S. and Gulf allies pursue a missile shield against Iranian attack. *The New York Times*. Available at www.nytimes.com/2012/08/09/world/middleeast/

us-and-gulf-allies-pursue-a-missile-shield-against-iranian-attack.html (accessed 20 February 2016).
Shapir, Y. Magen Z. and Perel, G. (2014, 1 May). MiG-35s for Egypt: A veritable change of direction? *INSS Insight* 544. Available at www.inss.org.il/index.aspx?id=4538&articleid=6946 (accessed 6 September 2016).
Sharp, J. and Blanchard, C. (2007). *Post-war Iraq: Foreign contributions to training, peacekeeping, and reconstruction*. Congressional Research Service: Foreign Affairs, Defense, and Trade Division.
Shushan, D. and. Marcoux, C. (2011). Arab aid allocation in the oil era, AidData, Brief 2. Available at http://aiddata.org/sites/default/files/arab-aid-allocation-in-the-oil-era.pdf (accessed 28 September 2016).
Simon, H. (1985). *Models of man: Social and rational*. New York: Wiley.
Simon, J. (2005). *Nato expeditionary operations: Impacts upon new members and partners*. Washington, DC: National Defence University Press.
Singer, J.D. (1961). The level of analysis problem in international relations, *World Politics*, 14(1): 77–92.
Sluglett, P. (2005). The Cold War in the Middle East, in L. Fawcett (ed), *International relations of the Middle East*. Oxford: Oxford University Press, pp. 55–6.
Snyder, J. (1991). *Myths of Empire: Domestic politics and international ambitions*. Ithaca, NY: Cornell University Press.
Snyder, R., Bruck, H.W. and Sapin, B. (1962). *Foreign policy decision-making: An approach to the study of international politics*. New York: Free Press/Macmillan.
Social & Economic Survey Research Institute (SESRI) (2012). *Annual omnibus survey: A survey of life in Qatar 2012*. Doha, Qatar: SESRI.
Solomon J. (2013, 29 November). Iran nuclear deal raises fears of proliferation among Arab States. *The Wall Street Journal*. Available at www.wsj.com/articles/SB10001424052702303332904579228214211545256 (accessed 20 February 2016).
Sons, S. and Wiese, I. (2015). The engagement of Arab States in Egypt and Tunisia since 2011 – Rationale and impact, *DGAP Analyse*, 9. Available at https://dgap.org/en/think-tank/publications/dgapanalysis/engagement-arab-gulf-states-egypt-and-tunisia-2011 (accessed 19 October 2016).
Soubrier, E. (2014a). Sécurité des monarchies du Golfe: De nouvelles règles du jeu?, *Moyen-Orient*, 23: 66–71.
Soubrier, E. (2014b). *Regional disorder and new geo-economic order: Saudi security strategies in a reshaped Middle East*. Geneva: Gulf Research Center (GRC).
Soubrier, E. (2014c). La diplomatie économique des pays du Golfe à l'aune du Printemps arabe: Du rayonnement à la puissance, in F. Charillon and A. Dieckhoff (eds), *Annuaire Afrique du Nord Moyen-Orient 2014–2015*. Paris: La Documentation Française, pp. 123–36.
Sovereign Wealth Fund Institute (2014). Source on sovereign wealth funds, pensions, endowments, superannuation funds, central banks and public funds. Available at www.swfinstitute.org/fund-rankings (accessed 31 October 2015).
Spyer, J. (2014, 1 January). Confidence game: Losing American support, the Gulf States scramble. *The Tower*. Available at www.thetower.org/article/confidence-game-losing-american-support-the-gulf-states-scramble/ (accessed 20 February 2016).
Steinmetz, R., Thorhallsson, B. and Wivel, A. (eds) (2010). *Small states in Europe: Challenges and opportunities*. Aldershot, UK: Ashgate.
Stevenson, A. (2010). *Oxford Dictionary of English*. Oxford: Oxford University Press.
Strange, S. (1996). *The retreat of the state: The diffusion of power in the world economy*. Cambridge, UK: Cambridge University Press.

Sundelius, B. (1989). National security dilemmas and strategies for the European neutrals, in M.H. Haltzel and J. Kruzel (eds), *Between the blocs: Problems and prospects for Europe's neutral and nonaligned states*. Cambridge, UK: Cambridge University Press, pp. 98–121.

Sutton, P. (1987). Political aspects, in Colin Clarke and Tony Payne (eds), *Politics, security and development in small states*. London: Allen & Unwin, pp. 3–25.

Swiss Political Science Review (2013). Natural born peacemakers? Ideas and identities in foreign policies of small states in Western Europe, *Swiss Political Science Review*, Special Issue, 19(3): 259–423.

Taliaferro, J.W., Lobell, S.E. and Ripsman, N.M. (2009). Introduction: Neoclassical realism, the state and foreign policy, in Jeffrey W. Taliaferro, Steven E. Lobell and Norrin M. Ripsman (eds), *Neoclassical realism, the state and foreign policy*. Cambridge, UK: Cambridge University Press, pp. 1–41.

Talmon, J.L. (1960). *The origins of totalitarian democracy*. London, UK: Secker & Warburg.

Taulbee, J.L. (2014). Lesser states and niche diplomacy, in James Larry Taulbee, Ann Kelleher and Peter C. Grosvenor (eds), *Norway's peace policy: Soft power in a turbulent world*. New York: Palgrave MacMilllan, pp. 1–22.

The Business Year (2012). A vision true. Available at www.thebusinessyear.com/uae-dubai-2012/a-vision-true/review (accessed 1 November 2015).

The Economist (2012, 20 October). Egypt's Salafists: Dogma and purity v worldly politics. Available at www.economist.com/news/middle-east-and-africa/21564911-will-egypt%E2%80%99s-salafists-manage-evolve-party-practical-politics (accessed 1 September 2016).

The Emirates Center for Strategic Studies and Research (ECSSR) (2012a, 26 January). The UAE and China: A strategic partnership. Abu Dhabi: ECSSR. Available at www.ecssr.ac.ae/ECSSR/print/ft.jsp?lang=en&ftId=/FeatureTopic/ECSSR/FeatureTopic_1500.xml (accessed 1 November 2015).

The Emirates Center for Strategic Studies and Research (ECSSR) (2012b, 8 March). UAE foreign policy: Dynamic activities and effective roles. ECSSR. Available at www.ecssr.ae/ECSSR/print/ft.jsp?lang=en&ftId=/FeatureTopic/ECSSR/FeatureTopic_1513.xml (accessed 1 November 2015).

The Guardian (2008, 1 March). US Embassy cables: Oman Sultan resists Iranian charm offensive. Available at www.theguardian.com/world/us-embassy-cables-documents/143790 (accessed 6 September 2016).

The Guardian (2013, 30 August). Oman's Sultan's Iran visit sparks hope of progress in nuclear standoff. Available at www.theguardian.com/world/iran-blog/2013/aug/30/iran-oman-nuclear-negotiations (accessed 6 September 2016).

The National (2013, 13 November). Qatar approves compulsory military service for men: Reports. Available at www.thenational.ae/world/middle-east/qatar-approves-compulsory-military-service-for-men-reports (accessed 19 October 2016).

The New York Times (2002, 26 September). War with Iraq is not in America's best interest. Available at http://web.mit.edu/cis/pdf/TimesAd_01.pdf (accessed 20 February 2016).

Theodoulou, M. (2013, 11 December). Iran's hardliners tell Zarif to steer clear of military issues. *The National*. Available at www.thenational.ae/world/middle-east/irans-hardliners-tell-zarif-to-steer-clear-of-military-issues (accessed 6 September 2016).

The Official Site of the President of The Islamic Republic of Iran (2015a, July 18). Retrieved from www.president.ir/fa/88210 (accessed 24 August 2016).

The Official Site of the President of The Islamic Republic of Iran (2015b). Retrieved from The World Forum for Proximity of Islamic Schools of Thought (2011, 21 September). Islamic Awakening Conference final communiqué. Retrieved from https://

web.archive.org/web/20131015210932/http://www.taqrib.info/english/index. php?option=com_content&view=article&id=385:islamic-awakening-conference-final-communique-&catid=35:2009-08-31-05-01-28&Itemid=63 (accessed 27 September 2016).

The Wall Street Journal (2014, 7 October). Biden's Apology Tour. Available at www.wsj.com/articles/bidens-apology-tour-1412636332 (accessed 20 February 2016).

The White House, Office of the Press Secretary (2003, 6 November). President Bush discusses freedom in Iraq and Middle East. Available at http://georgewbush-whitehouse.archives.gov/news/releases/2003/11/20031106-2.html (accessed 21 February 2016).

The White House, Office of the Press Secretary (2009, 4 June). Remarks by the President at Cairo University. Available at www.whitehouse.gov/the-press-office/remarks-president-cairo-university-6-04-09 (accessed 20 February 2016).

The White House, Office of the Press Secretary (2014a, 28 May). Remarks by the President at the United States Military Academy Commencement Ceremony. Available at www.whitehouse.gov/the-press-office/2014/05/28/remarks-president-united-states-military-academy-commencement-ceremony (accessed 15 February, 2016).

The White House, Office of the Press Secretary (2014b, 24 September). Remarks by President Obama in Address to the United Nations General Assembly. Available at www.whitehouse.gov/the-press-office/2014/09/24/remarks-president-obama-address-united-nations-general-assembly (accessed 21 February 2016).

The World Forum for Proximity of Islamic Schools of Thought (2011, 21 September). Islamic Awakening Conference final communiqué. Available at https://web.archive.org/web/20131015210932/http://www.taqrib.info/english/index.php?option=com_content&view=article&id=385:islamic-awakening-conference-final-communique-&catid=35:2009-08-31-05-01-28&Itemid=63 (accessed 6 September 2016).

Thorhallsson, B. (2000). *The role of small states in the European Union*. Aldershot, UK: Ashgate.

Thorhallsson, B. (2012). Small states in the UN Security Council: Means of influence?, *The Hague Journal of Diplomacy*, 7(2): 135–60.

Thorhallsson, B. (2015). How do little frogs fly? *NUPI Policy Papers*, Oslo: Norwegian Institute of International Affairs, no. 12.

Thorhallsson, B. and Wivel, A. (2006). Small states in the European Union: What do we know and what would we like to know?, *Cambridge Review of International Affairs*, 19(4): 651–68.

Tocqueville, A. (1838). *Democracy in America*. New York: Dearborn.

Toumi, H. (2015, 10 August). Iran uses Daesh as pretext to meddle in region. Gulf News. Available at http://m.gulfnews.com/news/gulf/bahrain/iran-uses-daesh-as-pretext-to-meddle-in-region-1.1563956 (accessed 6 September 2016).

Townsend, J. (1977). *Oman: The making of a modern state*. London/New York: Taylor & Francis.

Tunsjø, Ø. (2013). *Security and profit in China's energy policy: Hedging against risk*. New York: Columbia University Press.

Ulrichsen, K.C. (2009). The evolution of internal and external security in the Arab Gulf States, *Middle East Policy*, 16(2): 39–58.

Ulrichsen, K.C. (2011a). *Insecure Gulf*. Colombia, NY: Colombia University Press.

Ulrichsen, K.C. (2011b). Rebalancing global governance: Gulf States' perspectives on the governance of globalisation, *Global Policy*, 2(1): 65–74.

Ulrichsen, K.C. (2011c). Repositioning the GCC states in the changing global order, *Journal of Arabian Studies*, 1(2): 231–47.

Ulrichsen, K.C. (2012). *Small states with a big role: Qatar and the United Arab Emirates in the wake of the Arab Spring*. Durham, UK: Durham University, HH Sheikh Nasser al-Mohammad al-Sabah Publication Series 3.

Ulrichsen, KC. (2013, 19 December). The Gulf goes global: The evolving role of Gulf countries in the Middle East and North Africa and beyond. No. 121. FRIDE and Hivos. Available at http://fride.org/descarga/WP_121_The_Gulf_Goes_Global.pdf (accessed 29 October 2015).

Ulrichsen, K.C. (2014a). *Qatar and the Arab Spring*. Oxford: Oxford University Press.

Ulrichsen, K.C. (2014b, 14 May). The changing face of Gulf aid. *The Majjalla*. Available at www.majalla.com/eng/2014/05/article55249941 (accessed 6 September 2016).

Ulrichsen, K.C. (2016). The rationale and implications of Qatar's intervention in Libya, in Dag Henriksen and Ann Karin Larssen (eds), *Political rationale and international consequences of the war in Libya*. Oxford: Oxford University Press, pp. 118–35.

Underwood, L.J. (2013). *Cosmopolitanism and the Arab Spring – Foundations for the decline of terrorism*. New York: Peter Lang.

UN Development Program, Regional Bureau for Arab States (2009). *Arab Human Development Report: Challenges to human security in the Arab countries*. New York: UN Development Program.

United Arab Emirates Ministry of International Cooperation and Development (2014). United Arab Emirates foreign aid 2013, Abu Dhabi: UAE Ministry of International Cooperation and Development (MICAD).

United Nations (1945). *Charter of the United Nations and Statute of the International Court of Justice*. San Francisco, CA: United Nations.

United Press International (2013, 18 March). Emirates builds its own defense industry. Available at www.upi.com/Business_News/Security-Industry/2013/03/18/Emirates-builds-its-own-defense-industry/UPI-77731363633569/ (accessed 1 November 2015).

United States Institute of Peace (2015, 2 October). Regional leaders at UNGA: On Iran. Available at http://iranprimer.usip.org/blog/2015/oct/02/regional-leaders-unga-iran (accessed 24 August 2016).

Valeri, M. (2009). *Oman: Politics and society in the Qaboos state*. London: Hurst.

Valeri, M. (2013a). *Oman: Politics and Society in the Qaboos States*. New York: Oxford University Press.

Valeri, M. (2013b). Domesticating local elites: Sheikhs, Walis and state-building under Sultan Qaboos, in S. Wippel (ed.), *Regionalizing Oman: Political, economic and social dynamics*. Dordrecht: Springer Science+Business Media, pp. 267–77.

Valeri, M. (2013c). Oligarchy vs. Oligarchy: Business and Politics of Reform in Bahrain and Oman, in s. Hertog, G. Luciani & M. Valeri (eds), *Business politics in the Middle East*. London: Hurst and Company, pp. 17–42.

Valeri, M. (2014, 21 March). Oman's mediatory efforts in regional crises, Norwegian Peacebuilding Resource Centre (NOREF). Available at www.peacebuilding.no/Regions/Middle-East-and-North-Africa/The-Gulf/Publications/Oman-s-mediatory-efforts-in-regional-crises/(language)/eng-US (accessed 31 August 2016).

Vela, J. (2014, 9 December). GCC to set up regional police force based in Abu Dhabi. *The National*. Available at www.thenational.ae/world/gcc/gcc-to-set-up-regional-police-force-based-in-abu-dhabi. (accessed 29 October 2015).

Vital, D. (1966). *The unaligned small state in its foreign relations*. PhD Dissertation: University of Oxford.

Vital, D. (1971). *The survival of small states: Studies in small power/great power conflict*. London: Oxford University Press.

Vukadinovic, R. (1989). The various conceptions of European neutrality, in Michael H. Haltzel and Joseph Kruzel (eds), *Between the blocs: Problems and prospects for Europe's neutral and nonaligned states*. Cambridge, UK: Cambridge University Press, pp. 29–46.

Waever, O. (2004). *Aberystwyth, Paris, Copenhagen – New schools in security theory and their origins between core and periphery*. Paper presented at the annual meeting of the International Studies Association, Montreal.

Wagner, D. and Cafiero, G. (2015, 10 September). Iran exposes myth of GCC unity. *Huffington Post*. Available at www.huffingtonpost.com/daniel-wagner/iran-exposes-the-myth-of-_b_8102532.html?ir=Australia (accessed 24 August 2016).

Walt, S. (1985). Alliance formation and the balance of world power, *International Security*, 9(4): 3–43.

Walt, S.M. (1987). *The origins of alliances*. Ithaca, NY: Cornell University Press.

Waltz, K.N. (1959). *Man, the state and war: A theoretical analysis*. New York: Columbia University Press.

Waltz, K.N. (1979). *Theory of international politics*. London: Addison–Wesley.

Waltz, K.N. (2000). Structural realism after the Cold War, *International Security*, 25(1): 5–41.

Watanabe, L. (2014a). Qatar and the UAE in a changing Middle East. ISN ETH Zurich. Available at www.isn.ethz.ch/Digital-Library/Articles/Detail/?ots591=4888caa0-b3db-1461-98b9-e20e7b9c13d4&lng=en&id=184991 (accessed 29 October 2015).

Watanabe, L. (2014b). Sinking in shifting sands: The EU in North Africa, in O. Thränert and M. Zapfe (eds), *Strategic trends 2014: Key developments in global affairs*. Zurich: Center for Security Studies, ETHZ, pp. 31–48.

Wehrey, F. (2013, 14 June). The forgotten uprising in eastern Saudi Arabia. Carnegie Endowment for International Peace. Available at http://carnegieendowment.org/files/eastern_saudi_uprising.pdf (accessed 24 August 2016).

Wehrey, F. (2014, 10 March). A new U.S. approach to Gulf security, Carnegie Endowment for International Peace: Policy Outlook. Available at http://carnegieendowment.org/2014/03/10/new-u.s.-approach-to-gulf-security/h30d (accessed 18 February 2016).

Welch, D. (1992). The organizational process and bureaucratic politics paradigms, *International Security*, 17(2): 112–46.

Wendt, A. (1999). *Social theory of international politics*. Cambridge, UK: Cambridge University Press.

Wiberg, H. (1996). Security problems of small nations, in Werner Bauwens, Armand Clesse and Olav Knudsen (eds), *Small states and the security challenge in the new Europe*. London: Brassey's, pp. 21–41.

WikiLeaks (2009a, 25 February). US State Department Abu Dhabi. Strong words in private from MBZ at IDEX – Bashes Iran, Qatar, Russia. Available at https://wikileaks.org/plusd/cables/09ABUDHABI193_a.html (accessed 24 August 2016).

WikiLeaks (2009b, 9 July). US State Department Doha. Qatar: Balancing geographic interests with Iran, strategic interests with U.S. Available at https://wikileaks.org/plusd/cables/09DOHA442_a.html (accessed 6 September 2016).

WikiLeaks (2011, 15 February). Salafism on the Rise in Egypt. Passed to *The Telegraph* from WikiLeaks. Available at www.telegraph.co.uk/news/wikileaks-files/egypt-wikileaks-cables/8327088/SALAFISM-ON-THE-RISE-IN-EGYPT-CAIRO-00000202-001.2-OF-004.html (accessed 6 September 2016).

Wivel, A. (2003). Small states and alliances, *International Affairs*, 79(1): 176–7.

Wivel, A. (2005). The security challenge of small EU member states: Interests, identity and the development of the EU as a security actor, *Journal of Common Market Studies*, 43(2): 393–412.

Wivel, A., Bailes, A.J.K. and Archer, C. (2014). Setting the scene: Small states and international security, in C. Archer, A.J.K. Bailes and A. Wivel (eds), *Small states and international security: Europe and beyond*. Abingdon, UK/New York: Routledge, pp. 3–35.

World Bank (2010). Arab development assistance, four decades of cooperation, Middle East and North Africa Region, Concessional Finance and Global Partnerships Vice Presidency, June. Available at http://siteresources.worldbank.org/INTMENA/Resources/ADAPub82410web.pdf (accessed 27 September 2016).

World Bank (2011, 24 September). The World Bank and small states: Accelerating partnership, in Small States Forum: Sustainability of Small State's Development and Growth. Washington, World Bank. Available at http://siteresources.worldbank.org/PROJECTS/Resources/40940-1118776867573/TheWorldBankandSmallStates.pdf (accessed 6 September 2016).

Wright, S. (2011a). Foreign policy in the GCC states, in Mehran Kamrava (ed), *The international relations of the Persian Gulf*. Syracuse, NY: Syracuse University Press, pp. 72–93.

Wright, S. (2011b). Qatar, in C. Davidson (ed), *Power and politics in the Persian Gulf monarchies*. London: Hurst, pp. 113–35.

Wright, S. (2012). Foreign policies with international reach: The case of Qatar, in David Held and Kristian Ulrichsen (eds), *The transformation of the Gulf: Politics, economics and the global order*. London: Routledge, pp. 296–332.

Yom, S.L. (2005). Civil society and democratization in the Arab world, *Middle East Review of International Affairs*, 9(4): 14–33.

Youngs, R. (2009). *Impasse in Euro-Gulf relations*. Working Paper 80. FRIDE.

Yousef, D. (2011, 23 August). Iran sanctions pinch carpet sellers. Gulf News. Available at http://gulfnews.com/business/sectors/retail/iran-sanctions-pinch-carpet-sellers-1.855697 (accessed 29 October 2015).

Yousef, D.K. (2015, 2 June). Lower Saudi oil receipts won't stem record arms imports. Bloomberg Business. Available at www.bloomberg.com/news/articles/2015-06-01/lower-saudi-oil-receipts-won-t-stem-record-arms-imports-ihs-say (accessed 6 September 2016).

Zahariadis, N. (1994). Nationalism and small state foreign policy: The Greek response to the Macedonian issue, *Political Science Quarterly*, 109(4): 647–67.

Zahlan, R.S. (1998). *The making of the modern Gulf States*. Reading, UK: Ithaca Press.

Zaine, A. (1992). *Communication and freedom of expression in Yemen: 1974–1990*. Beirut: Contemporary Thought Press.

Zakaria, F. (2014, 12 June). Who lost Iraq? The Iraqis did, with an assist from George W. Bush, *Washington Post*.

Zarif, M.J. (2013, 21 November). Opinion: Our neighbors are our priority. *Asharq al-Awsat*. Available at http://english.aawsat.com/2013/11/article55323055 (accessed 6 September 2016).

Zarooni, M. (2015, 9 October). 8 reasons why UAE has to liberate Yemen. *Khaleej Times*. Available at www.khaleejtimes.com/nation/general/8-reasons-why-uae-has-to-liberate-yemen (accessed 10 November 2015).

Zayed, A. (2014, 22 November). HH Sheikh Abdullah binZayed gives interview to Bret Baier of US TV Channel Fox News, UAE Ministry of Foreign Affairs, www.mofa.gov.ae/mofa_english/portal/bf96f3d4-38b7-4a96-b902-e39faf416bf4.aspx (accessed 6 September 2016).

INDEX

Note: Table is indicated in bold; figure in italics.

Abdullah, King (Jordan) 89
Abdullah, King (Saudi Arabia) 95, 108, 188
Abu Dhabi Fund for Development 171
academic security discourses 48
ADIA (Abu Dhabi Investment Authority) 153
AFESD (Arab Fund for Economic and Social Development) 171, 176
Afghanistan 64, 68–9, 99, 119, 156, 161
AGFUND (Arab Gulf Program for United Nations Development Organizations) 171–2
Ahmadinejad, Mahmoud 73, 90, 93, 94, 95, 96; and the Arab Spring as an 'Islamic Awakening' 96, 101
aid development programmes 154–5, 156
Ajami, Fouad 71, 73–4
al-Akim, Hassan 20–1
Al Arabiya TV 3
al-Assad, Bashar 74, 97, 138
al-Attiyah, Khalid 97
al-Busa'idi, Hamud bin Faisal 115
Al Hinai, Imam Ghalib bin Ali 109
alignment policies and domestic stability 23
Al-Islah (Reform) societies 135, 174
Al Jazeera 3, 51, 174, 187
Al Khalifa family of Bahrain, the 55–6, 57, 94–5, 96
al-Khalili, Muhammad 108–9
alliances and the exercise of power 12–13, 38–9, 147, 169–70
al-Maktoum, Sheikh Mohammed bin Rashid 158
al-Maliki, Nouri 184
Almezaini, Khalid 172, 173
al-Nahyan, Sheikh Abdullah bin Zayed 94, 97, 100
al-Nahyan, Sheikh Khalifa bin Zayed 152
al-Otaiba, Yousef 80, 81
Al Qaeda 65, 69, 72, 78, 111
al-Qardhawi, Yusuf 40
al-Sabah, Emir Sabah Al-Ahmad Al-Jaber 98
al-Sabah, Mohammed 97
al-Sisi, General Abdel Fattah 79, 85n19, 97
Al-Suwaidi, Nasser 153
Al-Thani regime of Qatar, the 56–7, 60n4
al-Thani, Sheikh Tamim 57, 98
amity and enmity patterns between GCC states 36–8, 41
Analyzing Middle East foreign policies and the Relationship with Europe (book) 20
anarchic structure of a RSC 36
Ansar al-Sunna 177
Arab Human Development Report (2009), the 49
Arab League, the 150
Arab Monetary Fund, the 171
Arab solidarity and foreign aid 172
Arab Spring, the 23, 42n3, 50, 69, 74, 89–90; in Bahrain 55–6, 90, 96–7, 133; and change in security dynamic 3, 37–8, 40, 79, 89–90, 123, 149; as an Islamic Awakening 96, 101; impact on Qatari and Emirati security policy 2, 132–4, 135–8, 149, 159, 174–5, 184–6; and the

Index

media 51, 52; Qatari reaction to 57–8, 60n5; and US reaction to 39, 40, 42; *see also* Muslim Brotherhood
arms transfer agreements 140n4
autonomy and defensive security policy 5, *12*, 12–13, 14, 126, 155, 182

BADEA (Arab Bank for Economic Development in Africa) 171
Bahrain 44n15, 139, 183–4, 188, 189; and the al-Khalifa monarchy 49, 55–6, 57, 94–5, 96; and the Arab Spring 55–6, 90, 96–7, 133; and the Peninsula Shield Force intervention 32, 40, 91, 96, 133, 138–9, 150; pressures for reform 71, 74, 85n18; and relations with Iran 100, 101, 184; social divides in 54–6, 59, 101
balance-of-threat theory 43n4
balances of power in the Middle East 36–7
band-wagoning 12–13, 15, 169, 182; with Saudi Arabia 34, 126, 135, 137, 150; by the UAE 137, 144, 145, 150, 155, 157; with the US 130, 155, 157
Barnett, Michael N. 20, 33, 42n1, 43n12
bay'ah and Islamic political thought 60n2
Biden, Joe 84n4
bilateral alliances 15, 34, 42, 147
bilateral defence-cooperation agreements 126, 140n5
bilateral foreign aid 172, 175–6
bin Laden, Osama 72, 78
bounded rationality 17
British legacy on state formation 22
British relations with Oman 109, 111–12, 116, 117
Bromley, Simon 21
Brzezinski, Zbigniew 69
bureaucracies and foreign and security policy 17
Busa'idi tribe, the 11
Bush, George W. 71
Buzan, Barry 35, 36

Cairo speech by Barack Obama, June 2009 73, 75
Camp David agreement, the 113
Carter Doctrine, the 69, 74
Carter, Jimmy 84n15
China and trade 154
Clinton Doctrine, the 68
Clinton, Hillary 136
coalitions and the exercise of power 12
Cohen, Roger 77

Cold War, the 1, 3, 64, 66, 109, 125
colonialism and autocratic governance 49
communal affairs in Gulf states 49
communal consent and the social-contractual relationship 54, 56
conceptual foundation for a new security narrative since the Arab Spring 48–9, 50
constructivists and the small state 10–11, 13, 42n1
containment and US foreign policy *see* dual containment policy of the US
CP (Comparative Politics) 124, 127, 131
credibility as a state survival strategy 129, 130, 135
Crocker, Ryan 82

DAC (Development Assistance Committee) aid donors 170, 172
dawah (preaching) networks 177
decolonization period, the 8
defence expenditure in the UAE 159
defensive realism 129
democratic peace theory 17–18
democratization in the Middle East and Gulf 68, 74, 82–3
Dhofar Revolution, the 109, 111, 112, 115, 116, 121
Diwan of the Royal Court of Oman 112
Dorra/Arash gas field 95
dual containment policy of the US 37, 70, 75
Dubai 79, 89, 92, 94, 101, 156; and economic connections to Iran 148, 149
Dunford, David 118

economy of Oman, the 112–13
Egypt 85n19, 113, 178–9; economic assistance to 134, 149–50, 175, 176–7, 188; and the Muslim Brotherhood 136, 174, 177–8; *see also* Mubarak, Hosni; Muslim Brotherhood, the
Egyptian military, the 177
Ehteshami, Anoushiravan 20, 22
Eliot, T.S. 77, 78
Elman, M.F. 127
entrapment through alliances 13, 155
European Union (EU), the 3, 8–9, 154, 160, 168
Evan, Gareth 15–16
expat community of Qatar, the 56, 57, 128, 140n7
expats in the UAE 79, 128, 140n7, 148

external defense of GCC states 33, 34
extra-regional protection of the GCC 34–5, 41–2, 42n2

Facilities Access Agreement, the 110
Fahd, King 69, 76, 78
Federal National Council of the UAE 80
foreign aid 3, 23, 171–3, 185–6; and foreign policy 168, 170–1, 173, 177–9, 186; and project funding 171, 175–6
foreign and security policies of small Gulf states 2–3, 9, *12*, 12–15, 20–1, 24, 182–3
freedom of speech 60n1
French involvement in the UAE 44n17, 80, 126, 140n5, 147, 158
FSPA (foreign and security policy analysis) 8, 16, 18–19

Gaddhafi, Colonel Muammar 23, 40, 134, 135, 136, 150
Gamey'ah Shar'iah 177
Gargash, Anwar 157
gas deal between Iran and Oman 98
gas reserves of Iran 92
Gates, Robert 85n18
GCC (Gulf Cooperation Council), the 2–3, 20, 140n6, 182; amity and enmity patterns between 36–8, 41; and foreign policy 21, 147; impact of changes in the security dynamic 35–8, 123, 138–40, 186; military integration and the US security umbrella 38–41, 44n17, 151; and Oman 107, 110, 116–22, 189; parameters for alliance decisions of ruling elites 32–5, 43n4; and political integration 186, 187–8, 189; relations with Iran 75, 89, 90–4, 96–101, 128, 184; *see also* Qatar; UAE, the
Gervais, Victor 130–1, 184
global financial crisis (2007–8) 153, 160
globalization 3, 18, 20, 152, 159
Green Movement in Iran, the 73–4
Gulf War (1991), the 13, 34, 43n12, 70, 155

Habermas, Jürgen 50
Hadi, Abd, Rabbuh Mansur 99
Hamad, Tamim bin 131
Hamas 37
hedging strategies *12*, 14–15, 21, 31, 125, 126, 182, 184
Hezbollah 37, 44n20, 95–6
Hillal Dessouki, Ali 20

Hinnebusch, Raymond 20, 22
Hobbes, Thomas 52, 53, 54
Houthi war in Yemen, the 65, 114; involvement of small Gulf states in 23, 79, 119, 120, 136, 151, 186–7; and tensions with Iran 6, 99
Hussein, Saddam 44n14, 70, 71–2, 76, 89, 90, 95

Ibadi imamate, the 108–9
Ibadism in Oman 111
ICI (Istanbul Cooperation Initiative), the 147
Identity and foreign policy in the Middle East (book) 20
IDEX (International Defence Exhibition and Conference) 159
IMF (International Monetary Fund), the 91, 94, 153, 176
'immature anarchy' 125, 132
individualism and communal affairs in Gulf states 49–57, 58, 59, 60
internal security threats on the alliance model of GCC states 40–1, 42n3, 43n4
international finance and UAE risk-diversification policies 152–3
international institutions and trust 10
Internet and transnational interaction, the 51
intra-state war and the law of neutrality 14
IP (international politics) 140n1
IR (International Relations) 124
Iran 81; and the GCC 75, 89, 90–4, 96–101, 128, 184; and international sanctions 73, 94, 99, 100, 101, 148; and relations with Oman 92, 98, 99, 113, 116–17, 121, 185; and the UAE 91, 99, 100, 148
Iranian influence in the Gulf 37, 56, 75, 110, 184; and the Arab Spring 73–4, 96, 97, 98, 99, 101, 133; benefits from US invasion of Iraq 70, 71, 75, 95; and impact on small GCC states 32, 33, 40, 90–5, 100, 101; and the nuclear deal 74, 94, 99–100, 101, 108, 118; *see also* Iran–Saudi tensions
Iranian revolution (1979), the 69, 76, 107–8, 114; as a regional threat 64, 68, 91
Iran–Iraq War, the 68, 76, 91, 110, 116; and Saudi involvement 69, 89
Iran Sanctions Act (2006, Oman) 110
Iran–Saudi tensions 76, 77, 90–1, 100, 132; from the Bahraini uprising 96, 138–9; from the Houthi war in Yemen 6, 99; through the GCC 89, 94, 95, 98, 99, 101; *see also* Iranian influence in the Gulf

Index

Iraq 37, 44n14, 71–3, 125, 132, 156; and invasion of Kuwait 34, 68, 72, 119; and the Shi'a–Sunni divide 71, 75, 82; *see also* Gulf War (1991), the; US invasion of Iraq, the ISAF (International Security Assistance Force) in Afghanistan 156
IsDB (Islamic Development Bank) 171
ISIL *see* ISIS (Islamic State in Iraq and Syria)
ISIS (Islamic State in Iraq and Syria) 23, 44n20, 82, 98, 157, 177; creation of 65, 75; as Sunni extremists 37, 69, 77
Islam as a fascist threat 81, 83
Islamic Revolutionary Guard Corps (Iran) 100
Israel 37, 43n12, 68, 95, 113–14
Istanbul Cooperation Initiative, the 23

Jebel Akhdar rebellion, the 109
Johnson, Lyndon B. 82
Joint Comprehensive Plan of Action, the 4, 108

Kagan, Robert 66, 67
Kamrava, Mehran 21
Kechichian, Joseph 21
Kerry, John 117
KFAED (Kuwait Fund for Arab Development) 171
Khalfan, Lieutenant-General Dhahi 137
Khalifa, Hamad bin 131
Khomeini, Ayatollah 69, 76, 77, 89, 90, 91
Kirkpatrick, Jeane 84n15
Korany, Bahgat 20
Kuwait 49, 50, 114, 128, 140n4; and foreign aid and investment 119, 170, 171, 187, 188; Iraqi invasion of 34, 68, 72, 119, 125; relations with Iran 91, 95, 97

law of neutrality and intra-state war, the 14
Lefebvre, J.A. 110, 111
legitimacy as a state survival strategy 130
leverage of small states 3, 9, 12–13, 144, 147, 152, 154
liberalism and US foreign policy 76, 77, 81–2, 83, 84n15, 84n17, 183
Libya 39, 133, 135, 150, 174, 175; and the Arab Spring 52, 58, 90, 132–3, 135, 136; and Colonel Gaddhafi 23, 40, 134, 135, 136, 150; and UAE involvement in 23, 150, 151, 155, 156, 186
Libyan Constitution Drafting Assembly, the 114

'linkage politics' 127
Locke, Joseph 53, 54

mature anarchy through institutionalization 13
media influence in small Gulf states 3–4
mediatory role of Oman in foreign affairs 113–14, 117–18
MENA (Middle East and North Africa) region, the 23, 134, 139, 172–3, 182, 188; impact of the Arab Spring 123, 132, 134, 135, 138
merchant elites of Oman, the 115
'micro-states' 128
Migdal, Joel 112
military interventions through multinational coalitions 4, 12, 23
military investment of GCC states 34, 43n8, 44n17
monarchies and republics in the Gulf 23, 48, 49, 65
Morocco and foreign aid 175
Morsi, Mohammed 40, 96, 149, 169, 176; *see also* Muslim Brotherhood
Mubarak, Hosni 4, 39, 74, 96, 97, 183
multilateral forums and foreign aid assistance 171–2
Muslim Brotherhood 32, 38, 134, 135, 140n15, 186; and Qatari support for 40–1, 75, 84n6, 97, 136–7, 177–8, 186; viewed as a threat 173–4, 179; Western abettal of 44n15, 74, 75; *see also* Morsi, Mohammed

'narcissism of small differences,' the 132
Nasser, Gamal Abdel 174
NATO 4, 9, 23, 147, 150
natural resources of small states 169
neoclassical realism and foreign policy 19, 24, 124, 125
neoconservatism and US foreign policy 70–1, 81
neo-liberals and the power of small states 10
neo-realism and foreign policy 19
Neumayer, Eric 173
neutrality 14
niche strategies and niche diplomacy 15–16
Non-Aligned Movement, the 14
non-alignment and neutrality 14
Nonneman, Gerd 20, 92
norms entrepreneurship and adoption 13
nuclear deal with Iran 74, 94, 99–100, 101, 108, 118

Obama, Barack 65, 72–4, 75, 85n19, 183
OECD (Organization for Economic Cooperation and Development), the 160, 170
OFID (OPEC Fund for International Development) 171
oil and gas exports 22
oil prices and foreign policy 170, 187, 188–9, 190
oil revenues in Oman 112–13
oil revenues in the UAE 152, 187, 189
Oman 23, 108–9, 111–13; foreign policy of 21, 107–8, 109–11, 113–16, 117–22, 187, 189; relations with Iran 92, 98, 99, 113, 116–17, 121, 185
OPEC (Organization for Petroleum Exporting Countries) 113, 160
Oslo Accord (1993), the 37, 110
outline of the book 5–7

parameters for alliance decisions of GCC state ruling elites 31, 32–5
Partrick, Neil 23–4
PDO (Petroleum Development Oman) 109
peculiarities of Middle East states 21–4
Peterson, J.E. 109, 110
PFLOAG (People's Front for the Liberation of Oman and the Arabian Gulf) 120
'pivot to Asia' of US foreign policy 44n16, 74, 157, 173
PLO, the 37
power and the realist tradition 9–10, 145
power exercised by small states 11–12, 124, 144, 145–7, **146,** 152, 161
'Prince State,' the 124, 131, 132–3; see also Qatar; UAE, the
private security and regime security 53, 56, 57
proactive posture of small state security policy 147
project funding and foreign aid 171, 175–6
PSF (Peninsula Shield Force) intervention, the 32, 40, 91, 96, 133, 138–9, 150
psychological factors and foreign policy-making 17
public sphere, the 50–1, 52, 53, 57, 58
Putnam, Robert 127

Qaboos, Sultan 119, 120, 121–2, 185; and Iran 92, 93, 98, 110, 114, 116, 117; and reign in Oman 109–10, 111–13, 114–15, 121–2
Qatar 21, 23, 60n5, 140n15; expat community of 56, 57, 128, 140n7; and foreign aid 168, 173, 175–6, 178, 179; and foreign and security policy 3, 57–8, 123–4, 125–6, 128–32, 186–7; and the GCC 34, 39–40, 139; impact of Arab Spring on reshaping of security policy 2, 132–3, 134, 136–8, 174–5, 184–5; and individual-centric security policy 57, 58, 59, 60; relations with Iran 92–3, 97–8; social homogeneity of 56–7, 140n9, 183–4; and support for the Muslim Brotherhood 40–1, 75, 84n6, 97, 136–7, 177–8, 186
quantitative criteria for defining the small state 11

rationality and FPSA (foreign and security policy analysis) 16–17
Reagan, Ronald 70, 84n15
realist approach of US foreign policy 66–70, 72–4, 75, 76, 81, 183
realist tradition and power, the 9–10, 11, 16
realpolitik in US foreign policy 68, 69
reconfiguration of power in the Middle East 4
reform and Saudi Arabia 78–9
relational power 146, 147–8, 152
risk-diversification strategies in foreign policy 144, 145, **146,** 146–53, 156–61, 185
Roosevelt, Franklin D. 81–2
Roosevelt, Theodore 84
Rosenau, James 127
Rouhani, Hassan 90, 94, 98–9, 100, 184
Rousseau, Jean-Jacques 53, 54
RSCs (Regional Security Complexes) 35, 36, 38, 43n6, 43n9, 140n2
RSCT (Regional Security Complex Theory) 125
Russell, James A. 34

Salafism 78, 120, 175; and jihadism 79, 149
Salafist Nour Party, the 177
Salman, Prince Mohammed bin 78
sanctions on Iran 73, 94, 99, 100, 101, 148
Saouli, Adham 22
satellite TV and control of communications 51
Saudi Arabia 35, 43n8, 44n17, 50, 140n3; band-wagoning of by smaller states 34, 126, 132, 135, 150; and foreign aid 119, 168, 171, 173, 175–7, 178–9; and the Iraq–Iran war 69, 89, 91; and the Muslim Brotherhood 40, 41; and the PSF intervention in Bahrain 32, 40, 91, 96,

133, 138–9, 150; as regional hegemon 31, 34, 75, 120; relations with Oman 109, 118, 119, 120, 121; and terrorism 44n20, 75, 78, 137, 151; and US relations 64, 65, 66, 68, 71–2, 77–8, 118; and Wahhabism 66, 69–70, 77, 78, 98, 174; *see also* Iran–Saudi tensions
Second Gulf War, the 37, 39
Second World War, the 67–8
security dynamics and change in the Middle East 35–41, 186, 188–90
security interdependence 38, 43n9
security policy of smaller GCC states 31–5, 39, 41–2, 57–8, 59–60; *see also* Qatar; UAE, the
security threats to internal stability 4, 42n2, 43n4
security umbrella of the US, the 2, 38, 44n17, 133; and band-wagoning 130, 155, 157; and move for manoeuvre under the Saudi orbit 31, 35, 126; through agreements with the GCC 32, 33, 43n6; and the UAE 148–9, 155, 158
September 11 attacks, the 70
Shah of Iran, the 76, 83, 84n15, 109, 110, 116, 117
shared interests in natural resources between Iran, Qatar and Oman 92–3
Shi'a majority of Bahrain, the 55
Shi'a–Sunni divide, the 55–6, 76, 91, 183; in Iraq 71, 75, 82; as main source of regional instability 37, 139
Sluglett, Peter 69
small state, the 9–13, 124, 169
small states and international politics 1–2, 8–9, 182–3
smart policy approach to foreign policy *see* risk-diversification strategies in foreign policy
social cohesion and bonds between state and the individual 59
Social Contract theory 52–4, 56, 60n2
social media and transnational communication 51, 52, 60n1
societal security and the state 48, 49–52
soft-power and foreign and security policy 130, 131, 134
South Pars/North Dome gas field 93
Soviet invasion of Afghanistan, the 68–9
Soviet Union, the 68
state-branding 130, 131, 132, 136, 184
state-centric strategies and new security challenges 138–9
state legitimacy and security provision 53

state of nature, the 53
state security and public security 54–7
state security as national security 48
Strait of Hormuz, the 92, 110, 113, 117
strategic options for small states *12*, 12–15, 18, 124–5, 126–31, 135, 139–40; of the UAE 144–5, 147–8, 159–61
Sunni extremism 65, 66, 69–70, 77, 79
SWFs (sovereign wealth funds) 153
Syria 97, 138, 188; and the uprising and civil war 74–5, 76, 77

Taimur, Sayyid 108, 109
Taimur, Sultan Said 109, 118
Taliban, the 78
Talmon, J.L. 53
Telhami, Shibley 20
territorial dispute between Iran and the UAE 93–4, 117
Theros, Patrick 93
Tocqueville, Alexis de 53
tolerance and Westernization in the UAE 79–81
trade diplomacy and humanitarian projects 154–5
transnational influence and interdependency on foreign policy 18, 33, 42n2
tribalism of Gulf states 23–4, 49
Tunisia and foreign aid 175
Tunisian mass protests in December 2010 52

UAE, the 2, 21, 44n18, 64, 66, 121; and band-wagoning 34, 137, 144, 145, 150, 155, 157; demographics and the expat community of 79, 91, 128, 140n7, 140n9, 148; and foreign aid 168, 171, 173, 175–7, 178, 179, 185; and foreign and security policy 3, 39–40, 43n8, 44n18, 123–4, 125–6, 128–32; French involvement in 44n17, 80, 126, 140n5, 147, 158; and the Houthi war in Yemen 64, 99; impact of Arab Spring on reshaping of security policy 133–6, 137–8, 174, 184–5, 186; and involvement in Libya 23, 150, 151, 155, 156, 186; and Iran 91, 99, 100, 148; and liberal reform 77, 79–81; and the Muslim Brotherhood 40–1, 75; oil revenues of 152, 187, 189; risk-diversification strategies and foreign policy 144, 145, 146–53, 155–9, 160–1; risk-diversification strategies and global finance 152–5, 158, 159–60, 185;

security challenges from state-centric policy 138; strategic options of as a small state 144–5, 147–8, 159–61; territorial dispute with Iran 93–4, 117; and the US security umbrella 148–9, 155, 158
UAE–Egypt Task Force, the 176
UAE–US alliance, the 150, 151, 155–6, 158
Ulrichsen, Kristian Coates 48–9, 176, 187
UN, the 154, 155, 160
UN Charter, the 13
UNSCOM (UN Special Commission) 110
US, the 125; perceptions of 66, 71, 83
US defence spending 157
US foreign policy 64, 65, 71–2, 76–8, 84n7–8, 157–8; and the Arab Spring 32, 39, 40; and dual containment 37, 70, 75; and Iran 76, 100, 117; liberal approach to 76, 77, 81–2, 83, 84n15, 84n17, 183; and neoconservatism 70–1, 81, 84n15; and perceived disengagement 4, 72–3, 100; 'pivot to Asia' of 44n16, 74, 157, 173; realist approach to 66–70, 72–4, 75, 76, 81, 183; and realpolitik 68, 69; *see also* security umbrella of the US, the
US invasion of Iraq, the 70–1, 82, 132, 183; failure of 39, 44n14, 65, 72, 75

Valeri, Marc 111–12, 115
Vietnam War, the 82
volonté générale concept 53, 55, 60

Wahhabism in Saudi Arabia 69–70, 77, 78, 98, 174
Walt, Stephen 43n4
Western abettal of the Muslim Brotherhood 44n15, 74, 75
Wilson, Woodrow 84n17
World Bank, the 11
Wright, Steven 21, 22

Yemen 32, 40, 116, 134, 188, 189; *see also* Houthi war in Yemen, the

Zakaria, Fareed 44n14
Zarif, Javad 94, 98, 120
Zayed, Sheik Abdullah bin 137, 154
Zayed, Sheik Mohammed bin 75, 92, 131

Taylor & Francis eBooks

Helping you to choose the right eBooks for your Library

Add Routledge titles to your library's digital collection today. Taylor and Francis ebooks contains over 50,000 titles in the Humanities, Social Sciences, Behavioural Sciences, Built Environment and Law.

Choose from a range of subject packages or create your own!

Benefits for you
- Free MARC records
- COUNTER-compliant usage statistics
- Flexible purchase and pricing options
- All titles DRM-free.

Benefits for your user
- Off-site, anytime access via Athens or referring URL
- Print or copy pages or chapters
- Full content search
- Bookmark, highlight and annotate text
- Access to thousands of pages of quality research at the click of a button.

REQUEST YOUR FREE INSTITUTIONAL TRIAL TODAY

Free Trials Available
We offer free trials to qualifying academic, corporate and government customers.

eCollections – Choose from over 30 subject eCollections, including:

Archaeology	Language Learning
Architecture	Law
Asian Studies	Literature
Business & Management	Media & Communication
Classical Studies	Middle East Studies
Construction	Music
Creative & Media Arts	Philosophy
Criminology & Criminal Justice	Planning
Economics	Politics
Education	Psychology & Mental Health
Energy	Religion
Engineering	Security
English Language & Linguistics	Social Work
Environment & Sustainability	Sociology
Geography	Sport
Health Studies	Theatre & Performance
History	Tourism, Hospitality & Events

For more information, pricing enquiries or to order a free trial, please contact your local sales team: **www.tandfebooks.com/page/sales**

The home of Routledge books

www.tandfebooks.com